הגדה של פסח

Seder Secrets

The Mysteries Revealed

RABBI DOVID MEISELS

Translated by Rabbi Avraham Y. Finkel

SEDER SECRETS

First Published 2005

ISBN 1-931681-66-X

Other books by the author:

Shabbos Secrets
Bar Mitzvah and Tefillin Secrets
Rosh Hashanah and Yom Kippur Secrets

Distributed By:
ISRAEL BOOK SHOP
501 Prospect Street
Lakewood NJ 08701
Tel: (732) 901-3009
Fax: (732) 901-4012
Email: isrbkshp @ aol.com

Printed in E. Israel

This book is dedicated
to be a source of merit
in restoring the health
and in strengthening

ישכר דוב בן תמר נ"י

May Hashem send him from
heaven a speedy and complete
recovery of spirit and body
among the other sick people of
Israel.

In the *Zechus* of being
Mezakeh es Harabbim
may his parents
merit to have much
nachas from him and
from the entire family.

Acknowledgements

I wish to express my gratitude to Reb Avraham Yaakov Finkel, the well-known Torah themes, for his highly professional and meticulous translation from the Yiddish into lucid, conversational English. The original Yiddish text was published under the title Otzer Hamoadim.

I am forever thankful to a dear friend, R' Aryeh Schachter who's help at all times has enabled this book to become a reality.

My special appreciation to Mrs. E. Langer for her superb job of editing the manuscript.

I am indebted to my daughter-in-law, Mrs. S. R. Meisels for her proficiency and talent in arranging the page layout, and for all the work that was put into the pictures.

I want to express my hakoras hatov to R' Yaakov Moshe Berkowitz, a dedicated friend of my father, Harav Hagaon Rabbi Zalmen Leib Meisels, and a staunch supporter of his kehilla, and benefactor to *kol davar shebikedushah*. It was his suggestion to have this sefer translated into English. His generous support and encouragement enabled to bring this project to fruition, *kedei lezakos es harabbim.*

May Hashem grant much nachas, simchos, and good health to him and his entire mishpachah.

Table of Contents

Preface

It is with a profound sense of gratitude to Hashem that I present this volume dedicated to the Yom Tov of Pesach. This is the fourth in a series that has been enthusiastically received, and it is my hope that this book-a compilation of some of the most stirring and thought-provoking insights on the *mitzvos* and *minhagim* of Pesach-will also be enjoyed by the reading public.

Pesach recalls the time when the oppressed Jewish slaves in Egypt became the nation chosen by Hashem. "I will take you to Myself as a nation, and I will be to you as a G-d" (*Shemos* 6:7).

The Sages tell us that at the time of the Exodus, the Jews had descended to a very low level of spiritual impurity. Hashem gifted them with heavenly inspiration, lifting them in a single instant-from the depths of defilement to the heights of holiness.

How far had they fallen before the redemption? The Jews had sunk to the forty-ninth level of impurity. In fact, the slightest delay would have caused them to fall to the fiftieth level, the ultimate degree of impurity from which there is no escape! This is why when

the moment of redemption was at hand, the Jews were not allowed to tarry for even one instant.

What does this tell us? Even the smallest amount-the slightest bit of existence-is accountable. The smallest delay could have led to the ultimate degree of impurity. And this idea, the *Yismach Moshe* explains, is symbolized in the prohibition against eating even the slightest amount of *chametz* on Pesach.

It teaches us something else as well. It tells a Jew that even if he has slumped to the bottom, as long as there is a single small spark of *Yiddishkeit* left in him, Hashem will lift him from the depths of impurity-just as He elevated *Klal Yisrael* in an instant from the morass of Egyptian *tumah* to the glory of *taharah*.

For who was redeemed from Egypt? Clearly, the Jews were not great *tzaddikim*-they had sunk to nearly the lowest level of impurity. Yet Hashem lifted them and redeemed them. This is the significance of Passover. Hashem passes over our actual level, and looks only at our desire to come close to Him.

This concept applies to our current exile as well. We are but a mere shadow of the greatness of earlier generations-how can we possibly be redeemed? Yet if we have that desire, the slightest connection to Hashem, He will lift us up regardless of our current level. This idea, too, is symbolized in the prohibition against eating even the smallest amount of *chametz. (Tiferes Shlomo)* It is our task to maintain our *emunah* that when the time comes for us to be redeemed from our current exile, Hashem will take us out-without delaying even for a moment.

The *sefer Chesed LeAvraham* comments that this miracle of instantaneous transformation is repeated annually, throughout all generations. Thirty days before Pesach, every Jew feels a surge of *kedushah* entering his heart. This overpowering pull toward holiness culminates on the night of Pesach, when every Jew experiences his own personal Exodus. The spirit of Pesach cleanses him of unholy, Egyptian-like tendencies, granting him a new outlook of *kedushah* and purity.

The Gemara (*Berachos* 4b) asks, who merits *Olam Haba*? One who connects the *Geulah,* the *berachah* of *Ga'al Yisrael* in which we give thanks for our deliverance from Egypt, with the *Shemoneh esrei*. Asks Rabbeinu Yonah: why should saying the *Shemoneh esrei* immediately after the *berachah* of *Ga'al Yisrael* cause one to deserve the great reward of coming into *Olam Haba*?

Rabbeinu Yonah explains that G-d took us out of Egypt so we would become His servants who serve Him. How do we serve Hashem? Through prayer. As the Gemara says (*Bava Kamma* 92b), prayer is *avodah*-service of Hashem. "*V'avadta es Hashem Elokecha*"-the *avodah* of a Jew is *tefillah*.

In the *berachah* of *Ga'al Yisrael* we acknowledge the good that Hashem did for us, thereby admitting that we are now required to serve Him. As soon as we acknowledge our responsibility to serve Hashem, we immediately begin serving him through prayer-with the recitation of *Shemoneh esrei*. It is this understanding and acknowledgement that merits a person *Olam Haba*.

In truth, the entire *haggadah* is a representation of this concept-an acknowledgement that we are servants of Hashem. Because Hashem redeemed us from Egypt for the purpose of serving Him, we are now required to do so. By demonstrating our acknowledgement and willingness to serve Him we become worthy of *Olam Haba*.

Rabbeinu Yonah suggests yet another reason. Reciting the *Shemoneh esrei* and enunciating our needs demonstrates our faith in Hashem and our trust that He will answer our prayers. In this we emulate our ancestors, as it says, "*B'nei Yisrael* saw the great power that Hashem had unleashed against Egypt, and the people were in awe of Hashem. They believed in Hashem and in His servant Moshe" (*Shemos* 14:31). Yes, they were suffering-yet their faith remained strong. Though we are still in exile, if we can share the same strong *emunah* and *bitachon* we are worthy of inheriting *Olam Haba.*

★ ★ ★

The Torah commands, "On that day you must tell your child" (*Shemos* 13:8). For over three thousand years, Jews have retold the story of the Exodus from Egypt on the night of Pesach, discussing the miracles and the mighty deeds Hashem performed for our ancestors in Egypt and continues to perform to this day. By relating the wonders of the Exodus we etch our children's hearts with unquestioning *emunah* in Hashem.

Torah can be learned at many different levels. At the Pesach *Seder*, it is vital for children to hear the Exodus retold in a way *they* can understand. Reasons for the *Seder*, descriptions of the *Korban Pesach*, vivid imagery of the ten *makkos*-all are presented here in detail, to promote comprehension and understanding. And the pictures-worth well over a thousand words-will deepen the children's appreciation of the Exodus and their enjoyment of the holiday of Pesach: from *matzah* baking to arranging the *Seder* plate to preparing for Yom Tov.

The *Yismach Moshe* stresses that every year at the *Seder* one should make an effort to tell original ideas and commentaries about the deliverance from Egypt, making the text of the *Haggadah* stimulating through commentaries that stir the imagination. But how, after three thousand years, can we manage to find new concepts?

The wisdom of the Torah is inexhaustible; novel thoughts *can* be discovered year after year. And this *Haggadah* was designed to aid in this task. Presented in this volume are a variety of details about Pesach, the *Seder*, and the Exodus, leading to an almost limitless variety of insights to be explored.

It is with this in mind that I present this treasury of inspiration for Pesach and the *Seder*, in the hope that it will contribute to greater *ahavas Hashem* and *yiras Shamayim*.

Rabbi Dovid Dov Meisels

Chapter 1

Preparing for Pesach

בדיקת חמץ

On the evening before Pasach, one must search for chametz. Before the search has began, the following blessing is recited with joy:

הֲרֵינִי מוּכָן וּמְזוּמָּן לְקַיֵּם מִצְוַת עֲשֵׂה וְלֹא תַעֲשֶׂה שֶׁל בְּדִיקַת חָמֵץ. לְשֵׁם יִחוּד קוּדְשָׁא בְּרִיךְ הוּא וּשְׁכִינְתֵּיהּ, עַל יְדֵי הַהוּא טָמִיר וְנֶעְלָם בְּשֵׁם כָּל יִשְׂרָאֵל:
וִיהִי נוֹעַם אֲדֹנָי אֱלֹהֵינוּ עָלֵינוּ, וּמַעֲשֵׂה יָדֵינוּ כּוֹנְנָה עָלֵינוּ, וּמַעֲשֵׂה יָדֵינוּ כּוֹנְנֵהוּ:

בָּרוּךְ אַתָּה יְיָ, אֱלֹהֵינוּ מֶלֶךְ הָעוֹלָם,
אֲשֶׁר קִדְּשָׁנוּ בְּמִצְוֹתָיו, וְצִוָּנוּ עַל בִּעוּר חָמֵץ:

Upon completion of the chametz search,
the following declaration is then said three times:

כָּל חֲמִירָא וַחֲמִיעָא דְּאִיכָּא בִרְשׁוּתִי דְּלָא חֲמִתֵּהּ וּדְלָא בִעַרְתֵּהּ וּדְלָא יְדַעְנָא לֵיהּ. לִבָּטֵל וְלֶהֱוֵי הֶפְקֵר כְּעַפְרָא דְאַרְעָא:

יְהִי רָצוֹן מִלְּפָנֶיךָ יְיָ אֱלֹהֵינוּ וֵאלֹהֵי אֲבוֹתֵינוּ, שֶׁתְּזַכֵּנוּ לָתוּר וּלְחַפֵּשׂ בְּנִגְעֵי בָּתֵּי הַנֶּפֶשׁ, אֲשֶׁר נוֹאַלְנוּ בַּעֲצַת יִצְרֵנוּ הָרַע, וּתְזַכֵּנוּ לָשׁוּב בִּתְשׁוּבָה שְׁלֵימָה לְפָנֶיךָ, וְאַתָּה בְּטוּבְךָ הַגָּדוֹל תְּרַחֵם עָלֵינוּ, עָזְרֵנוּ אֱלֹהֵי יִשְׁעֵנוּ עַל דְּבַר כְּבוֹד שְׁמֶךָ, וְתַצִּילֵנוּ מֵאִיסוּר חָמֵץ אֲפִילוּ בְּכָל שֶׁהוּא, בְּשָׁנָה זוּ וּבְכָל שָׁנָה וְשָׁנָה כָּל יְמֵי חַיֵּינוּ, אָמֵן כֵּן יְהִי רָצוֹן:

שריפת חמץ

On the morning of erev Pesach, after the chametz has been burned,
the following declaration is made.

הֲרֵינִי מוּכָן וּמְזוּמָּן לְקַיֵּם מִצְוַת עֲשֵׂה שֶׁל שְׂרֵיפַת חָמֵץ. לְשֵׁם יִחוּד קוּדְשָׁא בְּרִיךְ הוּא וּשְׁכִינְתֵּיהּ, עַל יְדֵי הַהוּא טָמִיר וְנֶעְלָם בְּשֵׁם כָּל יִשְׂרָאֵל: וִיהִי נוֹעַם אֲדֹנָי אֱלֹהֵינוּ עָלֵינוּ, וּמַעֲשֵׂה יָדֵינוּ כּוֹנְנָה עָלֵינוּ, וּמַעֲשֵׂה יָדֵינוּ כּוֹנְנֵהוּ:

Recite three times.

כָּל חֲמִירָא וַחֲמִיעָא דְּאִיכָּא בִרְשׁוּתִי דַּחֲזִתֵּהּ וּדְלָא חֲזִתֵּהּ, דַּחֲמִתֵּהּ וּדְלָא חֲמִתֵּהּ, דְּבִעַרְתֵּהּ וּדְלָא בִעַרְתֵּהּ, לִבָּטֵל וְלֶהֱוֵי הֶפְקֵר כְּעַפְרָא דְאַרְעָא:

יְהִי רָצוֹן מִלְּפָנֶיךָ יְיָ אֱלֹהֵינוּ וֵאלֹהֵי אֲבוֹתֵינוּ, שֶׁתְּרַחֵם עָלֵינוּ וְתַצִּילֵנוּ מֵאִיסוּר חָמֵץ אֲפִילוּ מִכָּל שֶׁהוּא, לָנוּ וּלְכָל בְּנֵי בֵיתֵנוּ וּלְכָל יִשְׂרָאֵל, בְּשָׁנָה זוּ וּבְכָל שָׁנָה וְשָׁנָה כָּל יְמֵי חַיֵּינוּ, וּכְשֵׁם שֶׁבִּיעַרְנוּ הֶחָמֵץ מִבָּתֵּינוּ וְשָׂרַפְנוּהוּ, כַּךְ תְּזַכֵּנוּ

לְבַעֵר הַיֵּצֶר הָרָע מִקִּרְבֵּנוּ תָּמִיד כָּל יְמֵי חַיֵּינוּ, וּתְזַכֵּנוּ לִידָבֵק בָּךְ וּבְתוֹרָתְךָ וְאַהֲבָתְךָ וְלִידָבֵק בְּיֵצֶר הַטּוֹב תָּמִיד, אֲנַחְנוּ וְזַרְעֵנוּ וְזֶרַע זַרְעֵנוּ מֵעַתָּה וְעַד עוֹלָם, כֵּן יְהִי רָצוֹן אָמֵן:

יְהִי רָצוֹן מִלְּפָנֶיךָ יְיָ אֱלֹהֵינוּ וֵאלֹהֵי אֲבוֹתֵינוּ כְּשֵׁם שֶׁאֲנִי מְבַעֵר הֶחָמֵץ מִבֵּיתִי וּמֵרְשׁוּתִי כַּךְ יְיָ אֱלֹהֵינוּ וֵאלֹהֵי אֲבוֹתֵינוּ תְּבַעֵר אֶת כָּל הַחִיצוֹנִים וְאֶת רוּחַ הַטּוּמְאָה תְּבַעֵר מִן הָאָרֶץ, וְאֶת יִצְרֵנוּ הָרָע תְּבַעֲרֵהוּ מֵאִתָּנוּ, וְתִתֵּן לָנוּ לֵב בָּשָׂר לְעָבְדְךָ בֶּאֱמֶת, וְכָל הַסִּטְרָא אַחֲרָא וְכָל הָרִשְׁעָה כֻּלָּהּ כֶּעָשָׁן תִּכְלֶה וְתַעֲבִיר מֶמְשֶׁלֶת זָדוֹן מִן הָאָרֶץ, וְכָל הַמְעִיקִים לַשְּׁכִינָה תְּבַעֲרֵם בְּרוּחַ בָּעֵר וּבְרוּחַ מִשְׁפָּט, כְּשֵׁם שֶׁבִּעַרְתָּ אֶת מִצְרַיִם וְאֶת אֱלֹהֵיהֶם בַּיָּמִים הָהֵם וּבִזְמַן הַזֶּה, אָמֵן:

Cleaning out Chometz

Why does every Jewish homemaker invest so much time and effort in cleaning for Pesach? Cleaning for Pesach is not simply about collecting and removing all *chametz* from our possession. It is destroying the forces of evil, the *klipos*—the shells of impurity and wickedness from the world. As every homemaker sweeps the crumbs away, this is the thought that should be in the foremost of her mind.

(Yesod Yosef)

Chametz alludes to the *yetzer hara*, the evil inclination that constantly preys on every individual to sin, to forfeit their reward in the World to Come. Hashem commanded us to destroy not only the physical *chametz* from the world, but the spiritual *chametz* as well.

This is why the prohibition of eating and even owning *chametz* is far stricter than any other Torah prohibition. *Chametz* must be searched out from holes and cracks and then burned. It may not be seen or found through the entire holiday of Pesach. Eradicate all *chametz*! Remove the control of the *yetzer hara*!

(Radbaz, ResMponsa 546)

As each person searches for *chametz* in the nooks and crannies of his home, he must also examine the inner recesses of his heart for misdeeds. Just as he rids his home of every last crumb of leaven, he must evict every last trace of the *yetzer hara*. As he burns the last vestiges of *chametz*, he must destroy the misdeeds in his soul.

(Chida)

Preparing for the Holiday

Erev Yom Tov, the day before the holiday, has the same rules as *erev Shabbos*. Every individual should trim his nails and hair, preferably before midday. If one forgets, he may still cut his nails later in the afternoon, but only a non-Jew may cut his hair. *(Shulchan Aruch HaRav 468:4,6)* In preparation for the *Yom Tov*, he should shampoo his scalp and wash his entire body in warm water. If this is not possible, he should at least wash his face, hands and feet.

(Shulchan Aruch HaRav 529:2, Chayei Adam 79:1, Mishnah Berurah 260:5)

Although it is not obligatory, as it was during the time of the holy Temple, it is proper to immerse in a *mikveh* prior to *Yom Tov*. Even one who does not usually immerse before Shabbos should do so for *Yom Tov*, as the Jews did before each of the *shalosh regalim*, the three pilgrimage holidays, in order to enter the *Beis Hamikdash*. *(Chayei Adam 79:1, Kaf Hachaim 468:101)*, One must keep in mind that the immersion is in honor of the holiday. The cleansing water draws in the holiness of the day with joy and good feeling.

(Matteh Efrayim 625:14)

During the times of the Temple, utensils that would be used to prepare the *Korban Pesach* were also immersed, a rite referred to as "purification of the vessels." These vessels can also be interpreted as

ערוב תבשילין

When a festival falls on Friday (or Thursday and Friday), an eruv tavshilin is made on erev yom tov, and recite the following:

בָּרוּךְ אַתָּה יְיָ, אֱלֹהֵינוּ מֶלֶךְ הָעוֹלָם,
אֲשֶׁר קִדְּשָׁנוּ בְּמִצְוֹתָיו, וְצִוָּנוּ עַל מִצְוַת עֵרוּב:

בְּדֵין עֵרוּבָא יְהֵא שָׁרָא לָנָא, לַאֲפוּיֵי, וּלְבַשּׁוּלֵי, וּלְאַטְמוּנֵי, וּלְאַדְלוּקֵי שְׁרָגָא, וּלְתַקָּנָא, וּלְמֶעְבַּד כָּל צָרְכָנָא, מִיּוֹמָא טָבָא לְשַׁבַּתָּא לָנָא וּלְכָל יִשְׂרָאֵל הַדָּרִים בָּעִיר הַזֹּאת:

---

the vessels of the soul or the limbs of the body. As the body is cleansed of foreign substances, the heart, thoughts and actions are cleansed from the influences of the *yetzer hara*. The limbs of the body, which carry out the misleading instructions of the *yetzer hara*, are purified through immersion.

(Moreh B'etzba 204)

The *Korban Pesach* was brought after midday on the day before Pesach, earning *erev Pesach* the title of "holiday." It is proper to wear holiday clothing in honor of the occasion. *(Teshuvos V'hanhagos II, Orach Chaim 213)* On *Yom Tov*, one should don even nicer clothing than on Shabbos, since we have an extra obligation of rejoicing on *Yom Tov*.

(Shulchan Aruch, Orach Chaim 529:1, Mishnah Berurah ibid.)

הדלקת הנרות

The candles are lit and the blessings are recited.

בָּרוּךְ אַתָּה יְיָ, אֱלֹהֵינוּ מֶלֶךְ הָעוֹלָם, אֲשֶׁר קִדְּשָׁנוּ בְּמִצְוֹתָיו, וְצִוָּנוּ לְהַדְלִיק נֵר שֶׁל (שַׁבָּת וְשֶׁל) יוֹם טוֹב:

בָּרוּךְ אַתָּה יְיָ, אֱלֹהֵינוּ מֶלֶךְ הָעוֹלָם, שֶׁהֶחֱיָנוּ וְקִיְּמָנוּ וְהִגִּיעָנוּ לַזְּמַן הַזֶּה:

יְהִי רָצוֹן מִלְּפָנֶיךָ יְיָ אֱלֹהֵינוּ וֵאלֹהֵי אֲבוֹתֵינוּ שֶׁיִּבָּנֶה בֵּית הַמִּקְדָּשׁ בִּמְהֵרָה בְיָמֵינוּ. וְתֵן חֶלְקֵנוּ בְּתוֹרָתֶךָ: וְשָׁם נַעֲבָדְךָ בְּיִרְאָה כִּימֵי עוֹלָם וּכְשָׁנִים קַדְמוֹנִיּוֹת:

It is customary to recite the following prayer after the kindling.

יְהִי רָצוֹן מִלְּפָנֶיךָ יְיָ אֱלֹהַי וֵאלֹהֵי אֲבוֹתַי. שֶׁתְּחוֹנֵן אוֹתִי וְאֶת אִישִׁי [וְאֶת בָּנַי וְאֶת אָבִי וְאֶת אִמִּי] וְאֶת כָּל קְרוֹבַי, וְתִתֶּן לָנוּ וּלְכָל יִשְׂרָאֵל חַיִּים טוֹבִים וַאֲרֻכִּים, וְתִזְכְּרֵנוּ בְּזִכְרוֹן טוֹבָה וּבְרָכָה. וְתִפְקְדֵנוּ בִּפְקֻדַּת יְשׁוּעָה וְרַחֲמִים וּתְבָרְכֵנוּ בְּרָכוֹת גְּדוֹלוֹת, וְתַשְׁלִים בָּתֵּינוּ, וְתַשְׁכֵּן שְׁכִינָתְךָ בֵּינֵינוּ, וְזַכֵּנִי לְגַדֵּל בָּנִים וּבְנֵי בָנִים חֲכָמִים וּנְבוֹנִים, אוֹהֲבֵי יְיָ, יִרְאֵי אֱלֹהִים, אַנְשֵׁי אֱמֶת, זֶרַע קֹדֶשׁ בַּיְיָ, דְּבֵקִים וּמְאִירִים אֶת הָעוֹלָם בַּתּוֹרָה וּבְמַעֲשִׂים טוֹבִים וּבְכָל מְלֶאכֶת עֲבוֹדַת הַבּוֹרֵא, אָנָּא שְׁמַע אֶת תְּחִנָּתִי בָּעֵת הַזֹּאת, בִּזְכוּת שָׂרָה וְרִבְקָה וְרָחֵל וְלֵאָה אִמּוֹתֵינוּ, וְהָאֵר נֵרֵנוּ שֶׁלֹּא יִכְבֶּה לְעוֹלָם וָעֶד וְהָאֵר פָּנֶיךָ וְנִוָּשֵׁעָה. אָמֵן:

Chapter 2

The Seder

Why Seder, Order?

This special night is named Seder night for many reasons:

- The supernatural miracles recounted during the course of the *Seder* occurred in the exact order ordained by Hashem. *(Chiddushei Harim)*
- Everything that happens to the Jewish nation, from the Exodus from Egypt until this day, follows the order of Hashem. Every detail in the history of the Jewish people is overseen by loving *hashgacha pratis*, Divine Providence.

  (Maharal)
- Hashem illuminates the night of Pesach with a spiritual light that enables us to realize that any misfortunes we may have endured during the year have been with a purposeful, Divinely ordained design and order.

  (Zer Zahav, Mishpatim)
- The *Seder* lays down an important prerequisite to the orderly service of Hashem throughout the year. Many *mitzvos* are

hinged on the memory of the Exodus, that we were once slaves in Egypt and Hashem took us out from there.

(Beis Aharon)

- One who observes the *Seder* in all its proper details is privileged to receive exalted spiritual revelations from Above, revelations that must be absorbed in an orderly fashion.

(Haggada Dvar Tzvi)

Rabbi Yehuda Hanasi wept as he exclaimed, "There can be one who attains his [share in the future] World in one moment" (Avodah Zara 10b). Why did he not rejoice? A normally lengthy process can be accomplished in so short a time-surely that is reason to celebrate, not to weep!

The third Belzer Rebbe, Rabbi Yissachar Dov Ber Rokeach, explained Rabbi Yehuda's distress. "Whoever is greater than another, his yetzer hara too is greater" (Sukkah 52a). A Torah scholar advances in Torah and mitzvos daily, at a steady pace, while his yetzer hara gains strength as well. The struggle to overpower the yetzer is constant-when the scholar's resources finally expand sufficiently to overcome his enemy, the yetzer hara swells to greater power. And so the battle continues.

But if a righteous scholar is endowed from Above with an abundance of exalted spiritual revelations all at once, if he earns his World to Come in one fell swoop, it becomes much harder for him to overcome his yetzer hara, which has suddenly grown to great power. It was for such a situation that Rabbi Yehuda Hanasi wept.

When we properly observe the Seder and are endowed with an abundance of exalted spiritual revelations, we have to absorb them slowly, in an orderly manner. This ensures that the yetzer hara will not rule over us, G-d forbid. It is called the Seder to indicate this orderly manner of absorbing the spiritual flow from Above.

(Haggada Dvar Tzvi)

Preparing for the Seder

The Chazon Ish recommends opening all boxes of *matzah* prior to *Yom Tov*. It is forbidden to open a container that is closed on all sides on Shabbos or *Yom Tov*. When it is sealed, the box is not a utensil. When the box is opened, a new utensil has been created-a box that can now be opened and closed.

(Chazon Ish, Orach Chaim 51:11)

The *matzos* should be examined one by one for *kefulos,* parts that are doubled over, and *nefuchos*, swollen parts. These parts of the *matzos* may have become *chametz*, and must be discarded. *(Lechem Hapanim on Kitzur Shulchan Aruch 110:1; Shulchan Aruch, Orach Chaim 461:5)* Whole *matzos* must be prepared for *lechem mishneh*, the two loaves of *matzos* used to start every Shabbos or *Yom Tov* meal. Even if just a small piece is missing, it renders a *matzah* invalid for use as *lechem mishneh*.

The *Seder* should begin as soon as possible after nightfall. All preparations should be done in advance-candles for *Yom Tov*, wine for the Four Cups, three *shmura matzos*. The *Seder* plate should be arranged with all its adornments-the *zeroa* that symbolizes the *Korban Pesach*, the egg, *marror*, *charoses*, the *chazeres*, vegetable for *karpas* and salt water.

Plates and silverware should be prepared for the meal, nuts for the children, the white *kittel* donned by the father of the house. The table should be set in advance, with all its finery. On the evening of Pesach, we are no longer slaves; we are free men, royalty, whose table is set long before the feast.

(Aruch Hashulchan, Orach Chaim 472:2)

For the sake of the children, who are a central part of the *mitzvah* of the day, as it says, "And you shall tell your child on that day" *(Shemos 13:8)*, the *Seder* should begin as soon as possible, lest they fall asleep. *(Shulchan Aruch HaRav 472:1)* The sooner the *Seder* begins, the more likely the participants will partake of the *afikoman* before midnight, as the *halachah* requires.

(Maharil, Hilchos Haggada)

Pesach Finery

At the *Seder*, every husband and wife should conduct themselves as a king and queen, and their children as princes. Like royalty, we prepare silver and gold utensils, silk and embroidered clothing-to the extent that Hashem has granted us. *(Shelah)* Dressing in beautiful clothing and using fine utensils fills us with happiness, and outwardly conveys to others our joy and thanks for Hashem's kindness.

(Maharil, Shelah)

Torah study provides food for our soul-it is absorbed into our minds just as food is absorbed in the body. Observance of *mitzvos* creates clothing for our soul, for our deeds envelop us like clothing. Recounting the story of the Exodus from Egypt is not only Torah study-food for the soul-it is also a *mitzvah* in its own right. So on this evening, we wear special clothing.

(Bnei Yissaschar)

During the year, fine vessels are avoided as a remembrance of the destruction of the *Beis Hamikdash*. But on the night of Pesach, our table is set with the finest utensils, even if they are not needed for the meal. They testify to the fact that we are now free from slavery and entitled to use valuable vessels. *(Maharil, Shulchan Aruch HaRav 472:6)* They are also a remembrance of the "great wealth" *(Beraishis 15:14)* that the Children of Israel received when they left Egypt, as Hashem promised to our ancestor Avraham.

(Haggadas Chaim Larosh)

Tall Candles

Many have the custom to light tall candles at the *Seder* table, dubbed by some as "*Ma Nishtana* candles." The light of the candles increases joy for all the *Seder* attendants. They are large enough to burn the whole night, to fulfill the optimal obligation of recounting the miracles of the Exodus throughout the night.

The Zohar teaches that on the night of Pesach, while the Jews were preparing to leave slavery and amassing great riches from their Egyptian neighbors, the sun shone as bright as day. *(Zohar II 38a)* Tall candles, which burn an unusually long time, commemorate that miracle.

(Avudraham)

The White Kittel

G-d, the King of the universe, originally chose us as His special nation on Pesach night. In bygone times, white was the color of royal robes. We too wear white to openly proclaim our association with the King of Kings.

(Pe'er Aharon)

The Torah stipulates that in a court case between a wealthy and a poor man, the judges must view them equally to be able to judge their claims without bias. If necessary, the poor man should be clothed in rich garments like the wealthy man, so the judges can preserve this balance. Pesach is when G-d passes judgment concerning our harvests for the year. We therefore wear white clothing that is similar to Hashem's garb-"His garment is like white snow" *(Daniel 7:9)*.

(Agudas Eizov)

The *Haggada* states that when the Children of Israel were in Egypt, they remained distinct from the non-Jews in their language, in their names and in their clothing. The Torah scholars of Babylon also were distinguished from the masses by their clothing. *(Shabbos 114a)* What was different about their clothing? It was white. *(Rashi, Kiddushin 72a)* The Jewish people in Egypt also wore distinctive white garment, just like the *kittel* worn on *Seder* night.

(Malbim, Hagahos Maaseh Rav 1)

The *kohen gadol*, the holiest Jew of his generation, entered the Holy of Holies in the *Beis Hamikdash*, the holiest point on earth, for

the special Divine service every Yom Kippur, the holiest day in the year. At that time he would wear only white linen garments *(Vayikra 16:4)*. Our service of G-d at the Pesach *Seder* is comparable to the *kohen gadol's* sacred service in the Holy of Holies, and therefore we too don a white garment.

(Maharal)

During the dedication of the *mishkan* in the desert, Moshe Rabbeinu himself served as the sole *kohen* before he bequeathed this privilege, by G-d's command, to Aharon and his sons. While he served, Moshe wore the white linen garments of a regular *kohen*. Pesach commemorates the first time the Jews began to serve G-d, the very first *Korban Pesach* in Egypt. Pesach was the dedication of *avodas Hashem* much like the dedication of the *mishkan*. Moshe wore white at the dedication of the *mishkan*; we wear a white kittel at the dedication of *avodas Hashem*-Pesach.

(Dvar Aharon)

Our Days are Numbered...

As a purely white garment, the *kittel* is indicative of importance and freedom, reminding us of our promotion from the lowly status of slaves to free men and nobles. On the other hand, a *mes* (dead person) is buried in a *kittel*. To prevent us from getting caught up in the excitement and joy of the *Seder*, the *kittel* serves as a reminder that we do not live forever, and we must be mindful of our every action.

(Turei Zahav 472:3)

The *Seder* night is a backdrop for long-lasting memories. The unique *Seder* ambiance exerts a powerful influence on the children to remain faithful to G-d and His Torah. We want our children to remember that one day our bodies will be clothed in a simple white *kittel*, such as the one that the father of the house wears. At the end of our days in this world, we will have nothing to rely on except the merit of our good deeds.

(Haggadas Chasan Sofer)

When one passes on to the World of Truth, he is judged for all his misdeeds and condemned with an appropriate penance to purge his soul. In a *kittel* on *Seder* night, we envision ourselves in the World of Truth, standing before the Heavenly Tribunal. What will our verdict be? But wait-what's this? Hashem has granted us a special favor-we are still in this world! There is still time to repent and rectify our sins.

(Arugas Habosem, Tzav, quoting Rabbi Shmelke of Nikolsburg)

Three Matzos

There are three *matzos* at the *Seder*. Two are for *lechem mishneh*, in remembrance of the manna the Jewish people ate during their forty years in the desert. Every morning the manna would rain down-except for Shabbos. On Friday every Jew collected a double portion of manna for Shabbos. The *lechem mishneh* commemorates this miracle.

The third *matzah* at the *Seder* table is for the additional Torah commandment of eating *matzah* on this night. This *matzah* is broken in half-the smaller half is used for the *mitzvah* of *matzah*, while the larger half is reserved for the *afikoman*, the remembrance of the *Korban Pesach*.

(Tur, Turei Zahav 575)

The three *matzos* represent:

- Three patriarchs-Avraham, Yitzchak and Yaakov.

  (Rokeach 58, quoting Rav Sherira Gaon)

- Three measures of fine flour that Avraham told his wife Sarah to use for baking loaves, in honor of the three angels who came to visit them on Pesach.

  (Rokeach ibid.)

- Three separate shifts during which the Jews offered their *Korban Pesach*-their Pesach lamb-in the *Beis Hamikdash*,

inferred by our Sages *(Pesachim 64b)* from the threefold expression, "the entire congregation of the assembly of Israel shall slaughter it" *(Shemos 12:6)*.

(Pe'er Aharon)

- Three categories of Jewish people-Kohen, Levi and Yisroel.

(Pe'er Aharon)

- Three different times the Jews had *matzah*-while they were still slaves in Egypt, as we say at the beginning of the *Haggada*, "Here is the bread of suffering that our ancestors ate in the land of Egypt"; with the *Korban Pesach* on the original night of Pesach, "with *matzos* and bitter herbs they shall eat it" *(Shemos 12:8)*; and after leaving Egypt, "They baked the dough that they brought out of Egypt into *matzah* cakes" *(Shemos 12:39)*.

(Haggadas Beis Avraham)

- Three types of unleavened bread that were part of the *Korban Todah*, thanksgiving offering.

No slave had ever escaped from Egypt before the miraculous Exodus of the Jewish nation. One who is released from imprisonment is required to bring a Korban Todah in the Beis Hamikdash. Pesach marks the unprecedented redemption of the Jewish nation from Egyptian slavery. The three matzos used at the Seder symbolize our thanks to Hashem for freeing us from slavery.

The firstborn were designated as the kohanim on the night of Pesach, when G-d skipped over their homes, killing only the Egyptian firstborn. [The firstborn lost their status as priests due to the sin of the Golden Calf, and were replaced by Aharon and his sons.] Upon his initiation into service, every kohen was obligated to bring the Korban Todah. Pesach night commemorates the initiation of the firstborn to their priestly service.

(Hamanhig 69)

Why Four Cups?

The four cups represent:

- Four expressions of *geulah* (redemption) that G-d used to tell Moshe how He would take the Children of Israel out of Egypt *(Shemos 6:6-7)*:
  1. "*Vehotzeisi*-I shall bring you out from beneath the burdens of Egypt."
  2. "*Vehitzalti*-I shall rescue you from their service."
  3. "*Vegaalti*-I shall liberate you" from Pharaoh's rule.
  4. "*Velakachti*-I shall take you to Me for a people."

  (Talmud Yerushalmi, Pesachim 10:1)

- Four *tzitzis,* fringes, worn on four-cornered garments also represent the four expressions of *geulah*.

  (Rashi, Bamidbar 15:41)

- Four times Pharaoh's name is mentioned in the account of the cupbearer's dream and Yosef's subsequent interpretation.

  (Beraishis 40:11-13). (Talmud Yerushalmi, Pesachim 10:1)

- Four empires ruled over the Jewish people and persecuted them in exile-Babylon, Medea-Persia, Greece and Rome.

  (ibid.)

- Four cups of punishment G-d will give to the nations who persecuted the Jews in exile, and four corresponding cups of consolation He will give to His nation.

  (ibid.)

- Four special qualities the enslaved Jews maintained in Egypt, for which they merited the *geulah*: their names, their language, they did not marry anyone forbidden by the Torah, and they did not speak slanderous talk.

  (Bnei Yissaschar, quoting Chida)

- Four matriarchs in whose merit the Jews were liberated from Egypt-Sarah, Rivka, Rachel and Leah.

(Maharal)

- Four encampments of three tribes apiece, and their four banners by which the Jewish nation camped in the desert.

(Pe'er Aharon)

- Four different factions of Jews, each with their own idea of how to deal with the mighty Egyptian army that was closing in on them at the shores of the Red Sea.

(Talmud Yerushalmi, Taanis 2:5; Mechilta, Targum Yonasan, Shemos 14:10).

- Four fifths of the Jewish nation, Jews who were unwilling or undeserving to leave Egypt, perished during the ninth plague of darkness.

(Rashi, Shemos 13:18)

The Four Cups

The first cup, drunk for *Kadesh*, is a remembrance of G-d's appointment of our ancestor Avraham to be the father of the Jewish nation. The sequence of these events is described in the early part of the *Haggada*.

The second cup, drunk at the end of *Maggid*, the narration of the Exodus from Egypt, is to give thanks to G-d for bringing us out of Egypt.

The third cup, drunk after *birkas hamazon*, Grace after Meals, alludes to the lowly exile. *Birkas hamazon* follows the the festive meal of the *Seder*.

The fourth cup, drunk after we offer praise to G-d in *Hallel*, refers to the future Redemption of Moshiach.

(Matteh Moshe)

Chapter 3

Arranging the Seder Plate

סדר הקערה לפי מנהג האר״י ז״ל

הועתק מספר עץ חיים וז״ל:

סדר הקערה של השמורות יהי׳ כסדר הזה, והוא שתקח ג׳ מצות שמורות ותניח הכהן למעלה, ואחריו לוי, ולמטה ממנו ישראל, שהם כנגד ג׳ מוחין דאבא עילאה. ואח״כ תקח מרור, וכרפס, וחרוסת, וב׳ מיני תבשיל זרוע של טלה צלויה וביצה מבושלת. ותניח אלו החמשה דברים על הג׳ מצות, דהיינו זרוע שהוא **חסד** בימין שלך, ביצה שהוא **גבורה** בשמאל שלך, מרור שהוא רמז ל**תפארת** באמצע בין הזרוע והביצה, כי תפארת מכריע בין חסד לגבורה, ואח״כ החרוסת בקו ימין תחת הזרוע, מפני שהוא רומז ל**נצח**, ואח״כ הכרפס שהוא רומז ל**הוד** תניח תחת הביצה בקו השמאל שלך, ואח״כ תקח החזרת ותניח למטה מן המרור בקו האמצעי שהוא כנגד **יסוד**, והוא כדי לעשות אח״כ כריכה עם החזרת. והקערה בעצמה הכוללת כולם היא **המלכות**, הרי יו״ד ספירות דחכמה, ואל ישנה מזה הסדר, ואשרי לו מי שמכוין להנ״ל, עכ״ל:

The Contents of the Seder Plate

The *Seder* plate is arranged according to the great Kabbalist, the Arizal, Rabbi Yitzchak Luria. Although this order is based on profound mystical reasons, it does not preclude other simpler explanations.

Zeroa: An arm or foreleg commemorates the *Korban Pesach*, the Pesach lamb or kid goat sacrifice, which was the central observance of Pesach in the times of the Temple. As such, it is placed on the top right of the plate, at the one o'clock position.

Beitzah: The egg commemorates the *Korban Chagigah*, the festival celebration sacrifice, which was usually eaten first at the Seder to become satisfied before eating the *Korban Pesach*. It is placed on the top left of the plate, at eleven o'clock.

Marror: Bitter herbs were eaten together with the *Korban Pesach*, and are therefore placed below the *zeroa* in the middle of the second row, in the center of the plate.

Charoses: This mixture of chopped fruit and nuts is used as a dip for the *marror*. It is placed below the *marror* at the right side of the third row, at four o'clock.

Karpas: This vegetable is eaten in part to absolve us from saying another blessing on the *marror* when we eat it later. It is also placed in the third row, following the *marror*, but to the left, at the eight o'clock position. *Karpas's* connection to the *marror* is not as strong as *charoses*, which is eaten together with the *marror*.

Chazeres: The bitter herbs eaten in the *matzah* sandwich following the main *marror* course. It is placed at the end, in the middle of the fourth row, at six o'clock.

The Zeroa

In early generations it was customary to use the arm or foreleg of a lamb, as a true commemoration to the *Korban Pesach*. Today, to differentiate from the actual *Korban Pesach*, most homes have a chicken neck or other animal part on the *Seder* plate. Nevertheless, it is still referred to as a *zeroa* to allude to Hashem's "*zeroa netuya*-outstretched arm" *(Devarim 26:8)*, the miracles He did on behalf of the Jewish nation to liberate them from slavery.

(Beis Yosef; Avudraham; Orchos Chaim)

The Egg

The *Korban Chagiga* is commemorated with a cooked food. Why specifically an egg? The Aramaic word for egg is *beia*, which has the same root letters as the Aramaic word for "desire." The *zeroa* and the *beia* together remind us that G-d "desired" to liberate us with an "outstretched arm."

(Beis Yosef; Avudraham; Orchos Chaim)

The Charoses

What does the word *charoses* mean?

- Sharp and acidic.

(Rashi, Pesachim 30b)

- Crushed vegetables, in Aramaic.

(Ohr Zarua 456)

- Any dip for food.

(Machzor Vitri)

- From the word "*cheres*," earthenware, in memory of the earthen bricks the Children of Israel had to make in Egypt.

(Mordechai on Pesachim, Seder Haggada Hakatzer quoting Talmud Yerushalmi)

The most common Ashkenazic recipe for *charoses* today includes wine, apples, pears and nuts; ginger and cinnamon are optional. These ingredients are based on a quote from the Torah: "*U'vacharoshes even … u'vacharoshes eitz*-and with stone-cutting … and with woodcarving" *(Shemos 31:5)*. The Hebrew words "*even*" and "*eitz*" are acronyms for the Yiddish words *epel* (apples), *baren* (pears), *nis* (nuts), *ingbar* (ginger) and *tzimrind* (cinnamon).

Some people add other fruits to their *charoses,* fruits that the Scripture uses as a metaphor for the Jewish people. "Beneath the apple

tree I aroused Your love" *(Shir Hashirim 8:5)*. "As many as a pomegranate's seeds" *(ibid. 4:3)*. "The fig tree has formed its first figs" *(ibid. 2:13)*. "I shall ascend on your date-palm" *(ibid. 7:9)*. "To the nut-garden I went down" *(ibid. 6:11)*.

(Teshuvos HaGeonim, quoted by Tosfos, Pesachim 115a)

Rashi explains that Jews are like nuts. Only the wooden shell can be seen from the outside; the flavorful nut within is completely concealed. The Jew's inner qualities are sealed inside, for the Torah scholar does not wear his wisdom on the outside. Only when he enters into conversation does the extent of his wisdom show.

The *Midrash* says that just as a nut does not get dirty when it falls into mud, for it is protected by its shell, so the Jews, despite their exile among the nations who persecute them, remain pure and untarnished.

Almonds in Hebrew are "*shkeidim*," from the same root as "*shkida,*" diligence and speed. G-d promises to diligently speed up our Redemption.

The *charoses* is softened with wine, a red liquid reminiscent of the first plague of *dam*, blood. *(Yerushalmi, Pesachim 10:3)* The Jewish nation is like a good wine.

(Pri Eitz Chaim, Shaar Chag Hamatzos 6)

Chapter 4

The Simanim of the Seder

סימני הסדר

The order of the seder

קַדֵּשׁ. וּרְחַץ. כַּרְפַּס. יַחַץ. מַגִּיד. רָחְצָה. מוֹצִיא. מַצָּה. מָרוֹר. כּוֹרֵךְ. שֻׁלְחָן עוֹרֵךְ. צָפוּן. בָּרֵךְ. הַלֵּל. נִרְצָה:

Reciting the Simanim

Pesach is a preparation for our acceptance of the Torah on Shavuos seven weeks hence. "The Torah is acquired only through *simanim*-signs" *(Eruvin 54b, Shabbos 104a)*. *Simanim* are usually understood as mental notes, hints used to remember a given subject matter better. But this can also be interpreted as referring to the *simanim* of the *Seder*. Perform the *Seder* properly, remember the *simanim*; on Shavuos, you will then be ready to acquire the Torah. *(ibid.)*

קדש

Kiddush should be recited and the Seder begun as soon after synagogue services as possible-however, not before nightfall.

הִנְנִי מוּכָן וּמְזוּמָן לְקַיֵּים מִצְוַת קִידּוּשׁ וּמִצְוַת כּוֹס רִאשׁוֹן שֶׁל אַרְבַּע כּוֹסוֹת, לְשֵׁם יִחוּד קוּדְשָׁא בְּרִיךְ הוּא וּשְׁכִינְתֵּיהּ עַל יְדֵי הַהוּא טָמִיר וְנֶעְלָם בְּשֵׁם כָּל יִשְׂרָאֵל: וִיהִי נוֹעַם אֲדֹנָי אֱלֹהֵינוּ עָלֵינוּ וּמַעֲשֵׂה יָדֵינוּ כּוֹנְנָה עָלֵינוּ וּמַעֲשֵׂה יָדֵינוּ כּוֹנְנֵהוּ:

On Shabbos begin here:

וַיְהִי עֶרֶב וַיְהִי בֹקֶר:

יוֹם הַשִּׁשִּׁי. וַיְכֻלּוּ הַשָּׁמַיִם וְהָאָרֶץ וְכָל צְבָאָם: וַיְכַל אֱלֹהִים בַּיּוֹם הַשְּׁבִיעִי מְלַאכְתּוֹ אֲשֶׁר עָשָׂה וַיִּשְׁבֹּת בַּיּוֹם הַשְּׁבִיעִי מִכָּל מְלַאכְתּוֹ אֲשֶׁר עָשָׂה: וַיְבָרֶךְ אֱלֹהִים אֶת יוֹם הַשְּׁבִיעִי וַיְקַדֵּשׁ אֹתוֹ כִּי בוֹ שָׁבַת מִכָּל מְלַאכְתּוֹ אֲשֶׁר בָּרָא אֱלֹהִים לַעֲשׂוֹת:

The Torah stipulates that in order to reclaim a lost object, we must first declare what unique signs-*simanim*-distinguish it. As subjects in exile, over the course of the year we tend to fall from the desired levels of holiness. But on the evening of Pesach, an exalted spiritual light is revealed which can restore us to our previous levels. To attain those lofty heights, we must begin by declaring the *simanim*, the signs of the *Seder*.

(Tiferes Ish)

When Aharon Hakohen had to serve in the *Beis Hamikdash* for the first time, he was too embarrassed to step forward until his brother Moshe Rabbeinu urged him to go. We begin by reciting all the *simanim* out loud, ensuring that we know what to do so we won't be embarrassed to proceed with the exalted Divine service of the *Seder*. The recitation arouses the appropriate intentions for fulfilling the requirements of the *Seder*.

(Dvar Aharon)

On all nights other than Friday, begin here:

סַבְרִי מָרָנָן:

בָּרוּךְ אַתָּה יְהוָֹה אֱלֹהֵינוּ מֶלֶךְ הָעוֹלָם בּוֹרֵא פְּרִי הַגָּפֶן:

בָּרוּךְ אַתָּה יְהוָֹה אֱלֹהֵינוּ מֶלֶךְ הָעוֹלָם אֲשֶׁר בָּחַר בָּנוּ מִכָּל עָם וְרוֹמְמָנוּ מִכָּל לָשׁוֹן וְקִדְּשָׁנוּ בְּמִצְוֹתָיו. וַתִּתֶּן לָנוּ יְהוָֹה אֱלֹהֵינוּ בְּאַהֲבָה (לשבת: שַׁבָּתוֹת לִמְנוּחָה וּ) מוֹעֲדִים לְשִׂמְחָה חַגִּים וּזְמַנִּים לְשָׂשׂוֹן (אֶת יוֹם הַשַּׁבָּת הַזֶּה וְ) אֶת יוֹם חַג הַמַּצּוֹת הַזֶּה זְמַן חֵרוּתֵנוּ (בְּאַהֲבָה) מִקְרָא קֹדֶשׁ זֵכֶר לִיצִיאַת מִצְרָיִם. כִּי בָנוּ בָחַרְתָּ וְאוֹתָנוּ קִדַּשְׁתָּ מִכָּל הָעַמִּים. (וְשַׁבָּת) וּמוֹעֲדֵי קָדְשֶׁךָ (בְּאַהֲבָה וּבְרָצוֹן) בְּשִׂמְחָה וּבְשָׂשׂוֹן הִנְחַלְתָּנוּ. בָּרוּךְ אַתָּה יְהוָֹה מְקַדֵּשׁ (הַשַּׁבָּת וְ) יִשְׂרָאֵל וְהַזְּמַנִּים:

On all nights conclude here:

בָּרוּךְ אַתָּה יְהוָֹה אֱלֹהֵינוּ מֶלֶךְ הָעוֹלָם
שֶׁהֶחֱיָנוּ וְקִיְּמָנוּ וְהִגִּיעָנוּ לַזְּמַן הַזֶּה:

On Saturday night, add the following two blessings:

בָּרוּךְ אַתָּה יְהוָֹה אֱלֹהֵינוּ מֶלֶךְ הָעוֹלָם בּוֹרֵא מְאוֹרֵי הָאֵשׁ:

בָּרוּךְ אַתָּה יְהוָֹה אֱלֹהֵינוּ מֶלֶךְ הָעוֹלָם הַמַּבְדִּיל בֵּין קֹדֶשׁ לְחֹל בֵּין אוֹר לְחֹשֶׁךְ בֵּין יִשְׂרָאֵל לָעַמִּים בֵּין יוֹם הַשְּׁבִיעִי לְשֵׁשֶׁת יְמֵי הַמַּעֲשֶׂה. בֵּין קְדֻשַּׁת שַׁבָּת לִקְדֻשַּׁת יוֹם טוֹב הִבְדַּלְתָּ. וְאֶת יוֹם הַשְּׁבִיעִי מִשֵּׁשֶׁת יְמֵי הַמַּעֲשֶׂה קִדַּשְׁתָּ. הִבְדַּלְתָּ וְקִדַּשְׁתָּ אֶת עַמְּךָ יִשְׂרָאֵל בִּקְדֻשָּׁתֶךָ: בָּרוּךְ אַתָּה יְהוָֹה הַמַּבְדִּיל בֵּין קֹדֶשׁ לְקֹדֶשׁ:

One drinks the wine while reclining to his left side.

Kadesh

Red Wine

The best type of wine is red wine, for when Shlomo Hamelech warns about overindulging in wine, it says, "Do not look at wine when it becomes red" *(Mishlei 23:31)*.

(Talmud Yerushalmi 10:1)

Red wine is also reminiscent of blood:

- Every morning and every evening, Pharaoh would bathe in the blood of 150 Jewish children to cure his *tzoraas* skin infection.

(Ohr Zarua 256)

- The first plague that ravaged Egypt was blood-all the water in the land turned to blood.

(Pri Megadim 472; Eishel Avraham 13)

- To partake of the *Korban Pesach*, all the males in Egypt were circumcised.
- The blood of the *Korban Pesach* itself was smeared on the doorposts of every Jewish home.

(Ohr Zarua 256)

Making Kiddush

Usually only the head of the family recites *Kiddush* at a regular Shabbos or *Yom Tov* meal. If everyone around the table were to say *Kiddush* simultaneously, at least one person would inevitably confuse the words because of all the voices around him. But at the *Seder* everyone carefully follows along in the *Haggada*, so it is unlikely that anyone will get confused.

(Vayagged Moshe 15)

The *mitzvah* of the *Seder* is to recount the miracles that Hashem performed during the Exodus from Egypt. In the *Kiddush* we proclaim, "*zacher litzias Mitzrayim*-in remembrance of the Exodus from Egypt." Then we proceed to tell the long story of the Exodus. Normally such a long interruption between *Kiddush* and the meal would not be permitted. But in this case, the story of the *Haggada* is considered a continuation of the *Kiddush*, a remembrance of the Exodus.

(Haggada Chaim Larosh)

Reclining

Once *Kiddush* is made, we drink the whole cup in a reclining position. This is done quickly, just as the *Korban Pesach* was eaten in a hurry.

(Shemos 12:11).

We recline many times throughout the *Haggada*, notably while drinking the Four Cups and eating the *matzah*. In bygone times, important people would eat their meals while reclining on couches. At the *Seder* we adopt this custom to show that we are no longer slaves: we conduct ourselves as free men.

(Remah, Orach Chaim 472:2)

Reclining alludes to the way G-d led the Children of Israel through the desert. They reclined on their beds while Hashem escorted them with the seven Clouds of Divine Glory.

(Midrash Aggadas Shemos 13:18)

The Torah states, "G-d turned the people around" *(Shemos 13:18)*. But the verse can be interpreted differently-it can mean that G-d caused them to recline. Throughout the years of slavery of the Children of Israel in Egypt, they were not permitted to eat sitting or reclining-only standing or walking. The evening of the original Pesach in Egypt was the first time they were able to eat and recline at their tables in a normal, relaxed manner. The Sages require even the poorest Jew to recline at the *Seder*, for this position symbolizes G-d bringing us out of Egypt.

(Midrash Rabba Shemos 20:18; Eitz Yosef)

ורחץ

The head of the household washes his hands, but do not recite a blessing.

Urchatz

Why Wash Our Hands?

Prominent *halachic* authorities maintain that whenever we eat wet finger food, we must first wash our hands the way we do for bread. While some do not adhere to this opinion during the rest of the year, at the *Seder* everyone is strict in this observance. The blessing of *al netilas yodayim* is not recited in deference to the authorities who believe that this washing is not obligatory.

(Shulchan Aruch, Orach Chaim 473)

During the times of the *Beis Hamikdash*, our ancestors carefully observed the laws of *tumah* and *taharah,* ritual impurity and purity, including the obligation to wash their hands before eating wet food. On this evening, in remembrance of the *Korban Pesach*, we follow the practice of the days of yore.

(Shvach Pesach)

This unusual hand washing piques the children's interest, and they begin to question this practice. Once their curiosity is aroused the children will continue to ask questions about other observances as the *Seder* progresses, creating an excellent educational opportunity to share the miracles of the Exodus.

(Chok Yaakov; Orach Chaim 473:28)

On Yom Kippur, the *kohen gadol* used to purify himself by immersing in a *mikveh* between each of the stages of the Divine service in the *Beis Hamikdash*-some tasks which were also performed during the rest of the year, and others which were exclusive to the

כרפס

Everyone takes a piece of a vegetable, smaller in volume than an half an egg, dips it into salt water, and recites the following blessing (one should bear in mind that the blessing also applies to the Maror):

בָּרוּךְ אַתָּה יְהֹוָה אֱלֹהֵינוּ מֶלֶךְ הָעוֹלָם, בּוֹרֵא פְּרִי הָאֲדָמָה:

special Yom Kippur service. In a similar way, we start from *Kiddush*, which is performed every Shabbos and *Yom Tov*, and then move on to the *Seder* observances unique to Pesach night. We mark the transition by washing our hands to purify ourselves.

(Agudas Eizov)

Karpas

The Vegetable Course

Eating a vegetable before we start the meal, and dipping it in salt water prior to the main *seudah*, are practices which are unique to the Seder night *(Rashi, Pesachim 114b; Tur 473)*. Besides arousing the children's interest and curiosity, it also arouses an appetite for the *matzah*.

(Maharil)

Noblemen would eat an appetizer dipped in flavorful dressing before a meal. Tonight we conduct ourselves in the superior manner of high society. The vegetable also satiates us enough to relate the story of the Exodus comfortably, until it is time for the main meal.

(Pri Megadim, Mishbetzos Zahav 473:7)

The first and third letters in the word *karpas*, *kaf* and *pei*, allude to the *kesones pasim*, the fine woolen robe that Yaakov made for his son Yosef *(Beraishis 37:3)*. This robe caused the entire sequence of events that culminated with the great Exodus from Egypt. The brothers were jealous of Yosef's robe, and sold him as a slave to Egypt. Yosef became a ruler there, and the entire family eventually settled in Egypt, initially as honored citizens. Generations later, they became slaves; on Pesach, G-d took them out of Egypt with a mighty hand.

(Birkei Yosef 473:14)

Karpas commemorates the crushing labor-"*parech*" *(Shemos 1:13)*- that the Egyptians forced on the 600,000 Israelites who were eventually redeemed. Our Sages often refer to them as the "*shishim ribo*," sixty times 10,000. The letters in *karpas-kof*, *reish*, *pei*, *samech*-can be rearranged to spell out *samech-parech*. *Samech* has the numerical value of sixty. Sixty *parech-karpas*-represents the sixty times ten thousand Jewish males and the crushing labor they were subjected to in Egypt.

(Avudraham; Maharil)

There was a therapeutic vegetable called *karpas*, celery, that the Israelites used to eat after their heavy toil. The vegetable soothed their weary limbs and strengthened their tired bodies, enabling them to withstand the heavy yoke of labor during their bitter exile in Egypt. Others say the Egyptians used to feed the Israelites this vegetable so they could continue their hard work.

(Birkei Yosef 473:14)

The Blessing

We make the blessing *borei pri haadama* on the *karpas*, while having in mind the *marror* that we will eat later in the *Seder*.

The *marror* is actually eaten as part of the meal, after we have already washed for *hamotzi*. Normally, the *hamotzi* blessing exempts blessings on other foods eaten as part of the meal. The *marror*, however, cannot be considered part of the meal, since it is not eaten

to satisfy hunger. We eat *marror* at the *Seder* because we are obligated to eat it, not as a filling or tasty course. So even though the *marror* is eaten after we make *hamotzi*, it needs its own blessing of *borei pri haadama*.

Other authorities contend that *marror* is an integral part of the Seder because of the obligation to eat bitter herbs on this evening. According to this view, an additional blessing on the *marror* would be unnecessary, since the food is already included in the *hamotzi* blessing.

In order to satisfy both opinions, the *borei pri haadama* on the *karpas* covers the *marror* later in the meal. But we must eat less than a *k'zayis* of the vegetable. A *k'zayis* of *karpas* would require a concluding blessing of *borei nefashos*, and then the original blessing would no longer be valid for the *marror*.

(Tur, Shulchan Aruch 473)

Dipping the Karpas

Dipping is a sign of freedom, for a slave cannot allow himself the luxury of enhancing his food with a dip. *(Bayis Chadash 473)* The main obligation of dipping on this evening is to dip the *marror* in *charoses*. We first dip the *karpas* in salt water to satisfy our desire for a flavorful dipped appetizer; later, when we dip the *marror*, it is solely for the sake of the *mitzvah*. *(Gevuros Hashem 3)* The salt water reminds us of the Israelites' salty tears when they cried to Hashem in prayer on account of their suffering.

Dipping the *karpas* is reminiscent of the selling of Yosef, the very beginning of the Exodus. Before Yosef was sold, his brothers removed the special woolen robe he wore. They dipped the coat in goat's blood and showed it Yaakov, claiming that a wild animal had attacked him *(Beraishis 37:31)*.

(Maasei Hashem)

יחץ

The head of the household breaks the middle matzah in two unequal parts. The smaller part is replaced between the two whole Matzos, and the larger part is put away for later use as the Afikoman.

In order to be able to eat the first *Korban Pesach* in Egypt, the Israelites first had to circumcise themselves and then immerse in water, just as a convert does *(Pesachim 92a)*. Because so many men immersed in the Nile River, the water became polluted. We commemorate the occasion by dipping *karpas* in salt water, which is considered halachically polluted and unacceptable for ritual washing.

(Rabbi Sholom Rokeach, first Belzer Rebbe)

Matzah and Vegetables

At the beginning of *Maggid*, we proclaim, "*Ha lachma anya*-this is the bread of poverty that our ancestors ate in the land of Egypt." The Egyptians provided their Jewish slaves only with *matzah*, unleavened bread, which was difficult to digest. When the hail and locusts destroyed all vegetation, the Egyptians were appropriately punished for their callousness. To allude to this punishment, we specifically eat a vegetable, the *karpas*, and then announce, "*Ha lachma anya*," this is the bread of poverty that the Egyptians forced upon our ancestors-and they were duly punished.

(Pe'er Aharon)

Yachatz

Breaking the Matzah

During *Yachatz* we break the middle *matzah* into two slightly uneven parts-one slightly larger than the other. Hashem originally condemned Avraham's descendants to exile in a foreign land for 400 years *(Beraishis 15:13)*. But in His great mercy, Hashem cut the years by about half, much as the middle *matzah* is broken just about in half. The Jewish nation spent only 210 years in Egypt until the Exodus, instead of the full four hundred. *(Chida, Simchas Haregel, Rimzei Haseder 3)* Breaking the middle *matzah* is also reminiscent of the splitting of the Red Sea.

(Orchos Chaim)

Many times throughout the year there is a *mitzvah* from the Torah to eat, an obligation to have a festive meal or partake of a particular food. There are two aspects to this physical obligation, whether it be on Shabbos, *Yom Tov* or any day of the year. Half is for Hashem-for His sake, for spiritual purposes; and half for our own sake-the physical enjoyment involved. When we break the middle *matzah*, it signifies, "Half for Hashem, half for me."

(Olelos Efrayim)

When two beloved friends bid each other farewell, some have a custom to divide a ring in half, each keeping his half in remembrance of his affection for the other. Here, too, we break the middle *matzah* as a way of making a covenant with Hashem, promising to faithfully follow His ways and keep His commandments.

(Menachem Tzion, Rabbi Mendel of Riminov)

At the *Seder*, everything comes in groups of four: four cups of wine, four expressions of redemption, four questions, the four sons. But there are only three *matzos*! Break one *matzah* into two, and now there are four.

(Taamei Minhagim, quoting Rabbi Tzvi Hersh of Djikov)

Bread of a Poor Man

Normally bread is broken at the start of a meal, immediately before eating the bread or *matzah*. Why is it necessary to break the *matzah* so early on in the *Seder,* long before we are going to eat it?

The Torah says, "You shall eat upon it [the *Korban Pesach*] *lechem oni*, bread of suffering" *(Devarim 16:3)*. The word "*oni*" is written in the Torah without the letter *vav*. It can also be read "*ani*," a poor person. When we declare, "*Ha lachma anya*-this is the bread of poverty," we refer to the *matzah*, the *lechem oni*, the *lechem ani*. There must be a broken *matzah* lying on the table, because surely a poor man would not have a complete loaf-only a broken piece of bread.

(Beis Yosef, quoting Kol Bo)

"*Lechem oni*" can also be interpreted as the bread of answers. At the *Seder* we ask many questions and provide answers. As we point to the *matzah*, announcing "*Ha lachma anya*," we fulfill both interpretations of "*lechem oni*" simultaneously: as we provide the answers, the broken *matzah* of the poor man lies before us.

(Shulchan Aruch HaRav 473:36)

The Middle Matzah

When it is time for *Motzi*, the blessing on the *matzah*, the top *matzah* will be the first encountered. "We do not pass over *mitzvos*" *(Pesachim 64a)*, so we cannot skip over the first *matzah* and go to the second-we must perform the *mitzvah* as soon as it comes our way.

Whenever possible, blessings are pronounced over a whole, complete food. We are even more stringent on Shabbos and *Yom Tov*, when the blessing of *hamotzi lechem min haaretz* is pronounced on two whole uncut loaves of bread or *matzah*. Since the first *matzah* is the one over which the blessing will be pronounced, it

would not be appropriate for it to be broken. So we break the second *matzah* instead.

(Rosh, Pesachim)

According to *Kabbalah*, the middle *matzah* refers to the tribe of *Levi*. Just as the tribe of *Levi* was divided into two parts-*kohanim* and *levi'im*-the middle *matzah* is divided as well.

(Haggada Chodesh Haaviv)

In the Scriptures, the middle of something is often represented by the word heart: the heart of the heavens, the heart of the earth, the heart of the sea. Our holy sources tell us that "there is nothing so perfect as a broken heart," a heart broken by feelings of remorse and humility. We break the middle *matzah*, our hearts, subjugating our hearts and deeds to Hashem.

(Haggada Dvar Tzvi)

If the three matzos represent our forefathers, Avraham, Yitzchak and Yaakov, the middle matzah is Yitzchak. Before the ultimate redemption, G-d will call on each of the forefathers to propose merit for which their descendants should be redeemed. After all, they have sinned! Only Yitzchak will try to find merit for them.

The average human life span is only seventy years, Yitzchak will argue. The first twenty years are not punishable by the Heavenly court. Fifty years remain. Half of that time, Yitzchak will plead, is spent sleeping, and man cannot sin while he is sleeping. Twenty-five years remain. Twelve and a half years are devoted to eating and praying. Only twelve and a half years are left!

Based on this logic, Yitzchak will propose a deal: Hashem should forgive half of the remaining years, and Yitzchak would accept the rest upon himself. (Shabbos 89b) We break the middle matzah in half, in tribute to Yitzchak who will accept half of the Jewish sins upon himself.

(Shem Shlomo)

The Afikoman

The middle *matzah* is broken in half. The smaller piece will be used for *Motzi Matzah*. The larger half will be reserved for the *afikoman*, so it will be sufficient for the optimal requirement for the *afikoman*-two *k'zaisim* of *matzah*, the size of two olives.

The designated larger *matzah* is hidden away until *Tzafun*, when we eat the *afikoman* for dessert. Hiding the *matzah* provides entertainment for the children. *(Shulchan Aruch 473)* Also, if it is hidden, sufficient *matzah* will undoubtedly remain for the important *mitzvah* of *afikoman*.

(Siddur Yaavetz)

The fact that we have an *afikoman* at the *Seder* is a source of shame for us. The *afikoman* is a remembrance of the *Korban Pesach*, the sacrifice which was offered every Pesach in the holy Temple. We are ashamed that we can't bring a *Korban Pesach* in the *Beis Hamikdash* today, for the holy Temple was destroyed-on account of our own sins. We conceal the *afikoman*, the reminder of our grave sins.

(Divrei Yoel)

On Their Shoulders

When the Jews left Egypt, the verse states, "The people picked up their dough before it could rise, their leftovers bound up in their garments on their shoulders" *(Shemos 12:34)*. In remembrance, the *afikoman* at our *Seder* is wrapped in a cloth *(Shulchan Aruch HaRav 473:13, quoting Rokeach)*, and some people place it on their shoulders

(Shulchan Aruch HaRav 473:13, quoting Maharshal).

When someone has a cherished possession-an exquisite *Kiddush* cup purchased in Israel, for example-when he returns to America by

plane, he will insist on carrying the cup himself. He will not put it in his luggage that will be stowed far away in the belly of the airplane.

We want to show our children how much we cherish the *mitzvos*. Although every Israelite had ninety donkeys to carry his belongings out of Egypt *(Bechoros 5b)*, each Jew bundled his leftover dough on his own shoulder. In a display of fondness for the *mitzvah* of *matzah*, we place it on our shoulders before hiding it away.

(Haggada Chodesh Haaviv)

The *Korban Pesach*, too, was carried home from the *Beis Hamikdash* on the owner's shoulder. *(Pesachim 65b)* And the *afikoman* is a remembrance for the *Korban Pesach*.

(Vayagged Moshe 18)

Between Two Cushions

The *afikoman*, broken from the middle *matzah*, is often placed between two cushions. As a portion of Yitzchak's *matzah*, the *afikoman* represents the qualities of *gevura,* severity, and *din,* judgment. To temper the Divine Attribute of severity and judgment, it needs to be sweetened by a good dose of compassion-Yaakov's spiritual quality.

Yaakov was called "*ish tam*-a perfect, wholesome man" *(Beraishis 25:27)*. *Tam* is made of the letters *taf* and *mem*, giving it the numerical value of 440. *Kar*, the Hebrew word for cushion, is spelled *kaf, reish*, which equals 220. Two cushions (2 x 220) equal 440. We take the *afikoman*-a representation of severity and judgment-and place it between two cushions, sweetening it with Yaakov's quality of compassion.

(Haggada Dvar Tzvi)

Two cushions, twice *kar*, totaling 440, has the same numerical value as the word *nafshi*, my soul (*nun*=50, *fei*=80, *shin*=300, *yud*=10). *Matzah* equals 135 (*mem*=40, *tzaddik*=90, *hei*=5). When the

value of *matzah* is broken in half, the yield is two slightly uneven parts-67 and 68. The larger portion, 68, is designated for the *afikoman*. Sixty-eight is also the numerical value of the word *chaim*, life (*ches*=8, *yud*=10, *yud*=10, *mem*=40). By placing the *afikoman* between two cushions, we emphasize that the main aspect of life is the spiritual portion-our souls-which continue to exist beyond this world, in the World to Come.

(ibid.)

Stealing the Afikoman

Children everywhere anticipate the *Seder* night. Who will be able to steal the *afikoman*? The exciting promise of a prize in exchange for the stolen *afikoman* keeps the children awake. *(Chok Yaakov 472)* *Hallel*, the praises of G-d that we sing after the Pesach evening services, opens the gateway of Heaven that normally separates G-d from His chosen nation, revealing an exalted spiritual light. Parents desire that even their youngest children receive this special light. The game of stealing the *afikoman* keeps them awake until the end of the *Seder*, ensuring that they will be privileged to receive this revelation together with the adults.

(Avodas Yisroel)

Despite the great outcry in Egypt when all their firstborn died, a miracle happened that no dogs barked as the Children of Israel left the land *(Shemos 11:7)*. The Talmud recommends residing in a city where dogs bark, for their barks alert the residents to thefts *(Pesachim 114a)*. There must have been a lot of thefts when the Jews left Egypt-thieves who took advantage of the quiet dogs that night! By trying to steal the *afikoman*, the children allude to the great miracle of the dogs who did not bark when our people left the land of their enslavement.

(Rabbi Shimon Sofer of Cracow)

מַגִּיד

Recite the Haggadah.
Some recite the following passage frome the Zohar prior to beginning Magid:

הֲרֵינִי מוּכָן וּמְזוּמָּן לְקַיֵּם הַמִּצְוָה לְסַפֵּר בִּיצִיאַת מִצְרַיִם, לְשֵׁם יִחוּד קוּדְשָׁא בְּרִיךְ הוּא וּשְׁכִינְתֵּיהּ עַל יְדֵי הַהוּא טָמִיר וְנֶעְלָם בְּשֵׁם כָּל יִשְׂרָאֵל: וִיהִי נוֹעַם אֲדֹנָי אֱלֹהֵינוּ עָלֵינוּ וּמַעֲשֵׂה יָדֵינוּ כּוֹנְנָה עָלֵינוּ וּמַעֲשֵׂה יָדֵינוּ כּוֹנְנֵהוּ:

פִּקּוּדָא בָּתַר דָּא לְסַפֵּר בִּשְׁבָחָא דִיצִיאַת מִצְרָיִם, דְּאִיהוּ חִיּוּבָא עַל בַּר נָשׁ לְאִשְׁתָּעֵי בְּהַאי שְׁבָחָא לְעָלְמִין, הָכִי אוֹקִימְנָא, כָּל בַּר נָשׁ דְּאִשְׁתָּעֵי בִּיצִיאַת מִצְרַיִם וּבְהַהוּא סִפּוּר חָדֵי בְּחֶדְוָה, זַמִּין אִיהוּ לְמֶחֱדֵי בִּשְׁכִינְתָּא לְעָלְמָא דְּאָתֵי דְּהוּא חֵדוּ מִכֹּלָּא, דְּהַאי אִיהוּ בַּר נָשׁ דְּחָדֵי בְּמָרֵיהּ, וְקוּדְשָׁא בְּרִיךְ הוּא חָדֵי בְּהַהוּא סִפּוּר. בֵּיהּ שַׁעְתָּא כָּנִישׁ קוּדְשָׁא בְּרִיךְ הוּא לְכָל פַּמַלְיָיא דִילֵיהּ, וְאָמַר לוֹן זִילוּ וְשָׁמְעוּ סִפּוּרָא דִשְׁבָחָא דִילִי דְקָא מִשְׁתָּעוּ בָּנַי וְחָדָאן בְּפוּרְקָנִי. כְּדֵין כֻּלְּהוּ מִתְכַּנְשִׁין וְאָתְיָין, וּמִתְחַבְּרִין בַּהֲדֵיהוּ דְיִשְׂרָאֵל, וְשָׁמְעוּ סִפּוּרָא דִשְׁבָחָא דְקָא חָדָאן בְּחֶדְוָה דְפוּרְקָנָא דְמָרֵהוֹן, כְּדֵין אָתְיָין וְאוֹדָן לֵיהּ לְקוּדְשָׁא בְּרִיךְ הוּא עַל כָּל אִינוּן נִסִּין וּגְבוּרָן, וְאוֹדָאן לֵיהּ עַל עַמָּא קַדִּישָׁא דְּאִית לֵיהּ בְּאַרְעָא דַחֲדָאן בְּחֶדְוָה דְפוּרְקָנָא דְמָארֵהוֹן, כְּדֵין אִתּוֹסֵף חֵילָא וּגְבוּרְתָּא לְעֵילָּא וְיִשְׂרָאֵל בְּהַאי סִפּוּרָא יָהֲבִין חֵילָא לְמָארֵיהוֹן כְּמַלְכָּא דְאִתּוֹסַף חֵילָא וּגְבוּרְתָּא כַּד מְשַׁבְּחִין גְבוּרְתֵּיהּ וְאוֹדָן לֵיהּ וְכֻלְּהוּ דַחֲלִין מִקַּמֵּיהּ וְאִסְתַּלֵּק יְקָרֵיהּ עַל כֻּלְּהוּ. וּבְגִין כָּךְ אִית לְשַׁבָּחָא וּלְאִשְׁתָּעֵי בְּסִפּוּרָא דָא כְּמָה דְּאִתְּמַר. כְּגַוְנָא דָא חוֹבָא אִיהוּ עַל בַּר נָשׁ לְאִשְׁתָּעֵי תָּדִיר קַמֵּי קוּדְשָׁא בְּרִיךְ הוּא וּלְפַרְסוּמֵי נִיסָּא בְּכָל אִינוּן נִסִּין דְּעָבַד. וְאִי תֵימָא אַמַּאי אִיהוּ חוֹבְתָא וְהָא קוּדְשָׁא בְּרִיךְ הוּא יָדַע כֹּלָּא כָּל מַה דַּהֲוָה וְיֶהֱוֵי לְבָתַר דְּנָא, אַמַּאי פִּרְסוּמָא דָא קַמֵּיהּ עַל מַה דְּאִיהוּ עָבַד וְאִיהוּ יָדַע, אֶלָּא וַדַּאי אִצְטְרִיךְ בַּר נָשׁ לְפַרְסוּמֵי נִיסָּא וּלְאִשְׁתָּעֵי קַמֵּיהּ בְּכָל מַה דְּאִיהוּ עֲבַד, בְּגִין דְּאִינוּן מִלִּין סַלְקִין וְכָל פַּמַלְיָא דִלְעֵילָּא מִתְכַּנְשִׁין וְחָמָאן לוֹן וְאוֹדָאן כֻּלְּהוּ לְקוּדְשָׁא בְּרִיךְ הוּא, וְאִסְתַּלֵּק יְקָרֵיהּ עֲלַיְיהוּ עֵילָּא וְתַתָּא.
בָּרוּךְ יְהֹוָה לְעוֹלָם אָמֵן וְאָמֵן:

Maggid

Retelling the Exodus

The Exodus from Egypt is a great foundation and mighty pillar of our Torah and our faith. We constantly repeat in our blessings and prayers, "a remembrance of the Exodus from Egypt." This pivotal event serves as absolute proof that Hashem created the world. He is the original G-d Who desires and is able to bring all things into being, and He has the power to change His creations at any given time. And that is exactly what He did in Egypt. G-d changed the nature of this world for the Jewish people. He performed great and mighty miracles without precedent. This should be enough to silence any non-believer. Retelling the story of the Exodus reinforces our belief in Hashem's power and ability to affect all species and individual beings—great and small.

(Sefer Hachinuch 21)

When the Children of Israel were liberated from Egypt, Moshe said to them: "You are not being liberated for your own deeds but in order to tell about it to your sons, to give praise to Hashem that His children are telling about His glory among the nations." What is Hashem's glory? "Sing to Hashem a new song ... Tell among the nations His glory" *(Tehillim 96:1-3)*. When His children tell His glory among the nations, G-d is glorified.

(Midrash Tehillim Shochar Tov 44)

The Rambam teaches that we begin the *Haggada* with disgrace and conclude with praise. "Originally our ancestors used to be idol worshippers ..." The *Haggada* begins with our forefather's father-Terach. He and his comrades served idols; they pursued nothingness! We conclude with the true faith that G-d separated us from the nations, bringing us close to awareness of His Oneness.

The *Haggada* announces at the onset that "We were slaves to Pharaoh in Egypt," telling about all the evil he did to us. We conclude with the miracles and wonders that happened to us, and with our Divine liberation from there.

(Rambam, Hilchos Chametz Umatzah 7:4)

To Teach the Children

The commandment of telling the story of the Exodus from Egypt is highly cherished. No other *mitzvah* caters so much to the children. This is the only instance when the Torah commands, "And you shall tell your son on that day saying, 'Because of this, Hashem did it for me when I went out of Egypt'" *(Shemos 13:8)*.

(Maharil)

What is the message we must give over to our children at the *Seder*? "Because of this..." What's "this?" In what merit were we redeemed? Because one day in the future we will fulfill the commandments of Hashem's Torah. *(Rashi, Shemos 13:8)* And if we fulfill Hashem's commandments today, we will be redeemed from our present exile as well.

In addition to the specific commandment of telling the story of the Exodus on this evening, retelling the story also fulfills the positive commandment to teach children Torah. The Torah states, "And you shall teach them to your children" *(Devarim 11:19)*. What Torah shall you teach? Everything! "And you shall make them [the words of Torah] known to your children and your children's children" *(ibid. 4:9)*.

(Hagahos Maharif Perla on Sefer Hamitzvos of Rav Saadya Gaon, Mitzvos Asei 35; Maarchei Lev 64, based on Teshuvos Harosh)

In the merit of relating the miracles of the Exodus, Hashem will bless you with children to whom to tell the story.

(Ohr Hachaim, Shemos 13:8)

Unique to Pesach

There is an obligation every day of the year to remember the Exodus from Egypt, but on Pesach, there is an additional *mitzvah*. How does the obligation differ on Pesach?

- The story is retold in question and answer format.

  (Rambam, Hilchos Chametz Umatzah 7:4)

- The Egyptians' evil role is highlighted-how they tortured us, embittered our lives with heavy toil, and how G-d punished them.

  (Rambam, Sefer Hamitzvos)

- We praise G-d for all the miracles He did for us in Egypt.

  (Sefer Hachinuch 21)

- We expound on the sequence of events in detail, not just simply stating that G-d took us out of Egypt.

  (Maharal, Gevuros Hashem 2)

- The words are expressed orally on Pesach; it is not sufficient to simply think of it.

  (Sefer Hachinuch 21; Responsa B'samim Rosh 473)

- There is an obligation to repeat the story to our children if possible.

  (Sefer Hachinuch 21)

- It is chanted in a song.

  (Rashbatz)

- We must say and feel in our hearts that we ourselves have been liberated from Egypt today.

  (Moadim Uzmanim)

- *Matzah* and *marror* must lie in front of us.

  (Rabbi Shlomo Kluger)

No Blessing

In *shul* on Rosh Hashana, the Day of Judgment, hordes of congregants stand in awesome silence, listening as the *baal tokea* recites the blessing on the *shofar*. On Succos we take the four species in our hands; the *lulav* is in the right, the *esrog* is in the left, and we solemnly bless, "Blessed are You Hashem ... that sanctified us with His *mitzvos* ..." But on Pesach, on the magical night of the *Seder*, there is no blessing recited prior to fulfilling the *mitzvah* of *sippur yetzias Mitzrayim*, telling the story of the Exodus. Why?

When we make *Kiddush*, the very first *siman* in the *Seder*, we proclaim, "a remembrance of the Exodus from Egypt." According to the Rif, this proclamation exempts us from saying any further blessing for the *mitzvah*.

(Avudraham, quoting Rif)

Telling the story of the Exodus is secondary to the *mitzvos* of eating *matzah* and *marror*. After all, if a person has neither *matzah* nor *marror*, he is absolved from his obligation. The blessings on these Pesach essentials exempt a person from reciting a separate blessing on telling the story.

(Chesed L'Avraham, Orach Chaim 54)

Since, according to the instructions of the Rambam, we start the story of the Exodus with our disgrace-that our ancestors were idol-worshippers and we were slaves-we say no blessing for the obligation to relate this story.

(Rabbi Shlomo Kluger)

Certain *mitzvos* of the Torah are logical *mitzvos*, obligations that any feeling person could deduce on his own, such as honoring one's parents, giving charity, and visiting the sick. There are no blessings for commandments that fall into this category. The obligation of telling about the Exodus is also a logical *mitzvah*. We naturally express our gratitude to G-d for miraculously taking us out of Egypt

with a mighty hand. Gratitude is intuitive, and as such, requires no blessing.

(Sfas Emes, Pesach 5640)

Technically, the obligation of telling the story of the Exodus can be fulfilled with a single word. *(Avudraham, quoting Rashba)* If we were to pronounce the blessing, "that Hashem has commanded us to tell about the Exodus from Egypt," we would have already fulfilled the obligation! *(Binas Yissaschar)* It is preferable to expound on these unprecedented miracles and events, continuing into the wee hours of the night. For a *mitzvah* that has no minimum or maximum, there is no blessing.

(Avudraham, quoting Rashba)

On the evening of Pesach we are expected to personally re-experience the Exodus, just as if we ourselves had been slaves in Egypt and were liberated from there. As we start telling the story in the *Haggada*, we are transported back to the time when our ancestors served idols. How can we make a blessing that "He commanded us to tell the story" if Hashem did not give us the Torah yet? We have not yet been redeemed from Egypt! First we must relive all the miracles Hashem performed for us, how Hashem emancipated us from slavery and raised us out of the forty-nine levels of impurity. Then, after we have relived all these events, we recite the blessing: "Blessed are You, Hashem, Who has redeemed us ..."

(Chasam Sofer)

The prophet Yirmiyahu told the nation of Israel, "Days are coming, says G-d, when it will no longer be said, 'As G-d lives, Who brought out the Children of Israel from the land of Egypt'" (Yirmiyahu 16:14). Instead, G-d will be noted by the masses as the G-d Who redeemed the Jews from the present exile. The miracles that occurred at the Exodus from Egypt will pale in comparison to the great miracles of the Final Redemption. (Berachos 14b) We await the Final

Redemption at any given moment. The miracles of the Exodus will fade next to the miracles that we hope and pray will happen imminently. And so we refrain from making a blessing.

(Vay'lakeit Yosef)

With Intention

It is choicest to perform all *mitzvos* with specific intent to fulfill the commandment of Hashem. Authorities maintain that in most cases, even if there was no specific intent a person has still fulfilled the commandment. One exception is the *Shema* prayer in the morning and evening. One must concentrate on the meaning of at least the first verse to properly fulfill the *mitzvah*, "Hear, O Israel, G-d is our Master, G-d is One." It is the basis of our entire faith, reinforcing our belief in His sole control of the world.

Relating the Exodus is also a major cornerstone in the Jewish faith. *Halachic* authorities agree that one must have the same intentions that are required during *Shema* to fulfill the *mitzvah* in its true form.

(Maharal, Gevuros Hashem 62)

The Torah says, "You shall relate in the ears of your child and your grandchild that I made a mockery of Egypt and My miraculous signs that I placed among them, and you shall know that I am Hashem" *(Shemos 10:2)*. It is our obligation to teach the lessons learned from the Egyptians' punishment-that Hashem punishes the wicked who mistreat His people. With ten horrific yet miraculous plagues, G-d not only punished the wicked perpetrators, He demonstrated to the Jewish nation His dominion over the world. If one does not have this intention while saying the *Haggada*, he should preferably repeat it.

(Derech Pikudecha 21, Chelek Hamachshava 1)

Special Merits

If a Jew is in need of Divine assistance and miracles to rid himself of wicked enemies-on any day of the year-he should retell the miracles of the Exodus, how Hashem punished the Egyptians. This merit will arouse Divine vengeance upon his present enemies.

(Noam Elimelech, Bo)

"You shall surely remember what G-d your Master did to Pharaoh and to all Egypt" *(Devarim 7:18)*. By remembering the miracles Hashem performed in Egypt, a person will merit the miracles he needs in his everyday life-health, livelihood, and family.

(Igra D'kalla, Eikev)

By relating the miracles, our mouths become sanctified and we are privileged to speak only holy words before Hashem.

(Maor Vashemesh, Pesach, Avadim Hayinu)

Even in Exile

How can we tell the story of the way our nation was set free from slavery and redeemed from exile if we ourselves are still in exile? "Meanwhile, we are still serving Achashveirosh" *(Megillah 14a)*. We are still subservient to gentile rule!

There was once a penniless man who worked hard just to have a little food to eat. He certainly could not afford the luxury of sitting and studying Torah. Then he had a sudden change of fortune, and he became a wealthy man. He hired the best Torah scholar to open his mind to the beauties of Torah. For a period of time, he enjoyed "Torah and material prominence together." Every year, he celebrated the anniversary of his newfound wealth.

Years later his fortune changed. Once again the man was reduced to a penniless pauper. But he continued to celebrate the anniversary of his wealth. Though his money was gone, the Torah merit he earned while he was wealthy would always remain.

Although we are once again in exile, we can still celebrate the Torah we received upon our liberation from Egypt. We bequeath this treasure-the Torah-to our children, and they to their children. It brings us joy even in exile. "The more one tells about the Exodus from Egypt," even during these dark days of exile, "he is to be praised." He demonstrates his joy for the Torah we received from Hashem, even in times of darkness.

(Divrei Shaul)

The Torah's commandments are eternal; they never become invalid, even during exile. The Children of Israel were privileged to attain permanent and everlasting spiritual freedom when they were liberated from Egyptian slavery. Even if we are physically subservient to another nation, nothing can cancel the spiritual freedom that was permanently established at the Exodus from Egypt. As we say in our evening prayers, "... and He brought His people Israel from among them [the Egyptians] to everlasting freedom."

(Maharal, Gevuros Hashem)

Retelling the story of the Exodus strengthens our hope. G-d has not forsaken us! Just as He redeemed us from Egypt so many years ago "with a strong hand" and great miracles, G-d will redeem us from our present exile, wiping away all the troubles that beset us today.

Ha Lachma Anya

Throughout the evening, when reciting the Haggadah, the matzos should be uncoverd.

הֵא לַחְמָא עַנְיָא דִּי אֲכָלוּ אַבְהָתָנָא בְּאַרְעָא דְמִצְרָיִם. כָּל דִּכְפִין יֵיתֵי וְיֵיכוֹל. כָּל דִּצְרִיךְ יֵיתֵי וְיִפְסַח. הָשַׁתָּא הָכָא, לְשָׁנָה הַבָּאָה בְּאַרְעָא דְיִשְׂרָאֵל. הָשַׁתָּא עַבְדֵי, לְשָׁנָה הַבָּאָה בְּנֵי חוֹרִין:

Ha Lachma Anya

The Aramaic Introduction

Maggid begins with the recitation of "*Ha lachma anya*-this is the bread of affliction which our ancestors ate while they were enslaved in Egypt." This short paragraph in Aramaic invites the poor to come and participate in our *Seder*. Why do we begin the *Seder* in Aramaic?

After the exile of the Jews to Babylonia, Aramaic, the language of the land, became their spoken tongue. Even after Jews returned to the Holy Land, Aramaic prevailed as the language for everyday converstaion throughout the period of the *Tannaim*, the Sages of the *Mishnah*, and *Amoraim*, the Sages of Talmud. Hebrew was reserved for Torah study alone. We invite all the poor to join us using a language they could understand-Aramaic.

(Avudraham)

The Sages enacted this part of the *Haggada* after the first *Beis Hamikdash* was destroyed, when the Jews were exiled in Babylonia. We begin the *Haggada* in the foreign language of the exiled land, a sign of mourning for the destruction of the *Beis Hamikdash*.

(Maasei Hashem)

When Yaakov escaped with his family and possessions from his father-in-law's home in Aram, Lavan chased after him and caught up with him. Heeding Hashem's warning not to harm Yaakov and his family, Lavan made a peace agreement with his son-in-law Yaakov. They built two altars. Lavan called his altar "*Yigar Sahadusa*" *(Beraishis 31:47)*, Aramaic words meaning "a heap [of rocks to serve] as a testimony."

The Torah is exclusively written in the sacred Hebrew language-except these two words. Since Yaakov indirectly caused these two foreign words to be quoted in the Torah, his descendants were fated to erase the spiritual damage by enduring exile. We invite the "*galus* Jew," the poverty-stricken Jewish wanderer, to our *Seder* in Aramaic, insinuating that our poverty and exile were caused by that misplaced use of the Aramaic language.

(Chida, quoting Galia Razia)

The Zohar states that Hashem Himself is present in every Jewish home, listening directly to our prayers without any need for intermediary angels. Angels do not understand Aramaic. So we begin the *Seder* with "*Ha lachma anya*" to emphasize that we do not need the angels' service tonight; we are speaking directly to Hashem.

(Arugas Habosem)

While we recite "*Ha lachma anya*," the *Seder* plate is raised for everyone present to see:

- When the children see this unusual lifting of the plate prior to eating, they start asking questions.

(Rashbam, Pesachim 115b)

- When everyone present sees the *matzah*, it increases their fondness for the *mitzvah* of eating it.

(Leket Yosher 84a)

- The *Haggada* is recited over the *matzos* before us on the *Seder* plate, so we raise them up for everyone to see.

(*Hagahos Minhagim 96*)

- Raising the *Seder* plate demonstrates our joy, just as we raise our cup of wine for the paragraph "*Lefichach*-therefore," near the end of the *Haggada*.

(*Maharashal, Responsa 88*)

The Sequence

Why does the long story of the Exodus precede the main meal? The story of the Exodus has to be told when *matzah* and *marror* are lying in front of us. If the meal were eaten first, there would be no *matzah* or *marror* on the table anymore. (*Shulchan Aruch HaRav 473:3*) A filling meal often makes a person sleepy. We must be wide awake to tell the story of the *Haggada*.

(*Seder Hayom, beginning of Seder Hahaggada*)

Each of the Four Cups is related to a different segment of the *Seder*. The second cup corresponds with *Maggid*, but we we do not pour the cup when we are ready to begin *Maggid*. We wait until after "*Ha lachma anya*" is recited, immediately before we ask the Four Questions. Why?

"*Ha lachma anya*" is not part of the main *Haggada* enacted by our Sages. That begins with "*Avadim hayinu*." But the Four Questions are the essential introduction to the *Haggada*, which comes as a reply to those questions. Therefore we pour the second cup at that point, and not before.

(*Maglei Tzedek, Seder Pesach 127a*)

Ma Nishtanah

The second cup of wine is poured and the children ask the father the four Questions.

מַה נִּשְׁתַּנָּה הַלַּיְלָה הַזֶּה מִכָּל הַלֵּילוֹת

שֶׁבְּכָל הַלֵּילוֹת אָנוּ אוֹכְלִין חָמֵץ וּמַצָּה, הַלַּיְלָה הַזֶּה כֻּלּוֹ מַצָּה:

שֶׁבְּכָל הַלֵּילוֹת אָנוּ אוֹכְלִין שְׁאָר יְרָקוֹת, הַלַּיְלָה הַזֶּה (כֻּלּוֹ) מָרוֹר:

שֶׁבְּכָל הַלֵּילוֹת אֵין אָנוּ מַטְבִּילִין אֲפִילוּ פַּעַם אֶחָת, הַלַּיְלָה הַזֶּה שְׁתֵּי פְעָמִים:

שֶׁבְּכָל הַלֵּילוֹת אָנוּ אוֹכְלִין בֵּין יוֹשְׁבִין וּבֵין מְסֻבִּין, הַלַּיְלָה הַזֶּה כֻּלָּנוּ מְסֻבִּין:

Ma Nishtanah

The Four Questions

Many practices of the *Seder* night are designed to provoke the children into asking questions. Since Talmudic times, the children have asked four preestablished questions before the story of the Exodus is told. The adults recite these questions aloud if no children are present. Even when there are children, many adults still recite the questions to themselves.

Why do we eat *matzah* and no *chametz*? *Matzah* is bread of suffering, reminiscent of the hardships of slavery. It is food eaten by slaves who have no control over their own lives.

Why do we eat *marror*, the bitter herbs? To remind us of the suffering, the bitter lives we led in Egypt.

Why do we dip the *marror* in *charoses*? The sweetness of the *charoses* tempers the bitter herbs.

And why do we recline? Reclining is indicative of freedom. We were slaves in Egypt, but that is a thing of the past-now we are free men.

The Four Questions summarize the history of the suffering and eventual liberation. The *matzah* and *marror* allude to the long period of tortuous enslavement in Egypt. The last two questions allude to the sweetness and freedom we now have.

Hearing the Four Questions at the onset of the *Seder* stokes the memories of the Exodus-the slavery and the subsequent emancipation, the hardships and the subsequent glory-and we are inspired with gratitude to Hashem. Then we can proceed to tell the story in detail, fulfilling our obligation with enthusiasm.

The Talmud instructs us to start the story of the Exodus by first telling about our disgrace and then proceeding to the praise *(Pesachim 116a)*. If we do not start with the disgrace, we cannot fully appreciate the praise. When we expound on the disgrace, the slavery and the torture our people suffered in Egypt, then we are truly grateful for the praise, the great miracles, the redemption and the giving of the Torah.

(Malbim, Midrash Haggada)

Our obligation to tell the story of the Exodus on this evening is based on the verse, "And you shall tell your child on that day saying 'Because of this, G-d did it to me when I went out of Egypt'" *(Shemos 13:8)*. What is "this" that the verse refers to? Rashi explains that "this" refers to Hashem's commandments. For "this" we assemble at the *Seder* to retell the miracles of the Exodus. Because Hashem took us out of Egypt to fulfill His commandments, such as the *mitzvos* of *matzah* and *marror*.

Avadim Hayinu

The answer for the four questions.

עֲבָדִים הָיִינוּ לְפַרְעֹה בְּמִצְרָיִם, וַיּוֹצִיאֵנוּ יְהֹוָה אֱלֹהֵינוּ מִשָּׁם בְּיָד חֲזָקָה וּבִזְרֹעַ נְטוּיָה. וְאִלּוּ לֹא הוֹצִיא הַקָּדוֹשׁ בָּרוּךְ הוּא אֶת אֲבוֹתֵינוּ מִמִּצְרָיִם, הֲרֵי אָנוּ וּבָנֵינוּ וּבְנֵי בָנֵינוּ מְשֻׁעְבָּדִים הָיִינוּ לְפַרְעֹה בְּמִצְרָיִם. וַאֲפִילוּ כֻּלָּנוּ חֲכָמִים כֻּלָּנוּ נְבוֹנִים כֻּלָּנוּ זְקֵנִים כֻּלָּנוּ יוֹדְעִים אֶת הַתּוֹרָה מִצְוָה עָלֵינוּ לְסַפֵּר בִּיצִיאַת מִצְרָיִם. וְכָל הַמַּרְבֶּה לְסַפֵּר בִּיצִיאַת מִצְרַיִם הֲרֵי זֶה מְשֻׁבָּח:

מַעֲשֶׂה בְּרַבִּי אֱלִיעֶזֶר וְרַבִּי יְהוֹשֻׁעַ וְרַבִּי אֶלְעָזָר בֶּן עֲזַרְיָה וְרַבִּי עֲקִיבָא וְרַבִּי טַרְפוֹן שֶׁהָיוּ מְסֻבִּין בִּבְנֵי בְרַק וְהָיוּ מְסַפְּרִים בִּיצִיאַת מִצְרַיִם כָּל אוֹתוֹ הַלַּיְלָה, עַד שֶׁבָּאוּ תַלְמִידֵיהֶם וְאָמְרוּ לָהֶם רַבּוֹתֵינוּ הִגִּיעַ זְמַן קְרִיאַת שְׁמַע שֶׁל שַׁחֲרִית:

אָמַר רַבִּי אֶלְעָזָר בֶּן עֲזַרְיָה הֲרֵי אֲנִי כְּבֶן שִׁבְעִים שָׁנָה וְלֹא זָכִיתִי שֶׁתֵּאָמֵר יְצִיאַת מִצְרַיִם בַּלֵּילוֹת עַד שֶׁדְּרָשָׁהּ בֶּן זוֹמָא, שֶׁנֶּאֱמַר,

---

This explains the first two questions-*matzah* and *marror*, two Torah obligations. But the second two questions, regarding dipping and reclining, are obligations enacted by the Sages. What's the connection? The Sages wanted to demonstrate that we must be as careful fulfilling the instructions of our Sages-to dip and recline-as we are about the Torah obligations of *matzah* and *marror*.

Why did the Sages specifically choose questions regarding reclining and dipping? There are so many unusual practices tonight! It is simply because the children have already noticed dipping-*karpas* in salt water; and reclining-while drinking wine during *Kadesh*.

(Haggada Maaseh Nissim)

לְמַעַן תִּזְכּוֹר אֶת יוֹם צֵאתְךָ מֵאֶרֶץ מִצְרַיִם כֹּל יְמֵי חַיֶּיךָ. יְמֵי חַיֶּיךָ הַיָּמִים. כֹּל יְמֵי חַיֶּיךָ הַלֵּילוֹת. וַחֲכָמִים אוֹמְרִים יְמֵי חַיֶּיךָ הָעוֹלָם הַזֶּה. כֹּל יְמֵי חַיֶּיךָ לְהָבִיא לִימוֹת הַמָּשִׁיחַ:

בָּרוּךְ הַמָּקוֹם, בָּרוּךְ הוּא, בָּרוּךְ שֶׁנָּתַן תּוֹרָה לְעַמּוֹ יִשְׂרָאֵל, בָּרוּךְ הוּא. כְּנֶגֶד אַרְבָּעָה בָנִים דִּבְּרָה תוֹרָה: אֶחָד חָכָם. וְאֶחָד רָשָׁע. וְאֶחָד תָּם. וְאֶחָד שֶׁאֵינוֹ יוֹדֵעַ לִשְׁאוֹל:

חָכָם מָה הוּא אוֹמֵר. מָה הָעֵדוֹת וְהַחֻקִּים וְהַמִּשְׁפָּטִים אֲשֶׁר צִוָּה יְהֹוָה אֱלֹהֵינוּ אֶתְכֶם. וְאַף אַתָּה אֱמוֹר לוֹ כְּהִלְכוֹת הַפֶּסַח אֵין מַפְטִירִין אַחַר הַפֶּסַח אֲפִיקוֹמָן:

רָשָׁע מָה הוּא אוֹמֵר. מָה הָעֲבוֹדָה הַזֹּאת לָכֶם. לָכֶם וְלֹא לוֹ. וּלְפִי שֶׁהוֹצִיא אֶת עַצְמוֹ מִן הַכְּלָל כָּפַר בְּעִקָּר. וְאַף אַתָּה הַקְהֵה אֶת שִׁנָּיו וֶאֱמוֹר לוֹ. בַּעֲבוּר זֶה עָשָׂה יְהֹוָה לִי בְּצֵאתִי מִמִּצְרָיִם. לִי וְלֹא לוֹ. אִלּוּ הָיָה שָׁם לֹא הָיָה נִגְאָל:

תָּם מָה הוּא אוֹמֵר. מַה זֹּאת. וְאָמַרְתָּ אֵלָיו בְּחוֹזֶק יָד הוֹצִיאָנוּ יְהֹוָה מִמִּצְרַיִם מִבֵּית עֲבָדִים:

וְשֶׁאֵינוֹ יוֹדֵעַ לִשְׁאוֹל אַתְּ פְּתַח לוֹ. שֶׁנֶּאֱמַר, וְהִגַּדְתָּ לְבִנְךָ בַּיּוֹם הַהוּא לֵאמֹר בַּעֲבוּר זֶה עָשָׂה יְהֹוָה לִי בְּצֵאתִי מִמִּצְרָיִם:

יָכוֹל מֵרֹאשׁ חֹדֶשׁ, תַּלְמוּד לוֹמַר בַּיּוֹם הַהוּא. אִי בַּיּוֹם הַהוּא יָכוֹל מִבְּעוֹד יוֹם, תַּלְמוּד לוֹמַר בַּעֲבוּר זֶה. בַּעֲבוּר זֶה לֹא אָמַרְתִּי אֶלָּא בְּשָׁעָה שֶׁיֵּשׁ מַצָּה וּמָרוֹר מֻנָּחִים לְפָנֶיךָ:

מִתְּחִלָּה עוֹבְדֵי עֲבוֹדָה זָרָה הָיוּ אֲבוֹתֵינוּ, וְעַכְשָׁיו קֵרְבָנוּ הַמָּקוֹם לַעֲבוֹדָתוֹ. שֶׁנֶּאֱמַר, וַיֹּאמֶר יְהוֹשֻׁעַ אֶל כָּל הָעָם כֹּה אָמַר יְהֹוָה אֱלֹהֵי יִשְׂרָאֵל, בְּעֵבֶר הַנָּהָר יָשְׁבוּ אֲבוֹתֵיכֶם מֵעוֹלָם תֶּרַח אֲבִי אַבְרָהָם

וַאֲבִי נָחוֹר וַיַּעַבְדוּ אֱלֹהִים אֲחֵרִים: וָאֶקַּח אֶת אֲבִיכֶם אֶת אַבְרָהָם מֵעֵבֶר הַנָּהָר וָאוֹלֵךְ אוֹתוֹ בְּכָל אֶרֶץ כְּנָעַן וָאַרְבֶּה אֶת זַרְעוֹ וָאֶתֶּן לוֹ אֶת יִצְחָק, וָאֶתֵּן לְיִצְחָק אֶת יַעֲקֹב וְאֶת עֵשָׂו, וָאֶתֵּן לְעֵשָׂו אֶת הַר שֵׂעִיר לָרֶשֶׁת אוֹתוֹ, וְיַעֲקֹב וּבָנָיו יָרְדוּ מִצְרָיִם:

בָּרוּךְ שׁוֹמֵר הַבְטָחָתוֹ לְיִשְׂרָאֵל, בָּרוּךְ הוּא, שֶׁהַקָּדוֹשׁ בָּרוּךְ הוּא חִשַּׁב אֶת הַקֵּץ לַעֲשׂוֹת. כְּמָה שֶּׁאָמַר לְאַבְרָהָם אָבִינוּ בִּבְרִית בֵּין הַבְּתָרִים. שֶׁנֶּאֱמַר, וַיֹּאמֶר לְאַבְרָם יָדֹעַ תֵּדַע כִּי גֵר יִהְיֶה זַרְעֲךָ בְּאֶרֶץ לֹא לָהֶם וַעֲבָדוּם וְעִנּוּ אֹתָם אַרְבַּע מֵאוֹת שָׁנָה. וְגַם אֶת הַגּוֹי אֲשֶׁר יַעֲבֹדוּ דָּן אָנֹכִי וְאַחֲרֵי כֵן יֵצְאוּ בִּרְכוּשׁ גָּדוֹל:

Avadim Hayinu

The Answer: Avadim Hayinu

The Four Questions are based on apparent contradictions in the practices of this evening. We eat *matzah*, the bread of suffering, yet we recline like free men. We eat *marror*, alluding to our bitter experiences in Egypt, yet we dip, a practice of the wealthy.

These contradictions can be resolved. "*Avadim hayinu*-we were slaves to Pharaoh in Egypt, and G-d, our Master, brought us out with a strong hand and an outstretched arm." We were originally slaves, and then Hashem set us free. We eat *matzah*-while we recline; we take bitter *marror*-and dip it in sweet *charoses*. We were enslaved-but now we are liberated.

(Haggada Leshon Limudim 49)

The verse in *Devarim* reads: "If your child asks you tomorrow, saying, 'What are these testimonies and decrees and ordinances that

Hashem our G-d commanded you?' You shall say to your child, '*Avadim hayinu*-we were slaves to Pharaoh in Egypt ...'" *(Devarim 6:20-21)*.

The reasons for most individual *mitzvos* are concealed even from the wisest of men. But here the Torah states an overall answer. If a child questions the reason for *mitzvos*-any and all *mitzvos*-we are to tell him that Hashem gave us Torah and *mitzvos* because we were slaves to Pharaoh in Egypt, and then He took us out from there.

We ask the Four Questions. Why do we eat *matzah* and *marror*? Why do we dip and recline? Our Sages chose to answer the questions with the general answer in *Devarim*: we were slaves and G-d took us out. It is not our place to try to delve into the reasons for the commandments of this evening.

The verse does present some logical explanations-that Hashem skipped over our homes while the Egyptians were smitten *(Shemos 12:27)*, with a strong hand G-d took us out of Egypt *(ibid. 13:14)*, but the Sages preferred the blanket explanation.

As slaves to Pharaoh, we perforce observed his decrees without knowing the reasons behind them. We built cities that sunk into the ground, but build them we did. "We were slaves to Pharaoh in Egypt ..." *(Devarim 6:20)*.

But then G-d our Master brought us out of Egypt, from under the cruel jurisdiciton of the Egyptians. "Hashem our G-d took us out from Egypt ..." *(Devarim 6:21)*. Hashem emancipated us! This was all we needed to declare G-d's Supremacy, His Mastery over the world. Of course we could do anything Hashem requested of us-with joy.

Reliving the Exodus

Just as every Jew must imagine that he himself was emancipated from Egypt, he must imagine that he was enslaved there. A father tells his children, "I was a slave in Egypt."

(Chasam Sofer)

The redemption from slavery was twofold-a redemption of the body and a redemption of the spirit. The *Seder* commemorates both.

For the sake of the ordinary people, who feel the greatest thrill when recalling the Jews' physical release from slavery, the *Haggada* recounts-at great length-the back-breaking labor the Jews endured under the cruel Egyptian taskmasters. "They embittered their lives with harsh labor, involving mortar and bricks and all types of work in the field" *(Shemos 1:14)*. Without the mention of the misery of slavery, these people cannot taste the sweetness of the redemption, when the Jews were finally freed from Egyptian slavery.

Thinking people celebrate the Exodus as redemption from the spiritual decadence of Egypt. Dwelling on the physical suffering in Egypt is unnecessary. The *Haggada* says, "Therefore, if we were all wise, all men of understanding," people who do not focus on the physical suffering of the Jews, "it would still be our duty to tell the story of the departure from Egypt. And the more one elaborates on the story of the departure from Egypt, the more he is praised."

The more a person draws happiness from the redemption, the Jews' emergence from the decadence of Egypt, the more wise and discerning he must be. Only an inferior thinker needs to focus on the physical aspect of slavery to appreciate the joy in the redemption.

Five sages sat all night "telling the story of the departure from Egypt." They were not expounding on the bitterness of slavery. They were concentrating on the spiritual freedom brought about by the redemption.

(Arugas Habosem)

But most of us are ordinary people. Most of us have to concentrate on the era of slavery that our forefathers endured. And so we begin to examine the Egyptian exile.

Everlasting Benefit

"With a mighty hand ..." *(ibid.)*. Hashem brought us out with great miracles, for all the world to see. He could have orchestrated our release in a more natural way-Pharaoh could simply have assented to let us go, for instance. But the openly miraculous redemption was to our benefit, as the verse continues, "... for our good, all the days, to give us life, as this very day" *(Devarim 6:24)*. How is this so?

Hashem took us out of Egypt in the merit of our Patriarchs. "And Hashem heard their [the Jewish nation's] cries and He remembered His convenant with Avraham, Yitzchak and Yaakov" *(Shemos 2:24)*. But the Jews in the desert lamented, "Better for us to serve the Egyptians ..." *(Shemos 14:12)*. As a result of this complaint, G-d's chosen people deserved to go back to Egypt. Let them be slaves! The merit of their ancestors was exhausted; their eternal convenant already fulfilled. They could stay in Egypt for the rest of time.

But Moshe Rabbeinu defended them. How could the Almighty destroy the Jewish nation now? After all the open miracles, the world witnessing how Hashem had chosen the Jewish people, to destroy them would be a *chillul Hashem,* profanation of G-d's name! *(Shemos 32:12; Bamidbar 14:13)* If we had left slavery naturally, without the mighty hand of Hashem so evident, Moshe Rabbeinu would have been left without a defense against the Heavenly judgment.

"*V'ilu lo hotzi*-if He had not brought our ancestors out of Egypt, we would still be enslaved to Pharaoh in Egypt," continues the *Haggada*. Originally we were "*avadim*-slaves" to Pharaoh, but it was only temporary, like the term "*eved ivri*-Hebrew slave," who is due to be released after a maximum of six years. After 400 years in exile Hashem had promised our forefathers He would redeem us. But once the promise had been fulfilled, if we had returned to Egypt we would have been "*meshubadim*," permanently enslaved.

But even if the merit of the Patriachs was no longer valid, the honor of Hashem's name still remains. That cannot be desecrated. The "mighty hand" *(Devarim 6:21)* with which Hashem performed open miracles saved us from permanent slavery.

When a person invests great effort into a project, his honor becomes one with his project. If the project is successful, the person is esteemed. If it fails, his honor falls to the dirt. Hashem revealed to all the nations that we are His children and have been acquired by Him to be His servants. We are Hashem's project. If we obey His commandments, Hashem makes us successful and His name is glorified. But if we sin, and we are thrown into exile-it is the worst *chillul Hashem*.

Hashem Himself can always use this justification to protect us against all Heavenly accusations, recalling His explicit promises to us in the Scriptures. We are guaranteed that Hashem will renew our days-otherwise there will be a tremendous *chillul Hashem*.

The passage in the *Haggada* continues, "Even if all of us are wise, all of us understanding, all of us would know the whole Torah, it is still our obligation to tell about the Exodus from Egypt."

Simply repeating the story of the Exodus would be superfluous. We know what transpired, and besides, it happened so many thousands of years ago! The main obligation is to engrave the message in our hearts. Hashem intended this dramatic Exodus for our everlasting good. We are lowly and full of sins-we do not even deserve to exist! Yet Hashem exercised His tremendous kindness and compassion for our sake. We must examine every favor and realize that Hashem did it for our own eternal good and that of our descendants.

In *Hallel* we list Hashem's praises. After each one we declare, "For His kindness lasts forever!" Hashem did not perform kindness for the generation of the Exodus alone-His kindnesses last for all time.

"*Avadim hayinu*" concludes, "The more one tells about the Exodus from Egypt, the more praiseworthy he is." The more we examine His kind deeds on our behalf, the more we realize how it is good for us even now, "to give us life, like this very day" *(Devarim 6: 24)*.

(Haggada Maaseh Nissim)

Vehi Sheamdah

Tha Matzos are covered, and the cup is lifted,
as the following paragraph is proclaimed joyously.

וְהִיא שֶׁעָמְדָה לַאֲבוֹתֵינוּ וְלָנוּ. שֶׁלֹּא אֶחָד בִּלְבָד עָמַד עָלֵינוּ לְכַלּוֹתֵנוּ אֶלָּא שֶׁבְּכָל דּוֹר וָדוֹר עוֹמְדִים עָלֵינוּ לְכַלּוֹתֵנוּ, וְהַקָּדוֹשׁ בָּרוּךְ הוּא מַצִּילֵנוּ מִיָּדָם:

The cup is returned to the table and the Matzos uncoverd.

Vehi Sheamdah

Covered and Uncovered

While we recite the *Haggada* the *matzah* is partially uncovered. The Torah says, "You shall eat upon it *lechem oni*" *(Devarim 16:3)*. *Lechem oni* literally means "bread of suffering," the *matzah*. The Talmud in *Pesachim* 115b teaches that the word "*oni*" can also be interpreted as answer-"we must answer many words over it." To interpret the verse using the non-conventional translation, the *Korban Pesach* should be accompanied by many answers. As we teach the answers of the *Haggada*, as we tell the story, we have the *lechem oni* visible before us.

(Levush 473)

At "*Vehi sheamdah*," when we take the wine cup in our hands, the *matzah* is covered. Bread, the staple of our diet, is *halachically* more important than wine, which is why the *berachah* of *hamotzi* precedes the *berachah* on wine. On Shabbos or *Yom Tov*, when we make *Kiddush* before washing for bread, the bread is always

covered in respect for its importance. To avoid disrespect for the *matzah*, which normally ranks first, we cover it before raising the cup of wine.

(Magen Avraham 473)

Cup of Salvation

King David said, "I will raise the cup of salvations" *(Tehillim 116:13)*, I will raise a cup of wine and carry it into the Sanctuary to thank Hashem for saving me. When we reach "*Vehi sheamdah*," just as we are about to start sharing all the details of G-d's salvation of the Jews from Egypt, we raise our wine cup in thanks to Hashem for saving us from Egypt, and from enemies that sought to destroy us throughout the generations.

(Leket Yosher, quoting Rokeach)

The second cup represents the second of the four expressions of redemption that Hashem used, "*Vehitzalti*-I shall rescue you from their service." This cup expresses our praise of G-d specifically for having saved us from Pharaoh. We raise the wine cup in praise of Hashem to thank him for saving us from our enemies who seek to destroy us in our present exile.

(Maharal, Gevuros Hashem)

Since the destruction of the *Beis Hamikdash*, it is as if we are all in a state of intoxication, as it says, "Intoxicated, but not from wine" *(Yeshaya 51:21)*. One who is truly intoxicated is exempt from performing all Torah obligations. We raise our cup saying, "*Vehi sheamdah*-and this has stood." What has stood? The wine has stood us in good stead. We were intoxicated-and that makes us exempt. Hashem will not judge us harshly during our exile.

(Bnei Yissaschar)

Yetzias Mitrayim

Literally translated, "the departure of Egypt."

The departure of Egypt? Egypt did not depart to anywhere! It was the Jewish people who departed from Egypt. So why is the Exodus referred to as Yetzias Mitzrayim, the departure of Egypt? It should be Yetziah miMitzrayim, the departure from Egypt.

During the years of Egyptian slavery, the Jewish people were spiritually immature, easily swayed by the dictates of the evil inclination. Following selfish impulses, the Jews fell to the lowest degree of impurity-until they worshipped Egyptian idols. Mercifully, Hashem did not hold them fully responsible for their actions. Like juveniles, or alcoholics in a drunken stupor, they were not held fully accountable for their sins.

During the course of the Seder we raise our cups to commemorate Hashem's forgiving kindness, proclaiming, "Vehi sheamdah! This wine that imposed spiritual drunkenness and apathy upon the Jews-this wine saved our forefathers." Because of their sleepy, drunken state, Hashem exempted the Jews from their sins, for abandoning Him in favor of Egyptian worship.

"Mitzrayim" symbolizes the lethargy, the drunkenness, that dulled the minds of the Jews during the years of Egyptian slavery. The Exodus is called Yetzias Mitzrayim, the departure of Egypt-the departure of the Egyptian mindset: the idolatry, depravity, and materialism. The lifestyle called Egypt had poisoned the minds of the Jewish people; with the Exodus, that lifestyle departed-Yetzias Mitzrayim.

(Divrei Yoel)

Tzei Ulemad

צֵא וּלְמַד מַה בִּקֵּשׁ לָבָן הָאֲרַמִּי לַעֲשׂוֹת לְיַעֲקֹב אָבִינוּ. שֶׁפַּרְעֹה לֹא גָזַר אֶלָּא עַל הַזְּכָרִים וְלָבָן בִּקֵּשׁ לַעֲקוֹר אֶת הַכֹּל. שֶׁנֶּאֱמַר: אֲרַמִּי אֹבֵד אָבִי

וַיֵּרֶד מִצְרַיְמָה וַיָּגָר שָׁם בִּמְתֵי מְעָט, וַיְהִי שָׁם לְגוֹי גָּדוֹל עָצוּם וָרָב:

וַיֵּרֶד מִצְרַיְמָה אָנוּס עַל פִּי הַדִּבּוּר:

וַיָּגָר שָׁם, מְלַמֵּד שֶׁלֹּא יָרַד יַעֲקֹב אָבִינוּ לְהִשְׁתַּקֵּעַ בְּמִצְרַיִם אֶלָּא לָגוּר שָׁם. שֶׁנֶּאֱמַר, וַיֹּאמְרוּ אֶל פַּרְעֹה לָגוּר בָּאָרֶץ בָּאנוּ כִּי אֵין מִרְעֶה לַצֹּאן אֲשֶׁר לַעֲבָדֶיךָ כִּי כָבֵד הָרָעָב בְּאֶרֶץ כְּנָעַן, וְעַתָּה יֵשְׁבוּ נָא עֲבָדֶיךָ בְּאֶרֶץ גֹּשֶׁן:

בִּמְתֵי מְעָט, כְּמָה שֶׁנֶּאֱמַר, בְּשִׁבְעִים נֶפֶשׁ יָרְדוּ אֲבוֹתֶיךָ מִצְרָיְמָה וְעַתָּה שָׂמְךָ יְהֹוָה אֱלֹהֶיךָ כְּכוֹכְבֵי הַשָּׁמַיִם לָרוֹב: וַיְהִי שָׁם לְגוֹי, מְלַמֵּד שֶׁהָיוּ יִשְׂרָאֵל מְצֻיָּנִים שָׁם:

גָּדוֹל עָצוּם, כְּמָה שֶׁנֶּאֱמַר, וּבְנֵי יִשְׂרָאֵל פָּרוּ וַיִּשְׁרְצוּ וַיִּרְבּוּ וַיַּעַצְמוּ בִּמְאֹד מְאֹד וַתִּמָּלֵא הָאָרֶץ אֹתָם:

וָרָב, כְּמָה שֶׁנֶּאֱמַר, רְבָבָה כְּצֶמַח הַשָּׂדֶה נְתַתִּיךְ וַתִּרְבִּי וַתִּגְדְּלִי וַתָּבֹאִי בַּעֲדִי עֲדָיִים שָׁדַיִם נָכֹנוּ וּשְׂעָרֵךְ צִמֵּחַ וְאַתְּ עֵרֹם וְעֶרְיָה: וָאֶעֱבוֹר עָלַיִךְ וָאֶרְאֵךְ מִתְבּוֹסֶסֶת בְּדָמָיִךְ וָאֹמַר לָךְ בְּדָמַיִךְ חֲיִי וָאֹמַר לָךְ בְּדָמַיִךְ חֲיִי:

Tzei Ulemad

With Seventy Persons

When Yaakov Avinu heard that Yosef was alive, he deliberated, "Shall I leave the land of my forefathers, the place where I was born and where the *Shechinah* resides, to go to a depraved land and live among people who have no fear of G-d?" Hashem reassured him, "Have no fear of descending to Egypt … I shall descend with you to Egypt" *(Bereishis 46:3)*.

At the border, Yaakov and his family took a census. There were sixty-six males. Yosef and his two sons were already in Egypt, raising the total to sixty-nine. But the Torah says, "Your ancestors emigrated to Egypt with *seventy* persons" *(Devarim 10:22)*. How is the seventieth person accounted for? Hashem included Himself in the count, fulfilling the pledge He made to Yaakov, "I shall descend with you to Egypt" *(Bereishis 46:3)*.

(Pirkei D'Rebi Eliezer)

"*Beshivim … larov*, with seventy souls your ancestors descended to Egypt …" *(Devarim 10:22)*. The verse describing the Jews' initial descent to Egypt begins with the letter *beis* and ends with the letter *beis. Beis* stands for *bayis*, house. Yaakov cautioned his children to preserve the holiness of the *bayis*, the Jewish home. He cautioned them not to mingle with the Egyptians. This is why the Jewish people were called "*Beis Yaakov*," the house of Yaakov, the letter *beis* with which Yaakov warned his children to remain a separate nation.

(Baal Haturim, Eikev

Fertile and Prolific

"The children of Israel were fertile and prolific, they multiplied and increased very greatly, so the land was filled with

them" *(Shemos 1:7)*. The Jews' virility did not diminish during their years in Egypt. Not a single man or woman could not have children. Boys fathered children at thirteen years of age. *(Midrash Rabbah)* Like *sheretz*, swarming animals or insects, the Jews multiplied profusely. There were no miscarriages, no stillbirths, and no infant was born infirm.

After seven months of pregnancy *(Chomas Anach)*, every woman gave birth to multiples. Usually children of multiple births are frail, but these children progressed and developed into strapping youths, accumulating great wealth. No evil eye was cast against them. They were vigorous and in good health, more rugged and muscular than most Egyptian children. They lived, robust, to a ripe old age.

Some say the mothers bore twins; others say sextuplets. According to some, six boys *and* six girls-twelve were born at a time!

(Mechilta, Bo)

The largest swarming animal, the mouse, gives birth to six young at a time. The smallest swarming animal, the scorpion, gives birth to sixty young. The women bore six hundred babies at a time!

(Shach)

One woman gave birth to 600,000, fulfilling the blessing Yaakov bestowed upon his children, "May they increase in the land like fish" *(Bereishis 48:16)*. And the prophet Yechezkel said, "I have increased you like the plants of the field" *(Yechezkel 16:7)*.

(Aggadas Bereishis)

No sooner had the mothers given birth than they were once again with child. *(Alshich)* When the first babies were nine or ten months old, the mother gave birth again. Not one took sick or died. All grew tall, strong and sturdy, shooting up like plants in the field. A one-year-old toddler looked like a twenty-year-old man.

The Source of Anti-Semitism

Like reeds in a marsh, the Jewish people filled the land of Egypt. *(Midrash Rabbah, Shemos)* Initially, the Jews stayed in their own neighborhood, working diligently and learning Torah. But as time progressed they ventured out into public places in groups of ten or twenty, creating the impression that the entire country was filled with them.

(Sefer Chasidim)

Eventually the Jewish population spilled over the borders of their assigned territory of Goshen. They purchased every available living space in Egypt to accommodate their quickly growing numbers, disregarding Yaakov's command to settle exclusively in Goshen.

Living among the citizens of Egypt, the Jews assimilated with their neighbors, adopting their vile mentality. They discarded the one sign that distinguished Jew from Egyptian-circumcision. *(Shemos Rabbah)* But instead of becoming one with the Egyptians, the Jews incited their hatred. Upon discovering that the Jews were filling up their theaters and circuses, the Egyptians issued anti-Semitic decrees to keep the Jews away. *(Yalkut Shimoni)* As in every generation that followed, when the Jews became too intrusive, the host nation rejected them.

Distinguished

When the Torah recounts the history of the Jews, it says that Yaakov went down to Egypt, "and he became a nation there" *(Devarim 26:5)*. The *Haggada* quotes this verse and comments, "This teaches us that the Children of Israel were *metzuyanim*, distinguished there." How were they distinguished? What made the Jews different? They kept their identity separate from the non-Jews by not changing their Jewish names, language, religion and clothing.

(Abarbanel, Zevach Pesach)

Vayareiu Osanu Hamitzriyim

וַיָּרֵעוּ אֹתָנוּ הַמִּצְרִים וַיְעַנּוּנוּ וַיִּתְּנוּ עָלֵינוּ עֲבוֹדָה קָשָׁה:

וַיָּרֵעוּ אֹתָנוּ הַמִּצְרִים, כְּמָה שֶׁנֶּאֱמַר, הָבָה נִתְחַכְּמָה לוֹ פֶּן יִרְבֶּה וְהָיָה כִּי תִקְרֶאנָה מִלְחָמָה וְנוֹסַף גַּם הוּא עַל שׂוֹנְאֵינוּ וְנִלְחַם בָּנוּ וְעָלָה מִן הָאָרֶץ:

וַיְעַנּוּנוּ, כְּמָה שֶׁנֶּאֱמַר, וַיָּשִׂימוּ עָלָיו שָׂרֵי מִסִּים לְמַעַן עַנֹּתוֹ בְּסִבְלוֹתָם וַיִּבֶן עָרֵי מִסְכְּנוֹת לְפַרְעֹה אֶת פִּתֹם וְאֶת רַעַמְסֵס:

וַיִּתְּנוּ עָלֵינוּ עֲבוֹדָה קָשָׁה, כְּמָה שֶׁנֶּאֱמַר, וַיַּעֲבִדוּ מִצְרַיִם אֶת בְּנֵי יִשְׂרָאֵל בְּפָרֶךְ:

At this point, it should be explained to each child that the Jews were distinctive-they had beards and *peyos*. They had their own code of dress, including *tzitzis*, derived from the same root as the word "*metzuyanim*."

(Darchei Hayashar Vehatov 314)

Vayareiu Osanu Hamitzriyim

The New Pharaoh

"A new king who did not know Yosef came into power" *(Shemos 1:8)*. Who was this new king?

Perhaps he was simply a new king in the literal sense-a new Pharaoh came to power who was born after Yosef's death. Or perhaps he was new in the sense that he issued new decrees. When he saw how quickly the Jews were multiplying, he placed restrictions upon

them to curb the rapid birth rate. *(Sotah 11a)* Perhaps he was new to royalty, a king not born from royal lineage.

(Ibn Ezra)

Looking with malice at the rapid increase of the Jewish population, the ungrateful Egyptians resented the original royal dynasty and Yosef, the Jewish viceroy who had saved them from starvation. Spiteful and bitter, they overthrew the current king, crowning a vicious scoundrel in his place.

The Midrash explains that this new king came from a distant country. Far away in a foreign land, this new leader did not hear the story of Yosef and his rise to power. This foreign upstart invaded Egypt with a band of followers and overtook the monarchy.

Onkelos describes the new king as the new king "who did not fulfill the decree of Yosef." He knew Yosef, but he abolished Yosef's decree that all Egyptian males had to be circumcised. Yosef issued this decree to minimize the hatred between the Jews and Egyptians due to their physical differences. If the Egyptians were circumcised as well, they could not hate the Jews as much. But when the new Pharaoh abolished the decree, the Egyptians were free to resume their original hatred of the Jews. The Jews attempted to blur this distinction and abstained from circumcision as well.

Identifying the Enemy

"He announced to his people, 'Behold, the people of the children of Israel are becoming too numerous and strong for us. We must deal wisely with them. Otherwise they may increase so much that if there is a war, they will join our enemies and fight against us, driving [us] from the land"

(Shemos 1:9,10).

The new king, chosen for his hatred of the Jews, actually feared the Jews' power and strength. He was concerned that should there be

a war, the Jews, so great in number, would join the allies of the deposed ruler to topple the new regime.

Pharaoh observed that the Jews were multiplying at an amazing rate. They would outnumber the Egyptians in no time! *(Rabbi Avraham ben HaRambam)* And aside from sheer numbers, the Jews' physical strength would exceed the Egyptians'. *(Abarbanel)* The Jews were strong in wealth and in might, formidable in their intelligence. *(Rabbi Tuviah)* Something had to be done.

Parasites

"The Jews are becoming too numerous and strong!" *(Shemos 1:9)* raved Pharoah. "The Jews' power, their wealth-it is not of their own making. It is from Egypt. The Jews are flourishing because they took advantage of our hospitality during and after the famine. We have to reclaim what is rightfully ours!"

King Avimelech insinuated the same message to Yitzchak. "Go away from us for you have become rich from us" *(Bereishis 26:16)*. "You siphoned your wealth from our economy. You took money out of our pockets."

Anti-Semitic rabble-rousers are powerless against a government that is righteous and kind to Jews. But "if a ruler listens to falsehood, all his ministers will be wicked" *(Mishlei 29:12)*. Jews suffer greatly under governments that are swayed by prejudice, persecuted for no fault of their own.

(Pardes Yosef, Bo)

Taxation and Confiscation

Pharaoh and his advisors deemed it imprudent to kill the Jews by the sword. Slaying innocent people who had immigrated to the land at the invitation of a former king would be despicable. Besides, the people of Egypt would not allow the king to commit such an outrage.

The Jews were numerous and mighty-they would fight back ferociously.

Instead, Pharaoh planned wisely. He kicked off his campaign with an innocent tax. "They appointed tax collectors" *(Shemos 1:11)*. The Jews would not be able to discern the hateful racism. All foreigners paid a special tax to the government.

(Ramban)

Pharaoh hoped the individual head tax of one hundred coins for each family member would make the Jews think twice before having so many children. *(Haggada Baalei Tosafos)* Any Jew who was not able to pay the fixed tax-either annually or in monthly installments-was drafted into slave labor. Some Jews, affluent enough to afford the enormous tax, never performed slave labor.

(Ralbag)

Others maintain that the tax was not a universal tax that every citizen was obligated to pay. The Jews were at the mercy of insulting and abusive tax collectors, who would demand whatever their hearts desired. *(Pardes Yosef)* The Egyptians confiscated beautiful homes, vineyards and fields which Yosef had given his Jewish brethren.

(Sefer Hayashar)

Crushing Labor

Next step was enslavement. How did the Egyptians manage to enslave the Jews, even though the Jews outnumbered them?

With the hot sun beating on their backs in the fields all day, the Jewish men grew uncomfortably warm. They innocently removed their jackets to stay cool. The Egyptians stole their garments and brought them to the homes of their owners. "Look," they told the wives who responded to their knocks. "Your husband sent me to fetch his weapons. Here is his jacket as proof." The Egyptians seized

the weapons, leaving the Jews defenseless, unable to rise against the enemy.

(Ri of Vienna)

"The Egyptians enslaved the children of Israel with crushing labor" *(Shemos 1:13)*. Every Egyptian was permitted to force a Jew to work for him. They tyrannized the Jews, beating and cursing them while forcing them to work. *(Ramban)* What was the "crushing labor" the Jews endured? Constant, never-ending work. *(Yalkut Midrash Teiman)* They had to supply the sand to make the mortar and bricks that were needed to build cities. All they were given was the straw.

> *On the first day of labor Pharaoh announced, "Whoever produces ten bricks per day receives 10 silver coins; for 40 bricks, he receives 40 silver coins." Eager for the money, each Jew produced a maximum quantity of bricks. His output was duly recorded. The next day, Pharaoh threatened, "There will be no reward today-but whoever produces any less than yesterday will be flogged!"*
>
> *(Yalkut Midrashim, Kurdistan)*

Things got progressively worse. "They made their lives miserable with harsh labor ... as well as with all types of work in the field" *(Shemos 1:14)*. When a Jew finally finished his work with mortar and bricks and was ready to go home in the evening, his Egyptian taskmaster would stop him. "Go and gather some vegetables in my garden! Chop this block of wood! Fill up this barrel with water!"

(Rav Pinchas Hakohen bar Chama)

Brotherhood and Unity

Avraham was told that his descendants would be enslaved for four hundred years *(Bereishis 15:13)*, but in the end, the Jews were freed after two hundred and ten years in Egypt, one hundred-ninety

years before the appointed time. The excessive harshness of the slavery compensated for those one hundred-ninety missing years.

According to Ramban, the Egyptian tax collectors rounded up Jews to work as slaves for a month or two, after which they were free to do as they pleased. But if they worked for only two months, this was not excessive harshness! Why were they set free one hundred-ninety years early?

The Jews were redeemed in the merit of their unity. There was no quarreling or jealousy among them. Each Jew sympathized and commiserated with his brother's plight, feeling as if it were his own. As long as one Jew was being oppressed, every Jew agonized with him. The excessive harshness of the slavery was felt equally by all the Jewish people, even by those who were not engaged in slave labor. They were fully deserving of the premature redemption as they fully shared the pain and misery.

(Arugas Habosem, Vaeira)

Breaking the Jewish Spirit

The Egyptians tried to break the Jews with crushing labor. They made a woman do a man's job, and a man do a woman's job. To a Jewish male, the Egyptians would command, "Knead this dough and bake it!" Women were sent to carry water and tend to the fields.

(Midrash Tanchuma)

They piled more and more tasks upon the Jewish slaves-the demeaning tasks of digging ditches and spreading manure on the fields. Pharaoh's intention was to exhaust the Jews, thereby lowering their birth rate.

(Yalkut Midrash Teiman)

The Jews worked in the blazing sun. Cooling off in the shade was forbidden. The lice tormented the slaves incessantly, as they were not

permitted to bathe or launder their clothes. They ate their food with mud-stained hands.

At night, the Egyptian master forced his Jewish slave to carry a torch for him, lighting up the road to the market. The master trapped a deer, killed it and prepared it for a feast. At dinnertime, the Egyptian placed a lamp on the Jew's head. "Make sure you don't move or I'll chop off your head!" The master ate the flavorful meat before the longing and hungry eyes of the Jewish slave. The Jew did not receive even a single bite to still his hunger.

(Ramban, Midrash Rabbah, Shach, Tanchuma)

To contain the explosive growth, men were not allowed to sleep at home. The taskmasters told them, "If you go home at night, you lose too much time. You won't be able to finish your daily quota. You must sleep out in the field."

The Holy One, blessed be He, said to the Egyptians, "I promised their father Avraham, 'I will increase your offspring like the stars of the sky' (Bereishis 22:17), and you are trying to stop them from increasing. Let's see who succeeds, you or I."

(Midrash Rabbah)

Stamping out Shabbos

When Pharaoh said, "Let us deal wisely with them" *(Shemos 1: 10)*, he intended to do away with the observance of Shabbos. It made Pharaoh so angry to see the Jews endure suffering with such ease. *(Kuntres Zeir Zahav, Shemos)* "Because the Jews are so joyous and happy," reasoned Pharaoh, "their numbers and their strength increase at an unusual rate. What is the source of their joy and their happiness? Shabbos! Shabbos gives them the stamina to last for the whole week. Shabbos gives them the strength to put up with the suffering we inflict on them. If we abolish their Shabbos, we will kill their source of joy. Let us deal wisely with them-let us abolish their Shabbos!"

(Yetev Lev)

I will never forget the Shabbos when the German soldiers burst into our courtyard. At the top of their voices they announced, "You have five minutes to vacate your apartments and assemble in the courtyard! All of you-men, women, and children. Anyone remaining inside will be shot on the spot! Alle raus! Sofort!"

Rav Avraham Yaakov Braun, an outstanding Torah scholar who had studied at the Unsdorf Yeshiva, shared our living quarters. He went out into the courtyard dressed in his finest Shabbos clothes. Oblivious of the German hoodlums, he broke into a lively dance, singing a spirited song. His face radiated pure joy.

As he danced, he chanted, "Ribbono shel Olam! I accept upon myself the yoke of exile as You decreed! I am ready to give my life to sanctify Your name!" The Germans couldn't take it. Hopping mad, they beat him, they screamed at him to stop, but he kept dancing ...

(Rav Tzvi Hirsch Meisels, Sefer Mikdeshei Hashem)

The Egyptian taskmasters forced the Jews to violate the thirty-nine acts of work that are forbidden on Shabbos. When the Jews were redeemed from slavery they were commanded to keep Shabbos, to abstain from these thirty-nine modes of work. *Kiddush* on Shabbos and holidays commemorates this distinction between slavery and freedom, "a memorial of the Exodus from Egypt."

The purpose of all the commandments of the Torah is to keep us away from idolatry. *(Rambam, Moreh Nevuchim)* Every *mitzvah* bestows holiness upon its performer. Pagan codes instructed worshippers to do precisely the acts the Torah forbids, because violating a *mitzvah* draws impurity. Idol worshippers, eager to attain any impurities they could get their hands on, would violate as many *mitzvos* as possible.

Pharaoh, attempting to instill impurity in the Jewish people, forced them to perform the forbidden labors on Shabbos. He sought to deprive them of the holiness that is conferred on those who uphold Shabbos.

(Divrei Yoel III, 26)

Keeping the Faith

The Jews in Egypt pledged to be kind to each other, to keep the covenant of their fathers and worship only their Father in Heaven. They promised not to abandon the language of Yaakov, never to learn the Egyptians' spoken language.

The Egyptians watched the Jews converse among themselves in their own language. They watched them perform Hashem's will. They used these commitments to goad the Jews.

"Why don't you worship the Egyptian idols? If you do, we'll ease up on your workload."

The Jews answered, "How can you expect us to abandon our Father in Heaven? Did our forefathers Avraham, Yitzchak, and Yaakov abandon our Father in Heaven? They did not, and neither will we!"

When the Jews circumcised their infant boys, the Egyptians said, "If you will refrain from circumcising your children, we will let up on your work."

The Jews retorted, "Our forefathers did not stop circumcising their sons and neither will we!"

A Jewish father lovingly performed a circumcision on his infant son. A mocking Egyptian looked on with laughter. "Why bother? Your child will soon be cast into the Nile!"

"I will perform the circumcision, no matter what you do afterward!"

A Jew joyously celebrated his marriage for seven days with the seven blessings. The Egyptians looked on, scoffing. "Why are you having seven festive meals? Tomorrow you'll be breaking your back under harsh labor!"

The Jew shot back, "I am celebrating my marriage for seven days. What you choose to do afterward is up to you!"

So the Egyptians provoked and taunted the Jews. The Jews had no place to hide.

(Tanna Debei Eliyahu, 23)

Building Cities

Foreign and native laborers abounded. There were plenty of workers to carry out Pharaoh's city building plan. But Pharaoh needed a way to finance the project. For this massive construction effort, he had to raise taxes. So he turned to the Jews.

Pharaoh also needed overseers. Shrewdly, he again turned to the Jews. The Jews were appointed managers of the entire Department of Public Works. "So they appointed taskmasters over it ..." *(Shemos 1:11)*-the Egyptians appointed the Jews as the overseers of the project. Who could turn down such a prestigious assignment?

But it was a trick, designed "to afflict them with hard labor" *(ibid.)*. If the Egyptian laborers were unable to finish the daily task, the Jewish overseers had to fill the remaining quota. Gradually, the Jews did more and more of the work, eventually becoming slaves themselves, "building supply centers for Pharaoh" *(ibid.)*.

(Ohr Hachaim)

Storage Cities

What were these storage cities, *arei miskenos*? *Miskenos* may be related to *miskein*, poor and miserable, because a builder is likely to lose his money and become poor. *(Hadar Zekeinim)* Or *miskenos* may be from the root word *sikkein* or *sakanah*, to expose to danger. While working on these buildings, slaves fell from dizzying heights to their deaths. Some were crushed by collapsing structures. These cities were hazardous; they endangered the lives of the workers who built them.

(Yalkut Midrash Teiman)

Moshe prayed to Hashem, "Master of the World, why are You allowing the Jewish people to suffer at the hands of these Egyptian evildoers? Look at what they are doing to Your people!"

"I am pulling the weeds from the vineyard," Hashem replied. Fatal construction accidents were G-d's method of removing the sinners from among the Jews. "Let me show you. I will let one sinner survive, and you will see for yourself how much harm he will do."

Hashem revived one man who had been crushed in a building collapse. This was the notorious Micha, who crafted an idol that he smuggled across the Red Sea and eventually built an idolatrous shrine on the opposite side of the Jordan. (See Shoftim 17,18.)

(Haggada Baalei HaTosafos)

Pharaoh needed storage facilities for the crops that he collected as tax from the Egyptians. "Yosef imposed it as a statute until this day regarding the land of Egypt, one-fifth belonged to Pharaoh" *(Bereishis 47:26)*. But the Jews were exempt from the tax, because Yosef had settled them in the fertile land of Goshen, which they never sold to Egypt.

Now Pharaoh made a false accusation. "The Egyptian farmers are tenants of the king. They pay me one-fifth of their crop and half of all animals that are born. But you Jews aren't paying anything. So instead, you have to build the granaries to store the harvest."

(Rabbi Yosef B'chor Shor)

When Yosef arrested Binyamin, Yehuda became furious. The two brothers argued vehemently, raising their voices to such a pitch that the entire cities of Pisom and Raamses collapsed. That's why the Egyptians insisted the Jews were responsible to rebuild these cities.

(Sforno, Yalkut Reuveni)

Pisom and Raamses

The Talmud presents disputing opinions, Rav and Shmuel, about the two storage cities of Pisom and Raamses. *(Sotah 116a)*

They were both one city. According to one opinion, its real name was Pisom, but it was called Raamses because one building after another would collapse, *misroses*. The other said that its real name was Raamses, but it was called Pisom because as the buildings were erected, they would gradually sink into the mouth of the ground, *pi tehom*.

The soggy Egyptian soil did not provide stable ground for tall structures. Whatever the Jews built during the day fell apart that night. *(Midrash Bechiddush)* The next day, the Jews would rebuild again. The entire effort was senseless; the sole purpose was to weaken the Jews and stop them from having children. *(Midrash Avkir)* Others say that at night, the wicked Egyptians made the Jews tear down whatever they had built during the day.

(Midrash Rabbeinu Efraim)

Pharaoh asked Moshe, "Why is it that the buildings don't stand?"

"Every nation in the world has a day of rest. Only the Jews have to work all week long," Moshe defended his brethren.

"I'll give them off one day a week," conceded Pharaoh. "Go and cast lots to determine which day." The lot fell on Shabbos.

During the silent Shemoneh Esrei on Shabbos morning we say, "Moshe rejoiced in the gift of his portion." Moshe rejoiced on Shabbos, for Pharaoh granted the Jewish people permission to rest on that day.

And that is why the Torah commands, "You must remember that you were slaves in Egypt ... It is for this reason that Hashem your G-d commanded you to keep the Shabbos day" (Devarim 5:15). Because of the day of rest Hashem granted the Jews of Egypt, we must keep the Shabbos day.

(Shemos Rabbah 1:32)

Vanitzak El Hashem

וַנִּצְעַק אֶל יְהֹוָה אֱלֹהֵי אֲבוֹתֵינוּ, וַיִּשְׁמַע יְהֹוָה אֶת קֹלֵנוּ וַיַּרְא אֶת עָנְיֵנוּ וְאֶת עֲמָלֵנוּ וְאֶת לַחֲצֵנוּ:

וַנִּצְעַק אֶל יְהֹוָה אֱלֹהֵי אֲבוֹתֵינוּ, כְּמָה שֶׁנֶּאֱמַר, וַיְהִי בַיָּמִים הָרַבִּים הָהֵם וַיָּמָת מֶלֶךְ מִצְרַיִם וַיֵּאָנְחוּ בְנֵי יִשְׂרָאֵל מִן הָעֲבֹדָה וַיִּזְעָקוּ, וַתַּעַל שַׁוְעָתָם אֶל הָאֱלֹהִים מִן הָעֲבֹדָה:

וַיִּשְׁמַע יְהֹוָה אֶת קֹלֵנוּ, כְּמָה שֶׁנֶּאֱמַר, וַיִּשְׁמַע אֱלֹהִים אֶת נַאֲקָתָם וַיִּזְכֹּר אֱלֹהִים אֶת בְּרִיתוֹ אֶת אַבְרָהָם אֶת יִצְחָק וְאֶת יַעֲקֹב:

With Crushing Harshness

"All the work they made them do was intended to break them, *befarech*" *(Shemos 1:13)*. The word *befarech* is a contraction of *befeh rach*, with gentle talk. *(Sotah 11a)* For the first month the Egyptians worked alongside the Jews, paying them a daily salary. Then the Egyptians stopped working. Finally, they discontinued their wages.

They appointed Egyptian administrators and elderly Jews as foremen, one foreman for ten Jewish slaves and one administrator for ten foremen. The foremen were ordered to pressure the Jews to work harder. When a Jew did not fill his daily quota the administrators berated the Jewish foreman, beating him black and blue.

(Midrash Rabbah)

"They made their lives miserable with harsh labor, with mortar and with bricks and with all kinds of field labor; all their labor they made them labor with crushing harshness" *(Shemos 1:14)*. This verse mentions the word *avodah*, labor, four times because the Egyptian slavery was worse than all the other exiles-Babylonia, Persia, Greece, and Rome.

(Rabbeinu Yoel)

וַיַּרְא אֶת עָנְיֵנוּ, זוֹ פְּרִישׁוּת דֶּרֶךְ אֶרֶץ. כְּמָה שֶׁנֶּאֱמַר, וַיַּרְא אֱלֹהִים אֶת בְּנֵי יִשְׂרָאֵל וַיֵּדַע אֱלֹהִים:

וְאֶת עֲמָלֵנוּ, אֵלּוּ הַבָּנִים. כְּמָה שֶׁנֶּאֱמַר, כָּל הַבֵּן הַיִּלּוֹד הַיְאֹרָה תַּשְׁלִיכוּהוּ וְכָל הַבַּת תְּחַיּוּן:

וְאֶת לַחֲצֵנוּ, זוֹ הַדְּחַק. כְּמָה שֶׁנֶּאֱמַר, וְגַם רָאִיתִי אֶת הַלַּחַץ אֲשֶׁר מִצְרַיִם לוֹחֲצִים אוֹתָם:

Vanitzak El Hashem

Plan Thwarted

"The more they oppressed them, the more they proliferated and spread" *(Shemos 1:12)*. Hashem mocked Pharaoh's words. "You were worried, Pharaoh. You said, 'Let us make a plan, *pen yirbeh*, lest they increase.' Your devices will do no good. Despite the crushing labor, I say, '*Ken yirbeh*, so they will increase!'"

Hashem arranged for the Jewish people to be saved; that Moshe, the one who was destined to save His beloved nation, would be rescued. "He makes wise men retreat and makes their knowledge foolish" *(Yeshaya 44:25)*. In every generation our enemies devise evil plans to wipe us from the face of the earth, but Hashem shatters their plots.

(Rabbeinu Bachya, Ramban, Tur)

Disgusted

The Egyptians saw the Jews' unusual proliferation and "they became disgusted, *vayakutzu*" *(Shemos 1:12)*. The Jews were like a *kotz*, a thorn piercing the flesh of the Egyptians. It hurt them so much to see the Jews multiplying at such an astonishing rate.

(Be'er Yitzchak)

Confident in their numbers, the enslaved Jews boldly broke into the Egyptians' vineyards, orchards, and farms, and walked off with anything they could find. In the fisheries, they took all the fish they could carry. "We remember the fish we ate in Egypt free of charge" *(Bamidbar 11:5)*. Helpless in the face of the widespread break-ins, the Egyptians became disgusted with the losses brought on by the audacious Jewish slaves. *(Abarbanel)* So they redoubled their efforts to oppress the Jews.

Righteous Women

The righteous and devout Jewish women in slavery loyally cared for their husbands. When they went to draw water from the well, Hashem miraculously filled their pails with water and nutritious little fish. The women warmed the water, cooking the fish. Sneaking up to the men in the fields, the women would provide their husbands with luxuriously warm water to wash their hands and feet, delicious little fish to savor, and a glass of wine to relax with.

Trying to cheer up the men, the wives would take out their copper mirrors and show off their beauty, playfully poking fun, "Look how much prettier I am than you!" The wives would comfort their husbands soothingly. "This slavery won't last forever. Have faith! Hashem has promised to have mercy on us and redeem us."

When Hashem told Moshe to build the Tabernacle, the men willingly donated silver, gold, and gemstones. The women were heartsick. "What can we contribute to the *Mishkan*? All we own are our mirrors!" So they offered these.

Initially, Moshe rejected their modest gift. But Hashem said, "Moshe! Don't look down on those mirrors. With these mirrors the women encouraged their husbands. Thanks to the women, we have a mighty legion of children for this generation. Accept these mirrors and fashion them into the copper washstand from which the priests will wash their hands and feet."

(Midrash Tanchuma, Pekudei)

Rachel, daughter of Shuselach, was with child. Despite this she stood on her feet, helping her husband mix the mortar. Quite suddenly, she gave birth! The infant fell into the mortar-to his quick death. Rachel's heartbreaking screams rose to the Divine Throne, and a year later, on the very same night, Hashem revealed Himself, slaying all Egyptian firstborn.

(Pirkei D'Rebi Eliezer)

The Midwives' Role

Much to the Egyptians' chagrin, the imposed slavery did not stem the Jews' growth. Normally hard work weakens a man and reduces his virility. But "the more they oppressed them, the more they proliferated and spread"

(Shemos 1:12).

So Pharaoh decreed extermination. To avoid adverse publicity, the killings were carried out secretly. He delegated the mortifying task to the Jewish midwives, Shifrah and Puah-ordering them to kill all newborn boys. Pharaoh thought that if the Jewish midwives did the evil work, G-d would vent His anger on the midwives.

(Yalkut Ha'ezovi)

How could two midwives take care of the vast and ever-growing Jewish population? Customarily in Egypt, all women were attended by two midwives. One assisted in the delivery and tended to the

newborn infant. Her title was Shifrah, "because she *meshapperes*, beautifies the newborn infant." The other midwife guided, soothed and encouraged the mother, praying for an easy childbirth. Her title was Puah, for *puah* is an expression of "crying out," similar to, "I will cry out, *ef'eh*, like a woman in childbirth"

(Yeshaya 42:14).

"The king of Egypt said to the Hebrew midwives of whom the name of the first was Shifrah and the name of the second was Puah" *(Shemos 1:15)*. When Pharaoh spoke to the Hebrew midwives, he did not speak to two midwives named Shifrah and Puah. He spoke to all the Shifrahs and all the Puahs who attended the births of the Jewish mothers.

(Abarbanel)

Infanticide

Pharaoh knew Jewish boys. He knew that Jewish boys were obstinate and set in their ways. These rascals were to be drowned, but the girls-they could live. When these girls would be ready to marry, there would be no Jewish boys around. They would marry Egyptians and blend into their society, obliterating the Jewish people altogether.

"You must look carefully at the birthstool. If the infant is a boy, kill it, but if it is a girl, let it live" *(Shemos 1:16)*. Pharaoh instructed the midwives sternly, "If you place your finger on the infant's nose, it dies instantly. Tell the mothers their babies were stillborn." Or perhaps Pharaoh told them to kill the fetus while it was still in the mother's womb.

(Ibn Ezra, Be'er Yitzchak, Kol Eliyahu)

How did Pharaoh think that no one would notice all these dying infants? The midwives wouldn't tell the mothers if their stillborn was a boy or a girl. They would just say, "Your baby was stillborn." The

mothers would see that some of the babies lived and some did not. No one would suspect the midwives.

(Ohr Hachaim)

But the midwives feared G-d more than they feared the king. They did not listen to Pharaoh's orders. With great courage, they allowed the infant boys to live.

With the Help of the Angels

When she felt ready to give birth, every Jewish mother went out into the field. There she lay down under an apple tree, falling into a deep sleep. The baby was born miraculously, without labor pains.

There was no pillow to rest on, and no attendant for the birthing mother. But angels came down from heaven to cut the umbilical cord, attending to the mother better than any midwife. After gently washing and cleaning the infant, the angels dressed the baby. They gave the baby two small stones-one from which to suckle milk and honey, the other to massage the skin with soft oil.

Then the mother awoke. Her baby was dressed in silk clothing, clean and anointed. "Blessed be the Almighty, for not withdrawing His kindness and truth from the offspring of Avraham our father," she praised. "We place these children in Your hand, to do with them according to Your will." Then she walked away, leaving her baby behind.

The Egyptians would come looking for Jewish babies under the apple tree-but a miracle happened. The babies were swallowed up by the earth. The Egyptians brought oxen to plow the ground. Satisfied that no living being could survive this treatment, the Egyptians left. But the infants remained safe and unharmed.

The children sprouted like grass, growing into a mighty legion. An angel would lead each one to his home to reunite him with his

parents. "In this house you will find your father and mother. Their names are such-and-such, and your name is so-and-so," the angels would inform the youth.

When the child entered, his parents asked, "Where are you from?"

He replied, "My name is so-and-so, I am your son, and your names are such-and-such."

"How did you get here?" the parents asked.

"A young man brought me, and he is waiting outside," the boy answered. But no one was there.

Overjoyed, yet bewildered, the parents pressed further, "Tell us, who took care of you all this time?"

"A kind and handsome young man came and provided all my needs."

And so it says, "My Beloved is clear-skinned and ruddy, surrounded with myriad angels" *(Shir Hashirim 5:10)*. When G-d revealed Himself at the Red Sea, these same children saw Him in the form of a young man. They recognized Him immediately, crying out, "This is my G-d, and I will glorify Him"

(Shemos 15:2).

Drowning the Infants

The midwives were ineffective; Jewish boys continued to live. So Pharaoh revealed the decree to the general population. Everyone was to drown his baby boy in the river. *(Rabbeinu Bachya)* Even the Egyptian people were to cast their newborn boys in the Nile. As it says, "Pharaoh then gave orders to *all* his people"

(Shemos 1:22).

Onkelus translates the verse, "Every boy born to the Jews must be cast in the Nile," indicating that only Jewish babies were to be killed. How is this disparity resolved? At the outset the decree was

issued only against the Jews. But one day the astrologers announced, "Today the future savior of the Jews was born!" They did not know whether the savior of the Jews was Jewish or Egyptian. On that day alone, Pharaoh ordered that all babies-Jewish and Egyptian-be drowned in the Nile.

> *For three-and-a-half years, Jewish infants were thrown into the Nile-until Moshe was born. When Moshe was born, Pharaoh's astrologers told him, "The savior of the Jews is born, but he is hidden away. We don't know where he is."*
>
> *"Now that he is born," reasoned Pharaoh, "there is no point continuing to cast infants into the Nile. Instead, let's force the Jews to do hard labor and make their lives miserable."*
>
> *(Midrash Yalkut Sippurim, Shemos)*

"Catch us the foxes, the little foxes that ruin the vineyards" *(Shir Hashirim 2:15)*. The little foxes are the Egyptian babies. The Egyptians had a fiendish way of discovering hidden Jewish babies. They would make their own babies cry, and when the Jewish babies in their hiding places heard the crying, they would start crying too. The Egyptians would pounce on the Jewish babies and cast them into the Nile. Thus it was the Egyptian babies who betrayed the Jewish babies in hiding.

(Midrash Rabbah)

The children who were thrown into the Nile did not perish. The Nile expelled them and catapulted them into the Egyptian desert. Hashem placed one stone in their mouth and one at their side. The stone in their mouth nursed them with honey, and the stone at their side nursed them with oil, like a mother suckling her baby. As it says, "He would suckle them with honey from a stone and oil from a flinty rock" *(Devarim 32:13)*.

(Pirkei D'Rabi Eliezer)

Pharaoh Stricken With Leprosy

"A long time passed, and the king of Egypt died" *(Shemos 2:23)*. Pharaoh did not actually die; he was stricken with leprosy. *(Rashi, ibid.)* The Egyptian sorcerers told Pharaoh that the only cure for his leprosy was to bathe in the blood of Jewish infants-one hundred-fifty infants' blood in the morning and one hundred-fifty in the evening.

"And the children of Israel were groaning" *(Shemos 2:23)*, upon hearing the recommended treatment for Pharaoh's leprosy, "and their pleas went up before G-d" *(ibid.)*.

(Shemos Rabbah)

Day after day, Pharaoh's agents arrived in Goshen to tear away babies from their mothers' arms. The doctors slaughtered the babies, applying the blood to Pharaoh's leprosy lesions twice a day. Pharaoh slaughtered three hundred seventy-five babies altogether, but his leprosy only got worse.

Pharaoh suffered terribly from his illness for ten long years. Then Hashem increased his suffering, afflicting him with boils and blisters and a stomach ailment.

Crippled

Two of Pharaoh's agents arrived at the royal palace one day, reporting that the Jews in the land of Goshen were lazy and lying down on the job. Pharaoh seethed with anger. "I see! The Jews know I'm sick, so they make fun of me! Harness my horse. I want to go to Goshen to see for myself how they are mocking me!"

Pharaoh was too weak to mount his horse himself; his servants lifted him up. Accompanied by an escort of one hundred horsemen and ten foot soldiers, he arrived at the border between Egypt and Goshen. A deep ravine separated Egypt from its neighboring province. There was a narrow bridge flanked by a fence suspended over the ravine.

The large entourage began crossing. But with the crush of people, Pharaoh tumbled into the gorge, his horse and a chariot crashing down on top of him. His bones were broken. Bleeding from multiple cuts and lacerations, he lay helpless, howling with agony.

Pharaoh's servants carried him back to Egypt and put him to bed, but Pharaoh realized his end was near. Queen Alparanis wept at the sight of her husband crippled and cut. Pharaoh, too, wept uncontrollably. It was all Hashem's doing, for He had heard the Jews' outcry and seen their suffering.

Pharaoh Appoints a Successor

Pharaoh's ministers advised him to appoint one of his sons as his successor. Aside from the children of his concubines, Pharaoh and his wife Alparanis had three sons and two daughters-Esro, Adikam, and Morion; Basyah and Efuzi.

Esro, the firstborn, was a diligent and sensible fellow. Ostensibly, the round and stout Adikam was shrewd and intelligent. But beneath the veneer lay a truly cruel man. Pharaoh chose Adikam as his successor. Adikam married Gedudah, daughter of Avidal, and they had four sons. He married three more wives who bore him eight sons and three daughters.

Pharaoh Dies

Pharaoh's sickness took a turn for the worse. His flesh was decaying like a carcass in the blazing sun. Pharaoh knew his end was near, so he crowned his son Adikam, one hundred years old, as the ruler of Egypt. Pharoah suffered for three more years while Adikam ruled the country.

Pharaoh was buried in the royal burial ground in Tzoan. But he was not embalmed like all Egyptian kings. At the time of his death, his flesh was so putrid that the embalmers could not take the stench. G-d brought this curse on him to pay him back for the suffering he

inflicted on the Jewish people. Pharaoh died in disgrace, and Adikam succeeded him.

Adikam ascended the throne two hundred-six years after the Jews' arrival in Egypt. He reigned for four years. Of very short stature, Adikam was called Avuz by Egyptian historians, which means short in Egyptian. Adikam the Short was a vicious man, more depraved than all earlier kings. He oppressed the Jews even more than his father had.

(Midrash Yalkut Sippurim, Shemos)

Groaning

"During those many days, it happened that the king of Egypt died, and the children of Israel groaned ..." *(Shemos 2:23)* Why did the Jewish people groan at this particular juncture?

- Out of fear that the next king would be even worse.

(Rabbeinu Bachya)

- They did not groan because the king had died. It was their anguished cries and overwhelming groans of "Woe is me!" that killed the brutish king.

(Tzror Hamor)

- Customarily, with the death of the king, the government would declare a general amnesty for prisoners and slaves. The Jewish people hoped and prayed that Pharaoh would die, and they would be set free. But when Pharaoh died, their status as slaves continued to be enforced. Now the Jews despaired of ever being released.
- The king who passed away knew and loved Yosef. Out of respect for their ancestor, he did not force the Jews to worship the Egyptian idols. But the new king made idol worship mandatory and refusal punishable.

(Haggada shel Pesach)

- When a king runs the country, he governs according to a set policy, and even the most depraved king will not commit flagrant crimes. Now, lawless warlords and competing gang leaders battled for the throne. It was mob rule-total anarchy, chaos, and a reign of terror.

(Tosafos Hashalem, Yalkut Ha'ezovi, Rabbi Yehudah Hechasid)

Because of the Work

The Jewish people were in exile, and their power of speech was in exile, too. They groaned without articulating any words because they simply could not talk. *(B'nei Yissoschor)* "Their [wordless] outcry because of the work went up to G-d" *(Shemos 2:23)*. They groaned from the physical labor, an impulsive reaction to the anguish of hard work and beatings.

(Igra DePirka)

Though the appointed time for the redemption had not yet arrived, the Jewish people were worthy to be set free. G-d was swayed by their outcry "because of the work." This phrase is mentioned twice in one verse to teach that prayer stirred by pain and distress rises straight to the heavenly Throne.

(Rabbeinu Bachya)

Seeing the Truth

"*Vayar Elokim es*, G-d saw the children of Israel" *(Shemos 2:25)*. The last letters in the first words of the verse are *alef*, *mem*, *tav-emes*, truth. Hashem saw in *Toras emes*, the Torah of truth, that He commanded His nation to be fruitful and multiply. The Egyptians were preventing the Jewish people from properly fulfilling that command.

The Jews were *zera emes*, children of truth, servants of *Elokei emes*, the G-d of truth, worthy of receiving *Toras emes*, the Torah of truth. The Omniscient G-d knew that the time for the redemption had arrived, and He began to perform His signs and wonders in Egypt.

(Haggada Baalei HaTosafos)

To See Is To Know

"G-d saw the children of Israel and G-d knew" *(Shemos 2:25)*. If G-d saw the Jewish people, G-d obviously knew all. But not everything was so obvious to the average observer. Some decrees against the Jewish people were public and open; others were maliciously hidden. G-d not only saw the obvious torment and harassment, He knew the hidden abuse and vengefulness that no human being knew about.

(Rabbeinu Bachya)

"G-d saw the children of Israel" *(Shemos 2:25)*. G-d took a good look at the Jewish nation, brutally enslaved by the Egyptians. Was the merit of their forefathers, Avraham, Yitzchak and Yaakov, sufficient to redeem them from slavery? Or had they been totally corrupted by the Egyptian environment?

G-d saw that the Jews had not changed their names, their language, or their style of clothing. And then G-d knew that the Jews had retained the good traits of their forefathers. He knew they were worthy of redemption and He sent Moshe to lead them out of *golus*.

(Tzror Hamor)

G-d saw the Jewish people's suffering, and He knew He had to deliver them because of the covenant He had made with the forefathers.

Hashem acknowledged that the Jews' virtue was not just skin-deep. Hashem discerned that they were upright and noble-through and through. "And I have heard how they cry out because of what their slave drivers do, and because I am aware of their pain" *(Shemos 3:7)*.

Although the Jews cried from the torment of the taskmasters, not in prayer, Hashem understood their pain. Because of their intense suffering, they could not concentrate on praying.

(Divrei Yirmeyahu, Abarbanel)

Very often Jews cry out over minor annoyances. But in this instance, Hashem said, "I am aware of their pain" *(Shemos 3:7)*. The Jews were not crying over a petty inconvenience. Their outcry was sincere-Hashem testified that He was aware of their pain. Therefore, He responded to their pleas.

(Abarbanel)

"I also see the pressure to which Egypt is subjecting them" *(Shemos 3:9)*. The Jewish population was very large, and the Egyptians did not allow them to expand their neighborhood. All the Jews were squeezed into a few small houses in narrow alleys, like a ghetto. It was overcrowded; so many people in such a small area created pressure.

(Minchah Belulah, Rabbeinu Chananel)

Despite Their Sins

According to Resh Lakish, the expressions "G-d saw" and "G-d knew" *(Shemos 2:25)* refer to conflicting behavior later in the Jews' history. G-d saw that they were going to rebel at the Red Sea, as it says, "They rebelled by the sea, the Sea of Reeds" *(Tehillim 106:7)*. But G-d knew that they were going to sing, "This is my G-d, and I will build Him a sanctuary"

(Shemos 15:2).

R' Yehoshua ben Levi says that G-d saw the Jews would inaugurate the golden calf, declaring, "This, Israel, is your god" *(Shemos 32:4)*. Yet, He knew the Jews would proudly proclaim their unconditional and wholehearted acceptance of the Torah-"We will do and we will obey"

(Shemos 24:7).

Vayotzienu Hashem Mimitzrayim

וַיּוֹצִאֵנוּ יְהֹוָה מִמִּצְרַיִם בְּיָד חֲזָקָה וּבִזְרֹעַ נְטוּיָה וּבְמֹרָא גָּדוֹל וּבְאֹתוֹת וּבְמֹפְתִים:

וַיּוֹצִאֵנוּ יְהֹוָה מִמִּצְרַיִם, לֹא עַל יְדֵי מַלְאָךְ וְלֹא עַל יְדֵי שָׂרָף וְלֹא עַל יְדֵי שָׁלִיחַ. אֶלָּא הַקָּדוֹשׁ בָּרוּךְ הוּא בִּכְבוֹדוֹ וּבְעַצְמוֹ. שֶׁנֶּאֱמַר, וְעָבַרְתִּי בְאֶרֶץ מִצְרַיִם בַּלַּיְלָה הַזֶּה וְהִכֵּיתִי כָל בְּכוֹר בְּאֶרֶץ מִצְרַיִם מֵאָדָם וְעַד בְּהֵמָה וּבְכָל אֱלֹהֵי מִצְרַיִם אֶעֱשֶׂה שְׁפָטִים אֲנִי יְהֹוָה: וְעָבַרְתִּי בְאֶרֶץ מִצְרַיִם בַּלַּיְלָה הַזֶּה, אֲנִי וְלֹא מַלְאָךְ. וְהִכֵּיתִי כָל בְּכוֹר בְּאֶרֶץ מִצְרַיִם אֲנִי וְלֹא שָׂרָף. וּבְכָל אֱלֹהֵי מִצְרַיִם אֶעֱשֶׂה שְׁפָטִים אֲנִי וְלֹא הַשָּׁלִיחַ. אֲנִי יְהֹוָה, אֲנִי הוּא וְלֹא אַחֵר:

בְּיָד חֲזָקָה, זוֹ הַדֶּבֶר. כְּמָה שֶׁנֶּאֱמַר, הִנֵּה יַד יְהֹוָה הוֹיָה בְּמִקְנְךָ אֲשֶׁר בַּשָּׂדֶה בַּסּוּסִים בַּחֲמֹרִים בַּגְּמַלִּים בַּבָּקָר וּבַצֹּאן דֶּבֶר כָּבֵד מְאֹד:

G-d saw that the Jews would repent for these sins, but His Justice would have prevailed if not for the merit of the forefathers. All this is hinted at in Moshe's instructions to the Jews to smear their doorposts with the blood of the *Korban Pesach*.

"You will then have to take a bundle of hyssop ..." *(Shemos 12:22)*. In the process of repentance, the Jews humbled themselves like hyssop, a lowly herb. "And dip it into the blood that is in the basin" *(ibid.)*. The blood alludes to the Giving of the Torah, where it says, "Moshe took half of the blood [of the offerings]" *(Shemos 24:6)*.

"And touch the lintel and the two doorposts with some of the blood that is in the basin" *(Shemos 12:22)*. Avraham was the foremost convert, the greatest of the Patriarchs, appropriately represented by the lintel, the highest part of the door. The two doorposts symbolize Yitzchak and Yaakov. The Jewish people repented like the hyssop and were redeemed in the merit of the forefathers, the doorposts of our nation.

(Midrash Rabbah, Shemos)

וּבִזְרֹעַ נְטוּיָה, זוֹ הַחֶרֶב. כְּמָה שֶׁנֶּאֱמַר, וְחַרְבּוֹ שְׁלוּפָה בְּיָדוֹ נְטוּיָה עַל יְרוּשָׁלָיִם:

וּבְמוֹרָא גָּדוֹל, זוֹ גִּלּוּי שְׁכִינָה. כְּמָה שֶׁנֶּאֱמַר, אוֹ הֲנִסָּה אֱלֹהִים לָבֹא לָקַחַת לוֹ גוֹי מִקֶּרֶב גּוֹי בְּמַסּוֹת בְּאֹתֹת וּבְמוֹפְתִים וּבְמִלְחָמָה וּבְיָד חֲזָקָה וּבִזְרוֹעַ נְטוּיָה וּבְמוֹרָאִים גְּדוֹלִים כְּכֹל אֲשֶׁר עָשָׂה לָכֶם יְהֹוָה אֱלֹהֵיכֶם בְּמִצְרַיִם לְעֵינֶיךָ:

וּבְאֹתוֹת, זֶה הַמַּטֶּה. כְּמָה שֶׁנֶּאֱמַר, וְאֶת הַמַּטֶּה הַזֶּה תִּקַּח בְּיָדֶךָ אֲשֶׁר תַּעֲשֶׂה בּוֹ אֶת הָאֹתֹת:

וּבְמוֹפְתִים זֶה הַדָּם. כְּמָה שֶׁנֶּאֱמַר. וְנָתַתִּי מוֹפְתִים בַּשָּׁמַיִם וּבָאָרֶץ,:

When reciting each of these words and again when reciting the ten plagues and by each word of Rabbi Yehudah's mnemonic, a bit of wine is removed from the cup.

דָּם, וָאֵשׁ, וְתִמְרוֹת עָשָׁן:

Vayotzienu Hashem Mimitzrayim

The Hour Arrives

"Hashem said, 'I have indeed seen, *raoh raisi*, the suffering of My people in Egypt'" *(Shemos 3:7)*. Why did G-d use this repetitious expression of "I have indeed seen"? The Jewish people prayed to Hashem, and He listened. They continued to pray, and He heard their outcry.

"When they started to pray," said Hashem, "I thought of saving them from the Egyptian oppression; if they had not continued praying,

they would have had to stay there for the full four hundred years. But now that they persist in crying out to Me, I am listening to their lament. The hour of liberation has arrived. I will not delay it any longer!"

(Rabbi Yosef Yaavetz)

Meeting Pharaoh

"And now go and I am sending you to Pharaoh and take my nation, the children of Israel, out of Egypt" *(Shemos 3:10)*. "And afterward, Moshe and Aharon came and they said to Pharaoh, 'So said Hashem, G-d of Israel, 'Send My nation so they can celebrate for Me in the desert''" *(Shemos 5:1)*.

There are different accounts regarding the very first encounter between Moshe and Aharon and Pharaoh.

> *Two ferocious lions bound by heavy chains guarded the palace gate. No one could enter without the king's permission. When Moshe arrived at the gate, he lightly tapped the lions with his staff. The lions' chains fell off. Purring like kittens, the lions accompanied Moshe and Aharon to Pharaoh's royal chamber.*
>
> *Pharaoh was overwhelmed at the sight of the two saintly brothers, whose faces radiated purity. "Why did you come?" he asked timidly. "What do you want?"*
>
> *Moshe replied boldly, "Hashem, G-d of Israel, has sent me to you to tell you, 'Send out My people, so that they can serve Me.'"*
>
> *"Go home and come back tomorrow," the shaken Pharaoh responded.*
>
> *As soon as Moshe and Aharon left, Pharaoh summoned Bilam the sorcerer, the sorcerer's sons, Yanus and Yambrut, and all the magicians, sorcerers, and stargazers on the palace staff. Addressing the assemblage, Pharaoh related all that Moshe and Aharon had told him.*
>
> *"But how could these men get past the two lions at the gate?" the sorcerers asked.*

"They waved their staffs over the lions, removed their chains, and just walked in," Pharaoh answered. "The lions graciously showed them the way."

"I'm sure these men are sorcerers like us," Bilam replied confidently. "Invite them back, and let's put them to the test."

The Reception

Pharaoh was hosting a reception for all foreign ambassadors. All the kings of the east came to pay tribute to him, bringing him crowns as gifts, praising him as the world's most illustrious emperor. As they were exalting him, the presence of two strangers was announced. "There are two elderly gentlemen waiting at the gate," a page informed the king breathlessly.

"Let them come in," Pharaoh ordered brusquely. As Moshe and Aharon entered the reception room, Pharaoh wondered, "Are they bringing me a crown? Perhaps they bear a diplomatic message." But Moshe and Aharon did not even offer a greeting.

They faced Pharaoh like ministering angels, towering as cedars of Lebanon. Their eyes were radiant as the sun. Moshe held the staff of G-d, engraved with the ineffable Divine Name.

The Message

"Who are you?" Pharaoh demanded.

"We are emissaries of the G-d of Israel," Moshe replied. The words that emerged from his mouth were like blazing flames.

"What do you want?"

"Hashem wants you to let His people go."

"Who is Hashem that I should obey Him!" Pharaoh shouted, his eyes bulging with fury. "He doesn't even send me a crown. All I get is a message! I do not recognize Hashem. Nor will I let the Jews leave."

But then Pharaoh rethought his decision. "Wait just a minute. Let me take a look in my register of deities." Stepping into the palace library, he looked up the gods of each nation, beginning with the gods of Moav, Ammon, Tzidon, and on down the list.

"I've checked my register of deities," Pharaoh said, returning to face Moshe and Aharon. "I'm sorry, but your G-d is not listed."

"Fool!" replied Moshe scornfully. "How can you expect to find a living G-d among dead ones? The gods in your register are dead gods. Our G-d is a living G-d, the everlasting King of the universe!"

"Tell me," Pharaoh asked, "your G-d-is He young or old? How many cities has He conquered? How many years has He reigned?"

"Our G-d's strength and power fill the universe," Moshe explained. "He existed before the world came into being, and He will exist after all has ceased to be. He created you, and gave you the living spirit."

"What are His works?" Pharaoh inquired.

"He stretches out the skies and establishes the earth's foundation. His voice cleaves with shafts of fire. It splits mountains and shatters rocks. His bow is fire, His arrows are flames, His spear is a flash, His shield are clouds, His sword is lightning. He creates mountains and hills and covers them with herbs. He makes rain and dew descend; He answers the pleas of wild animals. He forms the fetus in its mother's womb and brings it out into the world. He humbles kings like you, and brings down kings that are greater than you. He exacts vengeance from the wicked and saves the righteous from their hands."

As Moshe spoke, Pharaoh became more and more distraught. Moshe's words drained him of his power of speech, and Pharaoh was unable to respond. So Moshe continued his soliloquy.

"This G-d-our G-d-will take the Jews out of your land, lead them in the wilderness, and provide them with all their needs. Evildoers like you will be punished with ten ferocious plagues. And He can do it. Because everything in Heaven and on earth belongs to Him. The entire world's resources and beyond are at His disposal."

Finally Pharaoh regained his composure. "Nothing but a pack of lies! I am the master of the world! I created myself, and I created the Nile!" As it says in *Yechezkel*, "Mine [Pharaoh's] is my Nile, and I have made myself" *(Yechezkel 29:3)*.

(Shemos Rabbah 8b; Midrash Yalkut Sippurim, Shemos)

Pharaoh's Counterattack

Just then Pharaoh excused himself to answer the call of nature. As he relieved himself in the bathroom, twelve mice attacked and bit him. All the assembled dignitaries heard his pitiful screams. After he recovered from the shock, he returned to face Moshe and Aharon. "Who are you? Where do you come from? By whom were you sent?" Pharaoh repeated his questions.

"The G-d of the Hebrews sent me," Moshe replied evenly.

"Who is Hashem that I should listen to His voice?" Pharaoh demanded *(Shemos 5:2)*.

Pharaoh was punished for his proclamation of denial. Upon hearing this heresy, Hashem said, "Wretch! You ask, '*Mi Hashem*, Who is Hashem?' You are going to be punished with *mi*, fifty plagues!" *Mi* is spelled *mem*, *yud* (40+10=50). As it says in the *Haggada*, "The hand of G-d at the Red Sea caused fifty plagues." *Mi* backwards spells *yam*, sea. Pharaoh asked, "Who is Hashem?" Moshe answered, "At the sea you will see '*Mi Hashem*,' who Hashem is!"

(Midrash Rabbah, Shemos)

"I do not recognize Hashem. He has never sent me greetings or gifts," Pharaoh contended. "It could not be G-d who guides events in this world-for it is I! How could the Jews be His chosen nation? *(Moshav Zekeinim)* No! I will not let the Jewish people go!" *(Shemos 5:2)*

Woe to wicked mortals like Pharaoh! They are nothing but worms and maggots when they leave the world-yet they have the audacity to contradict the words of G-d. G-d said to Pharaoh, "You won't let the

Jewish people go. I say-let the Jewish people go! And we shall see whose words will prevail."

Ultimately, Pharaoh came to Moshe, begging on his knees, crying, "Get moving! Get out from among my people, you and the Jews" (Shemos 12:31). At that time, Hashem said to him, "Nu, Pharaoh! Whose words came true-yours or Mine?"

(Midrash Rabbah, Shemos)

Work, Work, Work

"Moshe and Aharon, why are you distracting the people from their work? Get back to your own business, *lesivloseichem*!" *(Shemos 5:4)* The word *sivloseichem* may be related to *savlonus,* patience, to resign oneself. "You were resigned to the fate of your brothers without protesting until now. Just put up with it-tough luck."

(Ksav Sofer)

"The peasants are becoming more numerous, and you want them to take a vacation from their work! *(Shemos 5:5)* This work has to get done," Pharaoh ranted. "If the Jews take a vacation, the shutdown results in tremendous financial loss. Three days there and three days back plus at least one day's stay-that's seven days of vacation! I can't hire six hundred thousand laborers to fill in for them-that would empty my entire treasury. Maybe one thousand slaves, maybe even two, could go on furlough. But you have the nerve to request a leave of absence for six hundred thousand men!

(Midrash)

"When I first set the daily quota, as you well know, Moshe and Aharon, there was only a small number of slaves. But now the Jewish population has grown. There are so many more slaves, but the quota remains the same. By rights, with so many more workers, I should set a higher quota. And you are asking for time off!

(Abarbanel)

"You see for yourselves how profusely those Jews are increasing. And it's because of the hard work they do. The men of the tribe of Levi are exempt from work-and their families are not growing like the others. How can you demand a break? It will slow down their growth!"

(Shaarei Simcha)

Communicating with Pharaoh

Moshe and Aharon addressed Pharaoh in his native tongue out of respect for the king. He did not speak Hebrew, and the brothers would not sully the holy tongue by speaking Hebrew in spiritually polluted Egypt. That's why Moshe said, "I have a speech defect" *(Shemos 6:30)*-speaking Egyptian was difficult for him.

(Sefer Panim Yafos)

Aharon served as Moshe's spokesman. Moshe announced the warnings and plagues. Aharon, a talented orator, explained the details. *(Chasam Sofer)* According to other opinions, Moshe conveyed Hashem's message in Hebrew; Aharon translated.

(Mechilta)

"Hashem said to Moshe, 'See, I have made you a master over Pharaoh'" *(Shemos 7:1)*. Hashem granted Moshe the power to lord over Pharaoh, to punish him with plagues and pain, to impart the knowledge that man amounts to nothing in this world. Once Pharaoh saw Moshe perform supernatural deeds, he exalted and praised him, for he recognized that Moshe held control over the forces of nature.

(Chasam Sofer)

Increasing the Burden

"You shall not continue, *lo sosifun*, to give the people straw for bricks as before. Let them go and gather their own straw" *(Shemos 5:7)*. In response to Moshe's request on behalf of the Jewish slaves to

worship Hashem in the desert, Pharaoh doubled their workload. The Jews had to fetch the straw to make the bricks themselves. It was not provided as before.

Where did the Jews find straw? The Jews went searching for straw in nearby fields. But if an Egyptian found a Jew trespassing on his land, the farmer beat the trespasser senseless. Hashem arranged this decree so the Egyptians would harm the Jews and be undeniably deserving of the punishment of the ten plagues.

(Chizkuni)

Jews were forced to gather straw from distant, abandoned, untilled fields, where the straw was mixed with thorns and thistles that pierced the skin of their hands and feet, causing blood to spurt forth.

(Midrash Tanchuma)

"And make sure they do it" *(Shemos 5:9)*-themselves. "Don't let the Jews hire anyone to gather the straw for them," warned Pharaoh with a wagging finger. Pharaoh did not want the Jewish people to have spare time to dwell on freedom and liberation.

(Shaarei Simcha)

"Make the work heavier for the men ... then they will stop paying attention to false ideas" *(Shemos 5:9)*. Every Shabbos, Amram, Moshe's father, used to expound on the forthcoming redemption, consoling the oppressed Jews with words of hope and solace. To retaliate, Pharaoh ordered an increase in the workload, so they would not have time to listen to these subversive speeches.

(Midrash Rabbah, Vaeira, Rabbi C. Paltiel)

There are two similar verbs-*yasaf*, to continue, and *asaf*, to gather. The root of *sosifun* is *yasaf*; Pharaoh commanded the taskmasters not to continue to give the Jews straw. The root word should be *yud*, *samech*, *fei*. Yet the Torah adds an *alef*, as in the word *asaf*, to gather.

The Jews would gather on Shabbos and weekdays after work to encourage each other with the message that Hashem's promise of

redemption was close at hand. Since every Jew drew strength and faith from these gatherings, Pharaoh decided to put an end to them. So he said, "*Lo sosifun*, stop these gatherings!"

(Zeir Zahav 77)

Taskmasters and Foremen

"The foremen of the children of Israel, whom Pharaoh's taskmasters had appointed over them, were beaten" *(Shemos 5:14)*. The Egyptian taskmasters set the quotas and held the Jewish foremen responsible for enforcing compliance. But whenever the slaves fell short, which was often, the Egyptian taskmasters beat the Jewish foremen ruthlessly. The foremen accepted the beatings-they refused to retaliate against the overworked Jews. Because of their devotion to their brothers, the foremen were chosen to be the elders in the wilderness.

(Rashi, Alshich)

"The Jewish foremen came and protested to Pharaoh" *(Shemos 5:15)*. Long after they were beaten, the foreman were finally permitted an audience with the king. *(Tur)* "What did we do to deserve this?" the foremen protested. "You did not buy us as slaves. You did not capture us in war. We, the Jewish people, came on our own initiative. And yet, we have been your slaves ever since. Does it make sense for a master to kill his slaves?"

(Rabbi Menachem)

Lazy Jews

"'You are lazy!' Pharaoh said. 'Lazy! That's why you are saying that you want to sacrifice to G-d'" *(Shemos 5:17)*. When a laborer stops working, his arms and legs grow limp. "You are lazy in the service of the king and your limbs are lazy, too! You want to sacrifice to G-d so

He will energize your lazy limbs?" Pharaoh screamed at them. "You don't need sacrifices! Hard work makes you strong! Lying down on the job saps your strength.

(Rabbeinu Efraim)

"I released you from working on Shabbos, so now you want to bring sacrifices to thank G-d for your day of rest. Well then! I'll cancel your day of rest. Then you won't have to bring thanksgiving sacrifices. Now go! Get to work! You will not be given any straw, but you must deliver your quota of bricks *(Shemos 5:18)*."

(Yalkut Me'am Lo'ez)

"But without straw," the foremen argued, "the Jews cannot possibly produce the same number of bricks as before."

"No problem," replied Pharaoh. "I'll fix that. Let's see, there is one foreman for every ten slaves. Six hundred thousand Jewish slaves ... there are sixty thousand of you foremen. Until now, you did not have to work. I decree that from now on the foremen have to work, just like all the other slaves. That give us ten percent more workers and it reduces the individual quota by ten percent, too."

"The foremen of Israel realized they were in serious trouble" *(Shemos 5:19)*. There would be no reduction in the quota of bricks. The foremen were already working hard to fill the quota each day. Each Jew would have to produce the same amount.

(Ibn Ezra)

If a Jew's quota was short by one brick, the Egyptian taskmasters would snatch one of his small children and wedge him into the bricks of the building. The sadistic Egyptians then forced the father to apply the mortar around his child. The parents' bitter tears joined the child's cries. No one lifted a finger at this brutality. Not one Egyptian showed compassion. (Midrash Yalkut Sippurim, Shemos) Over two hundred seventy thousand children were immured that way.

(Sefer Hayashar)

Hashem miraculously saved the children encased in the walls. The building collapsed, and the children flew away like birds escaping from a snare. "Our souls escaped like a bird from a hunter's snare; the snare broke and we escaped" (Tehillim 124:7).

(Tanna DeBei Eliyahu)

An Indignant Moshe

"Moshe returned to Hashem and said, 'My Lord, why do You mistreat Your people? Why did You send Me? As soon as I came to Pharaoh to speak in Your name, he made things worse for these people. You have done nothing to help Your people'"

(Shemos 5:22,23).

With the worsening of the oppression, Moshe asked, "Why do You mistreat Your people? If the people deserve to be delivered, why are You punishing them? If they don't deserve it, why did You send me? I inflicted so much extra pain and misery on the people with my mission! What purpose did the mission serve? If the people are worthy of the redemption, and I am to be the redeemer, You, Hashem, must have the means to set us free. But meanwhile, the situation is worsening and You have done nothing to help Your people!" This entire debate was prompted by Moshe's love of Hashem and the Jewish people.

(Ibn Ezra, Tzror Hamor)

Moshe knew that Pharaoh would not let the Jews go immediately. But Moshe thought that everything would happen in quick succession. When Pharaoh asked, "Who is Hashem?" Moshe thought the process would begin. He would perform the sign of the serpent, Hashem would punish Egypt with His wondrous plagues, and the Jews would soon be set free. But three days passed. And each day, Pharaoh increased their suffering. No command was forthcoming from G-d. At least, Moshe thought, their suffering should ease!

(Ibn Ezra, Ramban)

Harbinger of the Future

But then Hashem appeared to him. "Very soon, you will begin to see what I will do to Pharaoh. The end is not as far off as you think! When I begin to bring the plagues down upon them, things will get much easier for the Jews." *(Shemos 6:1)* The end was close at hand!

(Ibn Ezra, Ramban)

"For by a strong hand will he let them go, and with a strong hand will he drive them out of his land" *(Shemos 6:1)*. Mortal men like Moshe were helpless before Pharaoh. No natural, worldly motivation would change Pharaoh's stubborn decision not to let the Jewish people go. To move Pharaoh required a "strong hand," the hand of Hashem.

Moshe who lisped, who was not charismatic, was the instrument of Hashem's hand. It was not Moshe, with all his physical shortcomings, who influenced Pharaoh. It was obvious to all that it was Hashem's hand.

(Rabbi Samson Raphael Hirsch)

The excessive harshness hastened the redemption. "Now you will see what I will do to Pharaoh" *(Shemos 6:1)*-immediately, because the Jews' suffering was so intense.

(Kli Yakar)

May this be a source of consolation for our own generation. Let us hope that the present-day suffering of the Jewish people will hasten the time of our redemption. May we merit to be redeemed through the coming of Mashiach speedily in our days.

The Ten Wondrous Plagues

דָּבָר אַחֵר, בְּיָד חֲזָקָה שְׁתַּיִם. וּבִזְרֹעַ נְטוּיָה שְׁתַּיִם. וּבְמֹרָא גָּדוֹל שְׁתַּיִם. וּבְאֹתוֹת שְׁתַּיִם. וּבְמוֹפְתִים שְׁתַּיִם. אֵלּוּ עֶשֶׂר מַכּוֹת שֶׁהֵבִיא הַקָּדוֹשׁ בָּרוּךְ הוּא עַל הַמִּצְרִים בְּמִצְרַיִם וְאֵלּוּ הֵן:

דָּם. צְפַרְדֵּעַ. כִּנִּים. עָרוֹב. דֶּבֶר. שְׁחִין. בָּרָד. אַרְבֶּה. חֹשֶׁךְ. מַכַּת בְּכוֹרוֹת:

רַבִּי יְהוּדָה הָיָה נוֹתֵן בָּהֶם סִמָּנִים:

דְּצַ"ךְ עֲדַ"שׁ בְּאַחַ"ב:

The Ten Wondrous Plagues

Hashem punished the Jews' afflictors in Egypt with ten tortuous plagues to redeem His chosen nation from slavery. But this was not the only purpose of the plagues. Hashem could have easily paralyzed Pharaoh and the Egyptians in a single instant, allowing *Am Yisroel* an immediate exit from the land of Egypt. What, then, was the purpose of the ten plagues?

The *makos,* plagues, were undeniable wonders that impressed upon all idol worshippers-Jews and non-Jews alike-the supremacy of Hashem. The idol worshippers suffered terrible afflictions, while their idols stood powerless-silent, both physically and spiritually. Everyone who witnessed or experienced these nature-defying plagues was forced to acknowledge that *HaKadosh Baruch Hu* alone created the world.

The Order of the Makos

The *Haggadah* divides the ten *makos* into three separate categories, with the tenth and final *makah* in a class by itself. Each unit proved a different facet of Hashem's supremacy.

Detzach, the first category, is an acronym for the first three *makos* of *dam* (blood), *tzephardaya* (frogs), and *kinim* (lice). Pharaoh heretically proclaimed, "Who is Hashem that I must heed His voice? I do not know Hashem." *(Shemos 5:2)* The first three *makos* proved that there is a Creator of the World, as it is says, "With this [the plague of blood] you will know that I am Hashem." *(Shemos 7:17)*

The second unit, *Adash*, is comprised of *arov* (wild animals), *dever* (sickness), and *sh'chin* (boils), the fourth, fifth, and sixth *makos*. The Egyptians agreed that Hashem presided over the spiritually superior heavens, but maintained that He left the rest of the material world to other powers. Hashem sent the message, "...in order that you will know that I am Hashem in the midst of this land." *(Shemos 8:18)* Hashem's jurisdiction extends from the heavens down to the lowliest particle of earth.

B'achav-barad (hail), *arbeh* (locusts), and *choshech* (darkness), *makos* seven, eight and nine, demonstrated that there is no power and strength other than that of *HaKadosh Baruch Hu*. "Because of this, you shall understand that there is none such as Me in the whole of the land." *(Shemos 9:14)* Pharaoh could no longer claim that he never heard of Hashem. Hashem's power was demonstrated to this mortal king in all its strength.

Pharaoh and his nation finally believed that Hashem created the world, rules over it, and that there is no other power. With the tenth *makah*, *makas bechoros* (the death of the firstborn), Pharaoh was forced to release the Jews from Egyptian slavery.

The warnings for each category of *makos* followed identical patterns. At the first *makah*, Moshe Rabbeinu accosted Pharaoh at the Nile during his morning bath to warn him of the upcoming plague. Pharaoh secretly relieved himself every morning in the river to

substantiate his claim that he was a god, without the needs of mortal flesh and blood.

At the second of each of the three sets of *makos*, Moshe warned Pharaoh in his royal palace, surrounded by his entire court in broad daylight. When the general public heard the warnings and witnessed their actualization, they considered it illogical not to accept Moshe's terms. This was a source of great embarrassment to Pharaoh.

For the third *makah* of each set, there was no warning. The first two *makos* themselves served as warnings to Pharaoh to accept the supremacy of *HaKadosh Baruch Hu*, and the third was the punishment for refusing to acknowledge Him. It is done the same way in every Jewish court-two warnings precede the punishment. When Pharaoh saw that the warnings had ceased, he would resume his daybreak baths in the Nile, allowing the cycle to begin again.

(Malbim)

Performing the Makos

Aharon HaKohen performed the first category of *makos-Detzach-* by striking an object with Moshe Rabbeinu's staff. These *makos* involved inanimate objects that had protected Moshe Rabbeinu during his lifetime. The Nile River, the source for *dam* and *tzephardaya*, shielded Moshe as a three-month-old baby when his mother attempted to save him from the drowning decreed for all Jewish baby boys. Moshe used the dust of the earth, the origin of *kinim*, to hide the Egyptian that he had killed, saving him from certain death at the hands of Pharaoh. Our sages teach us, "An oasis that quenched your thirst, you shall not harm." *(Baba Kama 92)*

Hashem performed *arov* and *dever*, the first two *makos* of *Adash*, and the last one, *sh'chin,* was performed collectively by Hashem, Moshe Rabbeinu, and Aharon HaKohen. The *makos* of *Adash* were executed with the word of Moshe. The third category, *B'achav*, was

performed by Moshe Rabbeinu using his staff, except *makas bechoros*, which was done by the hand of Hashem.

(Midrash Rabbah, Shemos 12:5)

In total, Hashem, Moshe, and Aharon performed three *makos* each, in addition to the *makah* of *sh'chin*, which was done jointly.

The names of all ten *makos* were inscribed on Moshe Rabbeinu's staff. During each *makah*, the name of that plague became more visible and distinct.

(M`hari Leyad)

Pouring Wine for the Plagues

At the *Seder* we pour a total of sixteen drops of wine from our cups: three times for the words, "*Dam, va'eish, vesimros ashan*-blood and fire and plumes of smoke" *(Yoel 3:3)*, ten times for each of the ten plagues, and three times for the acronym of the ten plagues-*Detzach, Adash, B'achav*.

Hashem's sword, so to speak, is called by one of His mystical names, *Yohach*. *Yohach* is spelled *yud* (10), *vav* (6), *hei* and *chaf*. *Yud* plus *vav* equals 16 and *hei-chaf* spells hach, to strike. We pour sixteen drops as a remembrance that Hashem struck the Egyptians with the holy name *Yohach*.

(Magen Avraham 473:29)

"When your enemy falls, do not rejoice" *(Proverbs 24:17)*. Although the Egyptians deserved their punishment of the ten plagues, nevertheless our own joy of redemption is incomplete—G-d's creations suffered. As we recite the name of each *makah*, a small portion of wine is removed from the cup. Wine symbolizes joy and happiness; each *makah* diminishes that joy.

(Abarbanel, Zevach Pesach)

The Maharil teaches that as we remove wine from the cup, whether by pouring, with a finger, or using a utensil, we should have

in mind that the same plagues should befall our enemies in all generations.

(Maharil)

The Four Cups allude to the four cups of punishment that Hashem will dole out to the nations who have persecuted us during our exile. Each *makah* represents just a tiny drop in that cup of punishment. The proportionately poisonous remainder will be poured down the throats of the nations at the end of the present exile.

(Haggadas Zecher Lapesach)

1. *Dam*: Waters Turn to Blood

When Hashem punishes a nation, He smites its idols first. The Egyptians worshipped the river, which used to overflow and sustain their crops. The nation was devastated when the very body of water they worshipped was transformed to blood-bringing death instead of life.

(Rashi, Shemos 7:17)

In days of old, warring nations would block all the waterways entering the enemy city, starving its inhabitants so they would surrender. Hashem used the same strategy, cutting off the Egyptians' water source so they would admit the strength of the Almighty.

(Rashi, Shemos 8:17)

Moshe's First Warning at the Nile

Pharoah was a strong and haughty king. He led his subjects to believe that he was a god. *(Rashi, Shemos 7:15)* When Yaakov Avinu first moved to Egypt, he blessed Pharaoh that the waters of the Nile should rise to greet him. Pharaoh proudly insisted that the waters rose

because he was a divine being. Pharaoh's palace was built without any outhouses to prove to the Egyptians that he was immortal.

When the rest of the nation was asleep, Pharaoh and his court would stroll down to the river. Explaining that he was discussing divine plans with the Nile, Pharaoh would order his servants to stand far enough away that he would not be visible to them. Pharaoh used this opportunity to perform his bodily functions for the day. *(Masiach Ilmin)* When he was done, he would exit the river and return to the palace. No one knew of his daily ritual until Hashem instructed Moshe Rabbeinu to confront him there.

Moshe Rabbeinu awaited Pharaoh's inevitable arrival at the Nile River. According to Hashem's command, Moshe Rabbeinu approached Pharaoh as a soldier approaches his enemy, speaking to him with deliberate effrontery. He showed none of the respect a king, especially a king like Pharaoh, was accustomed to. *(Ramban, Shemos 8:15)* Moshe approached the king, grabbing the edge of his gown to prevent him from going any further. Moshe detained Pharaoh long enough for his servants to come searching for him. The sight that greeted them was astonishing.

There was Moshe Rabbeinu holding onto Pharaoh's gown, with Pharaoh painfully begging to be released. The stomach cramps he was experiencing were becoming unbearable. Moshe challenged him before all the assembled: "Does any god exist that experiences bodily functions like mere mortals?" Pharaoh hung his head, shamed and embarrassed.

(Rabbeinu B'chai)

Moshe Rabbeinu conveyed Hashem's message to a silent Pharaoh. "Hashem has sent me here to the river to warn you. Here, not at your palace-Hashem knows you are a mere mortal. Know the truth, Pharaoh, you are *not* a god; you are flesh and blood like the rest of us.

(Or Hachaim)

"Hashem is the truthful G-d of the Jews, Pharaoh. And if you do not allow the Jews to leave Egypt, the waters of the precious Nile will become bloody. And then you'll be forced to admit the truth-Hashem is One G-d Alone!

"You ask me, 'Who is Hashem?' *(Shemos 5:12)* You don't want to serve Hashem? You will never allow the release of the Jews? First, hear this," Moshe continued. "Allow the Jews to leave the land of Egypt; let them go serve Hashem in the desert. If you don't, I will smite the Nile with my staff. I'll point my staff to all four corners of the world, and all the bodies of water in Egypt will turn to blood."

The First Makah Begins

Three weeks had elapsed since the warning. Aharon HaKohen raised the staff, and everything that Moshe had warned came to be. The heavenly angel of the Nile was punished too, because he had been lax in his duty to pray when Pharaoh decreed that all Jewish male infants be drowned.

All over Egypt the waters became blood. All the lakes, rivers, wells, and even all water that was stored in barrels before the *makah* began turned to blood. The transformation began with the topmost waters of the Nile, the part that was visible to people. Then the river turned itself over, so the bottom waters were now on top, which then became bloody. The river was like a slave being beaten by his master on his back. He turns over, hoping to get some reprieve, but his master continues to lash him on his stomach.

(Zohar, Shemos 28)

Egyptians at the border saw the Nile flowing clear from afar. Excited, they waited for the fresh water to reach them-but the water turned to blood when it flowed past the border.

Those who were in the middle of taking a bath found that the water they were sitting in was no longer water. Busy housewives were certainly surprised to see their simmering soups turn bloody. *(Sefer Hayosher)* The Egyptians employed countless ancient methods to heal

the water. They tried digging fresh wells, but all the water that arose was blood. Even fruits and their juices were spotted with blood-completely inedible.

The *makah* soon spread to the stones and wood of Egypt. Blood flowed from the faces of the cherished idols. *(Minchah Belulah)* When an Egyptian sat down on a bench or chair, or lay down in bed, the furniture beneath him immediately turned bloody. The expensive garments the Egyptians favored were soiled and smeared with blood.

(Shemos Rabbah)

The Egyptians cleverly tried to drink from a glass that a Jew was holding, but as soon as the water touched their lips, it immediately turned to blood. The only method they discovered that worked was if a Jew and an Egyptian drank from the same glass simultaneously-then the Egyptian would have clean, clear water. The Egyptians became very dependent on the Jews. Whenever an Egyptian was thirsty, he would have to seek out a Jew who was drinking at that very moment. The Jews avoided drinking in the presence of their former oppressors.

The Egyptians formulated a plan-they would force the Jews to share their water with them. Hashem foiled their plot, assuring that all water the Egyptians consumed became blood-even the water that they drank out of the glass of a Jew. Only one possible method remained to obtain fresh water: an Egyptian had to pay large sums of money to a Jew for a simple drink.

Some, left with no other choice, distastefully drank the blood, causing their intestines to split open. *(Zohar)* But even those who opted not to drink at all tasted blood in their mouths, produced from their saliva glands.

(Shemos Rabbah)

The Demise of the Fish

The waters of the Nile not only assumed the look of blood, but its entire makeup was that of blood. The naturally warm temperature of blood caused all the fish in the river to die. The worshipped Nile had no power to save them from death. The decaying fish emitted a strong stench that spread over the entire land of Egypt. The smell permeated foods, leaving the horrible aftertaste of rotten fish in the mouth of every Egyptian.

The Egyptians suffered physically and monetarily from the loss of the fish. Egypt always had an overabundance of fish. Fish constituted a major part of their daily meals, and now there was not much to eat. The economy was supported in large part by the sale of fish to foreign lands, but the flow of income from that market now ceased.

The Egyptians were very fond of physical beauty and would constantly perfume themselves with aromatic herbs. The smell of the rotting fish was so strong that no amount of perfumes could cover it up. By the end of the *makah*, the Egyptians had adopted a new posture-walking with their hands over their noses.

When the *makah* was finally over and the Nile River reverted to its original state, the water was still unfit for human consumption as the smell of rotten fish continued to linger. The Egyptians had to once again dig new wells to bring up fresh supplies of water.

Midah K'neged Midah

Righteous and fair, Hashem justly punished the oppressors for their cruelty. The blood that flowed through the land during the first *makah* rightfully should have been the blood of the Egyptians, falling in battle to a foreign nation. *HaKadosh Baruch Hu*, with pity for His chosen nation, did not want to cause unnecessary fright among the Jews. To a lesser degree, the Egyptians were punished in the same manner they had afflicted *Am Yisroel*.

Why were the Egyptians punished with a plague of blood?

- The Egyptians forbade every Jew to bathe in the river. The river became bloody, making it completely unfit for bathing.
- Pharaoh became wealthy at the expense of the hard labor of the Jews. But when there was no water available for the Egyptians, the Jews thrived on the profitable demand for inexpensive, clean water, regaining a considerable amount of their wealth.
- Pharaoh's doctors recommended that he bathe in blood to cure the leprosy Hashem had inflicted on him. Pharaoh mercilessly killed 350 Jewish children twice daily for this selfish purpose, and he was justly punished with an overabundance of blood.

2. *Tzephardaya*: Frogs Infest the Land

The *Midrash* explains that after a mortal king blocks the waterways of a city, he invades with loud noises and sounds of trumpets. The cacophony scares the inhabitants of the city, causing great confusion. Hashem blocked Egypt's waterways with blood, and now croaking frogs echoed throughout the land. Their incessant shrieks reached a pitch almost unbearable to human ears, maddening some residents to the point of insanity.

(Rashi, Shemos 8:17)

Pharaoh often stated that the Nile was an idol of his own creation. When Moshe Rabbeinu warned him of the upcoming *makah*, "And the river will produce frogs," *(Shemos 7:28)* he challenged the extent of Pharaoh's creative power. Only Hashem, the true Creator, can define the laws of nature that govern the Nile and spill forth a great gush of frogs from its bowels. Pharaoh clearly had no jurisdiction over the Nile River.

Still, Pharaoh hardened his heart and Moshe's warning went unheeded. Moshe could not perform the *makah* himself; while Hashem's instructions were to simply raise the staff above the river without hitting it, one who raises his hand to hit is considered to have done the deed. So Aharon HaKohen was appointed to raise the staff above the river. The instant he did, countless numbers of frogs emerged from every body of water in Egypt.

The Makah Begins

The *Gemara* in *Sanhedrin* 67 presents different opinions on how the *tzephardaya* emerged. R' Elozor and R' Akiva say that one enormous frog emerged from the river, and from him, numerous more were created. According to the *Midrash*, the Egyptians tried to eliminate the tremendous frog by beating at it with rods and sticks. After severe and endless beating, its stomach finally split open and thousands upon thousands of frogs spilled forth. R' Elozor ben Azariah states that the frog yelled and croaked so loudly that it called forth all the frogs in the entire world-and they convened in Egypt. Another opinion suggests that the *tzephardaya* were not really frogs at all; they were crocodiles capable of swallowing a few people at a time, *whole! (Rabbeinu B'chai)* The molecules of water themselves became frogs. If an Egyptian was drinking a glass of water, every last drop of water in that glass converted to a frog. *(Shemos Rabbah)* Even the vapor that condensed on the outside of the glass turned into frogs. Beads of sweat on a perspiring Egyptian transformed into frogs as soon as it was secreted from his glands.

(Sefer Hayosher)

Unlike normal frogs, the frogs that invaded the land of Egypt during the *makah* of *tzephardaya* had the power of speech. They tormented the Egyptians, "Our sole purpose on this Earth is to torture you, as punishment for your sins [the oppression of the Jews]!"

(Shach)

Immediately after they emerged from the river, the frogs headed straight to the palace of Pharaoh. No one pointed the way or showed them the imposing edifice. Until they reached their destination, they harmed no one whom they chanced to meet. *(Abarbanel)* Hashem had instructed the frogs to attack the land of Egypt in a certain order:

1. The royal palace
2. The bedchambers of Pharaoh
3. Pharaoh's bed
4. The houses of Pharaoh's servants
5. The homes of the Egyptian citizens
6. The ovens in the homes of the Egyptians
7. The dough being prepared for baking
8. Pharaoh's stomach
9. The stomachs of Pharaoh's servants

Pharaoh's palace was built to maximize the protection of the king. The walls that surrounded his palace were made of heavy, strong marble. When the frogs arrived at the palace they surrounded it, jumped upon the marble walls, and spoke directly to the walls. "Hashem the Almighty has sent us here. We are willing to sacrifice our lives for Hashem. We are willing to perish in fire and in water for Him, and thus, our names will be sanctified." The marble respected the words of the frogs and the walls split open, allowing the frogs to enter.

(Malbim)

The frogs came in two sizes: large and small. The larger frogs were designated to invade Pharaoh's palace, while the smaller ones dispersed over the entire land of Egypt. *(Midrash Rabbah)* The frogs covered the earth with a croaking carpet of green. It was impossible to take a single step without trodding upon a frog.

(Rabbeini Efraim z'tl)

Hashem instilled the frogs with a natural instinct to distinguish between gentile and Jew, oppressor and innocent. When the

Egyptians attempted to take cover in underground shelters, the frogs followed to inflict torture upon them. *(Baal Haturim)* The Jews, on the other hand, never became victims of the frogs. If a frog happened to meet a Jew, it ran in the other direction, but when it caught sight of an Egyptian, even from afar, it immediately attacked.

(Midrash Rabbah Noso 89)

The sight of the thousands of frogs in the sea and on land frightened the birds in the sky. They were afraid to descend and drink from the waters of the seas. Noticing their absence, the frogs called up to the birds, "Do not fear us. We will do you no harm. Hashem has sent us here to punish only the Egyptians."

Many Egyptians attempted to kill the frogs. Every time a frog was struck, it split into twelve or fifteen parts, and a whole new frog was born from each part. The frogs would angrily enter the body of the Egyptian who had struck him, biting at his internal organs. Greatly frightened, the Egyptians stopped trying to kill the frogs.

(Zohar)

People became deathly ill from frogs that were biting at their insides and consuming their guts and intestines. Sometimes the frogs died inside the intestines, producing a foul odor emitted through that unlucky person's digestive system. Many Egyptians tossed and turned night after night, listening to the nonstop croaking that came from inside their bodies. Nerves were frayed and days were spent in tears and lament.

(Lekach Tov)

The frogs were irritating, even painful. But most bothersome of all was the Egyptians' inability to hear. An Egyptian could not hear his friend above the din of the noisy frogs, even if he was screaming into his ear. Many women and children perished. Strong men, sapped of all their strength, lay inert on the floor until the *makah* finally ceased.

(Zohar)

Just like the *makah* of *dam*, the frogs brought famine to the land of Egypt. *(Midrash Rabbah)* Egyptian housewives, working hard to knead their dough, were attacked by armies of frogs that consumed their dough instantaneously. The Egyptians hastened to heat their ovens to bake their bread before the frogs arrived. But large groups of frogs would forcibly enter the ovens and fill them up, rendering them useless.

If someone was fortunate enough to bake bread, frogs would become encrusted within it, burnt to death for the name of Hashem. As frogs were burnt in the ovens, they sang songs of praise to Hashem, thanking Him for the opportunity to sacrifice their lives for His name. When Pharaoh heard of their selflessness he became utterly disgusted, and hastened to summon Moshe to pray for the end of the *makah*.

(Meor Vashemesh, Va'era)

The Frogs Die

As Pharaoh lay suffering from intense pain, he overheard a conversation between a frog in his own stomach and one in the intestines of his servant. The frog wanted to know when they were going to be allowed to leave. The other answered, "When ben Amrom [the son of Amrom, Moshe Rabbeinu] will pray to Hashem for our release."

During the *makah* of *dam*, Pharaoh refused to summon Moshe Rabbeinu. Rather than degrade himself by pleading with Moshe for an end to the torture, he silently suffered the *makah* in its entirety. But the torture of the frogs was too intense, the pain too severe. The word *tzephardaya* is mentioned ten times in the Torah; this *makah* was more painful than all ten *makos* combined. Pharaoh could not bear it and he finally called for Moshe Rabbeinu, begging him to end his misery.

Sorcery, very commonplace in Egypt, can only be used during its peak time, at certain hours of the day. Moshe Rabbeinu knew that

after the frogs left, Pharaoh would claim that they had disappeared through his skilled witchcraft and sorcery. Moshe Rabbeinu used this opportunity to prove to Pharaoh that his strength came from Hashem, not black magic. He promised Pharaoh to pray for the end of the *makah*-on one condition. Pharaoh must state the exact time that the frogs should disappear.

"This must be the very moment that Moshe has the powers needed to rid Egypt of the frogs," Pharaoh thought to himself. "By tomorrow, his power will be gone. He expects me to say that I want the frogs gone now!" Pharaoh's desire to prove Moshe Rabbeinu a liar was so strong, he chose to suffer a full extra day. "Pray now," he said aloud to Moshe, "and get rid of the frogs this time tomorrow."

Moshe assented. "Just as you say, so it will be. But," Moshe Rabbeinu stipulated, "frogs will remain in the Nile. The river that you worship has no power to aid itself. Anyone who comes near will hear the croaking frogs, and will never be able to forget the horror of this plague."

And so it was. The next day all the frogs expired, adhering to the surfaces where they lay. The entire land of Egypt was covered with thousands of frog corpses. The suffering of the Egyptians was far from over. The frogs had to be ripped off the bodies of the Egyptians, off their clothes, out of their pockets, off the walls of their homes, and off the crops of the fields, the trees of the forests, and the grasses of the meadows.

The *Midrash Rabbah* says that every Egyptian collected four large piles of frogs from his house and yard. The *Baal HaTurim* contests that it was not four piles, but ten large piles of frogs, each pile twenty feet high, weighing 1,890 pounds. According to the latter calculation, every Egyptian amassed a whopping eighteen thousand nine hundred pounds of frogs.

(Sechel Tov)

The Egyptians gathered the carcasses of the frogs, depositing them in one large pile on the street. Once they had all the corpses in one place it would be very simple to dispose of them elsewhere. But

Hashem speeded up the decaying process, and soon all the frogs were in various degrees of rot. The stench that spread over the land permeated the Egyptians' clothing, their food, and their utensils.

The frogs that sacrificed their lives by entering the hot ovens were justly rewarded. Some say that their corpses did not rot since they had sanctified Hashem. Or that these frogs did not die, and at the end of the *makah* they moved into the Nile. According to our sages, years later, Chananya, Mishael and Azariah learned a lesson from these frogs. These great men, too, would rather be burned with the fires of this earth than desecrate the name of Hashem.

Despite the constant reminders that remained from the *tzephardaya*, the carcasses in the street and the croaks from the Nile, Pharaoh nevertheless hardened his heart and refused to liberate the Jews.

Midah K'neged Midah

Why were the Egyptians punished with a plague of frogs?

- The Jews would shriek and yell under the heavy burden the Egyptians imposed on them. And the Egyptians would shout and scream at the Jews to awake early in the morning. Now the frogs came to yell at the oppressors.

  (Lekach Tov)

- The Egyptians would order the Jews to collect snakes, frogs, and other creatures for them. The animals were used as entertainment or prepared as a delicacy. Hashem sent the Egyptians more frogs than they could ever ask for.

  (Shemos Rabbah)

- When the Egyptians drowned the Jewish male infants, their mothers' wails were loud and long. From the very same river

the frogs emerged, whose croaks sounded like the cries of young pitiful infants.

(Abarbanel)

- Jewish infants, miraculously spared from drowning, were burnt at the stake instead by Pharaoh, who voiced his disbelief in One G-d. The frogs sacrificed themselves in fire and water for the sake of Hashem, sanctifying His name.

(Kli Yokor)

- The Jews, forbidden to wash their hands prior to meals, were forced to eat with hands dirtied from mortar and brick dust. Now the Egyptians were forced to eat with their hands dirtied from the blood of the frogs.

(Shach)

- The rancid smell of the decaying frogs disgusted the Egyptians, just as they openly showed their disgust for the Jewish people and their G-d.
- The Torah is compared to water. Just as water is the lifeblood of man, so the Torah is the lifeblood of the Jews. Since the Egyptians prevented the Jews from receiving the Torah, their lifeblood, in the dry desert, they were punished with the frogs, which breed in the water.

(Midrash Yalmadeinu)

3. *Kinim*: Lice Crawl in Egypt

After frightening the inhabitants of an enemy city with the sound of trumpets and various other loud noises, a mortal king will begin to employ more severe tactics, such as shooting arrows. After the plague of frogs wreaked confusion and havoc, Hashem brought an

infestation of lice which feed upon the flesh and sting the enemy, much as arrows do.

(Midrash R' Tanchuma)

The Makah Begins

When Aharon HaKohen struck the earth with Moshe's staff, lice emerged from the dust over the entire land of Egypt. Anything that contained any form of earth became infested with lice. The earthenware floors in the homes of the Egyptians were covered with lice, making it impossible to walk. The houses all looked identical, equally bedecked with lice. *(Baar Mayim Chaim Parshas Va'era)* Any place a person would tread, his foot sank deep into a bed of lice, one, two, or five cubits (approximately two, four or ten feet) deep. *(Sefer Hayosher, Tzyoni)* The lice continued to breed in the flesh of the people and the animals.

Egyptians in close vicinity to Aharon HaKohen when the *makah* began were covered with lice instantaneously, assuming the appearance of one who has been lying in dirt and rubbish many years. Fifty-two and a half pounds worth of lice ate at each Egyptian. *(Sodi Razyah)* The cattle also suffered from an infestation of these parasites, which stung like numerous needles. *(Mishnas Rabbeinu Elazar 19)* The tormented shrieks of the cattle created a cacophonous din. As soon as one tried to rid himself or his cattle of the lice, either by cutting or cleaning, more lice would immediately cover that particular spot.

The lice were classified into fourteen different groups *(Tanah Dabi Aliyo 7, Yalkut Vayeira 182)*, or according to other opinions, up to twenty-four different groups. They ranged in size from a chicken egg to larger than the egg of a goose.

(Yalkut Shimoni)

The wounds and bites that covered the Egyptians' bodies were painful to the touch. *(Midrash brought in Haggada Ksav Sofer)* They were so badly stung and bruised that their entire bodies itched. Not

knowing where to begin scratching first, they rubbed the length of their bodies against the wall. Their skin was so irritated that it literally began shredding from the constant scratching. As large strips of skin began to fall away, tormented Egyptians lost dangerous amounts of blood. Countless wounds and scars also changed the Egyptian's physical appearance, and some were permanently blinded because of the constant distress their eyes were subjected to.

(Midrash B'chidush)

The lice invaded the utensils, pots and pans, plates and even the food. *(Mishnas Reb Eliezer)* The lice in the food caused the Egyptians to regurgitate all they had just consumed, leading to hunger and illness. When they would reach the point of unbearable starvation, they would force themselves to eat the infested food, which they promptly threw up. The cycle fruitlessly continued.

(Midrash B'chidush)

Pharaoh's sorcerers were able to duplicate the previous two *makos* with their powers of sorcery. But they could not duplicate the *makah* of *kinim*. Sorcerers only have powers on objects larger than the size of a lentil. Though the lice during the *makah* were larger than this, since a natural, normal louse is smaller than a lentil, they could not employ their unnatural powers. *(Sanhedrin 67)* In addition, witchcraft can only be performed on solid ground, and the bed of lice that now covered the ground was impossible to stand on.

(Shach)

Midah K'neged Midah

Why were the Egyptians punished with a plague of lice?

- The Egyptians attempted to annihilate the Jews, who are compared to the dust of the earth; Hashem aptly punished them by converting the dust to lice.

(Yalkut Shimoni)

- The Egyptians forced the Jews to sweep the dusty streets of Egypt, but dust-turned-lice made it impossible to even walk the streets, much less sweep them.

(Shemos Rabbah)

- The Jews were forced to work all day and all night, with no break to wash and cleanse themselves, or to change out of their dirty and dusty clothes. The Egyptians intended that the Jews, their lowly slaves, should become infested with lice, and this is exactly what happened to the Egyptians.

(Baal HaTurim)

- The Egyptians employed all their witchcraft powers to prevent the Jews from escaping, but the lice were brought upon them—a *makah* that could not be duplicated with sorcery.
- The Jews were enslaved to work with earthenware materials, mortar and brick, so Hashem punished the Egyptians with lice, which came from the same source.

(Kli Yakar, Va'era)

- The Egyptians forced the Jews to cleanse their expensive clothing from lice.
- Since the Egyptians prevented the Jews from obeying the *mitzvos* of Hashem, the plague of lice prevented them from doing their daily work.

(Shach)

4. *Arov*: Wild Animals Abound

The fourth *makah* of *arov* is the first *makah* in the set of *Adash*. Once again Moshe Rabbeinu warned Pharaoh of the upcoming *makah* at the Nile River, where Pharaoh would bathe at daybreak. Pharaoh, in an attempt to avoid Moshe Rabbeinu, decided to bathe even earlier

in the morning than usual. But Hashem the Almighty can read the thoughts of man, and he ordered Moshe Rabbeinu to awake earlier as well.

(Shemos Rabbah)

Moshe Rabbeinu warned Pharaoh that a very severe plague awaited him. Wild animals of all types and sizes will converge upon his land—lions, bears, leopards, serpents and snakes, flying insects, crawling insects, rats and mice, wild fowl and other dangerous animals and mammals from the entire world. Plus, the dreaded frogs and lice will return.

The Makah Begins

Arov was an outright wondrous miracle. All the wild beasts swarmed in hordes to Egypt, and spread over the entire land. They did not step foot over the border. In less than twenty-four hours all the animals arrived, at the exact moment Moshe Rabbeinu said they would.

(Midrash)

Animals born into the wild tend to act tamer when they are outside their natural habitats. Hashem transformed Egypt into one large forest so the natural, animalistic instincts of the beasts surfaced. They attacked with ferocity, and after they inflicted their harm, Hashem ordered them to remain in Egypt-their new natural habitat.

(Shach)

In the wild there are predators and prey; the stronger animals attack the weak. In a joint goal to punish the Egyptians, the animals called a temporary truce. The mice did not fear the vulture; the deer was not frightened of the cheetah. The lion did not seek out the lamb, and the wolf did not chase the goat.

(Rashi)

The animals began with an attack on the palace of Pharaoh, as he was the one who ordered the harsh decrees on the Jews. They continued to the homes of Pharaoh's servants and then over the entire land of Egypt.

(Sechel Tov)

Hashem Himself directed the beasts to the palace of Pharaoh and to the homes of his servants. He ordered them to enter the homes of Egypt with ferocity. Hashem gave them free run of the streets and the fields, instructing them to destroy all crops and dig damaging ditches.

(Shach)

Bees stung Egyptian eyes and flew into their ears. The Egyptians attempted to escape this painful torture, but the bees followed with pointed stingers. The same bees blinded the Canaanites when the Jews entered the land of Israel.

(Sefer Hayasher)

Flying fowl blocked the rays of the sun. Those fleeing from an attacking beast would stumble and fall, unable to see where they were going.

(Midrash Bechidush)

The Egyptians locked themselves into their homes and barred all entrances. The birds would shatter the windows and fly into the house. There was a sea creature that resembled a man, with arms that were twenty feet long. Hashem sent these creatures to climb on top of the houses and rip the roofs right off. They reached into the homes and opened the doors from the inside. Egyptian children were killed before their parents' eyes. Egyptian mothers awoke in the morning, horrified to discover that their infants had been consumed by wild beasts during the night.

(Sefer Hayasher)

Even non-venomous, non-predator animals became hunters of the Egyptians. Hashem put venom into the glands of these animals and instilled them with the instinct to hunt and kill. The animals bit

the trees, dripping venom into their branches. When the fruits were subsequently consumed by unsuspecting Egyptians, they died of the poison.

(Or Hachaim)

The Egyptians noticed that the animals spared the Jews. Egyptians working their fields would beg a Jew to escort them home. But the animals were able to differentiate and attack only the Egyptians. Even among a group of children playing together, the beasts would pick on only the Egyptian children. *(Shemos Rabbah, Shach)* The animals' newly acquired divine instinct directed them to anyone who did not heed the word of Hashem, though Hashem reversed the instinct when a beast approached a non-observant Jew.

Young Jewish girls were appointed to act as nannies and governesses for Egyptian children. A nanny had to carry four Egyptian children at one time-one on each shoulder, and one in each hand. Now, when they feared for the lives of their children, the Egyptian mothers were especially stringent to enforce this method.

> *The Midrash describes a typical scenario between an Egyptian father of five and his Jewish governess. The Egyptian sent his five children out in the care of the Jewish girl. When she arrived home empty-handed, the father wailed, "Where are my children?"*
>
> *"Sit down," the governess replied. "I will tell you exactly what occurred. A group of animals attacked us-a lion ate up the eldest; another, a bear consumed; a tiger tore up the third; yet another was bitten to death by a wolf; and the youngest was carried away by an eagle."*
>
> *(Midrash Tanchuma)*

Animals Disappear

No one was willing to venture out in the streets, even to obey the command of Pharaoh. Left with no other choice, Pharaoh began to call over the constant roar of wild beasts. After much shouting and

screaming, people near the palace faintly heard his cries, and took up the call. "Moshe, Moshe! I have something vital to discuss with you! Come quickly!" Egyptian after Egyptian joined in the chant until it finally reached the ears of Moshe Rabbeinu.

Moshe Rabbeinu arrived at the palace, untouched by wild beasts. Pharaoh pleaded with him to end the *makah*. Moshe prayed and Hashem heeded. This time, the animals disappeared, denying the Egyptians the use of their precious furs and hides. *(Midrash)* There were no carcasses, but the streets were filled with so many holes and ditches that it was difficult to walk. Sweat dripping down their necks, the Egyptians filled the ditches the animals had created.

Animals gone, Pharaoh once again broke his vow to Moshe Rabbeinu. He hardened his heart and did not allow the Jews to leave Egypt.

Midah K'neged Midah

Why were the Egyptians punished with a plague of wild beasts?

- The Egyptians used to put Jewish lives in grave danger by forcing the Jews to go hunting wild animals. Ironically, wild beasts now abounded.

(Midrash Tanchuma, Bo 4)

- The guards who assigned hard labor to innocent Jews instilled them with the same fear caused by a wild animal. Hashem brought the wild beasts so the Egyptians experienced the same fright they had so easily inflicted.
- Egyptians who forcefully ruled the Jews were now mercilessly preyed upon by wild animals.
- Just as the Egyptians banded together to torture the Jews, so the beasts convened to torment and feast upon the Egyptians.

(Shemos Rabbah)

- Jews were forced to shepherd cattle-cattle that were killed by attacking beasts.

(Zevach Pesach)

- Since Pharaoh would bathe daily in the blood of innocent Jewish children, animals spilled the blood of Egyptian children.

(Shach)

- Egyptians cruelly forced Jews to eat milk cooked together with the meat of an animal, a direct transgression of the laws of *kashrus*. A melting pot of wild animals gathered to punish the Egyptians.

(Tiferes HaRishonim)

- The tribe of Yehudah is compared to a strong lion; a serpent is the symbol for the tribe of Don; Binyamin is represented by the wolf. The Jews are compared to an assortment of animals, all of which invaded the land of Egypt to attack their oppressors.

(Midrash brought in Shach)

5. *Dever*: Death of the Cattle

In step with the pattern, Hashem ordered Moshe Rabbeinu to warn Pharaoh of the upcoming *makah* at his palace. "Use very stern language when addressing Pharaoh-instill a fear of G-d in him. Enumerate every single animal that will die, and tell him that his cattle won't be spared either. Remind Pharaoh about the glorious horses that pull his regal coach, of how all citizens of Egypt turn their heads to stare in awe as the coach gallops by. His beautiful horses, the symbol of his greatness, his dignity, his pride. All these will be lost."

Moshe repeated the words of Hashem. But Pharaoh's reaction was cold.

The Makah Begins

The *makah* commenced as warned. Egypt's abundant donkeys followed the demise of the horses. Anyone riding an animal at the moment of its demise perished too, crushed by the sudden fall of the heavy animal. *(Mishnas Rabbeinu Eliezer, Perek 19)* Camels, the primary mode of long distance travel, were not spared. Precious oxen, vital to the farming of Egyptian lands for plowing, died. Wheat production fell dangerously short. Sheep perished, resulting in tremendous shortages of milk and wool. The ram, Egypt's most worshipped species, helplessly died, despite its so-called spiritual powers. Egyptian lives were not in danger, but the sight of the worshipped ram dying was enough to frighten Pharaoh.

(Sifsei Kohen)

Egyptians awoke one morning to discover that all their cattle had perished. *(Midrash Rabbah, Shemos 15:5)* It was difficult for the Egyptians to accept that all their cattle were dead, while the cattle of the despised Jews were still alive. The sudden death of the cattle caused great hardship. Egyptian-owned horses, donkeys, camels, oxen and sheep all died within a fraction of a second. *(Shemos 9:6)* There was no time for Moshe Rabbeinu to pray in favor of the Egyptians. There was not even enough time for Pharaoh to promise the release of the Jews.

Some Egyptians, fearing Moshe's warning, had sold their cattle to the Jews prior to the *makah*. They had no intention of allowing the Jews to retain their cattle; they expected it back as soon as the *makah* was over. These cattle perished along with the rest.

A normal plague is contagious and, carried by air and wind, germs spread quickly over a large area. But Jewish cattle were unaffected by this fatal plague. In fact, Jewish cattle that were close to

death before the plague were now healed. Even cattle that were in the same pen as those owned by Egyptians remained strong and germ-free. *(Midrash Rabbah, Shemos 11:5)* If a Jew and an Egyptian had shares in cattle, the cattle did not die, since it partially belonged to a Jew.

In the past, the Egyptians underhandedly stole cattle from the Jews. Now it was clear which cattle truthfully belonged to the Jews: the stolen cattle did not die. The Egyptians were finally forced to return the cattle to their rightful Jewish owners.

(Midrash Rabbah, Shemos 11:5)

Some *midrashim* say that only the cattle in the fields died; those in the homes did not. *(Rashi, Shemos 9:10)* The cattle, the Torah tells us, also suffered during the next *makah*, from *sh'chin*. The *Midrash* concludes that not all the cattle died during the *makah* of *dever*. One tenth of the cattle were left alive, so the Jews could take some Egyptian cattle along when they left the land.

(Sefer Hayosher)

Jewish cattle that were under forced contract to be remitted to the king died. Pharaoh used this as an excuse to harden his heart. He would not allow the Jews to go.

(M'Harilad)

Midah K'neged Midah

Why were the Egyptians punished with the death of their cattle?

- The Egyptians monopolized the Jews' time with hard labor day after day, leaving them no time to tend to their own cattle.

(Tana D'bai Eliyahu)

- Jews had served in place of oxen to pull the plows through their fields, so the Egyptian oxen would not be overtaxed.
  (Midrash Tanchuma, Raba)

- Since the Egyptians used to steal the cattle owned by Jews, Hashem punished them with the death of their own cattle.
  (Zevach Pesach)

- Before the *makah* of *arov*, when many Egyptian children died, these children shepherded the cattle. Now the job fell to the Jews, so Hashem redeemed them of the burden.
  (Midrash Tanchuma)

6. *Sh'chin*: Boils and Blisters

Three miraculous events occurred during the *makah* of *sh'chin* that impressed Egyptian and Jew alike:

1. Moshe Rabbeinu and his brother Aharon HaKohen each scooped up two handfuls of ash, and then transferred all the ash into one of Moshe Rabbeinu's hands-and none spilled.
   (Rashi)
2. Moshe Rabbeinu tossed the ash heavenward, and it reached the throne of Hashem, in the seventh and most distant heaven. *(Midrash Rabbah, Va'era 11:10)* Ash is feather-light, easily carried by the wind. Nevertheless, it proceeded directly to the heavens, and on until the sun, where the heat transformed it into a substance capable of causing blisters.
3. Four handfuls of ash were enough to spread over the entire land of Egypt, including its provinces and colonies, and fall on every citizen of Egypt and all the cattle.
   (Hurava'm)

The Makah Begins

All the Egyptians were in constant agony; blisters and boils covered every inch of their bodies. The few remaining cattle that were left in the aftermath of *dever* were afflicted with painful blisters. Homes, stone and wood, were also covered, resembling buildings afflicted by leprosy.

(Haggada Bais Avraham)

All of twenty-four types of blisters that exist were present on the bodies of the Egyptians during the *makah* of *sh'chin*. *(Midrash Hagodel)* These were not run-of-the-mill blisters. *Sh'chin* were dry on the outside and filled with fluid, requiring one treatment for the outside and another for the inside. Methods that provided relief for one type of blister were damaging to another type.

(Baba Kama,80)

Bolts of pain would shoot through their bodies in response to the slightest pressure. There was a burning sensation as skin and flesh beneath the boils cracked. No ointments or cures lessened the pain. The Egyptians attempted to soothe the boils with cold or hot water, but any contact with water intensified the pain.

Not one patch of skin was left unblemished, transforming the entire appearance of the Egyptians until they no longer resembled men. *(Haggada Bais Avraham)* Until their deaths the Egyptians never fully recovered from the *sh'chin*. *(Bechoros 41a, Pirkei D'Rebi Eliezer)* The sorcerers were particularly embarrassed to venture outdoors; their magic was no use to them now. To avoid meeting Moshe Rabbeinu, or anyone else, they steered clear of the royal palace.

(Ramban)

Until the fifth *makah*, Pharaoh hardened his own heart and did not allow the release of the Jews. From the sixth *makah* of *sh'chin* onward, Hashem hardened the heart of Pharaoh, denying him the option of letting the Jews go. Hashem, with His infinite mercy, allowed Pharaoh the opportunity to save himself from the *makos* until

the fifth one. When Hashem saw that Pharaoh obstinately refused, with absolutely no intention of letting the Jews leave Egypt, he declared that Pharaoh had lost his chance. He deserved to suffer all ten *makos* now, even if he were to change his mind and repent.

Midah K'neged Midah

Why were the Egyptians punished with a plague of boils?

- The Egyptians forced the Jews to labor so hard and so long that their skin would tear. Hashem punished them with *sh'chin*, boils that caused painful irritation and breakage of their skin.
- The Jews worked long hours under a scorching hot sun, blackening their skin. The boils and blisters left permanent black marks and scars on the Egyptians' skin.

(Shach)

- As slaves, women were forced to perform the labor of men and men did the women's work, violating the intrinsic laws of nature. The blisters that the Egyptians were punished with were unnatural as well.

(Haggada Bais Avraham)

- Because the Egyptians spilled innocent Jewish blood to cure Pharaoh's ills, Hashem drew blood from the Egyptians in the form of boils.

7. Barad: Torrents of Hail

Attempting to avoid Moshe Rabbeinu, Pharaoh chose a new location for his daily bath. It was a futile attempt before Hashem, the All-Knowing. Moshe Rabbeinu blocked Pharaoh's path, preventing him from continuing any further. According to the command of Hashem, Moshe Rabbeinu stood proudly before Pharaoh "just as a

larger, stronger man would stand in front of a weaker, frailer one." *(Or Hachaim)* In a forceful voice, Moshe warned Pharaoh of the upcoming *makah*.

"Pharaoh, be warned. A plague of great noise, torrents of rain, hail and fire awaits you. This storm will ruin all the Egyptian crops. Any shepherd brazen enough to remain in the fields when the *makah* is due to arrive will experience unprecedented fear. Hashem the Almighty is superior to all! Only He has the power to conduct all these wondrous events. Your sorcerers, Pharaoh? I think not!"

(Or Hachaim)

"If it would be the will of Hashem," Moshe Rabbeinu continued, "the Egyptian people would no longer be among the living. Think about it: if Hashem could bring a plague that massacred all the cattle at once, He could do the same to man. Recognize the superiority of Hashem!" Moshe thundered. "He is Master of this World!"

But it was not the will of Hashem to bring a single *makah* that would eradicate the Egyptian legacy in a single blow. Hashem's plan was to inflict suffering upon Pharaoh, forcing him to acknowledge Hashem's sovereignty and spread the name of Hashem over the entire world.

Moshe Rabbeinu made a firm mark in the wall where he and the king were standing. "When the sun's light reaches this mark at sunrise," Moshe Rabbeinu told Pharaoh, "a torrential hail will fall from the heavens. It will be a storm such as none that Egypt, or the entire world, has ever witnessed. You are warned!"

(Rashi, Shemos 9:18)

Hashem allowed Egypt a full day's warning: perhaps they would repent. *(Midrash Rabbah, Shemos 12:1)* Why did Hashem allow them this privilege? Hashem is a *baal rachamim* Who has pity on all of creation. The *barad* was intended to ruin only the crops, not the people or their cattle. During the twenty-four hours of warning,

Pharaoh and his shepherds had the opportunity to provide shelter for the cattle as they saw fit. *(Ramban)* When the Jews were finally allowed to leave Egypt, the Egyptians provided them with cattle to sacrifice to Hashem-it was necessary now to protect some of their cattle for this purpose. *(Minchu Belilu)* The Egyptians also needed horses to chase the Jews into the Red Sea, horses that were destined to drown in the pursuit. *(Me'am Loez)* All part of Hashem's grand plan.

Pharaoh chose to ignore the grace period he was allowed. Trying to disprove Moshe's words, Pharaoh's secretaries and servants decreed that all shepherds must remain in the fields with their cattle. *(Meshech Chochma)* The more G-d fearing and decent Egyptians, among them Job, did not heed the words of Pharaoh's servants, taking shelter for themselves and their cattle prior to the *makah*. The rest of the evil Egyptians left their cattle to graze in the fields, including Bilaam.

(Shemos Rabbah)

Even though the majority of the Egyptians did not believe that the storm, as Moshe Rabbeinu described it, could possibly happen, deep inside their hearts they knew that the prediction was sure to come true-and they took their idols indoors. They were subconsciously aware that their idols had no spiritual powers. To avoid embarrassment and confrontation, they sheltered the idols from the predicted damaging storm.

There was a tumult in the Heavenly Court when the *makah* of *barad* was about to begin. The plague was intended for the crops, not the people or the cattle! The cattle were still roaming the fields-how could the *makah* begin? But the entire Heavenly Court unanimously assented to begin the plague. The Egyptians had sufficient warning to house their cattle, and some chose not to. They had to suffer the consequences.

(Ramban)

The Makah Begins

The Egyptians awaited the arrival of the hail with anticipation. Even if it started hailing at the exact moment Moshe Rabbeinu had stated, it would still take a few seconds for the hailstones to reach the earth. And the thunder could not possibly be heard at the same moment that the storm and lightning arrived, for sound always travels slower than light. The Egyptians thought they would prove Moshe a liar. Hashem's power, however, supersedes the laws of nature, and the Egyptians were disappointed.

(Malbim)

At sunrise, Hashem lifted Moshe Rabbeinu to the skies, where he stretched his staff in the direction of the heavens. *(Rashi, Shemos 9:22)* Immediately it began to thunder and flash lightning. The earth quaked *(Midrash Hagadol)*, and hailstones as large as rocks fell from the sky.

When the storm initially left the clouds, the precipitation started out as soft rain. During its earthbound journey, lightning and crashes of thunder joined in. The noise of the thunder was loud and continuous, almost unbearable; the lightning, unnaturally bright. Great winds began to blow and the hail was created.

(Midrash Tanchuma)

According to the *Midrash*, when it first began hailing, the lightning was so bright that it lit up the entire world. The sounds of thunder were so strong and so loud, they caused the earth to tremor.

(Mishnas Rabbeinu Eliezer 19)

Egypt is situated in a desert area; rain is very infrequent there. The Nile was the only form of usable water that the Egyptians could depend on. Prior to the settlement of Egypt, its landscape was entirely flat, without any mountain ranges or hills. Later, when the sons of Cham arrived there, they dried out the wet earth and set up a civilized community, using the river as the main water source. The arrival of

the waters from heaven in Egypt's naturally dry climate was a miraculous event in itself.

(M'haria)

No form of precipitation, no lightning, no thunder had been seen or heard before in Egypt. Now *HaKadosh Baruch Hu* tallied all the thunderstorms and hailstorms that could have fallen in the land of Egypt since the beginning of time. All this, and more, was released in a fury during the *makah* of *barad*. All the sounds of thunder were combined into one deafening crash; all the flashes of lightning into one brilliant flash.

(Chasam Sofer)

The frightening sounds of thunder instilled terror in the heart of Pharaoh and the Egyptians. They began suffering from nervous diseases. *(Rabbeinu B'chai)* When Pharaoh summoned Moshe Rabbeinu to the palace, he did not initially ask for the cessation of the entire *makah*, but an end to the terrible noises. Even the Jews in Goshen heard the frightening thunder and saw the lightning, though the storm did not reach them. As the *Gemara* teaches, the Jews utilized the noise to instill within themselves *yiras Hashem*, fear of G-d, and to humble their hearts.

Fire and Water

What was the composition of the hailstones? On the outside they were hard, frozen ice, and on the inside they contained burning balls of fire. (*Rashi*) The unusual combination of cold and heat affected the weather in Egypt, causing the Egyptians to fall ill.

(Rabbeinu B'chai)

The *barad* were supernatural in a number of ways.

- Fire and water are naturally repellent, but now, in a temporary truce, the water did not extinguish the fire.

- The size of each hailstone was extraordinary-the width of six closed adult male fists.

(Lekach Tov)

- According to the laws of nature, fire and heat rise. The fire should have been on the outside or top of the hailstone, but it was within.
- Water, which normally pools together, should have gathered in the center of the ball of hail. Yet during the *makah* of *barad* the water remained frozen, surrounding the inner ball of fire.

(Shemos Rabbah)

R' Yehuda and R' Nechemiah had different opinions about the appearance of the hailstones. According to one, the ice on the outside encased the fire on the inside. The fire looked like the burning red seeds of a pomegranate, faintly visible through the translucent white shell of ice. The other countered that the hailstone resembled a *yahrtzeit licht*, a candle commemorating the anniversary of the death of a loved one. The ice on the outside was like the clear glass cup that holds the water and oil; floating at the surface was the flame.

(Midrash Raba)

Hail Damage

The hailstones that fell acted as saws and axes. When a hailstone hit a tree it tore the tree out at the roots, and the fire burned the tree to ashes. If the hailstones hit an Egyptian who dared to venture outdoors, he would die instantly, his body cremated by the fire. *(Shemos Rabbah)* Hashem would frighten any Egyptian trying to escape an oncoming hailstone with the mighty sound of thunder. The victim would be rendered inert from the overpowering sound, and he was paralyzed directly in the path of the hailstone.

(Midrash Hagodol, H'ravom)

The hailstones were like rocks with fire inside them. Within the fire lay more hail. The hailstone would drop upon trees, Egyptians, and various animals, ripping open the intended victim. The rock would explode, releasing burning fire. The sharp rocks within the fire wreaked the final torture.

(Mishnas D'Rebi Eliezer)

When the hail fell in the fields it formed a wall around the cattle; they were unable to seek shelter. Egyptian cattle grazing together with Jewish cattle were not protected. The huge hailstones would rain down and harm only the Egyptian-owned cattle, while the cattle owned by the Jew did not suffer the tiniest scratch.

(Midrash Raba, Naso 81)

When the Egyptians realized that their cattle were being killed and destroyed, they decided to slaughter the animals on their own. At least they could enjoy the meat! Hashem sent huge birds to snatch the flesh set aside after the slaughter, and they carried it away.

(Midrash Rabbah 12:4, Midrash Tehillim 79)

Among the crops, only the hard and ripe wheat, which ripen during Shevat and Adar, the months in which the *makah* took place, broke during the storm. Other crops were scheduled to ripen during Nissan and were still soft and pliable. According to the laws of nature, hard stalks break when they are bent by the wind, whereas soft matter springs right back when they are bent.

The young crops should have been ruined despite this, burned to a crisp from the ravaging fires. *HaKadosh Baruch Hu* saved these crops from the *makah* of *barad* in order to threaten Pharaoh with the eighth *makah* of locusts. Each additional plague provided an opportunity to prove Hashem's supremacy to Pharaoh, his nation, and the entire world.

Suffering Ends

Terrified to venture out himself, Pharaoh sent messengers to summon Moshe Rabbeinu to his palace. *(Sifsai Kohen)* "Moshe, Aharon," Pharaoh begged, "it's enough thunder! No more hail! Please put an end to this *makah*! I'll send your nation out ..."

Moshe Rabbeinu agreed to pray to end the *makah*, but he stipulated that he must pray outside the city. The Egyptians had brought all their cattle, which they regarded as idols, into the cities for protection. All other expensive idols had been sheltered in their homes while the destructive *barad* fell outside. Moshe could not pray in a city so full of false gods. He escaped to a *beis medrash* in the outskirts of the city, where he *davened* to Hashem that the *makah* conclude.

(Rashi, Shemos 9:29)

The instant Moshe Rabbeinu prayed, the hail immediately ceased falling. Hailstones that were en route to the ground remained suspended in midair until forty-one years later, when a portion fell on the *Givonim,* who were fighting against Joshua. The rest will fall on Gog and Magog in the Messianic era, when *Moshiach* will bring the ultimate redemption for all Jews.

(Midrash Rabbah, Shemos 12:7)

The sounds of thunder also remained suspended in the air, to be sounded five hundred years later during the times of Yehoram. *(Melachim II 5-7)* The people of Machaneh Arom were fighting against *bnei Yisroel*, and Hashem caused confusion among them with the sounds of thunder.

(Mishnas Rabbeinu Eliezer 19)

Witness to the extraordinary hail, Pharaoh admitted that "Hashem is the righteous One, and I and my nation are wicked." *(Shemos 9:27)* Hashem, in His infinite kindness, had explicitly warned the Egyptians to shelter their cattle and bring them into their homes. Pharaoh acted as evil people usually do: during hardship and suffering

he was willing to admit his mistakes, but once the hardship was removed he reverted to his old self-righteousness, heresy, and ingratitude.

(Midrash Rabbah, Shemos 12:7)

Pharaoh was nonetheless rewarded for his declaration of the righteousness of Hashem, even though it was under duress. The Torah prohibits a Jew from hating any Egyptian. *(Machilta)* Pharaoh himself was rewarded with a proper burial, one that did not befit a heretic such as he.

(Mechilta, Beshalach)

Midah K'neged Midah

Why were the Egyptians punished with a plague of hail?

- The Egyptians did not allow the Jews to enjoy the comforts that the shade of a tree offers, or even to cool off in a patch of fresh grass. Hashem destroyed the grass and trees, and now the Egyptians could not enjoy them either.

  (Shach)

- The Egyptians used to force the Jews to plow the fields, sow the seeds, and plant the grapevines. Now the hail ruined all their crops.

  (Midrash Rabbah, Shemos 12:5)

- The hail and winds whipped the Egyptians the same way guards would whip the Jews to work.

  (Haggada Bais Avraham)

- The Egyptians would shriek and yell at the Jews, throwing stones and pebbles to induce them to work harder. The thunder assaulted Egyptian ears, and the hail cut and bruised the Egyptians like rocks.

  (Me'am Loez)

- The Egyptians sadistically forced Jews to perform demeaning tasks, solely for the purpose of embarrassing them. Violated Jews would obey, their faces white with shame. Hashem frightened the Egyptians with hail and thunder, causing their faces to pale and whiten.
- When Hashem's beloved nation sins, Hashem absolves them of their sins, making them pure and white again. The Egyptians, who tried to annihilate an innocent nation, were punished with pure, white hail.

(Sifsai Kohen)

8. *Arbeh*: Hordes of Locust

Pharaoh had endured so much suffering—seven horrifying plagues. He even admitted, "Hashem is the righteous one, and I and my nation are wicked men." *(Shemos 9:27)* How could Pharaoh still harden his heart and refuse the appeal of Moshe to let the Jews go?

Hashem answers in *Shemos* 10:1-2, speaking to Moshe Rabbeinu. "Pharaoh only hardens his heart because I decreed that it should be so. I hardened the hearts of all his servants as well. I must inflict the remaining *makos* upon Pharaoh and the Egyptians. They will know that it is Hashem Who runs this world. And the miraculous events of the past few months will be repeated to all, worldwide, to the children of this generation, and the generations after them. *(Rashban)* My chosen nation will know, without a doubt, that I guard them with wondrous *nissim*, miracles."

(Malbim)

A Warning is Issued

Moshe Rabbeinu and Aharon HaKohen, emissaries of Hashem, presented themselves at Pharaoh's palace, reminding him of his vow during the plague of hail to release the Jews. Day in and day out, at each appearance, Pharaoh gave the same procrastinating answer, "Come to me tomorrow."

"How long will you continue to lie to us?" Moshe and Aharon finally protested. "We will not wait until tomorrow. If you do not liberate the Jews *now*, locusts will invade the borders tomorrow. *(Rashi, Ramban)* They will arrive in an abundance never seen before, never to be seen again. The earth underneath your feet will not be visible to your eyes because of the vast amount of locusts. *(Rashi)* The crowd of buzzing locusts will be a cloud between the skies and the earth, obliterating the sun's light. Darkness will descend. *(Targum Unkelos)* The locusts will consume everything that the *barad* spared. They will enter and fill the homes of the Egyptians, piling on top of each other until they reach the ceilings in the houses."

(Me'am Loez)

Moshe Rabbeinu ended his warning to Pharaoh and his servants. Against all laws of respect for a mortal king, he turned his back to Pharaoh and exited the palace, without waiting to be dismissed.

Pharaoh's servants dreaded yet another frightful *makah*. They begged and pleaded Pharaoh to spare their land more pain and suffering. "Send the men!" the servants advised. "Let them go and serve their G-d. Don't you realize that the nation of Egypt is practically lost?" *(Shemos 10:7)* Egypt's power within its own borders and in foreign lands had declined to almost naught.

Pharaoh resignedly summoned Moshe Rabbeinu to return to his palace, and offered Moshe this compromise. He would assent to the liberation of the men only-the women and children must remain in Egypt as collateral, so the men would return after three days of worship.

Through astrology, Pharaoh saw a star called *ra'ah* (bad) in the future of the Jewish nation, a very ominous warning of events to come. This star was an omen that blood would be spilled from the nation of Israel in the desert, and that they would suffer a mass demise. He predicted that all the Jews leaving Egypt would die in the desert, save for Joshua and Caleb. He argued with Moshe that the Jews would be better off remaining in Egypt.

Pharaoh was correct in his predictions-to an extent. The star represented the sin of the Golden Calf that the Jews later committed in the desert. Hashem wanted to punish *bnei Yisroel* by spilling their blood, but through the power of Moshe Rabbeinu's prayers, Hashem forgave His beloved nation. Instead of blood being spilled by death, the Jews were commanded to circumcise every Jewish male before entering the holy land of Israel.

The Makah Begins

Moshe Rabbeinu raised his staff heavenward, and strong gusts of wind began blowing from the east. The warm wind was very conducive for the locusts to increase their numbers. *(Paniach Ruzo)* The wind blew all day and all night, allowing the Egyptians sufficient opportunity to repent. *(Midrash Rabbah, Shemos 13:5)* By the next morning, an entire army of locusts had amassed from the seas.

(Rashbam)

There are eight different species of locusts, and each species has one hundred subspecies. One thousand of each subspecies arrived in Egypt, adding up to 800,000 locusts! And once they arrived, they kept right on increasing in number until the entire land of Egypt was filled. As the largest group, the species of *arbeh* earned the *makah* title.

(Haggada Bais Avraham)

R' Nechemiah describes the unique locusts that inflicted the destructive plague. Their mouths were sealed shut; had they been open,

any mortal standing before them would have been immediately destroyed. The saliva of the locusts was venomous-and fatal. The locusts' teeth were made of iron. They had horns that resembled the horns of an ox, and wings that resembled the wings of an eagle. Their eyes were like those of a calf. The front legs were similar to the paws of a lion. The throat was the throat of a horse. The heart beating within the locusts was the heart of a man. Their backsides resembled the backside of a fish, and the tail end was the same as a snake's. The knees of the locusts were like a camel's knees, and their hind legs like two large shields. As members of the army of Hashem, there was a spiritual life beating within them.

These horrific locusts entered Egypt via the border. They made a beeline for the palace of Pharaoh, passing over the homes of Pharaoh's servants and other Egyptians. When not a single additional locust could squeeze into Pharaoh's palace, they proceeded to the homes of Pharaoh's servants, and subsequently the homes of every Egyptian.

(Me'am Loez)

The locust's average journey across the vast land of Egypt normally would last about forty days. But with Hashem's infinite power, the locusts were able to spread from one corner of the land to another in a fraction of an instant. The locusts filled Egypt from border to border, from the ground until the height of an average man's eyes. The citizens' vision was marred and their eyes blinded by the mass of locusts. *(Haggada Bais Avraham)* The sun provided no benefit; all light and heat were blocked by the creatures.

(Sifsai Kohen)

Instead of pitying their fate, some Egyptians viewed this as a wonderful opportunity and joyous occasion. Crowds ventured outside and gathered the locusts in barrels to salt and pickle this delicacy. But at the end of the week, when the westerly wind began blowing the locusts away, the preserved locust were revived and whisked out of the land along with the active ones.

(Ramban)

People could not see the earth they were standing on. Nor could the locusts. Part of the satisfaction derived from food comes from viewing an appetizing meal. Since the locusts could not see what they were eating, they continued to consume without satisfying their hunger.

(Kli Yokor)

In their natural habitat, locusts prefer food sources that are soft and yielding. The locusts consumed all the soft wheat and fruits that remained from the *makah* of *barad*. But when those were gone, they did not continue on to a neighboring country as their natural instinct would have directed them. Instead, they entered the homes of the Egyptians and consumed all the food the Egyptians had hidden for themselves. *(Rabbeinu B'chai)* The Egyptians attempted to carry sacks of wheat to neighboring countries, to save them from the ever-seeking mouths of the locusts. But locusts formed a wall at the borders, preventing any Egyptian from exiting the land to hoard his wheat elsewhere.

(Haggada Bais Avrahom)

If a Jew had purchased a tree in the field of an Egyptian, the locusts would consume the roots of the tree and the grass around it, as this was considered the property of the Egyptian. But they assiduously protected the tree and its fruits, property of a Jew. If the situation was reversed, the locusts were equally careful. The locusts would hungrily consume the Egyptian tree and its fruits, but would not touch the roots or the surrounding growth.

(Eitz Chaim)

For the first three days, the locusts did not descend on the Egyptians themselves. But after all the food in the land of Egypt was consumed, the locusts began sampling the flesh of the Egyptians and ate it with relish. *(Midrash B'chidush)* The locusts picked at the clothing of the Egyptians, and then ate all their jewels. Egyptian noses, ears, eyes and mouths became a favorite perch for the locusts,

inflicting an unbearably unpleasant sensation. *(Hurie M'vien)* They gouged out and ate the eyes of many Egyptians.

(Sechel Tov)

The locusts did not come alone-they were accompanied by poisonous snakes and serpents. *(Baal Haturim)* A snake bite meant immediate death, their venom as poisonous as wild bees'. *(Midrash Hagodel)* Even the locusts spewed forth poisonous venom, fatal to their victims.

(Rabbeinu B'chai)

Prior to the *makah* of *arbeh*, the Egyptians and *bnei Cham* (*Cushim*, or Ethiopians) each claimed a portion of land at the border as their own. Now the limits of the *makah* of *arbeh* were a clear delineation of the border between the two countries. The *makah* of *tzephardaya* had also indicated the border, but the Egyptian sorcerers had argued that Moshe's magic cannot define a border-since they could conjure frogs with their magic too. But the plague of locusts could not be replicated, and the Egyptians were unable to debate the wall of locusts that formed at the border. *(Midrash Rabbah)* Even the Egyptians had to admit that this plague was decreed from Above, and not through nature or sorcery.

The Locusts Blow Away

Pharaoh summoned Moshe Rabbeinu and Aharon HaKohen to his palace once again. He confessed and admitted his sins against Hashem-that he had not liberated the Jews. Apologizing for cursing G-d's messengers and forcibly sending them from the palace, he vowed never again to transgress the will of Hashem.

"I promise, I give my oath to release your people from my land," Pharaoh declared. "Just please pray for an end to this death immediately! My entire nation will sink into the depths of a great famine and suffer terribly. I have given you my word, and I will

stand by it. It is futile to allow the Jews to remain-the suffering is too much to bear," Pharaoh sobbed as he ended his declaration. "Please pray to your G-d!"

In the outskirts of the city, Moshe prayed to Hashem to end the *makah* of *arbeh*. Strong, cold gusts of wind began blowing from the west. The wind lifted all the locusts and gently deposited them into the Red Sea. When Pharaoh and the Egyptians chased the Jews into the splitting sea, the locusts rose once again to plague and torment them.

Not one locust remained in the entire land of Egypt, and until this very day locusts do not inhabit the land of Egypt. The power of Moshe Rabbeinu's prayer was so great that it continues to be effective. Although there are locusts and grasshoppers in Egypt's neighboring countries, they do not step foot over the borders of Egypt. This power of prayer is a legacy that parents repeat to their children generation after generation.

(Rabbeinu B'chai)

When Pharaoh saw that the pickled locusts were also removed, he accused Moshe of using sorcery to eradicate the *makah*. His heart was hardened and he did not allow the Jews to go. Two remaining *makos* awaited.

(Midrash Rabbah)

In His humble way, Hashem discussed the situation during *makas arbeh* with His Heavenly Court. Although Hashem the Almighty is all-knowing, He nevertheless asked the Heavenly Court whether they believed the Egyptians deserved to be punished along with Pharaoh. After all, the Egyptian people were in favor of liberating the Jews. The Heavenly Court decreed the Egyptians guilty, as they had assented to the release of the men only, not the entire nation.

(Me'am Loez)

Midah K'neged Midah

Why were the Egyptians punished with a plague of locusts?

- The crops that the Egyptians forced the Jews to plant for them were consumed by the locusts.

(Shemos Rabbah)

- The Egyptians used to steal wheat and other crops from the Jews, and now their own crops were all destroyed by the *arbeh*.

(Zevach Pesach)

- Because the Egyptians would deprive the Jews of food and force them to go hungry, Hashem brought locusts that deprived the Egyptians of their own food.

(Chaim Lerosh)

- Jews were forced to bake bread for the Egyptians while they themselves went hungry. The *makah* of *arbeh* brought famine and starvation, this time for the Egyptians.

(Megala Tzifonos)

9. *Choshech*: Darkness Reigns

As the third *makah* in the set of *B'achav*, no warning was issued to Pharaoh. The Egyptians had no opportunity to hide all their valuables. Under the heavy cloak of darkness, away from the searching eyes of the Egyptians, all the wicked men of the Jewish nation were killed.

(Midrash Rabbah)

Before Hashem brought darkness on Egypt, He consulted with His Heavenly Court. All agreed unanimously to everything Hashem proposed.

(Midrash Rabbah, Bo, 14:1)

The Makah Begins

In the third hour of the day when the sun shines in its fullest strength, Moshe Rabbeinu raised his staff toward the heavens. No Egyptian could possibly entertain the heretic thought that the night was simply prolonged.

The darkness that presided was twice as dark as the average nighttime darkness. Hashem combined the nights of the Egyptians together with the nights of the Jews to create the darkness that reigned during the plague of *choshech*.

(Kli Yokor)

A thick, palpable cloud of darkness descended from the heavens and settled into a thick sheet. It spread out beneath the skies where the sun normally cast its rays onto the land. The darkness covered the entire land of Egypt.

(Midrash)

During the first three days of the *makah*, the darkness was so thick it was tangible, like no other darkness known to man. Even in the deepest valleys, far below sea level, one can faintly detect the outline of a man. But the consistency of this darkness extinguished any flame the Egyptians tried to light. Neither the sun nor the moon or stars lit up the skies.

(Me'am Loez)

It was during this period of time that Hashem killed all the wicked men of *bnei Yisroel*. These men collaborated with the Egyptians in the torture of the Jews, and forced them to work faster and more effectively. At the expense of their brethren, these wicked

people gained much wealth and power. They had no interest in leaving Egypt; life was pleasant for them there, fond as they were of their Egyptian neighbors and friends. Journeying to a new land and leaving their comforts behind were strange and frightening ideas. Above all, they were reluctant to abandon their great income and wealth in Egypt. All faith in Hashem was lost. Fellow Jews sadly buried their lost brothers under cover of the divine darkness.

The Sanzer Rebbe zt"l once stated that the burial of wicked men, though they may be Jewish, is not a mitzvah. How do we know this is true? When the Jews left Egypt they were devoid of any mitzvos. But they did have good deeds in their favor! They buried the wicked Jews who died during the plague of darkness, and they refused to leave Egypt stealthily in the dark because Hashem had not proclaimed that the hour had come. Yet these were not considered mitzvos. This proves that the burial of wicked men is not included in the obligation that the Torah states about burying the dead.

The Rebbe's son, the Galicia Rav, told his father, "Father, you are correct. It is not a mitzvah to bury the deceased rasha. But to figuratively bury a rasha, to subdue him and prevent him from spreading his venomous words of heresy-that is a mitzvah."

Six hundred thousand Jews were redeemed from Egypt. According to one opinion, only one out of every six hundred thousand Jews merited the exodus from Egypt. There were three hundred sixty billion Jews in Egypt before the *makah* of *choshech*. So many did not merit the redemption! Another opinion states that one out of every five hundred Jews merited to leave Egypt. Three hundred million Jews had been enslaved in Egypt, and 299,400,000 Jews died in the darkness.

A third opinion maintains that one out of every fifty Jews merited the exodus. Thirty million Jews were in Egypt during the era of the enslavement. 29,400,000 never left Egypt. Yet another opinion states

that one out of every five Jews merited leaving Egypt. 2,400,000 Jews out of the three million that were there did not merit the redemption.

Darkness Part Two

During the last three days of the *makah*, the darkness and its thick consistency quadrupled. The Egyptians were literally wrapped in a cloak of darkness so thick that they were rendered immobile, and remained so for three full days. If a person happened to be caught standing, he could not sit down. If he was sitting, he could not lift himself out of his chair. The Egyptians were paralyzed for three days. *(Rashi, Shemos 10:22)* Had this stage of darkness lasted any longer, they most certainly would have died.

There was only one thing that Hashem allowed the Egyptians to see. Frightening images passed before the eyes of the terrified Egyptians. *(Chasam Sofer)* The Egyptians feared that the Jews would now avenge themselves and rob them of their valuables and escape the tortures of slavery.

Darkness was accompanied by other visitors. Demons and evil spirits arrived to harm the Egyptians. *(Haggada Bais Avraham)* Lice and *sh'chin* returned. Their discomforts were intensified; they could not move to swat the lice, scratch their itching skins or soothe painful blisters.

(Yalkut Haruveini)

The Egyptians were hungry and thirsty, but they could do nothing to quench their thirst or ease their hunger pangs. Normally a person in such a trying situation would become so riddled with worries and phobias that he would go insane. Hashem deliberately kept their minds sharp and clear, so they would experience the pain of the *choshech* in its fullest extent.

The condensed darkness had the power to kill the Egyptians if it entered their bodies. Hashem blocked their airways, preventing them from inhaling the thick cloud, but miraculously enabled them to use their lungs.

(Me'am Loez)

While the Egyptians suffered in the darkness, the Jews enjoyed round-the-clock sunlight-the light that had been created during the six days of creation. The sunlight was so clear and bright that it allowed a view from one end of the world clear across to the other end. The Jews pinpointed all the gold and silver that the Egyptians had hidden, so they could demand and locate the vast wealth when it was time to leave Egypt. The special sunlight had been reserved until the time of *Moshiach*, but Hashem allowed it to shine now, when all the wicked Jews had died and the Egyptians were submerged in darkness. Only the righteous Jews were present to derive pleasure from it.

The *Targum Yonasan* states: The sunlight served to enable the Jews to bury the dead-the wicked who had died during the *makah*. It enabled them to perform *mitzvos* that can only be done during the day-wearing *tzitzis*, donning *tefillin*. Jews learned Torah, the true source of light, all day. "*Ki ner mitzvah v'torah ohr*-a mitzvah is a candle, and Torah is light."

(Mishlei 6:23)

The entire Jewish settlement of Goshen was bathed in light. A Jew who entered the home of an Egyptian was surrounded by a halo of light. *(Chizkuni)* The Egyptians were able to hear the Jews in their homes, rummaging through their possessions, but they were helpless.

The Jews faced many great ethical challenges during the period of darkness. The inert Egyptians were unable to defend themselves. The Jews could have easily robbed them of all their possessions. No one could have stopped them from escaping the hellish torments of Egypt. But the destined time had not yet come.

(Divrei Yoel)

All the previous *makos* lasted seven days, but the *makah* of *choshech* lasted only six days. Hashem reserved the seventh day to cast upon the Egyptians when they chased *bnei Yisroel* into the Red Sea.

(Midrash Rabbah, Bo, 14:3)

Pharaoh Offers a Compromise

Moshe Rabbeinu arrived at Pharaoh's palace in response to his summons. Pharaoh promised to release all Jews-men, women, and children-on one condition. The cattle owned by the Jews must stay in Egypt to guarantee that they will return. Moshe Rabbeinu, displeased with the plan, explained, "We will need our cattle to serve Hashem in the desert. And we won't know how many we will need until we get there. After all, it's been such a long time since we've had the opportunity to serve Hashem. And when the time comes," Moshe added, "you'll also be handing us your own cattle, begging us to leave!"

Pharaoh grew angry when he heard Moshe's heated speech. "Leave my palace immediately! The next time I see your face will be the day you die!"

Moshe Rabbeinu, unperturbed by Pharaoh's harsh words, retorted, "I will do just as you say, and never return. But be warned: There will come a day when *you* will come looking for *me*. You will bow down to me, pleading for mercy, begging me to take the Jews out of your land as quickly as I possibly can!"

Midah K'neged Midah

Why were the Egyptians punished with a plague of darkness?

- When Yaakov Avinu passed away, the darkness of slavery descended on the Jews.

  (Zera Shimshon)

- The Egyptians worshipped the sun and the moon, but during the *makah* of *choshech*, these supreme lights did not shine.

  (Yalkut Haruveini)

- Darkness descended on the Egyptians as punishment for locking Jews in dark, secluded towers.

  (Klai Chemda, Vayeira)

- Hashem blinded the Egyptians' eyes with darkness because they willingly closed their eyes to the pain and torturous labor of the Jews.

(Shach)

- Because the Egyptians forced the Jews to work all hours of the dark night, Hashem brought night upon them.
- Jews were forced to light and carry torches and lanterns for their masters during the dark hours of the night. Hashem cast a heavy darkness that the Egyptians could not dissipate with any form of light.
- When an Egyptian wanted to eat, he would instruct a Jew to stand at his side with a candle perched upon his head. The Jew was not permitted to move an inch; if he did, it was punishable by death. The *makah* of *choshech* snuffed out any candle that was lit.

(Lekach Tov)

- Because the Egyptians did not open their eyes to the previous *makos* to acknowledge the existence of Hashem, they were punished with a plague that blinded their eyes.

(Klai Chemda, Vayeira)

10. *Makas Bechoros*: Death of the Firstborn

Hashem wanted to speak with Moshe Rabbeinu before he retreated from the royal palace. *(Ramban)* Since he was in the company of so much impurity-Pharaoh, the Egyptians and all their idols-Hashem lifted Moshe ten *amos* (twenty feet) above the ground, and spoke with him there.

(Daas Zekeinim)

"I will soon inflict the tenth and final *makah* upon Pharaoh: the death of Pharaoh's firstborn and all firstborn males of Egypt. Pharaoh will chase you and all your cattle out of Egypt. He will pay you great sums of money to leave. *(Lekach Tov)* He will beg and plead for you to accept money to save the firstborns. Gather the Jews and quietly tell them to borrow the gold, silver and other valuables that they searched out during the plague of darkness. Tell Pharaoh what I said," Hashem instructed Moshe, "and then take your leave. Your people need you."

Moshe loudly repeated the warning to Pharaoh and all his servants. "Around midnight, Hashem Himself will descend into the land of Egypt and will strike all the firstborn children dead. None will be spared—the firstborn to their mothers and the firstborn to their fathers, the males and the females. They'll all die, from your beloved firstborn, Pharaoh, to the firstborns of the most common of men. The eldest of the precious animals you worship will die too. *(Rashi, Shemos 11:5)* You can try to hide the victims in your houses of worship, but your powerless idols will not aid them! The idols cast in gold and silver will melt, and those carved of stone will shatter into splinters of rock.

(Rashi, Shemos 12:12)

"A high-pitched, agonized wail will echo throughout your land," Moshe Rabbeinu continued. "Such a cry has never before been heard and will never be heard again. Everyone will be mourning the loss of a loved one. And amidst all the death in the dark of the night, not one dog will even whet its tongue. Then, Pharaoh, your servants will come running, begging me to leave together with the entire Jewish nation." With an insulting slap on King Pharaoh's cheek *(Zevachim 102a)*, Moshe turned and left the palace for the last time.

Word of the upcoming *makah* quickly spread. Firstborns gathered at the palace, begging Pharaoh to agree to Moshe's terms and save them from certain death. "Your Majesty is a firstborn as well," they pleaded.

Pharaoh reacted with great anger, ordering the rebellious crowd punished. He publicly embarrassed them, inflicting terrible tortures

on those who dared stand against him. A battle ensued and six hundred thousand people perished.

(Me'am Loez)

It was appropriate that Hashem chose to punish the Egyptians through their firstborns. Hashem has a special love for all firstborn creatures. The Torah prohibits the use of the eldest cattle to work the land, and the eldest sheep from shearing. *(Devarim 15:19)* Yet Pharaoh forced the eldest Jewish children to labor long and hard. He was justly punished.

(Midrash Rabbah)

Wealth Changes Hands

Meanwhile, Moshe Rabbeinu quietly conveyed Hashem's orders for the Jews to borrow expensive clothing, gold, silver and gems from their Egyptian neighbors.

Why waste valuable time collecting treasures? The righteous Jews thought. They preferred to hurry the ultimate exodus. When the time would finally arrive, they did not want the added bulk of wealth to impede their progress. Besides, the Egyptians would surely regret their decision to free the Jews and chase after them. Not only would these valuables slow them down, they would provide even more incentive for the Egyptians to catch them.

But Hashem had promised Avraham Avinu that the Jews would leave Egypt "in great wealth," *(Bereishis 15:13)* and He must fulfill his vow. The Jews did not derive pleasure from the newly gained wealth, but they obeyed the command of Moshe Rabbeinu. They ventured to their Egyptian neighbors and asked to borrow various valuable articles. If the Egyptians denied ever having owned such an item, the Jew identified the closet or drawer where he had seen it during the *makah* of *choshech*.

The Jews asked for clothing and valuables in a pleasant, neighborly fashion, innocently concealing the fact that they would be

escaping along with their belongings. The Egyptians had used similar tactics with the Jews many years before: they conned the Jews into accepting light work with the promise of great reward, then heavy labor was forced on them. The Egyptians were aptly punished chasing their "borrowed" possessions into the Red Sea.

Miraculously, the Egyptians handed over their valuables with smiles, and even offered to share more of their wealth with their Jewish neighbors. The Jews would eventually return with their gold and silver, they concluded. They were more concerned about their clothing. The Jews would never wear Egyptian-style clothing-they would cut it up and fashion it into a more modest covering, rendering it useless to the Egyptians. But they handed over their beautiful garments anyway.

One opinion states that the Jews visited their Egyptian neighbors on the very night of *makas bechoros*, when members of the household were mourning their lost loved ones, or fruitlessly tending to a victim in the throes of death. Even at this trying time, the Egyptians recognized the futility of their unwarranted hatred toward the Jews. They welcomed their former slaves with open arms, showering them with love and valuables.

The Sacrificial Lamb

The enslavement of the Jews in Egypt was preordained to last four hundred years. After only two hundred and ten years of slavery, Hashem was ready to redeem His people. But they had not accumulated nearly enough merit to earn the redemption. Therefore He ordered them to circumcise themselves, and to sacrifice a lamb as the *Korban Pesach*, the Pesach sacrifice.

And so came Shabbos, the tenth of Nissan, when every Jew sought the most exquisite lamb to sacrifice on the fourteenth day of the month, after four days of careful observation. The Egyptians noticed the Jews' unusual behavior.

"Why are you confining our revered lambs in your homes?" they inquired.

"Hashem has commanded us to slaughter these animals as sacrifices to Him in four days' time, in thanks that He will slaughter all the firstborn Egyptians," the Jews replied.

The Egyptians gritted their teeth at the response, inflicting more torture upon themselves than the torment of the *makos*. Enraged Egyptians prepared for war, collecting ammunition and sharpening their weaponry. "How dare they insult our gods this way!" they thought to themselves. Hashem smote them with pains so fierce that they could no longer stand on their feet and were forced to abandon their preparations.

(Kol Bo 47)

The Shabbos prior to Pesach is known as Shabbos HaGadol, the Great Shabbos, commemorating that Shabbos when the Egyptians were helpless to aid their idols.

(Tur Orach Chaim, 430)

Preparing for Pesach

The fourteenth day of Nissan was a frenzy of activity. The Jews were baking *matzos* and grating *marror*. During market hour, when the streets swarmed with Egyptians, the Jews busied themselves sacrificing their lambs. The pungent aroma of roasting lamb permeated the air, fulfilling the command, "The images of their idols you must burn in fire" *(Devarim 7:25)*. The quickly roasting meat alluded to the speed with which the Jews would leave Egypt less than twenty-four hours later.

(Chinuch, Chizkuni, Minchah Belulah)

Meanwhile, despite the blatant insult to their idol, the Egyptians were nervously trying to protect themselves from the fearful plague that was due. Some believing Egyptians begged their Jewish neighbors

to allow their eldest child to sleep in the protection of a Jewish home. It was to no avail. The Egyptian child died while the Jews slept peacefully.

(Shemos Rabbah 18:2)

The Jews were insructed to smear the blood of the *Korban Pesach* on the door frame of their homes. Not that the Omniscient needed the sign to differentiate Jew from Egyptian; it was to build merit for His beloved people to be redeemed from the land of *mitzrayim*.

The top and two sides of the door jamb formed the letter *ches*, for *chaim*, life, signifying that the deadly plague would not strike their homes. The blood on the two doorposts represented Moshe and Aharon, the pillars who supported the Jewish nation. The blood on the beam above the door alluded to Hashem, looking down on *klal Yisroel* with benevolence and kindness.

(Beer Mayim Chaim)

Some say the Jews inscribed the letters *yud, hei,* and *vav*, the Divine name of Mercy, on the doorposts: a *yud* on the beam above the door, a *vav* on the right doorpost and a *hei* on the left doorpost.

(Chizkuni)

According to Rabbi Shimon, the blood was placed on the inside of the house, because it says, "I will see the blood" *(Shemos 12:13)*. Only Hashem saw the blood, not the people passing by outside. Rabbi Yitzchak opined that the blood was placed on the outside so the Egyptians should see it, making them feel sick.

(Mechilta)

The Jews prepared for the *Korban Pesach* with celebration and happiness, following Moshe's orders to the letter. The Jews placed complete trust in Moshe, although they were unsure of their fate or what preparations they would need for an extended journey in the desert. As the messenger of Hashem, all that Moshe instructed was for the best.

Eating the Lamb

All Jews gathered to celebrate on the night of the fifteenth of Nissan, a day that would last thirty-six hours. *(Seder HaDoros)* A minimum of ten people per sacrifice assembled to feast on lamb, *matzos*, and bitter herbs. Though the *korban* had to be entirely consumed before midnight, they dined in total relaxation, leaning on their sides like kings. Their preparations were made, their canes poised in their hands, ready to leave at any given moment.

When they were about to begin eating, a Heavenly cloud descended. The cloud lifted and carried the exalted nation to Jerusalem, where they ate a portion of the *Korban Pesach* atop the *Har Habayis*, the Temple Mount. In a flash, they returned to Egypt.

(Targum Yonasan, Yisro)

The Jews were forbidden to leave their homes, since various evil spirits were given free reign to destroy on that night. The blood on their doorposts served as protection against the demons. Safe in their homes, the Jews anxiously awaited the moment of midnight; excitement for the redemption grew with each passing hour. As soon as the clock chimed twelve, Jews all over Egypt began singing praises to Hashem.

The angels, too, wanted to sing G-d's praises as they did every night at midnight. But G-d forbade it. "This is not the right time for you to sing. My children are singing because they are being delivered from *golus*." So all the ministering angels and Heavenly hosts gathered to listen to the Jewish nation singing as one, extolling the great miracles of G-d.

The sun shone all night for the Jews on the eve of the *makah*. *(Zohar)* But after their large meal they slumbered peacefully, fully aware that they must be rested for the trek through the desert the following morning. The high-pitched wails of mourning and suffering Egyptians did not awaken them. While they slept, they

dreamed of everything that was happening that night-Hashem wanted them to know all the miraculous wonders He performed on their behalf.

(Me'am Loez)

The Makah Begins

At the stroke of midnight, Hashem struck down the guardian angel of Egypt. The Jews had weakened the angel's power when they joyously sacrificed their lambs for the sake of Hashem. And then the *makah* began.

Some say that Hashem Himself descended to the land of Egypt to kill the firstborns, because destructive angels do not have the power to differentiate between Jew and non-Jew, or recall precisely who is a firstborn as dictated by Hashem. Or perhaps Hashem killed just the firstborn males, while the angel of death took care of the females. Others say that the angel of death killed all the firstborns. According to the *Zohar*, however, even the angel of death could not be present in a land so full of evil and unholy spirits.

> *G-d and His Heavenly Court came down to Egypt accompanied by ninety thousand terrifying destructive angels. The angels said to G-d, "Master of the universe! Give us free reign, and we will do Your will."*
>
> *Replied G-d, "Leave Me alone; I want to do the will of My children."*
>
> *"But, Master of the universe!" insisted the angels. "When a human king avenges his wrongs, he goes to war surrounded by guards who protect him and keep him safe. So let us and Your children go and take revenge against the Egyptians."*
>
> *But G-d retorted: "I will not have peace until I Myself go down and execute revenge against the Egyptians!"*

The sorcerers, who were comparable to dogs, were powerless against the hand of Hashem attacking them and their families. Their magic was as ineffective as the dogs' barks that night-entirely futile.

Some Egyptian firstborns did not die at the very stroke of midnight. They remained in the throes of death until the break of dawn, so the Jews could witness the deaths of their enemies. *(Mesechtas Simchos)* Other opinions state that all the firstborn children died at midnight, and the first one to die was King Pharaoh's very own firstborn. Egyptians who were not firstborn to either parent were struck with other troublesome ailments. *(Me'am Loez)* Every Egyptian home mourned the death of at least one loved one, sometimes many more.

A woman carrying her first child died along with her unborn fetus. *(Shemos Rabbah)* Many Egyptian women bore children for various men; one woman could have ten firstborn children-and all of them died during the *makah*. Some Egyptian men had a number of children, all firstborn to their young mothers. They, too, all perished.

A firstborn Egyptian in a different country at the time of the *makah* was not forgotten. And any visiting firstborns, even of foreign descent, died that night in Egypt. *(Rashi, Shemos 12:12)* These foreigners took pleasure in the sight of the Jews toiling. Non-Jewish firstborn prisoners, some of whom worked side by side with the Jews, preferred to suffer in their dark, dank cells than be released alongside the Jews. For this they were punished.

Hashem sent dogs to unearth the bones of firstborn Egyptians that had been buried in private homes and yards. The dogs ate the bones of these long-buried Egyptians, causing great emotional pain to their families.

(Sifri Bo 13)

To comfort themselves in times of mourning, Egyptians had a custom of engraving the image of deceased children into a wall of their home. During *makas bechoros*, images of firstborn children

shattered, spraying dust over the entire house, and reopening sad and painful memories for the whole family.

(Sifri Bo 13)

Pharaoh, a firstborn to his parents, was the only undeserving firstborn to remain among the living. Hashem desired him to witness the various miraculous events that occurred at the splitting of the Red Sea.

(Mechilta Bo 13)

Basya, Pharaoh's eldest daughter, was also spared in the merit of rescuing three-month-old Moshe from certain death in the Nile. She was a righteous woman in the eyes of Hashem. *(Shemos Rabbah 18:3)* A few firstborns who sympathized with the plight of the Jews, and even took part in the festivities when the Jews slaughtered the lambs as sacrifices for Hashem, were spared as well.

(Shemos Rabbah 13)

I'll Let Your People Go!

Thousands of Egyptians were dying. Egyptian citizens gathered outside the royal palace to protest the actions of Pharaoh, demanding that he release the Jews immediately.

Moshe Rabbeinu and Aharon HaKohen lived in Goshen, quite a distance from the capital city, but on the night of *makas bechoros*, Moshe and Aharon slept near the royal palace. They wanted to be readily available for Pharaoh when he would come running wildly through the streets in the middle of the night.

And so it was. Pharaoh and all his servants ran blindly, desperately searching for Moshe and his brother Aharon. They knocked on the doors of Jewish homes and checked the gates of the city. They shouted for Moshe and Aharon in pained, bitter tones.

The Jews mocked Pharaoh. When he asked them where Moshe Rabbeinu was, they directed him to some wild destination. "Oh, he's on this and this block, in such and such a house." When Pharaoh arrived there, he would find another helpful Jew, who would tell him, "Moshe Rabbeinu lives not here, but there and there."

Pharaoh ran all around town. Finally, he began yelling at the top of his lungs, "Moshe! Aharon! I grant you my full permission to take the Jews out of Egypt. Take your cattle-take *my* cattle! Please, I beg of you, pray to Hashem to end this *makah*! I fear for my life!"

Moshe Rabbeinu and Aharon HaKohen ignored the pleading voice of Pharaoh. They knew Pharaoh was still the same evil person he had always been, capable of going back on his word. Pharaoh intended for the Jews to leave Egypt for three days only.

The unruly mob of zealous Egyptians was growing larger and larger, ready to lynch their leader. A panicked Pharaoh enlisted the help of his strongmen to locate Moshe Rabbeinu and Aharon HaKohen.

Witness to Pharaoh's pitiful plight, Basya stepped in to help her father find Moshe. The leader of the Jewish people was enjoying the festive holiday meal, surrounded by family, friends and acquaintances. "I saved your life and raised you like my own child. You lived in my father's palace! Is this how you show your gratitude?" Basya reproached Moshe.

"It's your father's own fault," Moshe answered. "He brought this calamity upon himself. He refused to listen to G-d."

Pharaoh threw himself at Moshe's feet. "I beg you," he pleaded, "please leave the country and take your people with you."

"Now you see I was right," Moshe mocked him. "I told you that you and your officials would come and bow down to me!"

Pharaoh had to gulp back his pride not to respond to the obvious disrespect. "Go, go. You are free. Please go!" he implored.

"We have orders not to leave our houses until morning," Moshe replied. "We are not thieves who sneak away in the dark. Just be patient and wait until morning. Why, only a few days ago you refused to let us go. And now you can't wait a few hours!"

"I am afraid," Pharaoh replied meekly. "I'm afraid I will die. I myself am a firstborn."

"Oh, not to worry," Moshe assured him. "You will not die tonight. A fate far worse is in store for you."

"People are dying without letup! Please leave as soon as possible. Every minute counts!"

"I have one suggestion," Moshe countered. "Announce to all the Jews in Egypt that they are free."

Following Moshe's advice, Pharaoh proclaimed, "You are free to go! Your servitude has ended. From now on you are servants of no one but G-d. Go and worship Him!" Pharaoh's voice miraculously resounded throughout Egypt. As soon as the declaration was heard the Egyptian firstborns stopped dying.

Leaving the Land of Slavery

Once the royal word was given, the Egyptians turned their attention from Pharaoh to the Jews, encouraging them to leave as quickly as possible. They brought out their cattle and wagons, loading the Jews up with valuables. A Jew asked for one precious diamond; the Egyptian gave two. *(Rashi, Shemos 12:36)* It took ninety donkeys to carry the smallest haul a Jew had gathered. All the wealth Yosef had accumulated during the seven years of famine fell into the hands of his descendants.

A king asked his wise men, "What is the most powerful force in the world?"

The first wise man answered, "A woman is the most powerful force in the world. Eve brought death to the world by persuading Adam

to eat of the forbidden fruit. And it was a woman, Delilah, who subdued Shimshon, the strongest man that ever lived."

The second wise man offered, "Honor is the most powerful force in the world."

"You are quite right," the king declared. "Both women and honor are indeed powerful forces. But I think that the most irresistible force in all the world is money. In the final analysis, money is at the bottom of all wars, conflicts, and hostilities between individuals and nations."

"Egypt pressed the people strongly" *(Shemos 12:33)*. The Egyptians used the strongest possible force to make the Jews leave Egypt-money. The Jews were eager to leave, but they tarried, because G-d had prohibited them from leaving their homes until morning. So the Egyptians eagerly gave them their gold and silver, the most powerful means of persuasion, hoping it would encourage them to leave in a hurry.

(B'nei Yissos'chor, Nissan 12)

While the Jews amassed valuable articles, Moshe Rabbeinu was occupied with a very holy task. Mindful of the oath by which Yosef had bound his descendants, Moshe had been searching vainly for Yosef's coffin to accompany them to the Holy Land.

Elderly Serach, the daughter of Asher, met up with Moshe Rabbeinu. "Moshe, you look weary and worn-out. What's troubling you?"

"For three days and three nights I've been looking for Yosef's coffin," Moshe replied, exasperated. "And no one can tell me where it is."

"Come with me," Serach said soothingly. "I'll show you where it is hidden."

She led Moshe to the bank of the Nile. The Egyptians had deposited Yosef's coffin in the middle of the river to prevent the Jews'

escape. The tzaddik's watery grave brought blessing to Nile, making it overflow and irrigate the land.

Moshe called across the river in a loud voice, "Yosef, the hour of redemption has arrived! The Shechinah is waiting for you! The Jewish nation and the Clouds of Glory are waiting for you. You made us swear to take your bones with us. Pray that your coffin should rise to the surface. If your coffin comes afloat, we will take you with us; otherwise, we are absolved of our oath."

Moshe held a shard of rock in his hand. The shard was inscribed with Hashem's name, and the words, "Alei shor, rise up, O ox." Yosef is compared to an ox (Devarim 33:17). Moshe threw the shard into the water. Immediately, the coffin floated to the surface. Now the Jews could leave.

The Jews were leaving Egypt! For the Egyptians, there was a long-overdue sense of relief. "Egypt rejoiced when they left, for their fear had fallen on them" *(Tehillim 105:38)*. It was the height of the month of the ram, their god. And their god did nothing. The Jews' G-d ruled the world. No river, animal or rock had any power. They returned dejectedly to their homes, where their families-what was left of them-awaited.

There was a great dog carved into the widest gate that surrounded Egypt. In case a Jew attempted to escape, the sorcerers had empowered the dog to emit a howl that could be heard all over Egypt. But as the Jews exited Egypt en masse at this particular gate, not a sound was heard from the mouth of the great dog. *(Me'am Loez)* Pharaoh and his Egyptian followers shook their heads in amazement.

The hand of Hashem had shown itself in Egypt. Ultimately, all power and supremacy is His. Even Pharaoh himself proclaimed, "Nation of Israel, you are no longer my slaves. You are now the servants of Hashem!" The Jewish people left Egypt in broad daylight in full view of their former masters, revealing the might of Hashem and His sovereignty over the entire world.

Reb Yossi Haglili

רַבִּי יוֹסֵי הַגְּלִילִי אוֹמֵר, מִנַּיִן אַתָּה אוֹמֵר שֶׁלָּקוּ הַמִּצְרִים בְּמִצְרַיִם עֶשֶׂר מַכּוֹת וְעַל הַיָּם לָקוּ חֲמִשִּׁים מַכּוֹת. בְּמִצְרַיִם מָה הוּא אוֹמֵר, וַיֹּאמְרוּ הַחַרְטֻמִּים אֶל פַּרְעֹה אֶצְבַּע אֱלֹהִים הִיא. וְעַל הַיָּם מָה הוּא אוֹמֵר, וַיַּרְא יִשְׂרָאֵל אֶת הַיָּד הַגְּדוֹלָה אֲשֶׁר עָשָׂה יְהוָֹה בְּמִצְרַיִם וַיִּירְאוּ הָעָם אֶת יְהוָֹה וַיַּאֲמִינוּ בַּיהוָֹה וּבְמֹשֶׁה עַבְדּוֹ. כַּמָּה לָקוּ בְּאֶצְבַּע עֶשֶׂר מַכּוֹת. אֱמוֹר מֵעַתָּה, בְּמִצְרַיִם לָקוּ עֶשֶׂר מַכּוֹת וְעַל הַיָּם לָקוּ חֲמִשִּׁים מַכּוֹת:

רַבִּי אֱלִיעֶזֶר אוֹמֵר, מִנַּיִן שֶׁכָּל מַכָּה וּמַכָּה שֶׁהֵבִיא הַקָּדוֹשׁ בָּרוּךְ הוּא עַל הַמִּצְרִים בְּמִצְרַיִם הָיְתָה שֶׁל אַרְבַּע מַכּוֹת. שֶׁנֶּאֱמַר, יְשַׁלַּח בָּם חֲרוֹן אַפּוֹ עֶבְרָה וָזַעַם וְצָרָה מִשְׁלַחַת מַלְאֲכֵי רָעִים. עֶבְרָה אַחַת. וָזַעַם שְׁתַּיִם. וְצָרָה שָׁלֹשׁ. מִשְׁלַחַת מַלְאֲכֵי רָעִים אַרְבַּע. אֱמוֹר מֵעַתָּה, בְּמִצְרַיִם לָקוּ אַרְבָּעִים מַכּוֹת וְעַל הַיָּם לָקוּ מָאתַיִם מַכּוֹת:

רַבִּי עֲקִיבָא אוֹמֵר, מִנַּיִן שֶׁכָּל מַכָּה וּמַכָּה שֶׁהֵבִיא הַקָּדוֹשׁ בָּרוּךְ הוּא עַל הַמִּצְרִים בְּמִצְרַיִם הָיְתָה שֶׁל חָמֵשׁ מַכּוֹת. שֶׁנֶּאֱמַר, יְשַׁלַּח בָּם חֲרוֹן אַפּוֹ עֶבְרָה וָזַעַם וְצָרָה מִשְׁלַחַת מַלְאֲכֵי רָעִים. חֲרוֹן אַפּוֹ אַחַת. עֶבְרָה שְׁתַּיִם. וָזַעַם שָׁלֹשׁ. וְצָרָה אַרְבַּע. מִשְׁלַחַת מַלְאֲכֵי רָעִים חָמֵשׁ. אֱמוֹר מֵעַתָּה בְּמִצְרַיִם לָקוּ חֲמִשִּׁים מַכּוֹת וְעַל הַיָּם לָקוּ חֲמִשִּׁים וּמָאתַיִם מַכּוֹת:

כַּמָּה מַעֲלוֹת טוֹבוֹת לַמָּקוֹם עָלֵינוּ:

אִלּוּ הוֹצִיאָנוּ מִמִּצְרַיִם, וְלֹא עָשָׂה בָהֶם שְׁפָטִים דַּיֵּנוּ:

אִלּוּ עָשָׂה בָהֶם שְׁפָטִים, וְלֹא עָשָׂה בֵאלֹהֵיהֶם דַּיֵּנוּ:

אִלּוּ עָשָׂה בֵאלֹהֵיהֶם, וְלֹא הָרַג אֶת בְּכוֹרֵיהֶם דַּיֵּנוּ:

אִלּוּ הָרַג אֶת בְּכוֹרֵיהֶם, וְלֹא נָתַן לָנוּ אֶת מָמוֹנָם דַּיֵּנוּ:

אִלּוּ נָתַן לָנוּ אֶת מָמוֹנָם, וְלֹא קָרַע לָנוּ אֶת הַיָּם דַּיֵּנוּ:

אִלּוּ קָרַע לָנוּ אֶת הַיָּם, וְלֹא הֶעֱבִירָנוּ בְתוֹכוֹ בֶּחָרָבָה דַּיֵּנוּ:

אִלּוּ הֶעֱבִירָנוּ בְתוֹכוֹ בֶּחָרָבָה, וְלֹא שִׁקַּע צָרֵינוּ בְּתוֹכוֹ דַּיֵּנוּ:

אִלּוּ שִׁקַּע צָרֵינוּ בְּתוֹכוֹ, וְלֹא סִפֵּק צָרְכֵּנוּ בַּמִּדְבָּר אַרְבָּעִים שָׁנָה דַּיֵּנוּ:

אִלּוּ סִפֵּק צָרְכֵּנוּ בַּמִּדְבָּר אַרְבָּעִים שָׁנָה, וְלֹא הֶאֱכִילָנוּ אֶת הַמָּן דַּיֵּנוּ:

אִלּוּ הֶאֱכִילָנוּ אֶת הַמָּן, וְלֹא נָתַן לָנוּ אֶת הַשַּׁבָּת דַּיֵּנוּ:

אִלּוּ נָתַן לָנוּ אֶת הַשַּׁבָּת, וְלֹא קֵרְבָנוּ לִפְנֵי הַר סִינַי דַּיֵּנוּ:

אִלּוּ קֵרְבָנוּ לִפְנֵי הַר סִינַי, וְלֹא נָתַן לָנוּ אֶת הַתּוֹרָה דַּיֵּנוּ:

אִלּוּ נָתַן לָנוּ אֶת הַתּוֹרָה, וְלֹא הִכְנִיסָנוּ לְאֶרֶץ יִשְׂרָאֵל דַּיֵּנוּ:

אִלּוּ הִכְנִיסָנוּ לְאֶרֶץ יִשְׂרָאֵל, וְלֹא בָנָה לָנוּ אֶת בֵּית הַבְּחִירָה דַּיֵּנוּ:

עַל אַחַת כַּמָּה וְכַמָּה טוֹבָה כְּפוּלָה וּמְכֻפֶּלֶת לַמָּקוֹם עָלֵינוּ. שֶׁהוֹצִיאָנוּ מִמִּצְרַיִם. וְעָשָׂה בָהֶם שְׁפָטִים. וְעָשָׂה בֵאלֹהֵיהֶם. וְהָרַג אֶת בְּכוֹרֵיהֶם. וְנָתַן לָנוּ אֶת מָמוֹנָם. וְקָרַע לָנוּ אֶת הַיָּם. וְהֶעֱבִירָנוּ בְתוֹכוֹ בֶּחָרָבָה. וְשִׁקַּע צָרֵינוּ בְּתוֹכוֹ. וְסִפֵּק צָרְכֵּנוּ בַּמִּדְבָּר אַרְבָּעִים שָׁנָה. וְהֶאֱכִילָנוּ אֶת הַמָּן. וְנָתַן לָנוּ אֶת הַשַּׁבָּת. וְקֵרְבָנוּ לִפְנֵי הַר סִינַי. וְנָתַן לָנוּ אֶת הַתּוֹרָה. וְהִכְנִיסָנוּ לְאֶרֶץ יִשְׂרָאֵל. וּבָנָה לָנוּ אֶת בֵּית הַבְּחִירָה לְכַפֵּר עַל כָּל עֲוֹנוֹתֵינוּ:

Some congregations recite the Haggadah on the Great Shabbas (the Shabbas preceding Pesach) from after 'Ma Nishtanah' until here.

Rabban Gamliel

רַבָּן גַּמְלִיאֵל הָיָה אוֹמֵר, כָּל שֶׁלֹּא אָמַר שְׁלֹשָׁה דְבָרִים אֵלּוּ בַּפֶּסַח לֹא יָצָא יְדֵי חוֹבָתוֹ, וְאֵלּוּ הֵן:

פֶּסַח. מַצָּה. וּמָרוֹר:

One should look at the bone on the Seder plate (but not point at it or lift it), and then say the following:

פֶּסַח שֶׁהָיוּ אֲבוֹתֵינוּ אוֹכְלִים בִּזְמַן שֶׁבֵּית הַמִּקְדָּשׁ הָיָה קַיָּם עַל שׁוּם מָה. עַל שׁוּם שֶׁפָּסַח הַקָּדוֹשׁ בָּרוּךְ הוּא עַל בָּתֵּי אֲבוֹתֵינוּ בְּמִצְרַיִם. שֶׁנֶּאֱמַר, וַאֲמַרְתֶּם זֶבַח פֶּסַח הוּא לַיהוָֹה אֲשֶׁר פָּסַח עַל בָּתֵּי בְנֵי יִשְׂרָאֵל בְּמִצְרַיִם בְּנָגְפּוֹ אֶת מִצְרַיִם וְאֶת בָּתֵּינוּ הִצִּיל וַיִּקֹּד הָעָם וַיִּשְׁתַּחֲווּ:

The Matzah is lifted and displayed for all to see and the following paragraph is recited.

מַצָּה זוּ שֶׁאָנוּ אוֹכְלִים עַל שׁוּם מָה. עַל שׁוּם שֶׁלֹּא הִסְפִּיק בְּצֵקָם שֶׁל אֲבוֹתֵינוּ לְהַחֲמִיץ עַד שֶׁנִּגְלָה עֲלֵיהֶם מֶלֶךְ מַלְכֵי הַמְּלָכִים הַקָּדוֹשׁ בָּרוּךְ הוּא וּגְאָלָם. שֶׁנֶּאֱמַר, וַיֹּאפוּ אֶת הַבָּצֵק אֲשֶׁר הוֹצִיאוּ מִמִּצְרַיִם עֻגֹת מַצּוֹת כִּי לֹא חָמֵץ כִּי גֹרְשׁוּ מִמִּצְרַיִם וְלֹא יָכְלוּ לְהִתְמַהְמֵהַּ וְגַם צֵדָה לֹא עָשׂוּ לָהֶם:

The Maror is lifted and displayed for all to see and the following paragraph is recited.

מָרוֹר זֶה שֶׁאָנוּ אוֹכְלִים עַל שׁוּם מָה. עַל שׁוּם שֶׁמָּרְרוּ הַמִּצְרִים אֶת חַיֵּי אֲבוֹתֵינוּ בְּמִצְרָיִם. שֶׁנֶּאֱמַר, וַיְמָרְרוּ אֶת חַיֵּיהֶם בַּעֲבֹדָה קָשָׁה בְּחֹמֶר וּבִלְבֵנִים וּבְכָל עֲבֹדָה בַּשָּׂדֶה אֵת כָּל עֲבֹדָתָם אֲשֶׁר עָבְדוּ בָהֶם בְּפָרֶךְ:

בְּכָל דּוֹר וָדוֹר חַיָּב אָדָם לִרְאוֹת אֶת עַצְמוֹ כְּאִלּוּ הוּא יָצָא מִמִּצְרָיִם. שֶׁנֶּאֱמַר, וְהִגַּדְתָּ לְבִנְךָ בַּיּוֹם הַהוּא לֵאמֹר בַּעֲבוּר זֶה עָשָׂה יְהֹוָה לִי בְּצֵאתִי מִמִּצְרָיִם. לֹא אֶת אֲבוֹתֵינוּ בִּלְבָד גָּאַל הַקָּדוֹשׁ בָּרוּךְ הוּא, אֶלָּא אַף אוֹתָנוּ גָּאַל עִמָּהֶם. שֶׁנֶּאֱמַר, וְאוֹתָנוּ הוֹצִיא מִשָּׁם לְמַעַן הָבִיא אוֹתָנוּ לָתֶת לָנוּ אֶת הָאָרֶץ אֲשֶׁר נִשְׁבַּע לַאֲבוֹתֵינוּ:

Rabban Gamliel

Saying Why

"Rabban Gamliel used to say, 'Anyone who did not say these three things on Pesach has not fulfilled his obligation. And these three are: *Pesach*, *matzah* and *marror*.'"

Not only do we have to mention these three things, we must explain the reasons. If we do not state the reasons for the *Pesach*, *matzah* and *marror*, we have not fulfilled the commandment of telling the story of the Exodus from Egypt. *(Rambam, Hilchos Chametz Umatzah 7:6)* During the time of the *Beis Hamikdash*, the reasons for eating *Pesach*, *matzah* and *marror* had to be stated for a person to fulfill his obligation.

(Avudraham, Kol Bo 51)

A differing opinion maintains that Rabban Gamliel meant that one who does not enumerate the reasons has fulfilled the basic Torah obligation-this can be accomplished with just a few words-but he has not fulfilled the *mitzvah* with adornment.

(Ran, Pesachim 116a)

The Torah specifies the reason for the *Korban Pesach*, "And you shall say it is a *Pesach* sacrifice to G-d, because He passed (*pasach*) over the houses of the Children of Israel in Egypt" *(Shemos 12:27)*. Since the Torah commands us to eat *matzah* and *marror* together with the *Korban Pesach*, we can extrapolate that we should give reasons for eating them as well.

(Tosfos, Pesachim 116a)

Offerings in the *Beis Hamikdash* are accepted even if they were offered without explicit intent that they are for the sake of Hashem. *(Zevachim 2a)* There are two exceptions to this rule: the *Korban Chatas*, offering to atone for an inadvertent sin, and the *Korban Pesach*. These sacrifices are invalid if they were not offered explicitly for the sake of Hashem.

The *Korban Chatas* and *Korban Pesach* have one common demoninator: they are offered to draw nearer to Hashem's holiness. A person who has inadvertently sinned is greatly distanced from Hashem. The further from Hashem a person has become, the closer to Him one needs to get. The *Korban Chatas* has to be offered with an explicit intention that it is for Hashem's sake, to enable one to return to Him as closely as possible.

Rabban Gamliel says that the same applies to the *Korban Pesach*. It has to be explicitly for Hashem's sake, for it brings us closer to His holiness. Hashem Himself "passed over" the Israelite homes to liberate them from Egypt as soon as possible. Many of them had been worshipping idols and had become very distant from Hashem's holiness. The *Korban Pesach* was the vehicle used to draw these people close to G-d, and so it must be offered with specific intent.

The same applies to eating *marror*, the bitter herbs. The *marror* is a reminder of how the Israelites had strayed from Hashem's holiness. The Talmud says that originally the Egyptians gave them lighter work to do, and only later assigned them heavy work. This means that originally the Jews were permitted to serve Hashem, but later they were prohibited from doing so. As the Israelites grew further and

further away from Hashem, the heavier and more bitter their workload became.

The Torah tells us to eat *matzos* "so you will remember the day of your leaving the land of Egypt all the days of your life" *(Devarim 16:3)*. Realize that Hashem has taken you far away from the spiritual impurity of Egypt and brought you close to His holiness. How do we draw near to Hashem? By fulfilling His commandments-*Pesach, matzah, marror.*

(Maharasha, Chiddushei Halachos, Pesachim 116a)

The Order

If the *marror* is a remembrance of the bitterly heavy workload the Egyptians piled on the Jews, why does it come last? First the Jews were oppressed as slaves, then G-d "*pasach*-passed over" the homes of the Israelites, represented by the *Korban Pesach*. The heavy work the Israelites were subjected to actually accelerated their redemption. G-d told Avraham that his decsendants would be exiled for 400 years *(Beraishis 15:13)*, but because of the bitter oppression, the Jews spent only 210 years in Egypt. The *marror*, the bitter enslavement, was actually a part of the redemption process, just like the *Korban Pesach* and the *matzah*.

Rabban Gamliel maintains that one who does not recite *Pesach, matzah, marror* in their proper order implies that he does not consider the Israelites' heavy work in Egypt to be part of the process of their redemption. If so, the Jews had not lived out the prescribed 400 years in exile-and they were not yet entitled to leave Egypt! Such a person "has not fulfilled his obligation." He has a personal obligation to complete his years of enslavement in Egypt-he must return to Egypt to complete the 190 years missing from the full four hundred year term!

(Tzelach, Pesachim 116a)

Songs of Praise

The Matzos are coverd and the cup is held.

לְפִיכָךְ אֲנַחְנוּ חַיָּבִים לְהוֹדוֹת לְהַלֵּל לְשַׁבֵּחַ לְפָאֵר לְרוֹמֵם לְהַדֵּר לְבָרֵךְ לְעַלֵּה וּלְקַלֵּס לְמִי שֶׁעָשָׂה לַאֲבוֹתֵינוּ וְלָנוּ אֶת כָּל הַנִּסִּים הָאֵלּוּ. הוֹצִיאָנוּ מֵעַבְדוּת לְחֵרוּת, מִיָּגוֹן לְשִׂמְחָה, וּמֵאֵבֶל לְיוֹם טוֹב, וּמֵאֲפֵלָה לְאוֹר גָּדוֹל, וּמִשִּׁעְבּוּד לִגְאֻלָּה, וְנֹאמַר לְפָנָיו שִׁירָה חֲדָשָׁה הַלְלוּיָהּ:

Songs of Praise

Blessed is Our Redeemer

Toward the end of *Maggid* we begin to sing the praises of Hashem, cups raised, for "song is said only over a cup of wine" *(Berachos 35a)*.

(Tur 473)

Maggid concludes with a blessing similar to the seventh blessing in our daily *Shemoneh Esrei*-"Blessed are You, Hashem, *goel Yisroel*-Who redeems Israel," in the present tense. At the *Seder*, we bless, "that He has redeemed us and redeemed our ancestors from Egypt," in past tense. We believe with perfect faith that G-d redeemed Israel on Pesach thousands of years ago, and He continues to redeem Jews from their current strife every day.

This is a favorable moment on High for each individual to pray for redemption from his personal form of exile. Just as we believe that He redeemed our ancestors from Egypt, we also believe that He will soon redeem us from our present exile. Amen.

(Rabbi Avraham Yehoshua Heschel of Apta, Yalkut Ohev Yisroel, Likkutim)

The cup is replaced and the matzos uncovered.

הַלְלוּיָהּ הַלְלוּ עַבְדֵי יְהֹוָה הַלְלוּ אֶת שֵׁם יְהֹוָה: יְהִי שֵׁם יְהֹוָה מְבֹרָךְ מֵעַתָּה וְעַד עוֹלָם: מִמִּזְרַח שֶׁמֶשׁ עַד מְבוֹאוֹ מְהֻלָּל שֵׁם יְהֹוָה: רָם עַל כָּל גּוֹיִם יְהֹוָה עַל הַשָּׁמַיִם כְּבוֹדוֹ: מִי כַּיהֹוָה אֱלֹהֵינוּ הַמַּגְבִּיהִי לָשָׁבֶת: הַמַּשְׁפִּילִי לִרְאוֹת בַּשָּׁמַיִם וּבָאָרֶץ: מְקִימִי מֵעָפָר דָּל מֵאַשְׁפֹּת יָרִים אֶבְיוֹן: לְהוֹשִׁיבִי עִם נְדִיבִים עִם נְדִיבֵי עַמּוֹ: מוֹשִׁיבִי עֲקֶרֶת הַבַּיִת אֵם הַבָּנִים שְׂמֵחָה הַלְלוּיָהּ:

בְּצֵאת יִשְׂרָאֵל מִמִּצְרָיִם בֵּית יַעֲקֹב מֵעַם לֹעֵז: הָיְתָה יְהוּדָה לְקָדְשׁוֹ יִשְׂרָאֵל מַמְשְׁלוֹתָיו: הַיָּם רָאָה וַיָּנֹס הַיַּרְדֵּן יִסֹּב לְאָחוֹר: הֶהָרִים רָקְדוּ כְאֵילִים גְּבָעוֹת כִּבְנֵי צֹאן: מַה לְּךָ הַיָּם כִּי תָנוּס הַיַּרְדֵּן תִּסֹּב לְאָחוֹר: הֶהָרִים תִּרְקְדוּ כְאֵילִים גְּבָעוֹת כִּבְנֵי צֹאן: מִלִּפְנֵי אָדוֹן חוּלִי אָרֶץ מִלִּפְנֵי אֱלוֹהַּ יַעֲקֹב: הַהֹפְכִי הַצּוּר אֲגַם מָיִם חַלָּמִישׁ לְמַעְיְנוֹ מָיִם:

The Matzos are covered and the cup is held.

בָּרוּךְ אַתָּה יְהֹוָה אֱלֹהֵינוּ מֶלֶךְ הָעוֹלָם, אֲשֶׁר גְּאָלָנוּ וְגָאַל אֶת אֲבוֹתֵינוּ מִמִּצְרַיִם, וְהִגִּיעָנוּ הַלַּיְלָה הַזֶּה לֶאֱכָל בּוֹ מַצָּה וּמָרוֹר. כֵּן יְהֹוָה אֱלֹהֵינוּ וֵאלֹהֵי אֲבוֹתֵינוּ יַגִּיעֵנוּ לְמוֹעֲדִים וְלִרְגָלִים אֲחֵרִים הַבָּאִים לִקְרָאתֵנוּ לְשָׁלוֹם, שְׂמֵחִים בְּבִנְיַן עִירֶךָ, וְשָׂשִׂים בַּעֲבוֹדָתֶךָ, וְנֹאכַל שָׁם מִן הַזְּבָחִים וּמִן הַפְּסָחִים (*On Saturday nights say:* מִן הַפְּסָחִים וּמִן הַזְּבָחִים) אֲשֶׁר יַגִּיעַ דָּמָם עַל קִיר מִזְבַּחֲךָ לְרָצוֹן וְנוֹדֶה לְךָ שִׁיר חָדָשׁ עַל גְּאֻלָּתֵנוּ וְעַל פְּדוּת נַפְשֵׁנוּ:

בָּרוּךְ אַתָּה יְהֹוָה גָּאַל יִשְׂרָאֵל:

הִנְנִי מוּכָן וּמְזוּמָּן לְקַיֵּם מִצְוַת כּוֹס שֵׁנִי שֶׁל אַרְבַּע כּוֹסוֹת. לְשֵׁם יִחוּד קוּדְשָׁא בְּרִיךְ הוּא וּשְׁכִינְתֵּיהּ עַל יְדֵי הַהוּא טָמִיר וְנֶעְלָם בְּשֵׁם כָּל יִשְׂרָאֵל: וִיהִי נֹעַם אֲדֹנָי אֱלֹהֵינוּ עָלֵינוּ וּמַעֲשֵׂה יָדֵינוּ כּוֹנְנָה עָלֵינוּ וּמַעֲשֵׂה יָדֵינוּ כּוֹנְנֵהוּ:

בָּרוּךְ אַתָּה יְהֹוָה אֱלֹהֵינוּ מֶלֶךְ הָעוֹלָם בּוֹרֵא פְּרִי הַגָּפֶן:

The second cup is drunk while leaning on the left side.

רחצה

Wash the hands and recite the blessing.

בָּרוּךְ אַתָּה יְהֹוָה אֱלֹהֵינוּ מֶלֶךְ הָעוֹלָם אֲשֶׁר קִדְּשָׁנוּ בְּמִצְוֹתָיו וְצִוָּנוּ עַל נְטִילַת יָדָיִם:

Rachtzah

Washing Our Hands-Again

Although we have already washed our hands before *Karpas*, we wash them again now before the meal. While our minds were preoccupied with the story of the Exodus we were not taking special care to keep our hands clean. This diversion is considered an interruption between washing and eating and we are required to wash again.

(Pesachim 116a)

מוציא

Hold all three Matzahs, and recite:

הִנְנִי מוּכָן וּמְזוּמָן לְקַיֵּם מִצְוַת אֲכִילַת מַצָּה לְשֵׁם יִחוּד קוּדְשָׁא בְּרִיךְ הוּא וּשְׁכִינְתֵּיהּ עַל יְדֵי הַהוּא טָמִיר וְנֶעְלָם בְּשֵׁם כָּל יִשְׂרָאֵל: וִיהִי נוֹעַם אֲדֹנָי אֱלֹהֵינוּ עָלֵינוּ וּמַעֲשֵׂה יָדֵינוּ כּוֹנְנָה עָלֵינוּ וּמַעֲשֵׂה יָדֵינוּ כּוֹנְנֵהוּ:

בָּרוּךְ אַתָּה יְהוָה אֱלֹהֵינוּ מֶלֶךְ הָעוֹלָם הַמּוֹצִיא לֶחֶם מִן הָאָרֶץ:

Motzi

Which Matzah?

Authorities disagree as to which two of the three *matzos* we use for *lechem mishneh*. Some say that the *lechem oni*-the broken *matzah*-replaces one of the two loaves. Others say that the *lechem oni* is in addition to the usual two whole loaves. To fulfill both opinions, we hold the broken *matzah* between the two complete ones.

(Shulchan Aruch, Orach Chaim 475)

Which Berachah?

There are two blessings on the *matzah*: the usual *hamotzi* blessing and the special blessing for the *mitzvah* of *matzah*, *al achilas matzah*. The rule is, "Frequent and infrequent, frequent takes precedence" *(Pesachim 114a)*. *Hamotzi* is said all year round, whereas *al achilas matzah* is said only on the evening of Pesach. *Hamotzi* takes precedence; it is recited first.

מצה

The bottom Matzah is put down and the following blessing is recited. (Bearing in mind that the blessing shall also apply to the matzah of the Korech and Afikomen):

בָּרוּךְ אַתָּה יְהֹוָה אֱלֹהֵינוּ מֶלֶךְ הָעוֹלָם אֲשֶׁר קִדְּשָׁנוּ בְּמִצְוֹתָיו וְצִוָּנוּ עַל אֲכִילַת מַצָּה:

One them eats the matzah while leaning on the left side.

Matzah

The Obligation

It is a positive commandment of the Torah to eat a *k'zayis* (the size of an olive) of *matzah* on the first evening of Pesach, as the Torah says, "On the first day, on the fourteenth day of the month, in the evening you shall eat *matzos*" *(Shemos 12:18)*. The Torah also commands *(ibid. 12:8)* that the meat of the *Korban Pesach* should be eaten together with *matzos* and *marror*. Although there is no *Korban Pesach* today and the *mitzvah* of *marror* is no longer from the Torah, there is still an independent Torah obligation to eat *matzah* on the first night of Pesach.

(Pesachim 120a)

This is the only Torah obligation to eat that is applicable today. We can no longer eat the *Korban Pesach* or other offerings sacrificed in the *Beis Hamikdash*. *Terumah,* produce given to the *kohanim,* is discarded. *Maaser sheni*, tithes of produce eaten by the owner, no

longer have to be consumed in Jerusalem. Only the *mitzvah* of eating *matzah* remains today.

(Responsa Chasam Sofer, Choshen Mishpat 196, Hashmatos)

Two K'zeisim

At the outset, we should be strict and eat not just one but two *k'zeisim* of *matzah*, one from the top complete *matzah* and one from the second broken piece of *matzah*.

In order to fulfill the obligation, the *k'zayis* must be eaten from the *matzah* upon which *al achilas matzah* was recited. Some authorities maintain that this is the top one; others hold that this is the broken one. To fulfill both opinions, we eat a *k'zayis* from both. *(Shulchan Aruch HaRav 575:5)* The Vilna Gaon maintains that we fulfill the *mitzvah* of *matzah* with the *lechem oni*, the broken *matzah*, so we eat the *k'zayis* from the broken *matzah* first.

(Gra)

As with all blessings before eating food, we recite *hamotzi* to thank Hashem for the food He has given us before we derive benefit from it. When we recite *hamotzi* at the *Seder*, we imply that we will derive physical benefit from the *matzah*. On the other hand, the Talmud teaches that if a person eats the *Korban Pesach* to derive physical pleasure from the tasty meat, and not to fulfill the *mitzvah*, he has not fulfilled the *mitzvah* in the best way. *(Nazir 23a)* The same applies to the *mitzvah* of *matzah*.

Hamotzi is recited for the physical enjoyment of the food; *al achilas matzah* must be recited solely for the sake of the *mitzvah*. To avoid this contradiction, one *k'zayis* is designated for our physical benefit, and the second *k'zayis* to fulfill the *mitzvah* of *achilas matzah* with pure intentions.

(Haggadas Ohr Hachama 19-20)

The Torah commands, "And *matzos* upon bitter herbs shall they eat it" *(Shemos 12:8)*. Perhaps the Torah is indicating that we should eat the *matzos* the same way we eat the *marror*. Because of its bitter taste, the *marror* provides no physical enjoyment. The *matzah*, too, should be eaten without any enjoyment, solely to fulfill the *mitzvah*.

(Yeitav Panim, Shabbos Hagadol 28)

Food of Faith

The Torah introduces the *mitzvah* of *matzah* with a warning and an explanation. "And you shall guard the *matzos* [from leavening], for in the middle of this day [15 Nissan] I have taken out your legions from the land of Egypt" *(Shemos 12:17)*.

First the Torah instructs us to "guard the *matzos*," do not allow them to rise or become *chametz* on their own. Make sure they maintain the same flat shape as they were originally made. Why? "For in the middle of this day ..." *(ibid.)*. Because on the fifteenth of Nissan, Hashem took the Jews out of Egypt.

The zodiac of Nissan is represented by a lamb, the animal worshipped by the Egyptians. In the middle of the month, in the middle of the day-at the very height of the month, when the lamb should have had the most power, when their god should have been able to defend them against other powers of the world-the Egyptians' slaves walked out of their land right under their noses. Their precious lamb wielded no power that day. Only Hashem reigned supreme.

When eating the *matzah*, we should focus on Hashem's sovereignty. He and only He rules the world; there are no other powers. Even things that seem natural are from Hashem.

The Zohar calls *matzah* "food of faith" *(Zohar II 183b, 41a)* because *matzah* remains flat, as when it was first made-nothing happens to it on its own. Likewise the world, including the normal

processes of nature, are created and controlled by Hashem Himself. Only Hashem can make bread flat, or puffy and soft. While eating the *matzah*, one should focus on proper faith in Hashem, acknowledging that there is no power other than His.

(Bnei Yissaschar, Nissan, Maamar 4, Drush 1)

The Torah juxtaposes the *mitzvah* of *matzah*, remembering the Exodus, and *tefillin*. "And it shall be for you a sign on your arm and a reminder between your eyes [*tefillin*] so Hashem's Torah may be in your mouth-for with a strong hand Hashem took you out of Egypt" *(Shemos 13:9)*.

How is Hashem's Torah in our mouths? We fulfill the *mitzvah* of *matzah*-we eat the *matzah*. On Pesach this is the sign of our acceptance of G-d's sovereignty, just as *tefillin* are the sign of accepting the yoke of Heaven during the week.

(Maor Vashemesh)

Round and Sweet

The Torah recounts, "They baked the dough that they took out of Egypt into *ugos matzos*-unleavened cakes" *(Shemos 12:39)*. "*Ugos*" denotes a circular shape. *(Mahari Asad, Orach Chaim 159) Matzah* is also called the *lechem oni*, bread of poverty. Poverty is a wheel of fortune that turns; sometimes resting on one person, then rotating to another.

(Orach Chaim)

"In the evening [*ba'erev*] you shall eat *matzos*" *(Shemos 12:18)*. *Erev*, evening, can also be read *areiv*, sweet. The Torah tells us to cherish the *mitzvah* of eating *matzah*. It should be sweet, for we can fulfill this commandment only once a year.

(Tiferes Shlomo, Pesach)

In the Merit of Matzah

The mitzvah of eating matzah is so great that it reaches through the highest Heavenly worlds, where they hope and wait expectantly for the Jews to consume matzah with the proper intentions. The truly righteous tzaddikim have yearned so excitedly for this mitzvah that their souls almost left their bodies when they finally achieved it. Most Jews cannot perceive the enormity and sacredness of this mitzvah; but if they eat matzah simply because Hashem commanded it, they can still penetrate the highest Heavens. Because we lack the capacity to truly grasp this mitzvah's far-reaching effect on the highest spiritual worlds, we do not experience the amazing longing to fulfill this mitzvah.

(Haggada of Rabbi Yoel Teitelbaum, Satmar Rebbe)

- One who eats *matzah* in accordance with *halachah* all seven days of Pesach becomes a partner with Hashem in the creation of the world.

(Rokeach, Hilchos Pesach)

- Eating *matzah* for the sake of the *mitzvah* brings holiness to our limbs. The verse says, "*Matzos* shall be eaten in a holy place" *(Vayikra 6:9)*. We must prepare and sanctify our bodies and mouths to be a receptacle for the sacred *matzah*.

(Tiferes Shlomo, Pesach)

- If we eat *matzah* on Pesach, all the food we eat throughout the year can likewise become sanctified.

(Pri Tzaddik, Beraishis)

- "Three pilgrimage holidays shall you celebrate for Me during the year. You shall observe the holiday of *matzos* ..." *(Shemos 23:14-15)*. If we are careful to observe the *mitzvah* of eating *matzah* while we are in exile, perhaps we will merit to fulfill the preceeding *mitzvah* in the Torah-to

observe the three pilgrimage holidays in the holy *Beis Hamikdash*.

(Ohr Lashamayim)

- The Zohar calls *matzah* "the food of healing" *(Zohar II, 183b)*. Eating *matzah* has the same power as bringing sacrifices, *korbanos*, to Hashem. The word *korban*, sacrifice, is derived from a word that means to approach, come close. When a person brought a *korban* in the *Beis Hamikdash* he grew closer to Hashem. When a person eats *matzah* he heals his body's spiritual ailments, allowing him to grow closer to Hashem.

  (Tiferes Shlomo)

- When Moshe related the commandments of Pesach to the Children of Israel, including the commandment of eating *matzah*, he said, "You shall observe this matter as a *chok* for you and your children forever" *(Shemos 12:24)*. The word "*chok*" literally means decree, or a commandment we do not understand. In other contexts, "*chok*" can mean a stipend of food or livelihood *(Beraishis 47:22)*. Perhaps the Torah is indicating that by fulfilling the commandment to eat *matzah*, we, and all our descendants, will merit livelihood with ease.

  (Zera Kodesh)

- The *simanim* of the *Seder-matzah, marror, korech*-come together. *Marror* has the same numerical value as *maves*, death-446. *Korech* means wrapped up, concealed. In the merit of eating *matzah*, "*marror korech*"-death is concealed, and we are privileged to lead a good life. *(Yismach Yisroel, Pesach 21)*

- *Matzah* is *lechem oni*-the bread upon which we give many answers. Not only do we answer the children's questions-Hashem will answer our cries for help. "May Hashem answer you on the day of distress" *(Tehillim 20:2)*.

  (Rabbi Yehoshua Rokeach)

- The Zohar says that eating *matzah* saves a person from harsh judgment on Rosh Hashana. *(Zohar II 183b)* In reference to the Exodus, the verse says, "Today you are going out, in the spring month" *(Shemos 13:4)*. In *Iyov*, the word "today" is translated by the *Targum* as "the day of the great judgment" *(Iyov 2:1)*. To apply this translation, "Today," on the Day of Judgment, on Rosh Hashana, "you are going out," free of guilt, as a result of "the spring month," the *matzah* eaten on Pesach in the spring month of Nissan.

(Divrei Yechezkel, Bo)

- "Whoever does one *mitzvah* is treated well [from Above] and his life is lengthened" *(Kiddushin 39b)*. What is the one *mitzvah* the *Mishnah* refers to? Perhaps it is the very first *mitzvah* given to the Jewish nation as a whole *(Rashi, Beraishis 1:1)*. Which *mitzvah* was that? The *mitzvah* of *Korban Pesach*, which is in many ways synonymous with the current *mitzvah* of *matzah*. But we can no longer fulfill the *mitzvah* of *Korban Pesach*. So the "one *mitzvah*" that earns good treatment from Above and a lengthened life is now *matzah*.

(Tiferes Shlomo)

No Shehechiyanu?

The blessing of *shehechiyanu* that we recited at the end of *Kiddush* applies to all the *mitzvos* of the evening. *(Avudraham)* The blessing is a thanks to Hashem that He "granted us life and sustained us and enabled us to reach this occasion." In the blessing that concludes the story of the Exodus, we convey the same concept of gratitude: "Blessed is He Who has redeemed us ... and brought us to this night when we eat *matzah* and *marror* ..."

(Rokeach 371)

מרור

One takes a half-egg volume of the maror, dips it in the Charoses and recite the following:

הִנְנִי מוּכָן וּמְזוּמָן לְקַיֵּם מִצְוַת אֲכִילַת מָרוֹר לְשֵׁם יִחוּד קוּדְשָׁא בְּרִיךְ הוּא וּשְׁכִינְתֵּיהּ בִּדְחִילוּ וּרְחִימוּ עַל יְדֵי הַהוּא טָמִיר וְנֶעְלָם בְּשֵׁם כָּל יִשְׂרָאֵל: וִיהִי נוֹעַם אֲדֹנָי אֱלֹהֵינוּ עָלֵינוּ וּמַעֲשֵׂה יָדֵינוּ כּוֹנְנָה עָלֵינוּ וּמַעֲשֵׂה יָדֵינוּ כּוֹנְנֵהוּ:

בָּרוּךְ אַתָּה יְהֹוָה אֱלֹהֵינוּ מֶלֶךְ הָעוֹלָם אֲשֶׁר קִדְּשָׁנוּ בְּמִצְוֹתָיו וְצִוָּנוּ עַל אֲכִילַת מָרוֹר:

One then eats the Maror without reclining.

Marror

The Commandment

The Torah commands *(Shemos 12:8)* that the meat of the *Korban Pesach* should be eaten together with *matzos* and *marror*. Now that there is no *Beis Hamikdash* and we cannot offer the *Korban Pesach*, there is no Torah obligation to eat *marror*. Still, the *mitzvah* to eat *marror* is observed in our days as a separate Rabbinic ordination. *(Pesachim 120a)* The renowned Rabbi Akiva Eiger promised that whoever fulfills the obligation to eat *marror* eagerly and joyously will certainly not feel its bitter taste.

(Chut Hameshulash 205)

A *k'zayis* of *marror* is required to fulfill the obligation, for the term "eating" used in the verse above refers to a minimum olive sized amount. *(Sefer Yereim Hashalem 94)* Every *mitzvah* of eating requires a minimum of a *k'zayis*. *(Pri Megadim) Marror* is comparable to the

matzah and *Korban Pesach* with which it is eaten. Just as we must eat a *k'zayis* of these, we must eat a *k'zayis* of *marror* as well.

(Shaagas Aryeh, 100)

Other authorities contend that we do not need to eat a full *k'zayis* of *marror* just to fulfill our obligation, but since we have made a special blessing on it-*al achilas marror*-we have to eat the minimum amount. *(Rosh, Pesachim 10:25)* The *marror* is a remembrance of how the Egyptians embittered the lives of the Children of Israel. Less than a *k'zayis* of *marror* would not serve as a worthy remembrance.

(Mishnah Berurah, Shaar Hatziyun 475:12)

The Sequence

Matzah is a tribute to the miraculous redemption; *marror* is a remembrance of the bitter suffering. First the Jews suffered, then they were redeemed. Yet, at the *Seder*, the *matzah* comes before the *marror*. How can this contradiction be resolved?

The obligation to eat *matzah* is mentioned before the obligation to eat *marror*: "And *matzos* with bitter herbs shall they eat it" *(Shemos 12:8)*.

(Rashbam, Pesachim 114a)

Even after our liberation, even after we have eaten the *matzah*, we have not forgotten the bitterness of exile. We constantly thank Hashem for liberating us.

(Ahavas Yisroel)

While a person is in the midst of a troublesome life situation, it is best to avoid talking about his troubles-that will only serve to heighten his sorrow. Once he has emerged he can relive his troubles without sorrow, expressing gratitude to Hashem for saving him. On the *Seder* night, first we eat *matzah* and re-experience the liberation. Then we can look back on the bitter times, the troubles we had under Egyptian servitude, and properly thank Hashem for redeeming us from there.

(Divrei Yoel, Chanuka 24)

When the Children of Israel were in Egypt, they did not realize that their souls were in spiritual exile too. When they ate the *matzah*, the food of healing, their souls rose from the depths of spiritual devastation to the heights of holiness. From this lofty vantage point the Jews could perceive the dire spiritual danger to which they were exposed in Egypt. We eat the *matzah* first because only after we were liberated could we see the *marror*, how bitter the slavery truly had been.

(Migdalos Merkachim)

Dipping in Charoses

The *marror* used to contain a harmful poison. The sharp fluid of the *charoses* neutralized the poison. *(Pesachim 115b)* Since the poison is no longer prevalent these days, we dip the *marror* in *charoses* only to fulfill the injunction of our Sages, as a remembrance of the clay the Children of Israel used for making bricks in Egypt.

(Shulchan Aruch HaRav 475:11)

Perhaps we should make a blessing of *al achilas charoses*, if the *charoses* is also a *mitzvah*? Since the obligation to eat *charoses* is secondary to that of eating *marror*, the *charoses* is exempt by the blessing on the *marror*. *(Tur 475)* As a remembrance to the clay, it is only one small detail of the bitter enslavement the *marror* represents.

(Hamanhig)

The majority of the Sages maintained that the *charoses* was eaten only to neutralize the poison. Only one Sage contested that eating *charoses* was an independent *mitzvah (Mishnah Pesachim 114a)*.

(Pri Chadash 473:5)

After the *marror* is dipped in *charoses* the excess is shaken off and only a little *charoses* remains, so the bitterness of the *marror* is not drowned out by abundant *charoses*. We do not make a blessing on such a small amount.

(Siddur of Rabbi Yaakov Emden)

כורך

Take the bottom Matzah, put Maror on it, and recite the following passage:

זֵכֶר לְמִקְדָּשׁ כְּהִלֵּל. כֵּן עָשָׂה הִלֵּל. בִּזְמַן שֶׁבֵּית הַמִּקְדָּשׁ הָיָה קַיָּם הָיָה כּוֹרֵךְ פֶּסַח מַצָּה וּמָרוֹר וְאוֹכֵל בְּיַחַד לְקַיֵּם מַה שֶּׁנֶּאֱמַר עַל מַצּוֹת וּמְרוֹרִים יֹאכְלֻהוּ:

One then eats the Matzah-Maror 'sandwich' while reclining to the left.

During the time of the *Beis Hamikdash* we could not say a separate blessing on the *charoses* because it was an obligation enacted by our Sages, whereas *marror* was a *mitzvah* from the Torah itself. Now that we unfortunately no longer have the *Korban Pesach*, the *mitzvah* of *marror* too is only a Rabbinic obligation. Still, we continue the original practice of saying a blessing on the *marror* but not on the *charoses*.

(Responsa Radbaz III, 544)

Korech

The Sandwich

At the time of the *Beis Hamikdash*, Hillel Hazaken (the original Hillel, father of the dynasty of heads of the *Sanhedrin* for many generations) maintained that one could not fulfill the *mitzvos* of *Korban Pesach*, *matzah* and *marror* separately. According to Hillel, a *k'zayis* each of the *Korban Pesach*, *matzah* and *marror* were wrapped together and eaten simultaneously, derived from the Torah command, "… on *matzos* and bitter herbs they shall eat it"

(Bamidbar 9:11).

The other Sages maintained that the *mitzvos* could be fulfilled by eating each ingredient separately. Both opinions-Hillel's and the Sages'-are valid; neither view was ruled as the final *halachah*.

Without a *Korban Pesach*, we may not fulfill the *mitzvos* of *matzah* and *marror* simultaneously as Hillel recommended. The *matzah* is still a Torah commandment, while the *marror* is ordained by the Sages in memory of the times of the *Beis Hamikdash*.

Even Hillel Hazaken would agree that that in our times, the *matzah* must be eaten on its own to fulfill its separate Torah obligation. But to fulfill today's obligation to eat *marror*, Hillel would require that it be eaten together with *matzah*, just as he ate it with the *Korban Pesach*. In his opinion, when our Sages enacted the obligation to eat a *k'zayis* of *marror* now, they included an obligation to eat a *k'zayis* of *matzah* together with it, in addition to the Torah obligation of eating *matzah*.

The Sages who differed from Hillel allowed him to eat all three together-the *Korban Pesach*, *matzah*, and the *marror*-since they were all Torah obligations. But in regard to the Rabbinic obligation of eating *marror* today, that *mitzvah* is to eat the marror alone, not to eat a *k'zayis* of *matzah* with it. The extra *matzah*, they maintained, dilutes the bitterness of the *marror*.

To conform to all opinions, we first eat the *matzah* on its own to fulfill the Torah obligation. Then we make the blessing on a *k'zayis* of *marror* to fulfill the obligation according Hillel's contenders, the majority opinion. Then, according to Hillel's opinion, we eat a second *k'zayis* of *marror* together with another *k'zayis* of *matzah*.

(Tosfos Pesachim 115a; Shulchan Aruch HaRav 475:15-18)

Twice Bitter

The verse in *Eicha* says, "He filled me with bitter herbs, he satiated me with wormwood" *(Eicha 3:15)*. The *Midrash* comments that "He filled me with bitter herbs" refers to the night of Pesach; "he

satiated me with wormwood" refers to the night of Tisha B'Av, the anniversary of the destruction of the first and second *Beis Hamikdash*.

During the times of the *Beis Hamikdash* we used to eat only one *k'zayis* of *marror*, which was accompanied by the *matzah* and *Korban Pesach*. But now that the *Beis Hamikdash* is destroyed, we have to eat two *k'zeisim* of *marror*, one on its own and another together with *matzah*. "He filled me with bitter herbs"-we eat a double portion of *marror* on the night of Pesach because "he satiated me with wormwood"-on Tisha B'Av, when the *Beis Hamikdash* was destroyed.

(Gra)

Rabbi Pinchas HaLevi Horowitz, Rav of Frankfurt, Germany circa 1800, author of the Baal Hafla'a, was a disciple of the great Maggid of Mezritch, Rabbi Dov Ber, who succeeded the Baal Shem Tov as the leader of the chassidic movement. Rabbi Pinchas once asked his Rebbe how the Torah can expect one to "bless Hashem for the bad the same way as he blesses Him for the good" (Mishnah Berachos 9:4). The Maggid recommended that he ask this question of another great disciple, Reb Zusha of Anapoli.

Reb Zusha lived in extreme poverty and he suffered terribly during his lifetime. Rabbi Pinchas presented his conundrum to Reb Zusha, who replied, "I have never experienced anything bad in my life! Everything Hashem did for me was good, even if it may have seemed the opposite."

This is the lesson of *Korech*. The *marror* is wrapped with the *matzah*, the bitterness is concealed within the liberation. We cannot always perceive it, but even the bad, the bitter exile, is orchestrated by Hashem for our best interests. May we be *zocheh* to see the ultimate Redemption speedily in our days.

Pesach Sheini

There are two verses in the Torah that refer to the *Korban Pesach*. The first verse, in *Shemos*, refers to the *Korban Pesach* brought by the masses during Nissan. "They shall eat the meat [of the *Korban Pesach*] ... and *matzos*; on bitter herbs they shall eat it" *(Shemos 12:8)*. The Mechilta notes on this verse that one should eat the *Korban Pesach* even without *matzah* and *marror*. According to the Ramban, the *mitzvah* of this verse is to eat the meat of the *Korban Pesach* as well as the *matzos*, while the bitter herbs should be eaten with the *Korban Pesach*. These interpretations do not support Hillel's view-that all three must be eaten together.

The other verse in the Torah regarding the *Korban Pesach* occurs in *Bamidbar*, where the Torah discusses *Pesach Sheini*, the second Passover. If a person was unable to bring the Pesach sacrifice in Nissan, there was an alternate date during the following month of Iyar when he could bring his sacrifice. "On *matzos* and bitter herbs they shall eat it" *(Bamidbar 9:11)*. From this verse Hillel inferred that the *Korban Pesach* must be eaten together with *matzos* and bitter herbs. Hillel also deduced that this applies to the orginal *Korban Pesach* in Nissan as well.

(Rashash, Pesachim 115a)

The Belzer Rebbe once commented: As we eat the Korech on Pesach, we recite the verse that refers to the following month's Pesach Sheini. It is our sincerest hope and prayer to Hashem that even though we were unable to bring the Korban Pesach this month, may it be the will of Hashem that we merit to bring the Korban Pesach in the Beis Hamikdash during Iyar, on Pesach Sheini.

The Rav of Lemberg, Rabbi Yosef Shmuel Natansohn, renowned author of Shoel Umeishiv, heard the Belzer Rebbe's obversation. He commented, "The halachah rules that only individuals may offer a Pesach Sheini offering on 14 Iyar, not the whole Jewish people. So if

שלחן עורך

The meal should be eaten with great joy and happiness. Many eat a hard-boiled egg in remembrance of the Fastival Sacrifice and also in remembrance of the Holy Temple, since the night of the week that Pesach falls is always the same night that Tisha b'Av will fall.

---

the Moshiach does indeed come between 14 Nissan and 14 Iyar, we will still be unable to offer any Korban Pesach even on Pesach Sheini!"

But the Belzer Rebbe resolved this question, quoting Rabbi Yehuda in Talmud Yerushalmi (Pesachim 9:1). Rabbi Yehuda maintained that even a large public group may offer a Pesach Sheini sacrifice, just as King Chizkiyahu made a public Pesach Sheini celebration (Divrei Hayamim II 30:2). The Belzer Rebbe's observation was in accordance with the halachic view of Rabbi Yehuda.

(Haggada Kol Yehuda)

Two Pieces of Matzah

For the *afikoman* we eat two *k'zeisim* of *matzah*, one as a remembrance of the *Korban Pesach* and one as a remembrance of the *matzah* eaten with the *Korban Pesach*. Likewise for *Korech*: we eat one piece of *matzah* together with the *marror*, and throw in an extra piece of *matzah* in remembrance of the *Korban Pesach*, just as Hillel used to do it.

(Dvar Aharon)

Shulchan Orech

A Set Table

"This is the table (*shulchan*) which is before G-d" *(Yechezkel 41:22)*. When we eat for the sake of Heaven, our table is "before G-d" and it is a true table. But if a person eats merely to satisfy his physical desires, the letters of *shulchan-shin*, *lamed*, *ches*, *nun*-change into the word "*lanachash*," to a snake. His table belongs to the Satan and the forces of evil.

A *shulchan orech* is a table that is set sturdily on four legs, a table upon which people partake of food for the sake of Heaven. It is not, G-d forbid, a table turned upside down, sitting close to the ground like a snake.

(Avodas Yisroel)

The Egg Appetizer

Many people have the custom to begin the meal by eating an egg. Some flavor the egg with salt water, an antidote against the sharp taste of the *marror*. *(Imrei Pinchas)* The Vilna Gaon explains that it is in remembrance of the *Korban Chagiga*, eaten at the *Seder* before the *Korban Pesach*.

(Biur HaGra, Orach Chaim 476)

When Lot hosted the angels in Sodom he baked matzos for them. His wife defiantly borrowed salt from a neighbor and revealed the presence of guests in her home, a deed that was considered an abomination in Sodom (Beraishis Rabba 51:7). It was on the fifteenth of Nissan when Hashem destroyed Sodom with sulfur and fire, after which the city was flooded with the salty waters of the Dead Sea. As the

family was fleeing, Lot's wife looked back to see the destruction, and was befittingly turned into a column of salt

(Beraishis 19:26).

We, however, have no reason to fear the retribution Lot's wife earned, for we began our Seder with a hospitable invitation to guests: "Kol dichfin-whoever is hungry, let him come and eat." So we can use as much salt as we want.

(Seder Leil Pesach)

The Egyptians would not allow the Israelites to eat eggs *(Ibn Ezra, Shemos 8:22)*. By eating eggs at the meal, we actively acknowledge that we are free from their rule. In general, the more foods are cooked, the softer they get. Eggs get harder as they are cooked. The more the Egyptians oppressed us, the more our faith in Hashem solidified.

(Chasam Sofer)

For the *mitzvos* of *matzah* and *marror* on Pesach night, it is essential for us to know exactly how much a *k'zayis* is. How can we estimate the volume of a ripe olive? Olives do not grow in these areas, but eggs are readily available. Our Sages teach us that an egg is twice a *k'zayis*. So we have eggs on this night to properly calculate the size of a *k'zayis*.

(Imrei Emes)

"Any egg laid today was completed yesterday" *(Beitzah 2b)*. This should be our mindset on Pesach night. To partake in such holy and exalted activities, we need to have been "completed yesterday." We must prepare ourselves spiritually-in advance-in order to perceive and receive the exalted radiance of the holy day of Pesach.

(Likkutei Yehuda)

Quoting a differing opinion, the Talmud states, "An egg is completed when it is laid" *(Beitzah 6b)*. Even if we did not prepare ourselves spiritually for this night, we can still be privileged to receive the great holiness. Like the egg that is completed when laid, we can internalize the holiness as it emerges.

A Sign of Mourning, a Sign of Hope

Just as a mourner is comforted with eggs, so did Hashem comfort the Children of Israel after their suffering in Egypt by liberating them.

(Haggada Chaim Larosh)

Nissan is the time for redemption-from our present exile as well *(Rosh Hashana 11a)*. Every year that we celebrate Pesach in exile, we mourn that we have not yet been redeemed. We eat eggs to mourn the *Beis Hamikdash* and our inability to bring the *Korban Pesach* there. *(Haggada Chaim Larosh)* The first evening of Pesach always falls on the same evening of the week as does Tisha B'Av, the anniversary of the destruction of both the first and second *Beis Hamikdash*.

(Remah, Orach Chaim 476:6)

Several unfortunate and ominous occurrences took place on the fifteenth of Nissan, the day that later became Pesach. Hashem made a covenant with Avraham, the *bris bein habesarim*, promising his descendants the land of Israel, but at the same time warning that his children would suffer in slavery and exile

(Beraishis 15:13).

On this day, our matriarch Sarah was forcibly taken to Pharoah's palace *(ibid. 12:15)*. Yaakov Avinu appeared before Pharaoh after his reunion with his long lost son Yosef, lamenting his

difficult life *(ibid. 47:9)*. Thirty-three years were taken from his life because of his words and appearance

(Daas Zekeinim ibid.).

Many years later on the fifteenth of Nissan the Jews were forced to start their hard work as slaves in Egypt. Aharon and the tribe of Levi, who dodged the slave labor and were exempt from the work quotas of their brethren, used to keep this anniversary as a day of mourning. In remembrance of this, we too eat eggs on this night.

(Chasam Sofer)

The Arizal teaches that in the end of days, we will change the spelling of Hashem's name. Instead of *yud*, then *hei*, *vav*, *hei*, it will be spelled with two *yuds*: *yud* then *hei*, *yud* then *hei*, like the word "*yiheye*." The following verse supports this view: "*Bayom hahu yiheye Hashem echad ushmo echad*-on that day [when Moshiach comes] Hashem will be One and His Name will be One" *(Zechariah 14:9)*. *Yiheye* has the numerical value of 30. Together with the numerical value of Hashem's name *alef*, *dalet*, *nun*, *yud* (65)-which is how the *yud*, then *hei*, *vav*, *hei* is now pronounced-the two Divine Names total 95.

The word *beitzah*-egg-comprises four letters: *beis*, *yud*, *tzaddik*, *hei*. *Beis*, equivalent to the numerical value of two, is followed by the *yud*. Twice *yud* is the name of Hashem as it will be spelled during the time of Moshiach, with two *yuds*. The second half of the word *beitzah*, *tzaddik-hei*, has a numerical value of 95 (90+5), which is the sum of the two Divine Names, as they will be revealed in the time of Moshiach.

When we eat a *beitzah* at *Shulchan Orech*, we appear to indicate mourning. But upon closer examination, the *beitzah* really shows anticipation of Moshiach's arrival.

(Divrei Yechezkel Hechadash 30)

צָפוּן

One takes the Matzah that was set aside for the Afikomen and eats it, while reclining on the left side.

The following is said prior to eating the Afikomen.

הִנְנִי מוּכָן וּמְזוּמָּן לְקַיֵּם מִצְוַת אֲכִילַת אֲפִיקוֹמָן לְשֵׁם יִחוּד קוּדְשָׁא בְּרִיךְ הוּא וּשְׁכִינְתֵּיהּ בִּדְחִילוּ וּרְחִימוּ עַל יְדֵי הַהוּא טָמִיר וְנֶעְלָם בְּשֵׁם כָּל יִשְׂרָאֵל: וִיהִי נוֹעַם אֲדֹנָי אֱלֹהֵינוּ עָלֵינוּ וּמַעֲשֵׂה יָדֵינוּ כּוֹנְנָה עָלֵינוּ וּמַעֲשֵׂה יָדֵינוּ כּוֹנְנֵהוּ:

It is forbidden to eat anything after the Afikomen.

Tzafun

Remembrance of the Korban Pesach

Hidden, *tzafun*, within the *afikoman* is the holiness of the *Korban Pesach*. *(Haggada of Rabbi Yoel Teitelbaum, the Satmar Rebbe)* Just as the *Korban Pesach* was eaten after everyone was satisfied from the *Korban Chagiga*, the *afikoman* is eaten after a satisfying *Yom Tov* meal.

(Orach Chaim 476:1)

No other food follows the *afikoman*, as it says, "We do not conclude [the meal], after the *Korban Pesach*, with any *afikoman*" *(Pesachim 119b)*. Although this rule is mentioned in connection with

the *Korban Pesach*, today the rule applies to the *afikoman*, the *matzah* we eat in remembrance of the *Korban Pesach*.

The word *afikoman* is comprised of two Aramaic words-*afiku man*, bring out [more] food. Once we finish the *Korban Pesach*, we do not bring out any more food.

(Beis Yosef, Tur 478)

Afikoman can also be interpreted as "bring out sweet fruits." *Matzah* is as beloved to us as the sweetest fruits which are reserved for dessert.

(Levush 478)

When Hashem brought us out of Egypt, it was also a preparation for the future Redemption, when He will liberate us from our present bitter exile. We do not know exactly when the day will come, but we believe that He will bring the Redemption. We eat the afikoman at the end of our Seder to echo our belief that in the end, Hashem will redeem us from our present exile.

(Sfas Emes)

Two K'zeisim

During *Tzafun* we eat two *k'zeisim* of *matzah*. Eating double the minimum portion shows our fondness for this important Torah obligation. One *k'zayis* is in remembrance of the *Korban Pesach* offering, and the other is in remembrance of the minimum olive size of *matzah* that had to be eaten together with it. Alternatively, one *k'zayis* for the *Korban Pesach*, and one *k'zayis* in remembrance of the *Korban Chagiga*.

(Maharil, quoted by Turei Zahav, Orach Chaim 477:1)

The Tzanzer Rav, Rabbi Chaim Halberstam, known for his authorship of the great halachic work Divrei Chaim, recounted the following at his Seder. He quoted the Talmud (Arachin 13a) that the Chamber of Lambs in the Beis Hamikdash always had to have at least six lambs ready for offering. A minimum of six lambs had to be waiting, already checked for their perfection, with no disqualifying blemishes. "But now that the Beis Hamikdash unfortunately has been destroyed," the Tzanzer Rav asked, "where are these six lambs?"

"The six lambs were taken into the desert," he told the assembled, "where they have multiplied. Every day Eliyahu Hanovi takes two lambs from there, one for the morning offering and one for the afternoon offering.

"Once the Uiheler Rav, Rabbi Moshe Teitelbaum, author of Yismach Moshe, begged Hashem to be granted the privilege to see the heavenly Eliyahu Hanovi offer up the sacrifices. And his wish was granted. Eliyahu Hanovi was the kohen, and the angel Michael served as the kohen gadol.

"Every year on the afternoon before Pesach, Eliyahu Hanovi offers up the Korban Pesach. All the tzaddikim of the generation participate in this group offering. Eliyahu himself brings them each a piece of the Korban Pesach to eat. You might ask, the Korban Pesach must be eaten in Jerusalem-we are not in Jerusalem! But Eliyahu brings them the air of the Holy Land, of Jerusalem. The tzaddikim sit in the holy air and eat the Korban Pesach.

"Even those who are not on such a high level, as long as they are attached to a tzaddik of their generation, as long as they have faith-it is considered as if they have eaten from the holy Pesach lamb, too.

"You probably think that what I have described means a spiritual piece of the Korban Pesach. No! Tzaddikim actually eat a physical piece of meat from the Korban Pesach."

To prove his point, the Tzanzer Rav continued with a story: The Rebbe, Reb Zusha of Anapoli, once fell asleep in shul. When

he awoke, he tried to leave the building, but found himself locked in. There was no food to eat in the shul. Reb Zusha was resigned. "So-Zusha will fast."

As soon as Reb Zusha uttered those words, the angel Michael brought him a piece of fish from the livyasan and wine from the yayin hameshumar (foods reserved for the feast when Moshiach comes). Reb Itzikel Lantzuter, the Chozeh (Seer) of Lublin, testified that the angel Michael brought him a real drink of wine and real piece of fish.

"A real piece of the Korban Pesach is brought to the tzaddikim of each generation," the Divrei Chaim repeated with certainty. "How can we eat the offerings of the Beis Hamikdash? Everyone is impure, you ask? The Torah rule is that when the majority is tamei because of indirect contact with a dead body, they are allowed to offer the Korban Pesach.

"We [tzaddikim] are now in Jerusalem and we are eating of the Korban Pesach! And Jews who believe this are considered as if they have eaten of it themselves."

Rabbi Yoel Teitelbaum, the Satmar Rebbe zt"l, adds that when the holy Tzanzer Rav finished telling this and started to eat the afikoman, everyone present felt as if he was witnessing the Tzanzer Rav eating the Korban Pesach.

The Stropkover Rebbe, author of Divrei Menachem, added that after his declaration, all seventy people present longed to eat from the Tzanzer Rav's shirayim (leftovers). Amazingly, each and every participant received a piece of the afikoman that the Tzanzer Rav ate with meat of the Korban Pesach from Eliyahu Hanovi.

(A lengthy description of the Korban Pesach can be found in chapter 6)

ברך

One fills the third cup with wine and recites the Bircas HaMazon.

שִׁיר הַמַּעֲלוֹת, בְּשׁוּב יְהֹוָה אֶת שִׁיבַת צִיּוֹן הָיִינוּ כְּחֹלְמִים. אָז יִמָּלֵא שְׂחוֹק פִּינוּ וּלְשׁוֹנֵנוּ רִנָּה, אָז יֹאמְרוּ בַגּוֹיִם הִגְדִּיל יְהֹוָה לַעֲשׂוֹת עִם אֵלֶּה. הִגְדִּיל יְהֹוָה לַעֲשׂוֹת עִמָּנוּ, הָיִינוּ שְׂמֵחִים. שׁוּבָה יְהֹוָה אֶת שְׁבִיתֵנוּ כַּאֲפִיקִים בַּנֶּגֶב. הַזֹּרְעִים בְּדִמְעָה בְּרִנָּה יִקְצֹרוּ. הָלוֹךְ יֵלֵךְ וּבָכֹה נֹשֵׂא מֶשֶׁךְ הַזָּרַע, בֹּא יָבֹא בְרִנָּה, נֹשֵׂא אֲלֻמֹּתָיו:

הִנְנִי מוּכָן וּמְזוּמָּן לְקַיֵּם מִצְוַת עֲשֵׂה שֶׁל בִּרְכַּת הַמָּזוֹן, שֶׁנֶּאֱמַר וְאָכַלְתָּ וְשָׂבָעְתָּ וּבֵרַכְתָּ אֶת יְהֹוָה אֱלֹהֶיךָ עַל הָאָרֶץ הַטּוֹבָה אֲשֶׁר נָתַן לָךְ, לְשֵׁם יִחוּד קוּדְשָׁא בְּרִיךְ הוּא וּשְׁכִינְתֵּיהּ בִּדְחִילוּ וּרְחִימוּ עַל יְדֵי הַהוּא טָמִיר וְנֶעְלָם בְּשֵׁם כָּל יִשְׂרָאֵל: וִיהִי נֹעַם אֲדֹנָי אֱלֹהֵינוּ עָלֵינוּ וּמַעֲשֵׂה יָדֵינוּ כּוֹנְנָה עָלֵינוּ וּמַעֲשֵׂה יָדֵינוּ כּוֹנְנֵהוּ:

The leader begins:

רַבּוֹתַי נְבָרֵךְ:

The group responds:

יְהִי שֵׁם יְהֹוָה מְבוֹרָךְ מֵעַתָּה וְעַד עוֹלָם:

The leader continues:

בִּרְשׁוּת מָרָנָן וְרַבּוֹתַי נְבָרֵךְ (אֱלֹהֵינוּ) שֶׁאָכַלְנוּ מִשֶּׁלּוֹ:

The group responds:

בָּרוּךְ (אֱלֹהֵינוּ) שֶׁאָכַלְנוּ מִשֶּׁלּוֹ וּבְטוּבוֹ חָיִינוּ:

The leader Concludes:

והמזמן חוזר: בָּרוּךְ (אֱלֹהֵינוּ) שֶׁאָכַלְנוּ מִשֶּׁלּוֹ וּבְטוּבוֹ חָיִינוּ:

בָּרוּךְ הוּא וּבָרוּךְ שְׁמוֹ:

בָּרוּךְ אַתָּה יְהֹוָה אֱלֹהֵינוּ מֶלֶךְ הָעוֹלָם. הַזָּן אֶת הָעוֹלָם כֻּלּוֹ, בְּטוּבוֹ בְּחֵן בְּחֶסֶד וּבְרַחֲמִים. הוּא נוֹתֵן לֶחֶם לְכָל בָּשָׂר כִּי לְעוֹלָם חַסְדּוֹ. וּבְטוּבוֹ הַגָּדוֹל תָּמִיד לֹא חָסַר לָנוּ, וְאַל יֶחְסַר לָנוּ מָזוֹן לְעוֹלָם וָעֶד. בַּעֲבוּר שְׁמוֹ הַגָּדוֹל. כִּי הוּא אֵל זָן וּמְפַרְנֵס לַכֹּל וּמֵטִיב לַכֹּל וּמֵכִין מָזוֹן לְכָל בְּרִיּוֹתָיו אֲשֶׁר בָּרָא. כָּאָמוּר פּוֹתֵחַ אֶת יָדֶךָ וּמַשְׂבִּיעַ לְכָל חַי רָצוֹן. בָּרוּךְ אַתָּה יְהֹוָה הַזָּן אֶת הַכֹּל:

נוֹדֶה לְךָ יְהֹוָה אֱלֹהֵינוּ עַל שֶׁהִנְחַלְתָּ לַאֲבוֹתֵינוּ, אֶרֶץ חֶמְדָּה טוֹבָה וּרְחָבָה, וְעַל שֶׁהוֹצֵאתָנוּ יְהֹוָה אֱלֹהֵינוּ מֵאֶרֶץ מִצְרַיִם, וּפְדִיתָנוּ מִבֵּית עֲבָדִים, וְעַל בְּרִיתְךָ שֶׁחָתַמְתָּ בִּבְשָׂרֵנוּ, וְעַל תּוֹרָתְךָ שֶׁלִּמַּדְתָּנוּ, וְעַל חֻקֶּיךָ שֶׁהוֹדַעְתָּנוּ, וְעַל חַיִּים חֵן וָחֶסֶד שֶׁחוֹנַנְתָּנוּ, וְעַל אֲכִילַת מָזוֹן שָׁאַתָּה זָן וּמְפַרְנֵס אוֹתָנוּ תָּמִיד, בְּכָל יוֹם וּבְכָל עֵת וּבְכָל שָׁעָה:

וְעַל הַכֹּל יְהֹוָה אֱלֹהֵינוּ אֲנַחְנוּ מוֹדִים לָךְ, וּמְבָרְכִים אוֹתָךְ, יִתְבָּרַךְ שִׁמְךָ בְּפִי כָּל חַי תָּמִיד לְעוֹלָם וָעֶד. כַּכָּתוּב, וְאָכַלְתָּ וְשָׂבָעְתָּ, וּבֵרַכְתָּ אֶת יְהֹוָה אֱלֹהֶיךָ עַל הָאָרֶץ הַטֹּבָה אֲשֶׁר נָתַן לָךְ. בָּרוּךְ אַתָּה יְהֹוָה עַל הָאָרֶץ וְעַל הַמָּזוֹן:

רַחֵם נָא יְהֹוָה אֱלֹהֵינוּ, עַל יִשְׂרָאֵל עַמֶּךָ, וְעַל יְרוּשָׁלַיִם עִירֶךָ, וְעַל צִיּוֹן מִשְׁכַּן כְּבוֹדֶךָ, וְעַל מַלְכוּת בֵּית דָּוִד מְשִׁיחֶךָ, וְעַל הַבַּיִת הַגָּדוֹל וְהַקָּדוֹשׁ שֶׁנִּקְרָא שִׁמְךָ עָלָיו. אֱלֹהֵינוּ, אָבִינוּ, רְעֵנוּ, זוּנֵנוּ, פַּרְנְסֵנוּ, וְכַלְכְּלֵנוּ, וְהַרְוִיחֵנוּ,

וְהַרְוַח לָנוּ יְהֹוָה אֱלֹהֵינוּ מְהֵרָה מִכָּל צָרוֹתֵינוּ. וְנָא, אַל תַּצְרִיכֵנוּ יְהֹוָה אֱלֹהֵינוּ לֹא לִידֵי מַתְּנַת בָּשָׂר וָדָם, וְלֹא לִידֵי הַלְוָאָתָם, כִּי אִם לְיָדְךָ הַמְּלֵאָה, הַפְּתוּחָה, הַקְּדוֹשָׁה וְהָרְחָבָה, שֶׁלֹּא נֵבוֹשׁ וְלֹא נִכָּלֵם לְעוֹלָם וָעֶד:

On Shabbath add:

רְצֵה וְהַחֲלִיצֵנוּ יְהֹוָה אֱלֹהֵינוּ בְּמִצְוֹתֶיךָ וּבְמִצְוַת יוֹם הַשְּׁבִיעִי, הַשַּׁבָּת הַגָּדוֹל וְהַקָּדוֹשׁ הַזֶּה, כִּי יוֹם זֶה גָּדוֹל וְקָדוֹשׁ הוּא לְפָנֶיךָ, לִשְׁבָּת בּוֹ וְלָנוּחַ בּוֹ בְּאַהֲבָה כְּמִצְוַת רְצוֹנֶךָ, וּבִרְצוֹנְךָ הָנִיחַ לָנוּ יְהֹוָה אֱלֹהֵינוּ, שֶׁלֹּא תְהֵא צָרָה וְיָגוֹן וַאֲנָחָה בְּיוֹם מְנוּחָתֵנוּ, וְהַרְאֵנוּ יְהֹוָה אֱלֹהֵינוּ בְּנֶחָמַת צִיּוֹן עִירֶךָ, וּבְבִנְיַן יְרוּשָׁלַיִם עִיר קָדְשֶׁךָ, כִּי אַתָּה הוּא בַּעַל הַיְשׁוּעוֹת וּבַעַל הַנֶּחָמוֹת:

אֱלֹהֵינוּ וֵאלֹהֵי אֲבוֹתֵינוּ, יַעֲלֶה וְיָבֹא וְיַגִּיעַ, וְיֵרָאֶה וְיֵרָצֶה וְיִשָּׁמַע, וְיִפָּקֵד וְיִזָּכֵר זִכְרוֹנֵנוּ וּפִקְדוֹנֵנוּ, וְזִכְרוֹן אֲבוֹתֵינוּ וְזִכְרוֹן מָשִׁיחַ בֶּן דָּוִד עַבְדֶּךָ, וְזִכְרוֹן יְרוּשָׁלַיִם עִיר קָדְשֶׁךָ, וְזִכְרוֹן כָּל עַמְּךָ בֵּית יִשְׂרָאֵל לְפָנֶיךָ, לִפְלֵיטָה, לְטוֹבָה, לְחֵן וּלְחֶסֶד וּלְרַחֲמִים, לְחַיִּים טוֹבִים וּלְשָׁלוֹם, בְּיוֹם חַג הַמַּצּוֹת הַזֶּה:

זָכְרֵנוּ יְהֹוָה אֱלֹהֵינוּ בּוֹ לְטוֹבָה, וּפָקְדֵנוּ בוֹ לִבְרָכָה, וְהוֹשִׁיעֵנוּ בוֹ לְחַיִּים טוֹבִים. וּבִדְבַר יְשׁוּעָה וְרַחֲמִים, חוּס וְחָנֵּנוּ וְרַחֵם עָלֵינוּ וְהוֹשִׁיעֵנוּ, כִּי אֵלֶיךָ עֵינֵינוּ כִּי אֵל (מֶלֶךְ) חַנּוּן וְרַחוּם אָתָּה:

וּבְנֵה יְרוּשָׁלַיִם עִיר הַקֹּדֶשׁ בִּמְהֵרָה בְיָמֵינוּ. בָּרוּךְ אַתָּה יְהֹוָה בּוֹנֵה בְרַחֲמָיו יְרוּשָׁלָיִם, אָמֵן:

בָּרוּךְ אַתָּה יְהֹוָה אֱלֹהֵינוּ מֶלֶךְ הָעוֹלָם. הָאֵל, אָבִינוּ, מַלְכֵּנוּ, אַדִּירֵנוּ, בּוֹרְאֵנוּ, גּוֹאֲלֵנוּ, יוֹצְרֵנוּ, קְדוֹשֵׁנוּ קְדוֹשׁ יַעֲקֹב, רוֹעֵנוּ רוֹעֵה יִשְׂרָאֵל, הַמֶּלֶךְ הַטּוֹב וְהַמֵּטִיב לַכֹּל. שֶׁבְּכָל יוֹם וָיוֹם הוּא הֵטִיב הוּא מֵטִיב הוּא יֵיטִיב לָנוּ. הוּא גְמָלָנוּ הוּא גוֹמְלֵנוּ הוּא יִגְמְלֵנוּ לָעַד, לְחֵן וּלְחֶסֶד וּלְרַחֲמִים וּלְרֶוַח הַצָּלָה וְהַצְלָחָה, בְּרָכָה וִישׁוּעָה, נֶחָמָה, פַּרְנָסָה וְכַלְכָּלָה, וְרַחֲמִים וְחַיִּים וְשָׁלוֹם וְכָל טוֹב. וּמִכָּל טוּב לְעוֹלָם אַל יְחַסְּרֵנוּ:

הָרַחֲמָן הוּא יִמְלֹךְ עָלֵינוּ לְעוֹלָם וָעֶד: הָרַחֲמָן הוּא יִתְבָּרַךְ בַּשָּׁמַיִם וּבָאָרֶץ: הָרַחֲמָן הוּא יִשְׁתַּבַּח לְדוֹר דּוֹרִים. וְיִתְפָּאַר בָּנוּ לָעַד וּלְנֵצַח נְצָחִים. וְיִתְהַדַּר בָּנוּ לָעַד וּלְעוֹלְמֵי עוֹלָמִים: הָרַחֲמָן הוּא יְפַרְנְסֵנוּ בְּכָבוֹד: הָרַחֲמָן הוּא יִשְׁבּוֹר עֻלֵּנוּ מֵעַל צַוָּארֵנוּ וְהוּא יוֹלִיכֵנוּ קוֹמְמִיּוּת לְאַרְצֵנוּ: הָרַחֲמָן הוּא יִשְׁלַח לָנוּ בְּרָכָה מְרֻבָּה בַּבַּיִת הַזֶּה וְעַל שֻׁלְחָן זֶה שֶׁאָכַלְנוּ עָלָיו: הָרַחֲמָן הוּא יִשְׁלַח לָנוּ אֶת אֵלִיָּהוּ הַנָּבִיא זָכוּר לַטּוֹב וִיבַשֶּׂר לָנוּ בְּשׂוֹרוֹת טוֹבוֹת יְשׁוּעוֹת וְנֶחָמוֹת:

הָרַחֲמָן הוּא יְבָרֵךְ אֶת (אָבִי מוֹרִי) בַּעַל הַבַּיִת הַזֶּה, וְאֶת (אִמִּי מוֹרָתִי) בַּעֲלַת הַבַּיִת הַזֶּה, (אוֹתִי וְאֶת אִשְׁתִּי וְאֶת זַרְעִי) אוֹתָם וְאֶת בֵּיתָם וְאֶת זַרְעָם וְאֶת כָּל אֲשֶׁר לָהֶם. אוֹתָנוּ וְאֶת כָּל אֲשֶׁר לָנוּ. כְּמוֹ שֶׁנִּתְבָּרְכוּ אֲבוֹתֵינוּ אַבְרָהָם

יִצְחָק וְיַעֲקֹב בַּכֹּל מִכֹּל כֹּל כֵּן יְבָרֵךְ אוֹתָנוּ כֻּלָּנוּ יַחַד בִּבְרָכָה שְׁלֵמָה. וְנֹאמַר אָמֵן:

בַּמָּרוֹם יְלַמְּדוּ עֲלֵיהֶם וְעָלֵינוּ זְכוּת שֶׁתְּהֵא לְמִשְׁמֶרֶת שָׁלוֹם. וְנִשָּׂא בְרָכָה מֵאֵת יְהֹוָה וּצְדָקָה מֵאֱלֹהֵי יִשְׁעֵנוּ. וְנִמְצָא חֵן וְשֵׂכֶל טוֹב בְּעֵינֵי אֱלֹהִים וְאָדָם:

On Shabbath add:

הָרַחֲמָן הוּא יַנְחִילֵנוּ לְיוֹם שֶׁכֻּלּוֹ שַׁבָּת וּמְנוּחָה לְחַיֵּי הָעוֹלָמִים:

הָרַחֲמָן הוּא יַנְחִילֵנוּ לְיוֹם שֶׁכֻּלּוֹ טוֹב. לְיוֹם שֶׁכֻּלּוֹ אָרוּךְ, יוֹם שֶׁצַּדִּיקִים יוֹשְׁבִים וְעַטְרוֹתֵיהֶם בְּרָאשֵׁיהֶם וְנֶהֱנִים מִזִּיו הַשְּׁכִינָה וִיהִי חֶלְקֵנוּ עִמָּהֶם:

הָרַחֲמָן הוּא יְזַכֵּנוּ לִימוֹת הַמָּשִׁיחַ וּלְחַיֵּי הָעוֹלָם הַבָּא: מִגְדּוֹל יְשׁוּעוֹת מַלְכּוֹ וְעֹשֶׂה חֶסֶד לִמְשִׁיחוֹ לְדָוִד וּלְזַרְעוֹ עַד עוֹלָם: עֹשֶׂה שָׁלוֹם בִּמְרוֹמָיו הוּא יַעֲשֶׂה שָׁלוֹם עָלֵינוּ וְעַל כָּל יִשְׂרָאֵל וְאִמְרוּ אָמֵן:

יְראוּ אֶת יְהֹוָה קְדֹשָׁיו כִּי אֵין מַחְסוֹר לִירֵאָיו: כְּפִירִים רָשׁוּ וְרָעֵבוּ וְדֹרְשֵׁי יְהֹוָה לֹא יַחְסְרוּ כָל טוֹב: הוֹדוּ לַיהֹוָה כִּי טוֹב כִּי לְעוֹלָם חַסְדּוֹ: פּוֹתֵחַ אֶת יָדֶךָ וּמַשְׂבִּיעַ לְכָל חַי רָצוֹן: בָּרוּךְ הַגֶּבֶר אֲשֶׁר יִבְטַח בַּיהֹוָה וְהָיָה יְהֹוָה מִבְטַחוֹ: נַעַר הָיִיתִי גַּם זָקַנְתִּי וְלֹא רָאִיתִי צַדִּיק נֶעֱזָב וְזַרְעוֹ מְבַקֶּשׁ לָחֶם: יְהֹוָה עֹז לְעַמּוֹ יִתֵּן יְהֹוָה יְבָרֵךְ אֶת עַמּוֹ בַשָּׁלוֹם:

The blessing over the third cup is made after reciting the following:

הִנְנִי מוּכָן וּמְזוּמָּן לְקַיֵּם מִצְוַת כּוֹס שְׁלִישִׁי מֵאַרְבַּע כּוֹסוֹת. לְשֵׁם יִחוּד קוּדְשָׁא בְּרִיךְ הוּא וּשְׁכִינְתֵּיהּ בִּדְחִילוּ וּרְחִימוּ עַל יְדֵי הַהוּא טָמִיר וְנֶעְלָם בְּשֵׁם כָּל יִשְׂרָאֵל: וִיהִי נוֹעַם אֲדֹנָי אֱלֹהֵינוּ עָלֵינוּ וּמַעֲשֵׂה יָדֵינוּ כּוֹנְנָה עָלֵינוּ וּמַעֲשֵׂה יָדֵינוּ כּוֹנְנֵהוּ:

בָּרוּךְ אַתָּה יְהֹוָה אֱלֹהֵינוּ מֶלֶךְ הָעוֹלָם בּוֹרֵא פְּרִי הַגָּפֶן:

The third cup is then drunk while leaning on the left side.

Barech

Bentching

In the second blessing of *bentching* we thank Hashem "that You brought us out of Egypt, and You liberated us from the place of slaves." *Birkas hamazon* has a direct relation to Pesach and is worthy to be counted among the *simanim* of the *Seder.*

(Dvar Aharon)

Toward the end of *birkas hamazon*, we request that Hashem "send us Eliyahu Hanovi, remembered for the good." This request is especially applicable tonight, at the *Seder*, when we invite Eliyahu to join us. But to remember Eliyahu Hanovi for the good? Of course he will be remembered for the good!

While Eliyahu was staying with the widow of Tzarfas, her son passed away. She complained to Eliyahu Hanovi, "You have come to me to cause my sins to be remembered" *(Melachim I 17:18)*. Rashi

Shefoch Chamoscho

The cup of Elijah is poured at this point. The front door is then opened.

שְׁפוֹךְ חֲמָתְךָ אֶל הַגּוֹיִם אֲשֶׁר לֹא יְדָעוּךָ וְעַל מַמְלָכוֹת אֲשֶׁר בְּשִׁמְךָ לֹא קָרָאוּ: כִּי אָכַל אֶת יַעֲקֹב וְאֶת נָוֵהוּ הֵשַׁמּוּ: שְׁפָךְ עֲלֵיהֶם זַעְמֶךָ וַחֲרוֹן אַפְּךָ יַשִּׂיגֵם: תִּרְדוֹף בְּאַף וְתַשְׁמִידֵם מִתַּחַת שְׁמֵי יְהֹוָה:

(Beraishis 19:19) explains her intention: "Before you came," the widow said, "Hashem saw my deeds and the deeds of my people, and I was considered a righteous woman compared to them. But since you have come to stay with me, compared to your deeds I am wicked."

At the *Seder*, we ask that Hashem send us Eliyahu Hanovi in a manner that will be "remembered for good" and beneficial to our merits.

(Sichos Chachamim)

Shefoch Chamoscho

A Fifth Cup

After *bentching* the fourth cup of wine is poured. But an additional fifth cup of wine is poured in honor of Eliyahu Hanovi-the *kos shel Eliyahu*, the Cup of Eliyahu. The *halachic* authorities disagree whether or not a fifth cup should be drunk by all *Seder* participants. The final *halachah* has never been decided. We anxiously await the arrival of

Eliyahu Hanovi who will announce the coming of the Moshiach, who will render the final decisions on all Torah laws that remain in doubt.

(Gra)

The late Belzer Rebbe, Rabbi Aharon Rokeach, expounded further. Those who believe that a fifth cup of wine should be drunk at the Seder base their view on the words of Rabbi Eliyahu in Yalkut Shimoni. The fifth cup is called the "Cup of Eliyahu" after his name. And the Vilna Gaon (Gra) learned this information specifically because his name was Eliyahu too!

(Binas Aharon)

The Bris Milah Angel

Before the Jews of Egypt were allowed to partake of the *Korban Pesach*, Hashem commanded that they must have a *bris milah*. Eliyahu Hanovi is the angel who attends every Jewish circumcision. *(Pirkei d'Rebi Eliezer 29)* He comes to every *Seder* to testify before Hashem that even today, Jews still fulfill the *mitzvah* of *bris milah*. He blesses the Jews in their homes, combining their merits for the *mitzvos* of the *Seder* with the *mitzvah* of *bris milah*. Eliyahu praises the Jewish people before Hashem, acting as a defender on our behalf so Hashem should redeem us from our exile.

(Maamar Haminhagim, Maharam Chagiz)

Opening the Door

The Four Cups correspond to the four "cups" of punishment that Hashem will give the enemies of the Jewish people to drink. Now that the fourth cup has been poured, we open the door and ask Hashem to fulfill this promise: "*Shefoch chamascha*-pour out Your anger on the nations who do not know You ..." *(Tehillim 79:6-7)*.

(Matteh Moshe)

The *Seder* night is called "*leil shimurim*" *(Shemos 12:42)*. It is a night of special protection by Hashem; we fear nothing except Him. Surely no harm can befall us by leaving the door open. In the merit of our faith, we will soon be saved and Moshiach will take us out of exile. Then Hashem will pour out His anger upon the wicked nations who have persecuted the Jewish people.

(Remah 480, quoting Mahariv)

The meat of the *Korban Pesach* was only permitted to the designated group. Others were not allowed to join afterward, and no meat was allowed to leave the premises. To avoid these prohibitions, the doors of the home were locked to ensure that no one would enter or leave. Once everyone had finished eating and *bentched*, the doors were reopened. Everyone was free to come and go.

(Be'er Yosef, Bo)

As we know from the tradition of our prophets, the sign of the ultimate *geulah* is Eliyahu Hanovi. Before the coming of Moshiach, Eliyahu Hanovi will come and announce the good news of his imminent arrival. This is an important fundamental, for many impostors have come and claimed to be a Messiah. We must hand this tradition down to our children so they can avoid stumbling. When we open the door in honor of Eliyahu Hanovi and pour him a cup of wine, we impart this lesson to our children.

(Maharal)

The fathers send their children to open the door for the great prophet Eliyahu. "Behold, I am sending you Eliyahu the Prophet before the arrival of the great and awesome day of Hashem. And he [Eliyahu] will turn back [to Hashem] the hearts of fathers with their sons and the hearts of sons with their fathers" *(Malachi 3:23,24)*. With tender love, Eliyahu will encourage the children, "Please, go ask your parents to follow the ways of Hashem." *(Rashi, ibid.)* So the children go and open the door, for they will convey Eliyahu's message of repentance to their parents.

(Rabbi Yissachar Dov Rokeach of Belz)

Like Our Fathers Before Us

It was the night of Pesach when Yaakov usurped the firstborn blessings from his brother Eisav. Yaakov brought his father Yitzchak the meat of "two young goats" *(Beraishis 27:9)*-one for the *Korban Pesach* and the other for the *Korban Chagiga*. After Yitzchak finished eating the *afikoman* of the *Korban Pesach*, he gave Yaakov the blessings. "When Yitzchak finished blessing" *(ibid. 27:30)*, Yaakov left the house, and Eisav entered almost immediately.

Today, we perform the ritual the same way our Patriarchs did. When we finish blessing *birkas hamazon* we go open the door, just as Yaakov beat a hasty retreat. And why do we open the door? To recite "*Shefoch chamascha*," to pour out wrath on the cruel nations of the world, represented by their forefather Eisav.

(Menachem Tzion)

Another name for the *Beis Hamikdash* is *birah*, a palace *(Divrei Hayamim I 29:19)*. Our Sages tell us that the physical *Beis Hamikdash* in this world corresponds to the spiritual *Beis Hamikdash* in Heaven. When the physical *Beis Hamikdash* was destroyed its holiness ascended to the Heavenly realm. Now there are two *Batei Mikdash*-both called *birah*-in Heaven.

The numerical value of the word *birah-beis, yud, reish, hei*-equals 217 (2+10+200+5). Twice that equals 434, equivalent to the word *deles*, door (*dalet, lamed, taf*-4+30+400). We open the *deles* at the *Seder*, begging Eliyahu Hanovi to help bring the *geulah*. We pray to Hashem that He open the *deles* in Heaven-redivide the two palaces that He guards there-and allow one *Beis Hamikdash* to be rebuilt in this world.

(Rabbi Yissochor Dov Rokeach, third Belzer Rebbe)

It is advisable not to drink in pairs, for it can lead to danger. But if one has seen the outside between drinking one cup and the next, it is not dangerous. *(Pesachim 110a)* To avoid this danger at the *Seder*, we open the door and view the outdoors between the third and fourth cups, splitting up the second pair.

(Rabbi Yoel of Propaisk)

הלל

The fourth cup is poured, and the following paragraphs from the Hallel are recited.

לֹא לָנוּ יְהֹוָה לֹא לָנוּ. כִּי לְשִׁמְךָ תֵּן כָּבוֹד. עַל חַסְדְּךָ עַל אֲמִתֶּךָ: לָמָּה יֹאמְרוּ הַגּוֹיִם. אַיֵּה נָא אֱלֹהֵיהֶם: וֵאלֹהֵינוּ בַשָּׁמָיִם. כֹּל אֲשֶׁר חָפֵץ עָשָׂה: עֲצַבֵּיהֶם כֶּסֶף וְזָהָב. מַעֲשֵׂה יְדֵי אָדָם: פֶּה לָהֶם וְלֹא יְדַבֵּרוּ. עֵינַיִם לָהֶם וְלֹא יִרְאוּ: אָזְנַיִם לָהֶם וְלֹא יִשְׁמָעוּ. אַף לָהֶם וְלֹא יְרִיחוּן: יְדֵיהֶם וְלֹא יְמִישׁוּן. רַגְלֵיהֶם וְלֹא יְהַלֵּכוּ. לֹא יֶהְגּוּ בִּגְרוֹנָם: כְּמוֹהֶם יִהְיוּ עֹשֵׂיהֶם. כֹּל אֲשֶׁר בֹּטֵחַ בָּהֶם: יִשְׂרָאֵל בְּטַח בַּיהֹוָה. עֶזְרָם וּמָגִנָּם הוּא: בֵּית אַהֲרֹן בִּטְחוּ בַיהֹוָה. עֶזְרָם וּמָגִנָּם הוּא: יִרְאֵי יְהֹוָה בִּטְחוּ בַיהֹוָה. עֶזְרָם וּמָגִנָּם הוּא:

יְהֹוָה זְכָרָנוּ יְבָרֵךְ. יְבָרֵךְ אֶת בֵּית יִשְׂרָאֵל. יְבָרֵךְ אֶת בֵּית אַהֲרֹן: יְבָרֵךְ יִרְאֵי יְהֹוָה. הַקְּטַנִּים עִם הַגְּדֹלִים: יֹסֵף יְהֹוָה עֲלֵיכֶם. עֲלֵיכֶם וְעַל בְּנֵיכֶם: בְּרוּכִים אַתֶּם לַיהֹוָה. עֹשֵׂה שָׁמַיִם וָאָרֶץ: הַשָּׁמַיִם שָׁמַיִם לַיהֹוָה. וְהָאָרֶץ נָתַן לִבְנֵי אָדָם: לֹא הַמֵּתִים יְהַלְלוּ יָהּ. וְלֹא כָּל יֹרְדֵי דוּמָה: וַאֲנַחְנוּ נְבָרֵךְ יָהּ. מֵעַתָּה וְעַד עוֹלָם. הַלְלוּיָהּ:

אָהַבְתִּי כִּי יִשְׁמַע יְהֹוָה אֶת קוֹלִי תַּחֲנוּנָי: כִּי הִטָּה אָזְנוֹ לִי. וּבְיָמַי אֶקְרָא: אֲפָפוּנִי חֶבְלֵי מָוֶת. וּמְצָרֵי שְׁאוֹל מְצָאוּנִי. צָרָה וְיָגוֹן אֶמְצָא: וּבְשֵׁם יְהֹוָה אֶקְרָא. אָנָּה יְהֹוָה מַלְּטָה נַפְשִׁי: חַנּוּן יְהֹוָה וְצַדִּיק. וֵאלֹהֵינוּ מְרַחֵם: שֹׁמֵר פְּתָאיִם יְהֹוָה. דַּלּוֹתִי וְלִי יְהוֹשִׁיעַ: שׁוּבִי נַפְשִׁי לִמְנוּחָיְכִי. כִּי יְהֹוָה גָּמַל עָלָיְכִי: כִּי חִלַּצְתָּ נַפְשִׁי מִמָּוֶת. אֶת עֵינִי מִן דִּמְעָה. אֶת רַגְלִי מִדֶּחִי: אֶתְהַלֵּךְ לִפְנֵי יְהֹוָה. בְּאַרְצוֹת הַחַיִּים: הֶאֱמַנְתִּי כִּי אֲדַבֵּר. אֲנִי עָנִיתִי מְאֹד: אֲנִי אָמַרְתִּי בְחָפְזִי. כָּל הָאָדָם כֹּזֵב:

מָה אָשִׁיב לַיהֹוָה. כָּל תַּגְמוּלוֹהִי עָלָי: כּוֹס יְשׁוּעוֹת אֶשָּׂא. וּבְשֵׁם יְהֹוָה אֶקְרָא: נְדָרַי לַיהֹוָה אֲשַׁלֵּם. נֶגְדָה נָּא לְכָל עַמּוֹ: יָקָר בְּעֵינֵי יְהֹוָה. הַמָּוְתָה לַחֲסִידָיו: אָנָּה יְהֹוָה כִּי אֲנִי עַבְדֶּךָ. אֲנִי עַבְדְּךָ בֶּן אֲמָתֶךָ פִּתַּחְתָּ לְמוֹסֵרָי: לְךָ אֶזְבַּח זֶבַח תּוֹדָה. וּבְשֵׁם יְהֹוָה אֶקְרָא: נְדָרַי לַיהֹוָה אֲשַׁלֵּם. נֶגְדָה נָּא לְכָל עַמּוֹ: בְּחַצְרוֹת בֵּית יְהֹוָה. בְּתוֹכֵכִי יְרוּשָׁלָיִם. הַלְלוּיָהּ:

הַלְלוּ אֶת יְהֹוָה כָּל גּוֹיִם. שַׁבְּחוּהוּ כָּל הָאֻמִּים: כִּי גָבַר עָלֵינוּ חַסְדּוֹ. וֶאֱמֶת יְהֹוָה לְעוֹלָם. הַלְלוּיָהּ:

הוֹדוּ לַיהֹוָה כִּי טוֹב. כִּי לְעוֹלָם חַסְדּוֹ:

יֹאמַר נָא יִשְׂרָאֵל. כִּי לְעוֹלָם חַסְדּוֹ:

יֹאמְרוּ נָא בֵית אַהֲרֹן. כִּי לְעוֹלָם חַסְדּוֹ:

יֹאמְרוּ נָא יִרְאֵי יְהֹוָה. כִּי לְעוֹלָם חַסְדּוֹ:

מִן הַמֵּצַר קָרָאתִי יָּהּ. עָנָנִי בַמֶּרְחָב יָהּ: יְהֹוָה לִי לֹא אִירָא. מַה יַּעֲשֶׂה לִי אָדָם: יְהֹוָה לִי בְּעֹזְרָי. וַאֲנִי אֶרְאֶה בְשֹׂנְאָי: טוֹב לַחֲסוֹת בַּיהֹוָה. מִבְּטֹחַ בָּאָדָם: טוֹב לַחֲסוֹת בַּיהֹוָה. מִבְּטֹחַ בִּנְדִיבִים: כָּל גּוֹיִם סְבָבוּנִי. בְּשֵׁם יְהֹוָה כִּי אֲמִילַם: סַבּוּנִי גַם סְבָבוּנִי. בְּשֵׁם יְהֹוָה כִּי אֲמִילַם: סַבּוּנִי כִדְבוֹרִים. דֹּעֲכוּ כְּאֵשׁ קוֹצִים. בְּשֵׁם יְהֹוָה כִּי אֲמִילַם: דָּחֹה דְחִיתַנִי לִנְפֹּל. וַיהֹוָה עֲזָרָנִי: עָזִּי וְזִמְרָת יָהּ. וַיְהִי לִי לִישׁוּעָה: קוֹל רִנָּה וִישׁוּעָה בְּאָהֳלֵי צַדִּיקִים. יְמִין יְהֹוָה עֹשָׂה חָיִל: יְמִין יְהֹוָה רוֹמֵמָה. יְמִין יְהֹוָה עֹשָׂה חָיִל: לֹא אָמוּת כִּי אֶחְיֶה. וַאֲסַפֵּר מַעֲשֵׂי יָהּ: יַסֹּר יִסְּרַנִּי יָּהּ. וְלַמָּוֶת לֹא נְתָנָנִי: פִּתְחוּ לִי שַׁעֲרֵי צֶדֶק. אָבֹא בָם אוֹדֶה יָהּ: זֶה הַשַּׁעַר לַיהֹוָה. צַדִּיקִים יָבֹאוּ בוֹ: אוֹדְךָ כִּי עֲנִיתָנִי. וַתְּהִי לִי לִישׁוּעָה: אוֹדְךָ כִּי עֲנִיתָנִי. וַתְּהִי לִי לִישׁוּעָה: אֶבֶן מָאֲסוּ הַבּוֹנִים. הָיְתָה לְרֹאשׁ פִּנָּה: אֶבֶן מָאֲסוּ הַבּוֹנִים. הָיְתָה לְרֹאשׁ פִּנָּה: מֵאֵת יְהֹוָה הָיְתָה זֹּאת. הִיא נִפְלָאת

בְּעֵינֵינוּ: מֵאֵת יְהֹוָה הָיְתָה זֹּאת. הִיא נִפְלָאת בְּעֵינֵינוּ: זֶה הַיּוֹם עָשָׂה יְהֹוָה. נָגִילָה וְנִשְׂמְחָה בוֹ: זֶה הַיּוֹם עָשָׂה יְהֹוָה. נָגִילָה וְנִשְׂמְחָה בוֹ:

אָנָּא יְהֹוָה הוֹשִׁיעָה נָּא:	אָנָּא יְהֹוָה הוֹשִׁיעָה נָּא:
אָנָּא יְהֹוָה הַצְלִיחָה נָּא:	אָנָּא יְהֹוָה הַצְלִיחָה נָּא:

בָּרוּךְ הַבָּא בְּשֵׁם יְהֹוָה. בֵּרַכְנוּכֶם מִבֵּית יְהֹוָה: בָּרוּךְ הַבָּא בְּשֵׁם יְהֹוָה. בֵּרַכְנוּכֶם מִבֵּית יְהֹוָה: אֵל יְהֹוָה וַיָּאֶר לָנוּ. אִסְרוּ חַג בַּעֲבֹתִים. עַד קַרְנוֹת הַמִּזְבֵּחַ: אֵל יְהֹוָה וַיָּאֶר לָנוּ. אִסְרוּ חַג בַּעֲבֹתִים. עַד קַרְנוֹת הַמִּזְבֵּחַ: אֵלִי אַתָּה וְאוֹדֶךָּ. אֱלֹהַי אֲרוֹמְמֶךָּ: אֵלִי אַתָּה וְאוֹדֶךָּ. אֱלֹהַי אֲרוֹמְמֶךָּ: הוֹדוּ לַיהֹוָה כִּי טוֹב. כִּי לְעוֹלָם חַסְדּוֹ: הוֹדוּ לַיהֹוָה כִּי טוֹב. כִּי לְעוֹלָם חַסְדּוֹ:

הוֹדוּ לַיהֹוָה כִּי טוֹב.	כִּי לְעוֹלָם חַסְדּוֹ:
הוֹדוּ לֵאלֹהֵי הָאֱלֹהִים.	כִּי לְעוֹלָם חַסְדּוֹ:
הוֹדוּ לַאֲדֹנֵי הָאֲדֹנִים.	כִּי לְעוֹלָם חַסְדּוֹ:
לְעֹשֵׂה נִפְלָאוֹת גְּדֹלוֹת לְבַדּוֹ.	כִּי לְעוֹלָם חַסְדּוֹ:
לְעֹשֵׂה הַשָּׁמַיִם בִּתְבוּנָה.	כִּי לְעוֹלָם חַסְדּוֹ:
לְרוֹקַע הָאָרֶץ עַל הַמָּיִם.	כִּי לְעוֹלָם חַסְדּוֹ:
לְעֹשֵׂה אוֹרִים גְּדֹלִים.	כִּי לְעוֹלָם חַסְדּוֹ:
אֶת הַשֶּׁמֶשׁ לְמֶמְשֶׁלֶת בַּיּוֹם.	כִּי לְעוֹלָם חַסְדּוֹ:
אֶת הַיָּרֵחַ וְכוֹכָבִים לְמֶמְשְׁלוֹת בַּלָּיְלָה.	כִּי לְעוֹלָם חַסְדּוֹ:
לְמַכֵּה מִצְרַיִם בִּבְכוֹרֵיהֶם.	כִּי לְעוֹלָם חַסְדּוֹ:

וַיּוֹצֵא יִשְׂרָאֵל מִתּוֹכָם. כִּי לְעוֹלָם חַסְדּוֹ:
בְּיָד חֲזָקָה וּבִזְרוֹעַ נְטוּיָה. כִּי לְעוֹלָם חַסְדּוֹ:
לְגֹזֵר יַם סוּף לִגְזָרִים. כִּי לְעוֹלָם חַסְדּוֹ:
וְהֶעֱבִיר יִשְׂרָאֵל בְּתוֹכוֹ. כִּי לְעוֹלָם חַסְדּוֹ:
וְנִעֵר פַּרְעֹה וְחֵילוֹ בְיַם סוּף. כִּי לְעוֹלָם חַסְדּוֹ:
לְמוֹלִיךְ עַמּוֹ בַּמִּדְבָּר. כִּי לְעוֹלָם חַסְדּוֹ:
לְמַכֵּה מְלָכִים גְּדֹלִים. כִּי לְעוֹלָם חַסְדּוֹ:
וַיַּהֲרֹג מְלָכִים אַדִּירִים. כִּי לְעוֹלָם חַסְדּוֹ:
לְסִיחוֹן מֶלֶךְ הָאֱמֹרִי. כִּי לְעוֹלָם חַסְדּוֹ:
וּלְעוֹג מֶלֶךְ הַבָּשָׁן. כִּי לְעוֹלָם חַסְדּוֹ:
וְנָתַן אַרְצָם לְנַחֲלָה. כִּי לְעוֹלָם חַסְדּוֹ:
נַחֲלָה לְיִשְׂרָאֵל עַבְדּוֹ. כִּי לְעוֹלָם חַסְדּוֹ:
שֶׁבְּשִׁפְלֵנוּ זָכַר לָנוּ. כִּי לְעוֹלָם חַסְדּוֹ:
וַיִּפְרְקֵנוּ מִצָּרֵינוּ. כִּי לְעוֹלָם חַסְדּוֹ:
נוֹתֵן לֶחֶם לְכָל בָּשָׂר. כִּי לְעוֹלָם חַסְדּוֹ:
הוֹדוּ לְאֵל הַשָּׁמָיִם. כִּי לְעוֹלָם חַסְדּוֹ:

נִשְׁמַת כָּל חַי תְּבָרֵךְ אֶת שִׁמְךָ יְהוָֹה אֱלֹהֵינוּ. וְרוּחַ כָּל בָּשָׂר תְּפָאֵר וּתְרוֹמֵם זִכְרְךָ מַלְכֵּנוּ תָּמִיד: מִן הָעוֹלָם וְעַד הָעוֹלָם אַתָּה אֵל. וּמִבַּלְעָדֶיךָ אֵין לָנוּ מֶלֶךְ גּוֹאֵל וּמוֹשִׁיעַ. פּוֹדֶה וּמַצִּיל וּמְפַרְנֵס וְעוֹנֶה וּמְרַחֵם בְּכָל עֵת צָרָה וְצוּקָה. אֵין לָנוּ מֶלֶךְ עוֹזֵר וְסוֹמֵךְ אֶלָּא אָתָּה: אֱלֹהֵי הָרִאשׁוֹנִים וְהָאַחֲרוֹנִים. אֱלוֹהַּ כָּל בְּרִיּוֹת.

אֲדוֹן כָּל תּוֹלָדוֹת. הַמְהֻלָּל בְּכָל (בְּרוֹב) הַתִּשְׁבָּחוֹת. הַמְנַהֵג עוֹלָמוֹ בְּחֶסֶד וּבְרִיּוֹתָיו בְּרַחֲמִים: וַיהוָה עֵר. הִנֵּה לֹא יָנוּם וְלֹא יִישָׁן. הַמְעוֹרֵר יְשֵׁנִים. וְהַמֵּקִיץ נִרְדָּמִים. וְהַמֵּשִׂיחַ אִלְּמִים. וְהַמַּתִּיר אֲסוּרִים. וְהַסּוֹמֵךְ נוֹפְלִים. וְהַזּוֹקֵף כְּפוּפִים. וְהַמְפַעְנֵחַ נֶעֱלָמִים. וּלְךָ לְבַדְּךָ אֲנַחְנוּ מוֹדִים: וְאִלּוּ פִינוּ מָלֵא שִׁירָה כַּיָּם. וּלְשׁוֹנֵנוּ רִנָּה כַּהֲמוֹן גַּלָּיו. וְשִׂפְתוֹתֵינוּ שֶׁבַח כְּמֶרְחֲבֵי רָקִיעַ. וְעֵינֵינוּ מְאִירוֹת כַּשֶּׁמֶשׁ וְכַיָּרֵחַ. וְיָדֵינוּ פְרוּשׂוֹת כְּנִשְׁרֵי שָׁמָיִם. וְרַגְלֵינוּ קַלּוֹת כָּאַיָּלוֹת. אֵין אֲנַחְנוּ מַסְפִּיקִים לְהוֹדוֹת לְךָ יְהוָה אֱלֹהֵינוּ וֵאלֹהֵי אֲבוֹתֵינוּ. וּלְבָרֵךְ אֶת שִׁמְךָ מַלְכֵּנוּ. עַל אַחַת מֵאָלֶף אֶלֶף אַלְפֵי אֲלָפִים וְרִבֵּי רְבָבוֹת פְּעָמִים. הַטּוֹבוֹת נִסִּים וְנִפְלָאוֹת שֶׁעָשִׂיתָ עִם אֲבוֹתֵינוּ וְעִמָּנוּ: מִלְּפָנִים מִמִּצְרַיִם גְּאַלְתָּנוּ יְהוָה אֱלֹהֵינוּ. וּמִבֵּית עֲבָדִים פְּדִיתָנוּ. בְּרָעָב זַנְתָּנוּ. וּבְשָׂבָע כִּלְכַּלְתָּנוּ. מֵחֶרֶב הִצַּלְתָּנוּ. וּמִדֶּבֶר מִלַּטְתָּנוּ. וּמֵחֳלָיִם רָעִים וְרַבִּים וְנֶאֱמָנִים דִּלִּיתָנוּ: עַד הֵנָּה עֲזָרוּנוּ רַחֲמֶיךָ. וְלֹא עֲזָבוּנוּ חֲסָדֶיךָ יְהוָה אֱלֹהֵינוּ. וְאַל תִּטְּשֵׁנוּ יְהוָה אֱלֹהֵינוּ לָנֶצַח: עַל כֵּן אֵבָרִים שֶׁפִּלַּגְתָּ בָּנוּ. וְרוּחַ וּנְשָׁמָה שֶׁנָּפַחְתָּ בְּאַפֵּינוּ. וְלָשׁוֹן אֲשֶׁר שַׂמְתָּ בְּפִינוּ. הֵן הֵם. יוֹדוּ וִיבָרְכוּ וִישַׁבְּחוּ וִיפָאֲרוּ וִישׁוֹרְרוּ וִירוֹמְמוּ וְיַעֲרִיצוּ וְיַקְדִּישׁוּ וְיַמְלִיכוּ אֶת שִׁמְךָ מַלְכֵּנוּ תָמִיד: כִּי כָל פֶּה לְךָ יוֹדֶה. וְכָל לָשׁוֹן לְךָ תִשָּׁבַע. וְכָל עַיִן לְךָ תְצַפֶּה. וְכָל בֶּרֶךְ לְךָ תִכְרַע. וְכָל קוֹמָה לְפָנֶיךָ תִשְׁתַּחֲוֶה. וְכָל הַלְּבָבוֹת יִירָאוּךָ. וְכָל קֶרֶב וּכְלָיוֹת יְזַמְּרוּ לִשְׁמֶךָ. כַּדָּבָר שֶׁכָּתוּב. כָּל עַצְמוֹתַי תֹּאמַרְנָה יְהוָה מִי כָמוֹךָ. מַצִּיל עָנִי מֵחָזָק מִמֶּנּוּ. וְעָנִי וְאֶבְיוֹן מִגּוֹזְלוֹ. שַׁוְעַת עֲנִיִּים אַתָּה תִשְׁמַע. צַעֲקַת הַדַּל תַּקְשִׁיב וְתוֹשִׁיעַ: מִי יִדְמֶה לָּךְ. וּמִי יִשְׁוֶה לָּךְ. וּמִי יַעֲרָךְ לָךְ. הָאֵל הַגָּדוֹל הַגִּבּוֹר וְהַנּוֹרָא אֵל עֶלְיוֹן. קוֹנֵה שָׁמַיִם וָאָרֶץ: נְהַלֶּלְךָ וּנְשַׁבֵּחֲךָ וּנְפָאֶרְךָ וּנְבָרֵךְ אֶת שֵׁם קָדְשֶׁךָ. כָּאָמוּר. לְדָוִד. בָּרְכִי נַפְשִׁי אֶת יְהוָה. וְכָל קְרָבַי אֶת שֵׁם קָדְשׁוֹ:

הָאֵל בְּתַעֲצֻמוֹת עֻזֶּךָ. הַגָּדוֹל בִּכְבוֹד שְׁמֶךָ. הַגִּבּוֹר לָנֶצַח וְהַנּוֹרָא בְּנוֹרְאוֹתֶיךָ: הַמֶּלֶךְ הַיּוֹשֵׁב עַל כִּסֵּא רָם וְנִשָּׂא:

שׁוֹכֵן עַד מָרוֹם וְקָדוֹשׁ שְׁמוֹ. וְכָתוּב רַנְּנוּ צַדִּיקִים בַּיהֹוָה. לַיְשָׁרִים נָאוָה תְהִלָּה. בְּפִי יְשָׁרִים תִּתְרוֹמָם. וּבְשִׂפְתֵי צַדִּיקִים תִּתְבָּרַךְ. וּבִלְשׁוֹן חֲסִידִים תִּתְקַדָּשׁ. וּבְקֶרֶב קְדוֹשִׁים תִּתְהַלָּל:

וּבְמַקְהֲלוֹת רִבְבוֹת עַמְּךָ בֵּית יִשְׂרָאֵל. בְּרִנָּה יִתְפָּאֵר שִׁמְךָ מַלְכֵּנוּ בְּכָל דּוֹר וָדוֹר. שֶׁכֵּן חוֹבַת כָּל הַיְצוּרִים. לְפָנֶיךָ יְהֹוָה אֱלֹהֵינוּ וֵאלֹהֵי אֲבוֹתֵינוּ. לְהוֹדוֹת לְהַלֵּל לְשַׁבֵּחַ לְפָאֵר לְרוֹמֵם לְהַדֵּר וּלְנַצֵּחַ לְבָרֵךְ לְעַלֵּה וּלְקַלֵּס. עַל כָּל דִּבְרֵי שִׁירוֹת וְתִשְׁבְּחוֹת דָּוִד בֶּן יִשַׁי עַבְדְּךָ מְשִׁיחֶךָ:

וּבְכֵן יִשְׁתַּבַּח שִׁמְךָ לָעַד מַלְכֵּנוּ. הָאֵל הַמֶּלֶךְ הַגָּדוֹל וְהַקָּדוֹשׁ בַּשָּׁמַיִם וּבָאָרֶץ. כִּי לְךָ נָאֶה יְהֹוָה אֱלֹהֵינוּ וֵאלֹהֵי אֲבוֹתֵינוּ: שִׁיר וּשְׁבָחָה. הַלֵּל וְזִמְרָה. עוֹז וּמֶמְשָׁלָה. נֶצַח גְּדֻלָּה וּגְבוּרָה. תְּהִלָּה וְתִפְאֶרֶת. קְדֻשָּׁה וּמַלְכוּת: בְּרָכוֹת וְהוֹדָאוֹת לְשִׁמְךָ הַגָּדוֹל וְהַקָּדוֹשׁ. וּמֵעוֹלָם וְעַד עוֹלָם אַתָּה אֵל:

יְהַלְלוּךָ יְהֹוָה אֱלֹהֵינוּ עַל כָּל מַעֲשֶׂיךָ. וַחֲסִידֶיךָ צַדִּיקִים עוֹשֵׂי רְצוֹנֶךָ. וְכָל עַמְּךָ בֵּית יִשְׂרָאֵל. בְּרִנָּה יוֹדוּ וִיבָרְכוּ וִישַׁבְּחוּ וִיפָאֲרוּ וִישׁוֹרְרוּ וִירוֹמְמוּ וְיַעֲרִיצוּ וְיַקְדִּישׁוּ וְיַמְלִיכוּ אֶת שִׁמְךָ מַלְכֵּנוּ תָּמִיד. כִּי לְךָ טוֹב לְהוֹדוֹת. וּלְשִׁמְךָ נָאֶה לְזַמֵּר. כִּי מֵעוֹלָם וְעַד עוֹלָם אַתָּה אֵל: בָּרוּךְ אַתָּה יְהֹוָה מֶלֶךְ מְהֻלָּל בַּתִּשְׁבָּחוֹת:

Hallel

On the seventh day of Pesach, when the Egyptians were drowned in the Red Sea, the angels in Heaven wished to sing shira, a song of praise to Hashem. But Hashem told them, "My creations are drowning in the sea, and you want to sing shira?" Since our Exodus prevented one shira to Hashem from being sung in Heaven, we compensate by saying Hallel on the night of Pesach.

(Eizor Eliyahu)

At Night

Hallel, a litany of praises to Hashem, is normally recited only during the day. The Talmud *(Megillah 20b)* quotes two verses from *Tehillim* to support this rule: "From the rising of the sun to its setting ..." *(Tehillim 113:3)* and, "This is the day Hashem has made"

(Tehillim 118:24).

Pesach is an exception to the rule. In Egypt, when Hashem killed every firstborn Egyptian and havoc reigned outside, the Children of Israel stayed locked in their homes singing the praises of Hashem. Yeshaya the prophet said, "The song will be yours like the night when the holiday [of Pesach, in Egypt] became holy" *(Yeshaya 30:29)*. Our Sages deduced from here that we should say *Hallel* on the night of Pesach, just as the Jews in Egypt recited *Hallel* over their *Korban Pesach*.

(Chasam Sofer, Orach Chaim 51)

The night of Pesach is different from every other night. That night, according to the Zohar, is bright as daylight. Although not actually daytime, it is an appropriate time for *Hallel*.

(Sfas Emes 5644)

Dividing Hallel

At the *Seder* we divide *Hallel* into two, reciting the first two Psalms before the meal and the rest after the meal. Since it is divided into two sections, we say no blessing. A blessing is only recited on *Hallel* when it is recited all at once.

(Levush 472)

The Hallel said on Pesach night offers praise to Hashem for the miracle He did for us in Egypt on this night by killing all the Egyptian firstborn. It does not have the same halachic status as the obligatory Yom Tov Hallel. This Hallel is a shira, a spontaneous song of praise, and as such it does not require a blessing.

(Avudraham; Chiddushei Rabbi Yitzchak Zev Halevi Soloveitchik, Chanuka 3:6)

The first two Psalms of *Hallel* refer to the Exodus from Egypt, and appropriately belong with the story of the *Haggada*, the miracles of the Exodus. But the rest of *Hallel* refers to the redemptions from subsequent exiles, including the future *geulah*, the focus of the *Seder* after the meal.

(Levush 480)

We normally never interrupt in the middle of saying *Hallel*. But we do so on the night of Pesach to differentiate from our practice during the rest of the year. It prompts the children to ask questions.

(Seder Hayom, Seder Haggada)

Others contest that all the things we do in between the two parts of *Hallel* do not constitute a division. Drinking cups of wine, washing hands, eating *matzah*, *marror* and *charoses*, the *Yom Tov* meal, *bentching*- are all actions of spiritual content. The perfomance of *mitzvos* is not considered an interruption.

(Chiddushei Harim)

The Fourth Cup

The blessing over the fourth cup is recited.

הִנְנִי מוּכָן וּמְזוּמָן לְקַיֵּם מִצְוַת כּוֹס רְבִיעִי שֶׁל אַרְבַּע כּוֹסוֹת. לְשֵׁם יִחוּד קוּדְשָׁא בְּרִיךְ הוּא וּשְׁכִינְתֵּיהּ בִּדְחִילוּ וּרְחִימוּ עַל יְדֵי הַהוּא טָמִיר וְנֶעְלָם בְּשֵׁם כָּל יִשְׂרָאֵל: וִיהִי נוֹעַם אֲדֹנָי אֱלֹהֵינוּ עָלֵינוּ וּמַעֲשֵׂה יָדֵינוּ כּוֹנְנָה עָלֵינוּ וּמַעֲשֵׂה יָדֵינוּ כּוֹנְנֵהוּ:

בָּרוּךְ אַתָּה יְהֹוָה אֱלֹהֵינוּ מֶלֶךְ הָעוֹלָם בּוֹרֵא פְּרִי הַגָּפֶן:

Sitting Down

Normally we recite *Hallel* standing, for it is a testimony in praise of Hashem. All testimony must be given while standing, as our Sages derive from the verse referring to witnesses, "And the two men shall stand" *(Devarim 19:17)*. Why on Pesach do we sit?

- *Hallel* is divided at the *Seder*, and our Sages did not wish to bother us by making us stand up twice.

  (Shibbolei Haleket 173)

- It is not in the manner of free men to stand up and sit back down so many times.

  (ibid.)

- While we are saying both parts of Hallel, our cups of wine are on the table, and we are afraid they may be spilled if we have to get up.

  (Beis Yosef 422)

One then drinks this entire cup while reclining on the left side. After drinking the following blessing is recited:

בָּרוּךְ אַתָּה יְהֹוָה אֱלֹהֵינוּ מֶלֶךְ הָעוֹלָם עַל הַגֶּפֶן וְעַל פְּרִי הַגֶּפֶן וְעַל תְּנוּבַת הַשָּׂדֶה וְעַל אֶרֶץ חֶמְדָּה טוֹבָה וּרְחָבָה שֶׁרָצִיתָ וְהִנְחַלְתָּ לַאֲבוֹתֵינוּ לֶאֱכוֹל מִפִּרְיָהּ וְלִשְׂבּוֹעַ מִטּוּבָהּ. רַחֶם נָא יְהֹוָה אֱלֹהֵינוּ עַל יִשְׂרָאֵל עַמֶּךָ וְעַל יְרוּשָׁלַיִם עִירֶךָ וְעַל צִיּוֹן מִשְׁכַּן כְּבוֹדֶךָ וְעַל מִזְבְּחֶךָ וְעַל הֵיכָלֶךָ. וּבְנֵה יְרוּשָׁלַיִם עִיר הַקֹּדֶשׁ בִּמְהֵרָה בְיָמֵינוּ וְהַעֲלֵנוּ לְתוֹכָהּ וְשַׂמְּחֵנוּ בְּבִנְיָנָהּ וְנֹאכַל מִפִּרְיָהּ וְנִשְׂבַּע מִטּוּבָהּ וּנְבָרֶכְךָ עָלֶיהָ בִּקְדֻשָּׁה וּבְטָהֳרָה. (בשבת: וּרְצֵה וְהַחֲלִיצֵנוּ בְּיוֹם הַשַּׁבָּת הַזֶּה) וְשַׂמְּחֵנוּ בְּיוֹם חַג הַמַּצּוֹת הַזֶּה. כִּי אַתָּה יְהֹוָה טוֹב וּמֵטִיב לַכֹּל וְנוֹדֶה לְּךָ עַל הָאָרֶץ וְעַל פְּרִי הַגָּפֶן: בָּרוּךְ אַתָּה יְהֹוָה עַל הָאָרֶץ וְעַל פְּרִי הַגָּפֶן:

The Fourth Cup

The Fourth Cup

After the fourth cup has been drunk, a concluding blessing is recited. Why don't we recite a concluding blessing of *al hagafen* for the other cups of wine? The first two cups belong to the meal, and are covered by Grace After Meals: *Kiddush*, the first cup, is always recited at the place of the meal, and the second cup immediately precedes the main meal. The third cup, drunk at the end of *birkas hamazon*, is covered by the concluding blessing recited after the fourth cup.

(Turei Zahav 473:2)

נרצה

If all was performed in the correct manner, then one is favored by God and this merit will last forever.

חֲסַל סִדּוּר פֶּסַח כְּהִלְכָתוֹ. כְּכָל מִשְׁפָּטוֹ וְחֻקָּתוֹ. כַּאֲשֶׁר זָכִינוּ
לְסַדֵּר אוֹתוֹ. כֵּן נִזְכֶּה לַעֲשׂוֹתוֹ. זָךְ שׁוֹכֵן מְעוֹנָה. קוֹמֵם קְהַל
עֲדַת מִי מָנָה. בְּקָרוֹב נַהֵל נִטְעֵי כַנָּה. פְּדוּיִם לְצִיּוֹן בְּרִנָּה:

לְשָׁנָה הַבָּאָה בִּירוּשָׁלָיִם ג״פ:

Nirtzah

A Plea to Hashem

As we come to the end of the *Seder* we may become dejected, thinking that perhaps we have not fulfilled all its *mitzvos* properly. If only we could start the *Seder* all over again, we would conduct it more devoutly! Hashem accepts these thoughts, as if we have indeed conducted the whole Seder again correctly. Many recite the verse, "*Vihi noam*-May the pleasantness of Hashem, our Master, be upon us, and establish the accomplishment of our hands upon us." Please, Hashem, accept our deeds and intentions of this evening.

(Rabbi Yissochor Dov Rokeach, third Belzer Rebbe)

The word *nirtzah-nun, reish, tzaddik, hei*-is itself a prayer to Hashem. The first two letters spell *ner*, a lamp or candle. The second two letters-*tzaddik, hei*-equal 95, the sum of the two names of Hashem that will be revealed in the time of Moshiach *(see above-Shulchan Orech)*. In the merit of the *mitzvos* of the *Seder*, we ask Hashem that He should allow the lamp, the *ner*, to shine forth for the Final Redemption.

(Dvar Tzvi)

Next Year in Jerusalem!

One of the rousing excerpts that conclude the *Seder* is a fervent prayer that we recite with much hope and anticipation: "*L'shana haba biYerushalayim*!" Why isn't this part of the standard prayer services more often? This verse is said only twice a year-on Pesach and Yom Kippur.

The Talmud cites two different months in which the Final Redemption will take place-Nissan and Tishrei. Since both views are part of the Torah, both views must be true. But how can the *geulah* take place twice, in two separate months? Perhaps in Nissan there will be redemption on an individual level. And in Tishrei, Hashem will "remove the spirit of impurity from the world," so the entire world population will recognize Hashem as the One Creator.

At the apex of each month-at the end of the *Seder* in Nissan and at the end of *Neilah* on Yom Kippur-we proclaim with fervent prayer, "May we be next year in the rebuilt Jerusalem!"

(Yismach Moshe, Pesach)

But why do we ask for "next year?" We await the *geulah* every single day-why push it off another whole year? Moshiach will arrive with miracles that will exceed even those of the Exodus from Egypt *(Berachos 4a)*. The purpose of the world's creation will be revealed, and accordingly, a new system for counting the years will be instituted-the years since the *geulah*. That is what we mean when we say "next year." Let Moshiach arrive immediately and allow us the privilege to begin counting the years anew. May it be speedily in our days. Amen.

(Divrei Yoel)

The Jewish people were not even aware of G-d's existence; their outcry rose to the Heavens of its own accord.

(Rabbi Yaakov Sakili)

On the first night recite the following.

וּבְכֵן וַיְהִי בַּחֲצִי הַלַּיְלָה:

אָ ז רוֹב נִסִּים הִפְלֵאתָ בַּלַּיְלָה.

בְּ ראשׁ אַשְׁמוֹרֶת זֶה הַלַּיְלָה.

גֵּ ר צֶדֶק נִצַּחְתּוֹ כְּנֶחֱלַק לוֹ לַיְלָה.

וַיְהִי בַּחֲצִי הַלַּיְלָה:

דַּ נְתָּ מֶלֶךְ גְּרָר בַּחֲלוֹם הַלַּיְלָה.

הִ פְחַדְתָּ אֲרַמִּי בְּאֶמֶשׁ לַיְלָה.

וַ יָּשַׂר יִשְׂרָאֵל לָאֵל וַיּוּכַל לוֹ לַיְלָה.

וַיְהִי בַּחֲצִי הַלַּיְלָה:

זֶ רַע בְּכוֹרֵי פַּתְרוֹס מָחַצְתָּ בַּחֲצִי הַלַּיְלָה.

חֵ ילָם לֹא מָצְאוּ בְּקוּמָם בַּלַּיְלָה.

טִ יסַת נְגִיד חֲרוֹשֶׁת סִלִּיתָ בְּכוֹכְבֵי לַיְלָה.

וַיְהִי בַּחֲצִי הַלַּיְלָה:

יָ עַץ מְחָרֵף לְנוֹפֵף אִוּוּי הוֹבַשְׁתָּ פְּגָרָיו בַּלַּיְלָה.

כָּ רַע בֵּל וּמַצָּבוֹ בְּאִישׁוֹן לַיְלָה.

לְ אִישׁ חֲמוּדוֹת נִגְלָה רָז חֲזוֹת לַיְלָה.

וַיְהִי בַּחֲצִי הַלַּיְלָה:

מִ שְׁתַּכֵּר בִּכְלֵי קֹדֶשׁ נֶהֱרַג בּוֹ בַּלַּיְלָה.
נ וֹשַׁע מִבּוֹר אֲרָיוֹת פּוֹתֵר בִּעֲתוּתֵי לַיְלָה.
שִׂ נְאָה נָטַר אֲגָגִי וְכָתַב סְפָרִים בַּלַּיְלָה.

וַיְהִי בַּחֲצִי הַלַּיְלָה:

עוֹ רַרְתָּ נִצְחֲךָ עָלָיו בְּנֶדֶד שְׁנַת לַיְלָה.
פּ וּרָה תִדְרוֹךְ לְשׁוֹמֵר מַה מִלַּיְלָה.
צָ רַח כַּשּׁוֹמֵר וְשָׂח אָתָא בֹקֶר וְגַם לַיְלָה.

וַיְהִי בַּחֲצִי הַלַּיְלָה:

קָ רֵב יוֹם אֲשֶׁר הוּא לֹא יוֹם וְלֹא לַיְלָה.
רָ ם הוֹדַע כִּי לְךָ הַיּוֹם אַף לְךָ הַלַּיְלָה.
שׁ וֹמְרִים הַפְקֵד לְעִירְךָ כָּל הַיּוֹם וְכָל הַלַּיְלָה.
תָּ אִיר כְּאוֹר יוֹם חֶשְׁכַת לַיְלָה.

וַיְהִי בַּחֲצִי הַלַּיְלָה:

On the second night recite the following.

וּבְכֵן וַאֲמַרְתֶּם זֶבַח פֶּסַח:

א וֹמֶץ גְּבוּרוֹתֶיךָ הִפְלֵאתָ בַּפֶּסַח.
בְּ רֹאשׁ כָּל מוֹעֲדוֹת נִשֵּׂאתָ פֶּסַח.
גִּ לִּיתָ לְאֶזְרָחִי חֲצוֹת לֵיל פֶּסַח.

וַאֲמַרְתֶּם זֶבַח פֶּסַח:

דְּ לָתָיו דָּפַקְתָּ כְּחוֹם הַיּוֹם בַּפֶּסַח.
הִ סְעִיד נוֹצְצִים עֻגוֹת מַצּוֹת בַּפֶּסַח.
וְ אֶל הַבָּקָר רָץ זֵכֶר לְשׁוֹר עֵרֶךְ פֶּסַח.

וַאֲמַרְתֶּם זֶבַח פֶּסַח:

ז וֹעֲמוּ סְדוֹמִים וְלֹהֲטוּ בָּאֵשׁ בַּפֶּסַח.
חֻ לַּץ לוֹט מֵהֶם וּמַצּוֹת אָפָה בְּקֵץ פֶּסַח.
טִ אטֵאתָ אַדְמַת מוֹף וְנוֹף בְּעָבְרְךָ בַּפֶּסַח.

וַאֲמַרְתֶּם זֶבַח פֶּסַח:

יָ הּ רֹאשׁ כָּל אוֹן מָחַצְתָּ בְּלֵיל שִׁמּוּר פֶּסַח.
כַּ בִּיר עַל בֵּן בְּכוֹר פָּסַחְתָּ בְּדַם פֶּסַח.
לְ בִלְתִּי תֵּת מַשְׁחִית לָבֹא בִּפְתָחַי בַּפֶּסַח.

וַאֲמַרְתֶּם זֶבַח פֶּסַח:

מְ סֻגֶּרֶת סֻגָּרָה בְּעִתּוֹתֵי פֶּסַח.
נִ שְׁמְדָה מִדְיָן בִּצְלִיל שְׂעוֹרֵי עוֹמֶר פֶּסַח.
שׂ וֹרְפוּ מִשְׁמַנֵּי פּוּל וְלוּד בִּיקַד יְקוֹד פֶּסַח.

וַאֲמַרְתֶּם זֶבַח פֶּסַח:

עֽ וֹד הַיּוֹם בְּנוֹב לַעֲמוֹד עַד גָּעָה עוֹנַת פֶּסַח.
פַּ ס יָד כָּתְבָה לְקַעֲקֵעַ צוּל בַּפֶּסַח.
צָ פֹה הַצָּפִית עָרוֹךְ הַשֻּׁלְחָן בַּפֶּסַח.

וַאֲמַרְתֶּם זֶבַח פֶּסַח:

קָ הָל כִּנְסָה הֲדַסָּה צוֹם לְשַׁלֵּשׁ בַּפֶּסַח.

רֹ אשׁ מִבֵּית רָשָׁע מָחַצְתָּ בְּעֵץ חֲמִשִּׁים בַּפֶּסַח.

שְׁ תֵּי אֵלֶּה רֶגַע תָּבִיא לְעוּצִית בַּפֶּסַח.

תָּ עוֹז יָדְךָ וְתָרוּם יְמִינְךָ כְּלֵיל הִתְקַדֵּשׁ חַג פֶּסַח.

וַאֲמַרְתֶּם זֶבַח פֶּסַח:

On both nights continue here:

כִּי לוֹ נָאֶה. כִּי לוֹ יָאֶה:

אַדִּיר בִּמְלוּכָה. **בָּ**חוּר כַּהֲלָכָה. **גְּ**דוּדָיו יֹאמְרוּ לוֹ: לְךָ וּלְךָ. לְךָ כִּי לְךָ. לְךָ אַף לְךָ. לְךָ יְהוָֹה הַמַּמְלָכָה.

כִּי לוֹ נָאֶה. כִּי לוֹ יָאֶה:

דָּגוּל בִּמְלוּכָה. **הָ**דוּר כַּהֲלָכָה. **וָ**תִיקָיו יֹאמְרוּ לוֹ: לְךָ וּלְךָ. לְךָ כִּי לְךָ. לְךָ אַף לְךָ. לְךָ יְהוָֹה הַמַּמְלָכָה.

כִּי לוֹ נָאֶה. כִּי לוֹ יָאֶה:

זַכַּאי בִּמְלוּכָה. **חָ**סִין כַּהֲלָכָה. **טַ**פְסְרָיו יֹאמְרוּ לוֹ: לְךָ וּלְךָ. לְךָ כִּי לְךָ. לְךָ אַף לְךָ. לְךָ יְהוָֹה הַמַּמְלָכָה.

כִּי לוֹ נָאֶה. כִּי לוֹ יָאֶה:

יָחִיד בִּמְלוּכָה. **כַּ**בִּיר כַּהֲלָכָה. **לִ**מּוּדָיו יֹאמְרוּ לוֹ: לְךָ וּלְךָ. לְךָ כִּי לְךָ. לְךָ אַף לְךָ. לְךָ יְהוָֹה הַמַּמְלָכָה.

כִּי לוֹ נָאֶה. כִּי לוֹ יָאֶה:

מֶלֶךְ בִּמְלוּכָה. נוֹרָא כַּהֲלָכָה. סְבִיבָיו יֹאמְרוּ לוֹ: לְךָ וּלְךָ. לְךָ כִּי לְךָ. לְךָ אַף לְךָ. לְךָ יְהֹוָה הַמַּמְלָכָה.

כִּי לוֹ נָאֶה. כִּי לוֹ יָאֶה:

עָנָיו בִּמְלוּכָה. פּוֹדֶה כַּהֲלָכָה. צַדִּיקָיו יֹאמְרוּ לוֹ: לְךָ וּלְךָ. לְךָ כִּי לְךָ. לְךָ אַף לְךָ. לְךָ יְהֹוָה הַמַּמְלָכָה.

כִּי לוֹ נָאֶה. כִּי לוֹ יָאֶה:

קָדוֹשׁ בִּמְלוּכָה. רַחוּם כַּהֲלָכָה. שִׁנְאַנָּיו יֹאמְרוּ לוֹ: לְךָ וּלְךָ. לְךָ כִּי לְךָ. לְךָ אַף לְךָ. לְךָ יְהֹוָה הַמַּמְלָכָה.

כִּי לוֹ נָאֶה. כִּי לוֹ יָאֶה:

תַּקִּיף בִּמְלוּכָה. תּוֹמֵךְ כַּהֲלָכָה. תְּמִימָיו יֹאמְרוּ לוֹ: לְךָ וּלְךָ. לְךָ כִּי לְךָ. לְךָ אַף לְךָ. לְךָ יְהֹוָה הַמַּמְלָכָה.

כִּי לוֹ נָאֶה. כִּי לוֹ יָאֶה:

אַדִּיר הוּא יִבְנֶה בֵיתוֹ בְּקָרוֹב.

בִּמְהֵרָה בִּמְהֵרָה בְּיָמֵינוּ בְּקָרוֹב. אֵל בְּנֵה אֵל בְּנֵה. בְּנֵה בֵיתְךָ בְּקָרוֹב:

בָּחוּר הוּא. גָּדוֹל הוּא. דָּגוּל הוּא. יִבְנֶה בֵיתוֹ בְּקָרוֹב. בִּמְהֵרָה בִּמְהֵרָה בְּיָמֵינוּ בְּקָרוֹב.

אֵל בְּנֵה אֵל בְּנֵה. בְּנֵה בֵיתְךָ בְּקָרוֹב:

הָדוּר הוּא. וָתִיק הוּא. זַכַּאי הוּא. חָסִיד הוּא. יִבְנֶה בֵיתוֹ בְּקָרוֹב. בִּמְהֵרָה בִּמְהֵרָה בְּיָמֵינוּ בְּקָרוֹב.

אֵל בְּנֵה אֵל בְּנֵה. בְּנֵה בֵיתְךָ בְּקָרוֹב:

טָהוֹר הוּא. יָחִיד הוּא. כַּבִּיר הוּא. לָמוּד הוּא. מֶלֶךְ הוּא. נוֹרָא הוּא. סַגִּיב הוּא. עִזּוּז הוּא. פּוֹדֶה הוּא. צַדִּיק הוּא. יִבְנֶה בֵיתוֹ בְּקָרוֹב. בִּמְהֵרָה בִּמְהֵרָה בְּיָמֵינוּ בְּקָרוֹב.

אֵל בְּנֵה אֵל בְּנֵה. בְּנֵה בֵיתְךָ בְּקָרוֹב:

קָדוֹשׁ הוּא. רַחוּם הוּא. שַׁדַּי הוּא. תַּקִּיף הוּא. יִבְנֶה בֵיתוֹ בְּקָרוֹב. בִּמְהֵרָה בִּמְהֵרָה בְּיָמֵינוּ בְּקָרוֹב. אֵל בְּנֵה אֵל בְּנֵה. בְּנֵה בֵיתְךָ בְּקָרוֹב:

סדר ספירת העומר:

On the 16th day of nissan, the second evening of Pesach, one begins to Count the Omer. Outside the Holy Land this takes place on the night of the Second Seder. Some begin counting in the synagogue at the conclusion of the Evening Service, but, according to the ARI, one should count at the seder.

Prior to Counting the Omer the following is said:

לְשֵׁם יִחוּד קוּדְשָׁא בְּרִיךְ הוּא וּשְׁכִינְתֵּיהּ בִּדְחִילוּ וּרְחִימוּ. לְיַחֵד שֵׁם י״ה בו״ה בְּיִחוּדָא שְׁלִים בְּשֵׁם כָּל יִשְׂרָאֵל הִנְנִי מוּכָן וּמְזוּמָן לְקַיֵּם מִצְוַת עֲשֵׂה שֶׁל סְפִירַת הָעוֹמֶר. כְּמוֹ שֶׁכָּתוּב בַּתּוֹרָה. וּסְפַרְתֶּם לָכֶם מִמָּחֳרַת הַשַּׁבָּת מִיּוֹם הֲבִיאֲכֶם אֶת עוֹמֶר הַתְּנוּפָה. שֶׁבַע שַׁבָּתוֹת תְּמִימוֹת תִּהְיֶינָה. עַד מִמָּחֳרַת הַשַּׁבָּת הַשְּׁבִיעִית תִּסְפְּרוּ חֲמִשִּׁים יוֹם. וְהִקְרַבְתֶּם מִנְחָה חֲדָשָׁה לַיהוָה:וִיהִי נוֹעַם אֲדֹנָי אֱלֹהֵינוּ עָלֵינוּ. וּמַעֲשֵׂה יָדֵינוּ כּוֹנְנָה עָלֵינוּ. וּמַעֲשֵׂה יָדֵינוּ כּוֹנְנֵהוּ:

בָּרוּךְ אַתָּה יְהֹוָה אֱלֹהֵינוּ מֶלֶךְ הָעוֹלָם. אֲשֶׁר קִדְּשָׁנוּ בְּמִצְוֹתָיו וְצִוָּנוּ עַל סְפִירַת הָעוֹמֶר:

הַיּוֹם יוֹם אֶחָד לָעוֹמֶר:

אלהים ישמחו **אנא** **חסד שבחסד**

הָרַחֲמָן. הוּא יַחֲזִיר לָנוּ עֲבוֹדַת בֵּית הַמִּקְדָּשׁ לִמְקוֹמָהּ בִּמְהֵרָה בְּיָמֵינוּ. אָמֵן סֶלָה:

לַמְנַצֵּחַ בִּנְגִינוֹת מִזְמוֹר שִׁיר: אֱלֹהִים יְחָנֵּנוּ וִיבָרְכֵנוּ יָאֵר פָּנָיו אִתָּנוּ סֶלָה: לָדַעַת בָּאָרֶץ דַּרְכֶּךָ בְּכָל גּוֹיִם יְשׁוּעָתֶךָ: יוֹדוּךָ עַמִּים אֱלֹהִים יוֹדוּךָ עַמִּים כֻּלָּם: יִשְׂמְחוּ וִירַנְּנוּ לְאֻמִּים כִּי תִשְׁפֹּט עַמִּים מִישֹׁר וּלְאֻמִּים בָּאָרֶץ תַּנְחֵם סֶלָה: יוֹדוּךָ עַמִּים אֱלֹהִים יוֹדוּךָ עַמִּים כֻּלָּם: אֶרֶץ נָתְנָה יְבוּלָהּ יְבָרְכֵנוּ אֱלֹהִים אֱלֹהֵינוּ: יְבָרְכֵנוּ אֱלֹהִים וְיִירְאוּ אוֹתוֹ כָּל אַפְסֵי אָרֶץ:

אָנָּא בְּכֹחַ. גְּדֻלַּת יְמִינְךָ. תַּתִּיר צְרוּרָה: קַבֵּל רִנַּת עַמְּךָ. שַׂגְּבֵנוּ טַהֲרֵנוּ נוֹרָא: נָא גִבּוֹר. דּוֹרְשֵׁי יִחוּדְךָ. כְּבָבַת שָׁמְרֵם: בָּרְכֵם טַהֲרֵם. רַחֲמֵי צִדְקָתְךָ. תָּמִיד גָּמְלֵם: חֲסִין קָדוֹשׁ. בְּרוֹב טוּבְךָ. נַהֵל עֲדָתֶךָ: יָחִיד גֵּאֶה. לְעַמְּךָ פְּנֵה. זוֹכְרֵי קְדֻשָּׁתֶךָ: שַׁוְעָתֵנוּ קַבֵּל. וּשְׁמַע צַעֲקָתֵנוּ. יוֹדֵעַ תַּעֲלוּמוֹת:

בָּרוּךְ שֵׁם כְּבוֹד מַלְכוּתוֹ לְעוֹלָם וָעֶד:

רִבּוֹנוֹ שֶׁל עוֹלָם. אַתָּה צִוִּיתָנוּ עַל יְדֵי מֹשֶׁה עַבְדֶּךָ לִסְפּוֹר סְפִירַת הָעוֹמֶר כְּדֵי לְטַהֲרֵנוּ מִקְּלִפּוֹתֵינוּ וּמִטּוּמְאוֹתֵינוּ. כְּמוֹ שֶׁכָּתַבְתָּ בְּתוֹרָתֶךָ. וּסְפַרְתֶּם לָכֶם מִמָּחֳרַת הַשַּׁבָּת מִיּוֹם הֲבִיאֲכֶם אֶת עוֹמֶר

הַתְּנוּפָה שֶׁבַע שַׁבָּתוֹת תְּמִימוֹת תִּהְיֶינָה. עַד מִמָּחֳרַת הַשַּׁבָּת הַשְּׁבִיעִית תִּסְפְּרוּ חֲמִשִּׁים יוֹם. כְּדֵי שֶׁיִּטָּהֲרוּ נַפְשׁוֹת עַמְּךָ יִשְׂרָאֵל מִזֻּהֲמָתָם:

וּבְכֵן יְהִי רָצוֹן מִלְּפָנֶיךָ יְהֹוָה אֱלֹהֵינוּ וֵאלֹהֵי אֲבוֹתֵינוּ שֶׁבִּזְכוּת סְפִירַת הָעוֹמֶר שֶׁסָּפַרְתִּי הַיּוֹם יְתֻקַּן מַה שֶּׁפָּגַמְתִּי בִּסְפִירָה (השייך לאותו הלילה). וְאֶטָּהֵר וְאֶתְקַדֵּשׁ בִּקְדֻשָּׁה שֶׁל מַעְלָה. וְעַל יְדֵי זֶה יֻשְׁפַּע שֶׁפַע רַב בְּכָל הָעוֹלָמוֹת וּלְתַקֵּן אֶת נַפְשׁוֹתֵינוּ וְרוּחוֹתֵינוּ וְנִשְׁמוֹתֵינוּ מִכָּל סִיג וּפְגָם. וּלְטַהֲרֵנוּ וּלְקַדְּשֵׁנוּ בִּקְדֻשָּׁתְךָ הָעֶלְיוֹנָה. אָמֵן סֶלָה:

אֶחָד מִי יוֹדֵעַ.

אֶחָד אֲנִי יוֹדֵעַ. אֶחָד אֱלֹהֵינוּ שֶׁבַּשָּׁמַיִם וּבָאָרֶץ:

שְׁנַיִם מִי יוֹדֵעַ. שְׁנַיִם אֲנִי יוֹדֵעַ. שְׁנֵי לוּחוֹת הַבְּרִית. אֶחָד אֱלֹהֵינוּ שֶׁבַּשָּׁמַיִם וּבָאָרֶץ:

שְׁלֹשָׁה מִי יוֹדֵעַ. שְׁלֹשָׁה אֲנִי יוֹדֵעַ. שְׁלֹשָׁה אָבוֹת. שְׁנֵי לוּחוֹת הַבְּרִית. אֶחָד אֱלֹהֵינוּ שֶׁבַּשָּׁמַיִם וּבָאָרֶץ:

אַרְבַּע מִי יוֹדֵעַ. אַרְבַּע אֲנִי יוֹדֵעַ. אַרְבַּע אִמָּהוֹת. שְׁלֹשָׁה אָבוֹת. שְׁנֵי לוּחוֹת הַבְּרִית. אֶחָד אֱלֹהֵינוּ שֶׁבַּשָּׁמַיִם וּבָאָרֶץ:

חֲמִשָּׁה מִי יוֹדֵעַ. חֲמִשָּׁה אֲנִי יוֹדֵעַ. חֲמִשָּׁה חוּמְשֵׁי תוֹרָה. אַרְבַּע אִמָּהוֹת. שְׁלֹשָׁה אָבוֹת. שְׁנֵי לוּחוֹת הַבְּרִית. אֶחָד אֱלֹהֵינוּ שֶׁבַּשָּׁמַיִם וּבָאָרֶץ:

שִׁשָּׁה מִי יוֹדֵעַ. שִׁשָּׁה אֲנִי יוֹדֵעַ. שִׁשָּׁה סִדְרֵי מִשְׁנָה. חֲמִשָּׁה חוּמְשֵׁי תוֹרָה. אַרְבַּע אִמָּהוֹת. שְׁלֹשָׁה אָבוֹת. שְׁנֵי לוּחוֹת הַבְּרִית. אֶחָד אֱלֹהֵינוּ שֶׁבַּשָּׁמַיִם וּבָאָרֶץ:

שִׁבְעָה מִי יוֹדֵעַ. שִׁבְעָה אֲנִי יוֹדֵעַ. שִׁבְעָה יְמֵי שַׁבַּתָּא. שִׁשָּׁה סִדְרֵי מִשְׁנָה. חֲמִשָּׁה חוּמְשֵׁי תוֹרָה. אַרְבַּע אִמָּהוֹת. שְׁלֹשָׁה אָבוֹת. שְׁנֵי לוּחוֹת הַבְּרִית. אֶחָד אֱלֹהֵינוּ שֶׁבַּשָּׁמַיִם וּבָאָרֶץ:

שְׁמוֹנָה מִי יוֹדֵעַ. שְׁמוֹנָה אֲנִי יוֹדֵעַ. שְׁמוֹנָה יְמֵי מִילָה. שִׁבְעָה יְמֵי שַׁבַּתָּא. שִׁשָּׁה סִדְרֵי מִשְׁנָה. חֲמִשָּׁה חוּמְשֵׁי תוֹרָה. אַרְבַּע אִמָּהוֹת. שְׁלֹשָׁה אָבוֹת. שְׁנֵי לוּחוֹת הַבְּרִית. אֶחָד אֱלֹהֵינוּ שֶׁבַּשָּׁמַיִם וּבָאָרֶץ:

תִּשְׁעָה מִי יוֹדֵעַ. תִּשְׁעָה אֲנִי יוֹדֵעַ. תִּשְׁעָה יַרְחֵי לֵידָה. שְׁמוֹנָה יְמֵי מִילָה. שִׁבְעָה יְמֵי שַׁבַּתָּא. שִׁשָּׁה סִדְרֵי מִשְׁנָה. חֲמִשָּׁה חוּמְשֵׁי תוֹרָה. אַרְבַּע אִמָּהוֹת. שְׁלֹשָׁה אָבוֹת. שְׁנֵי לוּחוֹת הַבְּרִית. אֶחָד אֱלֹהֵינוּ שֶׁבַּשָּׁמַיִם וּבָאָרֶץ:

עֲשָׂרָה מִי יוֹדֵעַ. עֲשָׂרָה אֲנִי יוֹדֵעַ. עֲשָׂרָה דִבְּרַיָּא. תִּשְׁעָה יַרְחֵי לֵידָה. שְׁמוֹנָה יְמֵי מִילָה. שִׁבְעָה יְמֵי שַׁבַּתָּא. שִׁשָּׁה סִדְרֵי מִשְׁנָה. חֲמִשָּׁה חוּמְשֵׁי תוֹרָה. אַרְבַּע אִמָּהוֹת. שְׁלֹשָׁה אָבוֹת. שְׁנֵי לוּחוֹת הַבְּרִית. אֶחָד אֱלֹהֵינוּ שֶׁבַּשָּׁמַיִם וּבָאָרֶץ:

אַחַד עָשָׂר מִי יוֹדֵעַ. אַחַד עָשָׂר אֲנִי יוֹדֵעַ. אַחַד עָשָׂר כּוֹכְבַיָּא. עֲשָׂרָה דִבְּרַיָּא. תִּשְׁעָה יַרְחֵי לֵידָה. שְׁמוֹנָה יְמֵי מִילָה. שִׁבְעָה יְמֵי שַׁבַּתָּא. שִׁשָּׁה סִדְרֵי מִשְׁנָה. חֲמִשָּׁה חוּמְשֵׁי תוֹרָה. אַרְבַּע אִמָּהוֹת. שְׁלֹשָׁה אָבוֹת. שְׁנֵי לוּחוֹת הַבְּרִית. אֶחָד אֱלֹהֵינוּ שֶׁבַּשָּׁמַיִם וּבָאָרֶץ:

שְׁנֵים עָשָׂר מִי יוֹדֵעַ. שְׁנֵים עָשָׂר אֲנִי יוֹדֵעַ. שְׁנֵים עָשָׂר שִׁבְטַיָּא. אַחַד עָשָׂר כּוֹכְבַיָּא. עֲשָׂרָה דִבְּרַיָּא. תִּשְׁעָה יַרְחֵי לֵידָה. שְׁמוֹנָה יְמֵי מִילָה. שִׁבְעָה יְמֵי שַׁבַּתָּא. שִׁשָּׁה סִדְרֵי מִשְׁנָה. חֲמִשָּׁה חוּמְשֵׁי תוֹרָה. אַרְבַּע אִמָּהוֹת. שְׁלֹשָׁה אָבוֹת. שְׁנֵי לוּחוֹת הַבְּרִית. אֶחָד אֱלֹהֵינוּ שֶׁבַּשָּׁמַיִם וּבָאָרֶץ:

שְׁלשָׁה עָשָׂר מִי יוֹדֵעַ. שְׁלשָׁה עָשָׂר אֲנִי יוֹדֵעַ. שְׁלשָׁה עָשָׂר מִדַּיָּא. שְׁנֵים עָשָׂר שִׁבְטַיָּא. אַחַד עָשָׂר כּוֹכְבַיָּא. עֲשָׂרָה דִבְּרַיָּא. תִּשְׁעָה יַרְחֵי לֵידָה. שְׁמוֹנָה יְמֵי מִילָה. שִׁבְעָה יְמֵי שַׁבַּתָּא. שִׁשָּׁה סִדְרֵי מִשְׁנָה. חֲמִשָּׁה חוּמְשֵׁי תוֹרָה. אַרְבַּע אִמָּהוֹת. שְׁלשָׁה אָבוֹת. שְׁנֵי לוּחוֹת הַבְּרִית. אֶחָד אֱלֹהֵינוּ שֶׁבַּשָּׁמַיִם וּבָאָרֶץ:

חַד גַּדְיָא, חַד גַּדְיָא:

דְּזַבִּין אַבָּא בִּתְרֵי זוּזֵי. חַד גַּדְיָא, חַד גַּדְיָא:

וְאָתָא שׁוּנְרָא, וְאָכְלָה לְגַדְיָא, דְּזַבִּין אַבָּא בִּתְרֵי זוּזֵי. חַד גַּדְיָא, חַד גַּדְיָא:

וְאָתָא כַלְבָּא, וְנָשַׁךְ לְשׁוּנְרָא, דְּאָכְלָה לְגַדְיָא, דְּזַבִּין אַבָּא בִּתְרֵי זוּזֵי. חַד גַּדְיָא, חַד גַּדְיָא:

וְאָתָא חוּטְרָא, וְהִכָּה לְכַלְבָּא, דְּנָשַׁךְ לְשׁוּנְרָא, דְּאָכְלָה לְגַדְיָא, דְּזַבִּין אַבָּא בִּתְרֵי זוּזֵי. חַד גַּדְיָא, חַד גַּדְיָא:

וְאָתָא נוּרָא, וְשָׂרַף לְחוּטְרָא, דְּהִכָּה לְכַלְבָּא, דְּנָשַׁךְ לְשׁוּנְרָא, דְּאָכְלָה לְגַדְיָא, דְּזַבִּין אַבָּא בִּתְרֵי זוּזֵי. חַד גַּדְיָא, חַד גַּדְיָא:

וְאָתָא מַיָּא, וְכָבָה לְנוּרָא, דְּשָׂרַף לְחוּטְרָא, דְּהִכָּה לְכַלְבָּא, דְּנָשַׁךְ לְשׁוּנְרָא, דְּאָכְלָה לְגַדְיָא, דְּזַבִּין אַבָּא בִּתְרֵי זוּזֵי. חַד גַּדְיָא, חַד גַּדְיָא:

וְאָתָא תוֹרָא, וְשָׁתָה לְמַיָּא, דְּכָבָה לְנוּרָא, דְּשָׂרַף לְחוּטְרָא, דְּהִכָּה לְכַלְבָּא, דְּנָשַׁךְ לְשׁוּנְרָא, דְּאָכְלָה לְגַדְיָא, דְּזַבִּין אַבָּא בִּתְרֵי זוּזֵי. חַד גַּדְיָא, חַד גַּדְיָא:

וְאָתָא הַשּׁוֹחֵט, וְשָׁחַט לְתוֹרָא, דְּשָׁתָה לְמַיָּא, דְּכָבָה לְנוּרָא, דְּשָׂרַף לְחוּטְרָא, דְּהִכָּה לְכַלְבָּא, דְּנָשַׁךְ לְשׁוּנְרָא, דְּאָכְלָה לְגַדְיָא, דְּזַבִּין אַבָּא בִּתְרֵי זוּזֵי. חַד גַּדְיָא, חַד גַּדְיָא:

וְאָתָא מַלְאַךְ הַמָּוֶת, וְשָׁחַט לְשׁוֹחֵט, דְּשָׁחַט לְתוֹרָא, דְּשָׁתָה לְמַיָּא, דְּכָבָה לְנוּרָא, דְּשָׂרַף לְחוּטְרָא, דְּהִכָּה לְכַלְבָּא, דְּנָשַׁךְ לְשׁוּנְרָא, דְּאָכְלָה לְגַדְיָא, דְּזַבִּין אַבָּא בִּתְרֵי זוּזֵי. חַד גַּדְיָא, חַד גַּדְיָא:

וְאָתָא הַקָּדוֹשׁ בָּרוּךְ הוּא, וְשָׁחַט לְמַלְאַךְ הַמָּוֶת, דְּשָׁחַט לְשׁוֹחֵט, דְּשָׁחַט לְתוֹרָא, דְּשָׁתָה לְמַיָּא, דְּכָבָה לְנוּרָא, דְּשָׂרַף לְחוּטְרָא, דְּהִכָּה לְכַלְבָּא, דְּנָשַׁךְ לְשׁוּנְרָא, דְּאָכְלָה לְגַדְיָא, דְּזַבִּין אַבָּא בִּתְרֵי זוּזֵי. חַד גַּדְיָא, חַד גַּדְיָא:

שִׁיר הַשִּׁירִים

Many recite the Song of Songs after the Haggadah.

א שִׁיר הַשִּׁירִים אֲשֶׁר לִשְׁלֹמֹה: יִשָּׁקֵנִי מִנְּשִׁיקוֹת פִּיהוּ כִּי טוֹבִים דֹּדֶיךָ מִיָּיִן: לְרֵיחַ שְׁמָנֶיךָ טוֹבִים שֶׁמֶן תּוּרַק שְׁמֶךָ עַל כֵּן עֲלָמוֹת אֲהֵבוּךָ: מָשְׁכֵנִי אַחֲרֶיךָ נָּרוּצָה הֱבִיאַנִי הַמֶּלֶךְ חֲדָרָיו נָגִילָה וְנִשְׂמְחָה בָּךְ נַזְכִּירָה דֹדֶיךָ מִיַּיִן מֵישָׁרִים אֲהֵבוּךָ: שְׁחוֹרָה אֲנִי וְנָאוָה בְּנוֹת יְרוּשָׁלִָם כְּאָהֳלֵי קֵדָר כִּירִיעוֹת שְׁלֹמֹה: אַל תִּרְאוּנִי שֶׁאֲנִי שְׁחַרְחֹרֶת שֶׁשְּׁזָפַתְנִי הַשָּׁמֶשׁ בְּנֵי אִמִּי נִחֲרוּ בִי שָׂמֻנִי נֹטֵרָה אֶת הַכְּרָמִים כַּרְמִי שֶׁלִּי לֹא נָטָרְתִּי: הַגִּידָה לִּי שֶׁאָהֲבָה נַפְשִׁי אֵיכָה תִרְעֶה אֵיכָה תַּרְבִּיץ בַּצָּהֳרָיִם שַׁלָּמָה אֶהְיֶה כְּעֹטְיָה עַל עֶדְרֵי חֲבֵרֶיךָ: אִם לֹא תֵדְעִי לָךְ הַיָּפָה בַּנָּשִׁים צְאִי לָךְ בְּעִקְבֵי הַצֹּאן וּרְעִי אֶת גְּדִיֹּתַיִךְ עַל מִשְׁכְּנוֹת הָרֹעִים: לְסֻסָתִי בְּרִכְבֵי פַרְעֹה דִּמִּיתִיךְ רַעְיָתִי: נָאווּ לְחָיַיִךְ בַּתֹּרִים צַוָּארֵךְ בַּחֲרוּזִים: תּוֹרֵי זָהָב נַעֲשֶׂה לָּךְ עִם נְקֻדּוֹת הַכָּסֶף: עַד שֶׁהַמֶּלֶךְ בִּמְסִבּוֹ נִרְדִּי נָתַן רֵיחוֹ: צְרוֹר

הַמֹּר דּוֹדִי לִי בֵּין שָׁדַי יָלִין: אֶשְׁכֹּל הַכֹּפֶר דּוֹדִי לִי בְּכַרְמֵי עֵין גֶּדִי: הִנָּךְ יָפָה רַעְיָתִי הִנָּךְ יָפָה עֵינַיִךְ יוֹנִים: הִנְּךָ יָפֶה דוֹדִי אַף נָעִים אַף עַרְשֵׂנוּ רַעֲנָנָה: קֹרוֹת בָּתֵּינוּ אֲרָזִים רַהִיטֵנוּ בְּרוֹתִים:

ב אֲנִי חֲבַצֶּלֶת הַשָּׁרוֹן שׁוֹשַׁנַּת הָעֲמָקִים: כְּשׁוֹשַׁנָּה בֵּין הַחוֹחִים כֵּן רַעְיָתִי בֵּין הַבָּנוֹת: כְּתַפּוּחַ בַּעֲצֵי הַיַּעַר כֵּן דּוֹדִי בֵּין הַבָּנִים בְּצִלּוֹ חִמַּדְתִּי וְיָשַׁבְתִּי וּפִרְיוֹ מָתוֹק לְחִכִּי: הֱבִיאַנִי אֶל בֵּית הַיָּיִן וְדִגְלוֹ עָלַי אַהֲבָה: סַמְּכוּנִי בָּאֲשִׁישׁוֹת רַפְּדוּנִי בַּתַּפּוּחִים כִּי חוֹלַת אַהֲבָה אָנִי: שְׂמֹאלוֹ תַּחַת לְרֹאשִׁי וִימִינוֹ תְּחַבְּקֵנִי: הִשְׁבַּעְתִּי אֶתְכֶם בְּנוֹת יְרוּשָׁלַם בִּצְבָאוֹת אוֹ בְּאַיְלוֹת הַשָּׂדֶה אִם תָּעִירוּ וְאִם תְּעוֹרְרוּ אֶת הָאַהֲבָה עַד שֶׁתֶּחְפָּץ: קוֹל דּוֹדִי הִנֵּה זֶה בָּא מְדַלֵּג עַל הֶהָרִים מְקַפֵּץ עַל הַגְּבָעוֹת: דּוֹמֶה דוֹדִי לִצְבִי אוֹ לְעֹפֶר הָאַיָּלִים הִנֵּה זֶה עוֹמֵד אַחַר כָּתְלֵנוּ מַשְׁגִּיחַ מִן הַחַלֹּנוֹת מֵצִיץ מִן הַחֲרַכִּים: עָנָה דוֹדִי וְאָמַר לִי קוּמִי לָךְ רַעְיָתִי יָפָתִי וּלְכִי לָךְ: כִּי הִנֵּה הַסְּתָו עָבָר הַגֶּשֶׁם חָלַף הָלַךְ לוֹ: הַנִּצָּנִים נִרְאוּ בָאָרֶץ עֵת הַזָּמִיר הִגִּיעַ וְקוֹל הַתּוֹר נִשְׁמַע בְּאַרְצֵנוּ: הַתְּאֵנָה חָנְטָה פַגֶּיהָ וְהַגְּפָנִים סְמָדַר נָתְנוּ רֵיחַ קוּמִי לָךְ רַעְיָתִי יָפָתִי וּלְכִי לָךְ: יוֹנָתִי בְּחַגְוֵי הַסֶּלַע בְּסֵתֶר הַמַּדְרֵגָה הַרְאִינִי אֶת מַרְאַיִךְ הַשְׁמִיעִנִי אֶת קוֹלֵךְ כִּי קוֹלֵךְ עָרֵב וּמַרְאֵיךְ נָאוֶה: אֶחֱזוּ לָנוּ שֻׁעָלִים שֻׁעָלִים קְטַנִּים מְחַבְּלִים כְּרָמִים וּכְרָמֵינוּ סְמָדַר: דּוֹדִי לִי וַאֲנִי לוֹ הָרֹעֶה בַּשּׁוֹשַׁנִּים: עַד שֶׁיָּפוּחַ הַיּוֹם וְנָסוּ הַצְּלָלִים סֹב דְּמֵה לְךָ דוֹדִי לִצְבִי אוֹ לְעֹפֶר הָאַיָּלִים עַל הָרֵי בָתֶר:

ג עַל מִשְׁכָּבִי בַּלֵּילוֹת בִּקַּשְׁתִּי אֵת שֶׁאָהֲבָה נַפְשִׁי בִּקַּשְׁתִּיו וְלֹא מְצָאתִיו: אָקוּמָה נָּא וַאֲסוֹבְבָה בָעִיר בַּשְּׁוָקִים וּבָרְחֹבוֹת אֲבַקְשָׁה אֵת שֶׁאָהֲבָה נַפְשִׁי בִּקַּשְׁתִּיו וְלֹא מְצָאתִיו: מְצָאוּנִי הַשֹּׁמְרִים הַסֹּבְבִים בָּעִיר אֵת שֶׁאָהֲבָה נַפְשִׁי רְאִיתֶם: כִּמְעַט שֶׁעָבַרְתִּי מֵהֶם עַד שֶׁמָּצָאתִי אֵת שֶׁאָהֲבָה נַפְשִׁי אֲחַזְתִּיו וְלֹא אַרְפֶּנּוּ עַד שֶׁהֲבֵיאתִיו אֶל בֵּית אִמִּי וְאֶל חֶדֶר הוֹרָתִי: הִשְׁבַּעְתִּי אֶתְכֶם בְּנוֹת יְרוּשָׁלַם בִּצְבָאוֹת אוֹ בְּאַיְלוֹת הַשָּׂדֶה אִם תָּעִירוּ וְאִם תְּעוֹרְרוּ אֶת הָאַהֲבָה עַד שֶׁתֶּחְפָּץ: מִי זֹאת עֹלָה מִן הַמִּדְבָּר כְּתִימְרוֹת עָשָׁן מְקֻטֶּרֶת מֹר וּלְבוֹנָה מִכֹּל אַבְקַת רוֹכֵל: הִנֵּה מִטָּתוֹ שֶׁלִּשְׁלֹמֹה שִׁשִּׁים גִּבֹּרִים סָבִיב לָהּ מִגִּבֹּרֵי יִשְׂרָאֵל: כֻּלָּם אֲחֻזֵי חֶרֶב מְלֻמְּדֵי מִלְחָמָה אִישׁ חַרְבּוֹ עַל יְרֵכוֹ מִפַּחַד בַּלֵּילוֹת: אַפִּרְיוֹן עָשָׂה

לוֹ הַמֶּלֶךְ שְׁלֹמֹה מֵעֲצֵי הַלְּבָנוֹן: עַמּוּדָיו עָשָׂה כֶסֶף רְפִידָתוֹ זָהָב מֶרְכָּבוֹ אַרְגָּמָן תּוֹכוֹ רָצוּף אַהֲבָה מִבְּנוֹת יְרוּשָׁלָםִ: צְאֶינָה וּרְאֶינָה בְּנוֹת צִיּוֹן בַּמֶּלֶךְ שְׁלֹמֹה בָּעֲטָרָה שֶׁעִטְּרָה לּוֹ אִמּוֹ בְּיוֹם חֲתֻנָּתוֹ וּבְיוֹם שִׂמְחַת לִבּוֹ:

ד הִנָּךְ יָפָה רַעְיָתִי הִנָּךְ יָפָה עֵינַיִךְ יוֹנִים מִבַּעַד לְצַמָּתֵךְ שַׂעְרֵךְ כְּעֵדֶר הָעִזִּים שֶׁגָּלְשׁוּ מֵהַר גִּלְעָד: שִׁנַּיִךְ כְּעֵדֶר הַקְּצוּבוֹת שֶׁעָלוּ מִן הָרַחְצָה שֶׁכֻּלָּם מַתְאִימוֹת וְשַׁכֻּלָה אֵין בָּהֶם: כְּחוּט הַשָּׁנִי שִׂפְתוֹתַיִךְ וּמִדְבָּרֵךְ נָאוֶה כְּפֶלַח הָרִמּוֹן רַקָּתֵךְ מִבַּעַד לְצַמָּתֵךְ: כְּמִגְדַּל דָּוִיד צַוָּארֵךְ בָּנוּי לְתַלְפִּיּוֹת אֶלֶף הַמָּגֵן תָּלוּי עָלָיו כֹּל שִׁלְטֵי הַגִּבּוֹרִים: שְׁנֵי שָׁדַיִךְ כִּשְׁנֵי עֳפָרִים תְּאוֹמֵי צְבִיָּה הָרוֹעִים בַּשּׁוֹשַׁנִּים: עַד שֶׁיָּפוּחַ הַיּוֹם וְנָסוּ הַצְּלָלִים אֵלֶךְ לִי אֶל הַר הַמּוֹר וְאֶל גִּבְעַת הַלְּבוֹנָה: כֻּלָּךְ יָפָה רַעְיָתִי וּמוּם אֵין בָּךְ: אִתִּי מִלְּבָנוֹן כַּלָּה אִתִּי מִלְּבָנוֹן תָּבוֹאִי תָּשׁוּרִי מֵרֹאשׁ אֲמָנָה מֵרֹאשׁ שְׂנִיר וְחֶרְמוֹן מִמְּעוֹנוֹת אֲרָיוֹת מֵהַרְרֵי נְמֵרִים: לִבַּבְתִּנִי אֲחוֹתִי כַלָּה לִבַּבְתִּנִי בְּאַחַת מֵעֵינַיִךְ בְּאַחַד עֲנָק מִצַּוְּרֹנָיִךְ: מַה יָּפוּ דֹדַיִךְ אֲחֹתִי כַלָּה מַה טֹּבוּ דֹדַיִךְ מִיַּיִן וְרֵיחַ שְׁמָנַיִךְ מִכָּל בְּשָׂמִים: נֹפֶת תִּטֹּפְנָה שִׂפְתוֹתַיִךְ כַּלָּה דְּבַשׁ וְחָלָב תַּחַת לְשׁוֹנֵךְ וְרֵיחַ שַׂלְמֹתַיִךְ כְּרֵיחַ לְבָנוֹן: גַּן נָעוּל אֲחוֹתִי כַלָּה גַּל נָעוּל מַעְיָן חָתוּם: שְׁלָחַיִךְ פַּרְדֵּס רִמּוֹנִים עִם פְּרִי מְגָדִים כְּפָרִים עִם נְרָדִים: נֵרְדְּ וְכַרְכֹּם קָנֶה וְקִנָּמוֹן עִם כָּל עֲצֵי לְבוֹנָה מֹר וַאֲהָלוֹת עִם כָּל רָאשֵׁי בְשָׂמִים: מַעְיַן גַּנִּים בְּאֵר מַיִם חַיִּים וְנֹזְלִים מִן לְבָנוֹן: עוּרִי צָפוֹן וּבוֹאִי תֵימָן הָפִיחִי גַנִּי יִזְּלוּ בְשָׂמָיו יָבֹא דוֹדִי לְגַנּוֹ וְיֹאכַל פְּרִי מְגָדָיו:

ה בָּאתִי לְגַנִּי אֲחֹתִי כַלָּה אָרִיתִי מוֹרִי עִם בְּשָׂמִי אָכַלְתִּי יַעְרִי עִם דִּבְשִׁי שָׁתִיתִי יֵינִי עִם חֲלָבִי אִכְלוּ רֵעִים שְׁתוּ וְשִׁכְרוּ דּוֹדִים: אֲנִי יְשֵׁנָה וְלִבִּי עֵר קוֹל דּוֹדִי דוֹפֵק פִּתְחִי לִי אֲחֹתִי רַעְיָתִי יוֹנָתִי תַמָּתִי שֶׁרֹּאשִׁי נִמְלָא טָל קְוֻצּוֹתַי רְסִיסֵי לָיְלָה: פָּשַׁטְתִּי אֶת כֻּתָּנְתִּי אֵיכָכָה אֶלְבָּשֶׁנָּה רָחַצְתִּי אֶת רַגְלַי אֵיכָכָה אֲטַנְּפֵם: דּוֹדִי שָׁלַח יָדוֹ מִן הַחוֹר וּמֵעַי הָמוּ עָלָיו: קַמְתִּי אֲנִי לִפְתֹּחַ לְדוֹדִי וְיָדַי נָטְפוּ מוֹר וְאֶצְבְּעֹתַי מוֹר עֹבֵר עַל כַּפּוֹת הַמַּנְעוּל: פָּתַחְתִּי אֲנִי לְדוֹדִי וְדוֹדִי חָמַק עָבָר נַפְשִׁי יָצְאָה בְדַבְּרוֹ בִּקַּשְׁתִּיהוּ וְלֹא מְצָאתִיהוּ קְרָאתִיו וְלֹא עָנָנִי: מְצָאֻנִי הַשֹּׁמְרִים הַסֹּבְבִים בָּעִיר הִכּוּנִי פְצָעוּנִי נָשְׂאוּ אֶת רְדִידִי מֵעָלַי שֹׁמְרֵי הַחֹמוֹת: הִשְׁבַּעְתִּי

אֶתְכֶם בְּנוֹת יְרוּשָׁלָם אִם תִּמְצְאוּ אֶת דּוֹדִי מַה תַּגִּידוּ לוֹ שֶׁחוֹלַת אַהֲבָה אָנִי: מַה דּוֹדֵךְ מִדּוֹד הַיָּפָה בַּנָּשִׁים מַה דּוֹדֵךְ מִדּוֹד שֶׁכָּכָה הִשְׁבַּעְתָּנוּ: דּוֹדִי צַח וְאָדוֹם דָּגוּל מֵרְבָבָה: רֹאשׁוֹ כֶּתֶם פָּז קְוֻצּוֹתָיו תַּלְתַּלִּים שְׁחוֹרוֹת כָּעוֹרֵב: עֵינָיו כְּיוֹנִים עַל אֲפִיקֵי מָיִם רֹחֲצוֹת בֶּחָלָב יֹשְׁבוֹת עַל מִלֵּאת: לְחָיָו כַּעֲרוּגַת הַבֹּשֶׂם מִגְדְּלוֹת מֶרְקָחִים שִׂפְתוֹתָיו שׁוֹשַׁנִּים נֹטְפוֹת מוֹר עֹבֵר: יָדָיו גְּלִילֵי זָהָב מְמֻלָּאִים בַּתַּרְשִׁישׁ מֵעָיו עֶשֶׁת שֵׁן מְעֻלֶּפֶת סַפִּירִים: שׁוֹקָיו עַמּוּדֵי שֵׁשׁ מְיֻסָּדִים עַל אַדְנֵי פָז מַרְאֵהוּ כַּלְּבָנוֹן בָּחוּר כָּאֲרָזִים: חִכּוֹ מַמְתַקִּים וְכֻלּוֹ מַחֲמַדִּים זֶה דוֹדִי וְזֶה רֵעִי בְּנוֹת יְרוּשָׁלָם:

ו אָנָה הָלַךְ דּוֹדֵךְ הַיָּפָה בַּנָּשִׁים אָנָה פָּנָה דוֹדֵךְ וּנְבַקְשֶׁנּוּ עִמָּךְ: דּוֹדִי יָרַד לְגַנּוֹ לַעֲרוּגוֹת הַבֹּשֶׂם לִרְעוֹת בַּגַּנִּים וְלִלְקֹט שׁוֹשַׁנִּים: אֲנִי לְדוֹדִי וְדוֹדִי לִי הָרוֹעֶה בַּשּׁוֹשַׁנִּים: יָפָה אַתְּ רַעְיָתִי כְּתִרְצָה נָאוָה כִּירוּשָׁלָם אֲיֻמָּה כַּנִּדְגָּלוֹת: הָסֵבִּי עֵינַיִךְ מִנֶּגְדִּי שֶׁהֵם הִרְהִיבֻנִי שַׂעְרֵךְ כְּעֵדֶר הָעִזִּים שֶׁגָּלְשׁוּ מִן הַגִּלְעָד: שִׁנַּיִךְ כְּעֵדֶר הָרְחֵלִים שֶׁעָלוּ מִן הָרַחְצָה שֶׁכֻּלָּם מַתְאִימוֹת וְשַׁכֻּלָה אֵין בָּהֶם: כְּפֶלַח הָרִמּוֹן רַקָּתֵךְ מִבַּעַד לְצַמָּתֵךְ: שִׁשִּׁים הֵמָּה מְלָכוֹת וּשְׁמֹנִים פִּילַגְשִׁים וַעֲלָמוֹת אֵין מִסְפָּר: אַחַת הִיא יוֹנָתִי תַמָּתִי אַחַת הִיא לְאִמָּהּ בָּרָה הִיא לְיוֹלַדְתָּהּ רָאוּהָ בָנוֹת וַיְאַשְּׁרוּהָ מְלָכוֹת וּפִילַגְשִׁים וַיְהַלְלוּהָ: מִי זֹאת הַנִּשְׁקָפָה כְּמוֹ שָׁחַר יָפָה כַלְּבָנָה בָּרָה כַּחַמָּה אֲיֻמָּה כַּנִּדְגָּלוֹת: אֶל גִּנַּת אֱגוֹז יָרַדְתִּי לִרְאוֹת בְּאִבֵּי הַנָּחַל לִרְאוֹת הֲפָרְחָה הַגֶּפֶן הֵנֵצוּ הָרִמֹּנִים: לֹא יָדַעְתִּי נַפְשִׁי שָׂמַתְנִי מַרְכְּבוֹת עַמִּי נָדִיב:

ז שׁוּבִי שׁוּבִי הַשּׁוּלַמִּית שׁוּבִי שׁוּבִי וְנֶחֱזֶה בָּךְ מַה תֶּחֱזוּ בַּשּׁוּלַמִּית כִּמְחוֹלַת הַמַּחֲנָיִם: מַה יָּפוּ פְעָמַיִךְ בַּנְּעָלִים בַּת נָדִיב חַמּוּקֵי יְרֵכַיִךְ כְּמוֹ חֲלָאִים מַעֲשֵׂה יְדֵי אָמָּן: שָׁרְרֵךְ אַגַּן הַסַּהַר אַל יֶחְסַר הַמָּזֶג בִּטְנֵךְ עֲרֵמַת חִטִּים סוּגָה בַּשּׁוֹשַׁנִּים: שְׁנֵי שָׁדַיִךְ כִּשְׁנֵי עֳפָרִים תָּאֳמֵי צְבִיָּה: צַוָּארֵךְ כְּמִגְדַּל הַשֵּׁן עֵינַיִךְ בְּרֵכוֹת בְּחֶשְׁבּוֹן עַל שַׁעַר בַּת רַבִּים אַפֵּךְ כְּמִגְדַּל הַלְּבָנוֹן צוֹפֶה פְּנֵי דַמָּשֶׂק: רֹאשֵׁךְ עָלַיִךְ כַּכַּרְמֶל וְדַלַּת רֹאשֵׁךְ כָּאַרְגָּמָן מֶלֶךְ אָסוּר בָּרְהָטִים: מַה יָּפִית וּמַה נָּעַמְתְּ אַהֲבָה בַּתַּעֲנוּגִים: זֹאת קוֹמָתֵךְ דָּמְתָה לְתָמָר וְשָׁדַיִךְ לְאַשְׁכֹּלוֹת: אָמַרְתִּי אֶעֱלֶה בְתָמָר אֹחֲזָה

בְּסַנְסִנָּיו וְיִהְיוּ נָא שָׁדַיִךְ כְּאֶשְׁכְּלוֹת הַגֶּפֶן וְרֵיחַ אַפֵּךְ כַּתַּפּוּחִים: וְחִכֵּךְ
כְּיֵין הַטּוֹב הוֹלֵךְ לְדוֹדִי לְמֵישָׁרִים דּוֹבֵב שִׂפְתֵי יְשֵׁנִים: אֲנִי לְדוֹדִי וְעָלַי
תְּשׁוּקָתוֹ: לְכָה דוֹדִי נֵצֵא הַשָּׂדֶה נָלִינָה בַּכְּפָרִים: נַשְׁכִּימָה לַכְּרָמִים
נִרְאֶה אִם פָּרְחָה הַגֶּפֶן פִּתַּח הַסְּמָדַר הֵנֵצוּ הָרִמּוֹנִים שָׁם אֶתֵּן אֶת דֹּדַי
לָךְ: הַדּוּדָאִים נָתְנוּ רֵיחַ וְעַל פְּתָחֵינוּ כָּל מְגָדִים חֲדָשִׁים גַּם יְשָׁנִים דּוֹדִי
צָפַנְתִּי לָךְ:

ח מִי יִתֶּנְךָ כְּאָח לִי יוֹנֵק שְׁדֵי אִמִּי אֶמְצָאֲךָ בַחוּץ אֶשָּׁקְךָ גַּם לֹא יָבֻזוּ
לִי: אֶנְהָגְךָ אֲבִיאֲךָ אֶל בֵּית אִמִּי תְּלַמְּדֵנִי אַשְׁקְךָ מִיַּיִן הָרֶקַח מֵעֲסִיס
רִמֹּנִי: שְׂמֹאלוֹ תַּחַת רֹאשִׁי וִימִינוֹ תְּחַבְּקֵנִי: הִשְׁבַּעְתִּי אֶתְכֶם בְּנוֹת
יְרוּשָׁלָם מַה תָּעִירוּ וּמַה תְּעֹרְרוּ אֶת הָאַהֲבָה עַד שֶׁתֶּחְפָּץ: מִי זֹאת עֹלָה
מִן הַמִּדְבָּר מִתְרַפֶּקֶת עַל דּוֹדָהּ תַּחַת הַתַּפּוּחַ עוֹרַרְתִּיךָ שָׁמָּה חִבְּלַתְךָ
אִמֶּךָ שָׁמָּה חִבְּלָה יְלָדַתְךָ: שִׂימֵנִי כַחוֹתָם עַל לִבֶּךָ כַּחוֹתָם עַל זְרוֹעֶךָ כִּי
עַזָּה כַמָּוֶת אַהֲבָה קָשָׁה כִשְׁאוֹל קִנְאָה רְשָׁפֶיהָ רִשְׁפֵּי אֵשׁ שַׁלְהֶבֶתְיָה:
מַיִם רַבִּים לֹא יוּכְלוּ לְכַבּוֹת אֶת הָאַהֲבָה וּנְהָרוֹת לֹא יִשְׁטְפוּהָ אִם יִתֵּן
אִישׁ אֶת כָּל הוֹן בֵּיתוֹ בָּאַהֲבָה בּוֹז יָבוּזוּ לוֹ: אָחוֹת לָנוּ קְטַנָּה וְשָׁדַיִם אֵין
לָהּ מַה נַּעֲשֶׂה לַאֲחוֹתֵנוּ בַּיּוֹם שֶׁיְּדֻבַּר בָּהּ: אִם חוֹמָה הִיא נִבְנֶה עָלֶיהָ
טִירַת כָּסֶף וְאִם דֶּלֶת הִיא נָצוּר עָלֶיהָ לוּחַ אָרֶז: אֲנִי חוֹמָה וְשָׁדַי
כַּמִּגְדָּלוֹת אָז הָיִיתִי בְעֵינָיו כְּמוֹצְאֵת שָׁלוֹם: כֶּרֶם הָיָה לִשְׁלֹמֹה בְּבַעַל
הָמוֹן נָתַן אֶת הַכֶּרֶם לַנֹּטְרִים אִישׁ יָבִא בְּפִרְיוֹ אֶלֶף כָּסֶף: כַּרְמִי שֶׁלִּי
לְפָנָי הָאֶלֶף לְךָ שְׁלֹמֹה וּמָאתַיִם לְנֹטְרִים אֶת פִּרְיוֹ: הַיּוֹשֶׁבֶת בַּגַּנִּים
חֲבֵרִים מַקְשִׁיבִים לְקוֹלֵךְ הַשְׁמִיעִנִי: בְּרַח דּוֹדִי וּדְמֵה לְךָ לִצְבִי אוֹ לְעֹפֶר
הָאַיָּלִים עַל הָרֵי בְשָׂמִים:

רִבּוֹן כָּל הָעוֹלָמִים יְהִי רָצוֹן מִלְּפָנֶיךָ יְיָ אֱלֹהַי וֵאלֹהֵי אֲבוֹתַי
שֶׁבִּזְכוּת שִׁיר הַשִּׁירִים אֲשֶׁר קָרִיתִי וְלָמַדְתִּי שֶׁהוּא קֹדֶשׁ קָדָשִׁים
בִּזְכוּת פְּסוּקָיו וּבִזְכוּת תֵּבוֹתָיו וּבִזְכוּת אוֹתִיּוֹתָיו וּבִזְכוּת נְקֻדּוֹתָיו
וּבִזְכוּת טְעָמָיו וּבִזְכוּת שְׁמוֹתָיו וְצֵרוּפָיו וּרְמָזָיו וְסוֹדוֹתָיו הַקְּדוֹשִׁים
וְהַטְּהוֹרִים הַנּוֹרָאִים הַיּוֹצְאִים מִמֶּנּוּ שֶׁתְּהֵא שָׁעָה זוּ שְׁעַת רַחֲמִים

שְׁעַת הַקְשָׁבָה שְׁעַת הָאֲזָנָה וְנִקְרָאֲךָ וְתַעֲנֵנוּ נַעְתִּיר לְךָ וְהֵעָתֵר לָנוּ
שֶׁיִּהְיֶה עוֹלֶה לְפָנֶיךָ קְרִיאַת וְלִמּוּד שִׁיר הַשִּׁירִים כְּאִלּוּ הִשַּׂגְנוּ כָּל
הַסּוֹדוֹת הַנִּפְלָאוֹת וְהַנּוֹרָאוֹת אֲשֶׁר הֵם חֲתוּמִים בּוֹ בְּכָל תְּנָאָיו
וְנִזְכֶּה לְמָקוֹם שֶׁהָרוּחוֹת וְהַנְּשָׁמוֹת נֶחֱצָבוֹת מִשָּׁם וּכְאִלּוּ עָשִׂינוּ כָּל
מַה שֶּׁמּוּטָל עָלֵינוּ לְהַשִּׂיג בֵּין בְּגִלְגּוּל זֶה בֵּין בְּגִלְגּוּל אַחֵר וְלִהְיוֹת
מִן הָעוֹלִים וְהַזּוֹכִים לָעוֹלָם הַבָּא עִם שְׁאָר צַדִּיקִים וַחֲסִידִים וּמַלֵּא
כָּל מִשְׁאֲלוֹת לִבֵּנוּ לְטוֹבָה וְתִהְיֶה עִם לְבָבֵנוּ וְאִמְרֵי פִינוּ בְּעֵת
מַחְשְׁבוֹתֵינוּ וְעִם יָדֵינוּ בְּעֵת מַעְבָּדֵינוּ וְתִשְׁלַח בְּרָכָה וְהַצְלָחָה בְּכָל
מַעֲשֵׂה יָדֵינוּ וּמֵעָפָר תְּקִימֵנוּ וּמֵאַשְׁפּוֹת דַּלּוּתֵנוּ תְּרוֹמְמֵנוּ וְתָשִׁיב
שְׁכִינָתְךָ לְעִיר קָדְשֶׁךָ בִּמְהֵרָה בְיָמֵינוּ אָמֵן:

Chapter 5

After the Exodus

Day 1 - 15 Nissan

Redemption

The Jews had earned unprecedented freedom. The redemption had finally arrived! The spring weather was pleasant on the fifteenth of Nissan. Hurriedly wrapped sacks of unleavened bread and leftover marror were lovingly hoisted onto their shoulders. Six hundred thousand men, accompanied by their wives and families, joyously marched from the land where they had been enslaved for over two hundred years. It was a new beginning.

During their travels, the Jews were surrounded on all sides by the seven Clouds of Glory, spiritual clouds in which the presence of G-d resided, clouds that radiated the sublime light of the six days of creation.

(Hakesav Vehakabbalah, Shelach)

Four clouds on four sides protected the Jews from attackers and blustering winds. The fifth cloud hovered over them, shielding them from rain and hot sun. The sixth cloud below them kept away poisonous snakes. The seventh cloud moved in front of them, leading the way and leveling the path. At night a pillar of fire moved before them, brightening the road ahead like daylight.

Recognizing the nobility of the Jews, a contingent of foreigners joined the newly redeemed nation. Some say they were the Egyptian sorcerers who had ridiculed Moshe Rabbeinu. Moshe accepted them without asking G-d. This eirav rav, mixed multitude, caused all the unfortunate tragedies that befell the Jews during their forty years of wandering in the wilderness.

What Year?

The Jews were enslaved for 116 years, from the death of the last survivor of the original tribe of Levi until the Exodus. They labored 86 years, from the day Miriam was born. She was given the name Miriam from the root mar, bitter, because the enslavement began at her birth. (Seder Olam Rabbah) The Jews departed Egypt on the fifteenth of Nissan, 2448 years from Creation.

(Seder Olam)

According to Rabbeinu Bachya, the Exodus took place 430 years after the birth of Yitzchak, in the year 2478.

The Jews lived in Egypt for 215 years. Thus they departed in the Jewish year 2453.

(Pirkei d'Rabbi Eliezer)

No Turning Back

The abrupt freedom from extended golus and the yoke of physical work paradoxically caused the Jews to feel listless and

depressed. The initial feeling of euphoria after gaining their freedom gave way to a deep sense of distress.

They heard the sweet song of the angels praising and exalting the Almighty, but they were too downcast to enjoy it. G-d sought to infuse them with a new spirit of hope, enthusiasm and vitality-so He sent Pharaoh to accompany them on their way out of Egypt. The sight of the powerful tyrant Pharaoh escorting his slaves to the edge of the wilderness inspired the Jews with courage. Setting aside the misery of the past, they enjoyed the singing of the angels.

Bilam, the evil prophet, was exasperated. All his black magic, sorcery and evil schemes had been unable to prevent the Jews from leaving Egypt. Deeply despondent, he fled to the Mountains of Darkness where he futilely attempted to cast more spells on the Jews, using the latest witchcraft. He stayed there until the Giving of the Torah, when he finally gave up.

In Heaven, the guardian angel of Egypt stepped forward to accuse the Jews of sinfulness. "They only sinned because you enslaved them," rebutted the Judge. "Just look how beautifully and unselfishly they are fulfilling the mitzvos of Korban Pesach and milah now that they are free!"

Day 2 - 16 Nissan

Wandering

Originally, G-d was going to lead the Jews directly to Israel via the land of the Philistines. But G-d was concerned that if the nation confronted armed resistance, they would lose heart and return to Egypt. So G-d directed them circuitously through the desert, to erase any possible consideration of return.

Upon leaving Egypt the Jews traveled from Ramses to Sukkos. In Sukkos they stopped to bake their matzos by the heat of the blazing

sun. The matzos stayed fresh until the sixteenth of Iyar, the day the manna began to fall. For thirty-one days, sixty-one meals, the Jews enjoyed the crisp matzah.

(Rashi, Beshalach)

From Sukkos, the Jews continued on to Eisam. They were ready to pack up and leave again when Pharaoh's agents, who had accompanied them, informed them, "Time's up! You agreed to come back to Egypt after three days!"

But the Jews protested. "G-d miraculously delivered us from Egypt. Pharaoh begged us to leave. Just let us be already! Besides," they continued, "G-d assured us that we would never return to Egypt, and that we would go on to the land that He had promised to our ancestors."

"Whether you like it or not," the agents insisted, "you must obey Pharaoh's orders and return to Egypt." The Jews attacked the arrogant agents, beating them and even killing a number of them.

The surviving agents ran for their lives, back to their king in Egypt. "They refused to come back!" they testified, revealing their injuries as proof. Pharaoh conferred with his advisers-including Dasan and Aviram, Moshe's archenemies, members of the Jewish nation. They had been destined to die during the plague of darkness, but Moshe prayed on their behalf. Hashem conceded, allowing them to live, but He warned, "You will see how much trouble they will cause."

Pharaoh and his advisers concurred that it had been foolish to let the Jews go. He was especially distraught about the mixed multitude who had joined the Jews.

At that time Egypt was the dominant power of the entire world, exacting tribute from all countries in the region. "If we don't act," Pharaoh's advisers argued, "all the countries will follow the Jews' lead, hold us in contempt, and rebel against us. Some individuals already tried it!"

Day 3 - 17 Nissan

Turning Back

On the third day of Pesach, Shabbos, G-d told Moshe to turn back toward Egypt and encamp at Pisom, the city the Jewish nation built during their years of slavery. In Pisom, they were to camp facing the only idol left in all of Egypt since makas bechoros. It was shaped like an angry dog-the Baal Tzefon.

Most of the people followed Moshe's directives without question. The doubtful few were reassured by Moshe. Moshe blew the trumpet, and the Jews found themselves instantly in Pisom. The city was renamed Pi Hachiros, Dawn of Freedom.

In Pi Hachiros, the Jews discovered a vast treasure house built near the idol. The silver and gold that Yosef had collected during the famine, the riches of foreign kings, were all stored there. The Egyptians falsely believed that the mighty Baal Tzefon would protect the treasure from looters.

Now the Jews freely helped themselves, emptying the tremendous storehouse. The treasure they found there outweighed all the silver and gold they had taken from their Egyptian neighbors. It was actually their rightful fortune, inherited from their ancestor Yosef. As G-d had promised Avraham, "and they will then leave with great wealth" (Bereishis 15:14).

The Egyptians heard that the Jews set up camp opposite their idol. "Our powerful idol has prompted the Jews to turn back!" they thought. It had been foolish to let them go, they decided. Egypt's enormous wealth and power was derived from Yosef's management of the food supply during the seven years of famine. Jews were smart; it was a pity to give up all that brain power.

"They must be lost now," Pharaoh and his advisers agreed. "See how they backtracked to Pisom? How can they enter the desert, where the sand is crawling with poisonous snakes? We'll get them yet."

Day 5 - 19 Nissan

Rallying the Forces

On Monday, the fifth day of Pesach, Pharaoh made a proclamation before all his subjects. "My fellow countrymen! The Baal Tzefon has assembled all the lions of the desert and set them upon the Jews. Even our guardian angel came down from heaven to do battle with the Jews.

"Let us all march together! I won't be like other kings who stay in the rear of the troops. I'll be in the vanguard. And I won't grab all the spoils, as other kings do. I will divide them equally with you. Follow me to battle!"

To establish the truthfulness of his promise, Pharaoh opened the royal treasury. "Come one, come all-help yourselves!"

Pharaoh had kept a record of every Jew living in his kingdom, an exact tally of every Jewish slave in his possession. But he was unaware of the great percentage of Jews who had perished during the plague of darkness. To insure victory, Pharaoh recruited three hundred soldiers, including many foreign soldiers, for each Jew on his list.

It was a great miracle that the Egyptians were willing to pursue the Jews. After experiencing the horrors of the ten plagues, they surely knew that G-d would save the Jews. Any attempt to harm His chosen nation was asking for disaster. But they did not consider the fatal consequences of chasing the Jews.

In fact, Pharaoh was so zealous to recapture the Jewish nation that he did not wait for his servants to harness his three-horse chariot-the king did the work himself. (Me'am Loez) Chariots were normally pulled by two horses, but in Pharaoh's army, each chariot had three horses for increased speed. The distance the Jews traversed over three days, Pharaoh's mighty army covered in one.

(Bnei Yissos'chor)

Day 6 - 20 Nissan

The Egyptians Close In

Tuesday, the 20th of Nissan, was the sixth day of Pesach. On the breathtaking banks of the Red Sea, the Jews gathered diamonds and pearls washed ashore by the waves. These precious gems originated from the River Pishon which flows into Gan Eden (Bereishis 2:11). From there the jewels floated into the Gichon, ultimately passing into the Red Sea.

(Targum Yonasan)

But the peaceful stay did not last long.

"The Egyptians are coming!" terrified Jews screamed. The Egyptian army was approaching from behind, their guardian angel hovering over them. "The angel of Egypt has been granted permission to destroy us. We are not worthy to be saved!"

What were they to do now? Righteous Jews turned to G-d with tefillah and teshuvah, praying for help in their hour of distress. Other bands of unfaithful Jews attacked Moshe. "Why did you have to bring us out here to die in the desert?"

Waving at the Egyptians, they signaled their willingness to return as slaves. They hoped to curry favor with the Egyptians, so they could side with whoever emerged victorious. "It is because of you," they accused Moshe Rabbeinu, their humble leader. "They are coming to kill us and get back at us for the plagues they suffered and for the property we took from them on your orders."

The situation did seem desperate. The Jews were trapped. In front of them lay the menacing sea. Behind, the mighty Egyptian army was poised to strike. Snakes and hordes of wild animals hissed

and growled at them on either side. And there stood the Jews-helpless, powerless and defenseless.

The tribes were divided in their reactions. Reuven, Shimon, and Yissochor wanted to march into the sea and drown rather than be killed by the Egyptians. Zevulun, Binyamin, and Naftali argued, "Let's go back to Egypt. Better to be slaves than dead!" The mighty tribes of Yosef and Yehuda were prepared to fight back. Levi, Gad and Asher hoped to confuse the enemy with terrifying noises.

Moshe reassured the apprehensive crowd. "Do not fear!" he told them confidently. "Stand fast and see the salvation of Hashem that He will perform for you today; for as you have seen Egypt today, you will never see them again. Hashem will battle for you, and you should remain silent" (Shemos 14:13,14). Everyone looked up to the heavens to see legions of ministering angels ready to help them.

The Egyptians Attack

On the eve of the seventh day of Pesach, the Egyptians attacked. The Jews were greatly outnumbered, but G-d was on their side. The pillar of cloud and the pillar of fire that had been guiding the Jews by day and by night were now stationed behind them, forming a barrier between the Jews and their enemy.

The cloud protected the Jews from the barrage of arrows and boulders, absorbing the weapons and boomeranging them back to the Egyptians. G-d pelted the enemy with fiery coals and hailstones to bewilder them.

The cloud split into two parts. The portion of the cloud that faced the Jews lit up their camp, while the portion facing the Egyptians blocked out all light, causing palpable darkness.

(Midrash Tehillim; Targum Yonasan)

Egyptians, suddenly struck with blindness, stumbled over each other, wreaking havoc and chaos that caused a great number of casualties. They couldn't reach their positions or aim their arrows. But there was one thing they could clearly see-the Jews rejoicing and celebrating.

(Mechilta)

Challenging the Decree

Satan appeared before the Heavenly Throne. "Ribbono shel Olam," he began respectfully, "didn't the Jews worship idols together with the Egyptians? Why do You perform miracles for them? Yes, they did teshuvah, underwent milah, and brought the Korban Pesach. But these were atonement for the sins they committed in Egypt. They are not worthy of a miracle that overturns the laws of nature!"

The guardian angel of the sea was listening to Satan's accusations, growing more and more agitated. Outraged, he cried out, "Let me drown those Jews!"

"Fool!" G-d reproved. "Do you think they willingly worshipped idols? Of course not. The agony of slave labor and the daily whippings of their taskmasters dulled their minds-they could not think straight. You are judging an inadvertent sinner as an intentional sinner!"

In an effort to divert Satan's attention, G-d sent him to test Iyov's faith. Iyov, an advisor to Pharaoh, was a perfectly righteous man. But he committed one grave sin-he was silent. When Pharaoh asked his advisory council whether he should enslave the Jews, Iyov abstained and did not speak out against the proposition. Satan became so preoccupied in delivering dreadful afflictions to Iyov, he forgot to bring additional charges against the Jews.

Uzza, Egypt's guardian angel, also spoke up on behalf of his people. "Ribbono shel Olam, You Who cannot be bribed, why do You want to drown the Egyptians? My people did not drown or kill Your nation-they merely followed Pharaoh's orders. Yes, they did enslave the Jews, but they repaid the Jews already with gold and silver."

"Let all the Heavenly angels assemble-they will answer you," G-d replied.

"Whatever G-d does is just. His will should be done," the angels announced their conclusion.

"I know that the Egyptians are guilty. But please," Uzza begged, "have mercy on them."

The guardian angels of the other nations echoed Uzza's request. The angels conceded. But Michoel, the guardian angel of the Jewish nation, could not allow the Heavenly Tribunal to come to such an erroneous verdict.

Signaling to the angel Gavriel to join him, Michoel flew to Egypt to retrieve concrete evidence. They brought back a brick into which a Jewish baby had been pressed. Stepping forward, Gavriel said, "Ribbono shel Olam, look what they did to Your children!"

Then the Attribute of Justice exclaimed, "Deal with them with strict justice!" The guardian angel of Egypt had no rebuttal. The decree was final-the Egyptians would drown.

Mount Moriah, the site of the Akeidah, came to the sea to ignite the merit of the Akeidah. An image appeared-Yitzchak bound on the altar, with Avraham holding the slaughtering knife, ready to slit his son's throat. Yaakov and his twelve sons emerged from their caskets to witness the great miracle.

All three patriarchs-Avraham, Yitzchak, and Yaakov-came to witness the miraculous splitting of the sea that released their descendants from the iron grip of Egyptian rule. The Jews carried the remains of their brethren who had perished in Egypt so they could be buried in the Holy Land. Their souls witnessed the miracles, too.

Day 7 - 21 Nissan

The Waters Split

Moshe Rabbeinu faced the stormy waters of the Red Sea, in a quandary. As a baby, the waters of the Nile had saved his life when his mother sheltered him there among the rushes. How could he split these waters now?

"The sea is raging, the enemy is ready to strike-My precious children are in danger!" G-d reprimanded him. "Now is not a time for prayer! Go and tell the Jewish people to start moving. The sea will split in the merit of their forefathers and because they believed in you. Tell them not to be afraid, but to march forward!"

At the time of creation, Hashem enjoined the sea to split during the Exodus from Egypt. The sea agreed. Now the time had come for the sea to live up to her word. Moshe approached. "I am the agent of G-d who created the world," he declared. "I want you to split before the Jews so they will be able to pass."

The sea refused. "I am older than you," declared the sea. "I was created on the third day of creation; man was created on the sixth. I don't take orders from you! Besides, the Jews do not have enough merits."

Moshe was not ready to step down. He showed the sea the staff upon which G-d's ineffable Name was engraved; he showed her Yosef's coffin. "We have the tremendous merits of milah and the Korban Pesach," Moshe contended.

Still, the sea stubbornly refused. So Moshe turned to G-d. "What shall I do now?" Moshe cried. "The sea refuses to split. Why don't You tell it to split? The sea shall surely obey Your command!"

"If I tell the sea to part, it will never return to its normal flow," G-d explained. "Tell it to split and assure it that afterward its normal flow will be restored."

Accompanied by G-d on his right, Moshe approached the sea once more. Overwhelmed with awe, the sea said to the earth, "Open an escape route for me; I am terrified seeing the Master of the universe approach."

"Earlier when I asked you, you did not give in. What alarmed you, O sea, that you fled?" Moshe asked curiously.

The sea replied, quoting Kind David's psalm, "Before the presence of the G-d of Yaakov who created the world. It is before Him that I flee" (Tehillim 114:5,6).

(Mechilta)

G-d said to Moshe, "Lift your staff and raise your hand over the sea and you will split it; and the children of Israel will cross over on dry land" (Shemos 14: 16). Moshe lifted his staff, but he stretched the hand without the staff over the sea. For the staff did not lend Moshe his power; it was the power of G-d.

G-d generated a powerful east wind, accompanied by thundering noise. The east wind caused the sea to split only partially, not all the way down to the seabed. The upper third of the sea parted, while the lower two-thirds froze to the level of the land. The Jews marched straight across without going down to the seabed and climbing back up again.

(Ohr Hachaim)

According to other commentators, the entire height of the sea's waters split. The east wind dried the seabed, leaving a dry and firm surface for the Jewish nation to walk on. (Rabbeinu Bachya) Amazingly, the surface was clean and smooth, without pits or mounds.

The windy storm provided a natural guise for the supernatural splitting of the sea. An undeniable miracle would make G-d's power so indisputable as to take away man's free choice. Anyone who wanted to deny G-d's obvious involvement could point to the wind and explain the wonder away. G-d gave everyone the option of

believing in Him or denying His power. Those who chose to believe earned His reward.

First In

Twelve tribes stood by the sea. According to some accounts, each tribe fought for the privilege to enter the sea first. Yehuda, the most prominent tribe, argued that when G-d said, "Speak to the children of Israel and let them journey forth" (Shemos 14:15), G-d intended the tribe of Yehuda. Binyamin countered that "the children of Israel" referred to his tribe, since Binyamin was Yaakov's youngest child.

Yehuda argued that the Jews should enter the sea only once it split, whereas Binyamin wanted to jump into deep waters. Impatient for the outcome of the debate, the tribe of Binyamin broke into a lively dance, spinning and whirling joyously into the sea. "There Binyamin, the youngest, rules them, the princes of Yehuda stoned them; the princes of Zevulun, the princes of Naftali" (Tehillim 68:28).

In reward for their valiant leap of faith, the holy Beis Hamikdash was built in Binyamin's territory; the Shechinah rested among them. Binyamin merited to have a descendant like Mordechai, who was instrumental in saving the Jews in the days of Purim.

(Midrash)

The Talmud says each tribe wanted the other to enter the sea first. "We don't want to go in first. Let them go in first," each tribe refused, motioning to their neighbors. But pioneering Nachshon ben Aminadav from the tribe of Yehuda bravely waded into the sea, followed by the entire tribe of Yehuda. When the water reached Nachshon's nose, he cried out, "Save me, O G-d, for the waters have reached my neck" (Tehillim 69:2). (Sotah 37a) In reward for this heroic sanctification of G-d's name, Nachshon was the first to offer a sacrifice at the dedication of the Mishkan.

(Bamidbar 7:12)

Ten Miracles

Ten miracles were performed at the sea, corresponding to the merit of the ten trials of Avraham.

1. When Moshe struck the sea with his rod, tunnels formed.
2. The sea was turned into a valley.
3. The sea was cut into twelve passageways, one for each tribe.
4. The water piled up and turned into frozen clay.
5. The sea became a wilderness.
6. The wall of frozen clay broke up into many pieces.
7. The sea turned into hard rocks.
8. A flame passed between the walls of frozen water, drying the bottom of the sea. Yet the frozen walls of water did not melt.
9. The walls of water rose to a height of three hundred miles.
10. Fresh water came forth from the sea from which the Jews drank while crossing. The leftover water froze into the walls.

(Avos d'Rabi Nosson, 33)

Across the Globe

The thundering noise of the tempestuous storm was heard from one end of the world to the other. "Nations heard-they shuddered; terror gripped the dwellers of Philistia. The chiefs of Edom panicked; the heroes of Moav were seized with trembling; Canaan's residents melted away" (Shemos 15:14,15).

All the nations of the world were witness to the parting of the sea. Nothing like it had ever happened before and they shook with fear. (Targum Yonasan) Rivers, lakes, oceans, wells-every body of water on the face of the earth split. Even water in drinking glasses and water

pitchers parted, forming twelve small tunnels. (Mechilta) No one could deny Hashem's mighty hand.

Not a single ship in rivers and oceans survived the parting of the sea. When the waters split, the ships were stranded-half in the water, half in the dry area-and shipwrecked.

(Baal Haturim)

Alarmed, the nations of the world turned to Bilam, the heathen prophet, for an explanation. "G-d has taken the Jews out of Egypt to bring them to Israel," Bilam informed them. "It is for their sake that He split the sea." And so all the nations learned of G-d's power and His love for His chosen nation.

(Shach)

Partial Parting

When the Jews set foot in the sea, the water parted only as far as they were walking; it did not split all the way across. As they progressed, the water continued to part open before them. What a glorious act of faith! The Jews saw only water ahead, but all that night, they marched on into the sea.

According to other commentators, the sea parted all the way from the start. The Jews did not even notice that they were walking in the middle of the sea. Then they arrived on the opposite shore and turned to see the water crashing down on the Egyptians. Only then did they recognize the great miracle.

(Shach)

The verses imply that the Jews began crossing the sea in the evening, and when they arrived on the opposite shore early the next morning, they sang Shirah (Song by the Sea). Considering the number of elderly and infirm, this expeditious crossing was surely the hand of G-d.

According to the Ohr Hachaim, the Jews entered the sea just before daybreak on the seventh day of Pesach, not the previous evening. If so, the parting of the sea lasted only a few minutes. Six hundred thousand Jews, with their families and possessions, young and old, healthy and infirm, crossed the sea during a few brief moments. What a miracle!

The Twelve Tunnels

The water of the sea moved aside, forming two huge walls of ice, tall as mountains. But that wasn't all. The wall of water became a dam. Water continued its normal flow, but when it reached the dam, the water piled up, reaching a height of six thousand cubits (approximately twelve thousand feet, or 2.27 miles).

The sea split into twelve individual pathways, one for each tribe. Each path was twelve miles wide, equivalent to the encampment of the Jews in the wilderness, allowing the six hundred thousand men with their families and possessions to pass comfortably. (Rabbeinu Avraham ben HaRambam) A canopy of ice covered each tunnel, sheltering the tribes like a tent. In the middle of the sea, G-d spread His protective wings over His beloved nation.

The walls of seawater were transparent, glistening like diamonds from the light of the pillar of fire. For reassurance, the people were able to simply look through the wall to see their fellow tribes walking safely to shore. The muddy and soggy morass that formed the seabed was transformed into a smooth road, paved with beautiful slabs of marble upon which the Jews tread.

The Jews inhaled the fragrant air of Gan Eden. To drink, they just pushed a finger into the wall and fresh water, not the brackish water of the sea, burst forth like a fountain. When they were done drinking, the remaining water froze into the wall once more.

The walls dripped with oil and honey, eagerly lapped up by babies and small children. If a child was hungry, the mother simply

plucked the sweetest fruits from the trees that sprouted. The earth brought forth fresh vegetation to feed the animals.

The Jews did not traverse the sea from coast to opposite coast. They entered on one side and walked the shape of an arc into the sea, emerging further south, on the very same side which they had entered. The splitting of the sea was not a shortcut for the Jews; it was a guise to draw the Egyptians into the water to drown them.

(Midrash Lekach Tov)

When the Jews emerged from the sea, their faith in G-d faltered. "Just as we are coming up on this side, so will the Egyptians go up on the other side, and will pursue us," they complained to G-d.

The Holy One, blessed be He, said to the angel in charge of the sea, "Cast out the Egyptians on the dry land so the Jews will see that they drowned!"

But the sea answered, "Master of the universe! Is there a slave to whom his master gives a gift and then takes it away from him again?" The sea considered the Egyptians and their six hundred chariots a gift from Hashem and did not want to give them up.

Replied the Holy One, "I will give you afterward one and a half times as many of them." Later, in the days of Devorah, during the battle at Kishon Brook, nine hundred chariots plunged to the depths of the sea-G-d's repayment.

(Arachin 15a)

The mixed multitude did not go into the sea with the rest of the Jews, for there were only twelve paths. They rejoined the Jews when they emerged from the water further down the shore.

(Chiddushei Torah)

Revived From the Nile

When Pharaoh decreed that Jewish boys be cast into the Nile, the mothers attempted to conceal their infants in cellars where the Egyptians could not find them. But the Egyptians were crafty. They brought their own babies to visit Jewish homes. When their babies began to cry, the Jewish babies responded. The Egyptians cruelly stole the infants and drowned them, as Pharaoh had commanded.

Ten thousand infants were drowned, as it says, "Ten thousand [children] were handed over like grass in the field" (Yechezkel 16:7). As soon as ten thousand children were killed, another ten thousand were born who grew up as quickly as grass in the field.

"Moshe said, 'Six hundred thousand footmen are the people in whose midst I am'" (Bamidbar 11:21). According to Rabbi Levi, for each of six hundred thousand, one child was thrown into the river.

Rabbi Shimshon of Ostropoli commented that every child lived in the water like a fish, flourishing for eighty years. When the sea parted, the children emerged from the water, alive and well. Each child recognized his parents and was joyfully reunited.

The same will happen when Moshiach comes. "And he will turn back [to G-d] the hearts of fathers with [their] children, and the hearts of children with their fathers" (Malachi 3:24).

The illustrious Rav Tzvi Hirsch Meisels of Veitzen zt"l, this author's grandfather, derived hope from this idea. In Auschwitz, he tried to lift the spirits of the broken and despondent, people who watched the Germans cruelly cast children and parents into a fiery furnace.

"Six hundred thousand children were thrown into the Nile, and G-d sustained them like fish," he would tell his fellow inmates. "Our murdered children and our loved ones-they will also live on. We see our children being thrown into the furnace, but one day, the prophecy will come true, 'As in the days when you left the land of Egypt, I will show wonders' (Michah 7:15)."

(Zeir Zahav, Yisro)

Following the Jews Into the Sea

Despite the imposing darkness and the Egyptian casualties, despite the mighty hand of G-d they saw in Egypt, Pharaoh and his vast legions blindly chased the Jews straight into the Red Sea. G-d had hardened their hearts. They allowed themselves to be deceived by the weather conditions, thinking that perhaps it was the wind which froze the water, not Hashem.

The Egyptian army was normally very disciplined, always marching in exact formation, generals and officers followed by their loyal troops. But G-d startled and confused them. It was dark; they couldn't light their lamps. The whole world seemed to be blowing away by the wind. They didn't know if they should advance or retreat. Powerlessly watching the Jews carry off their precious possessions made them sick.

And then G-d grabbed Egypt's guardian angel-and flung him into the sea. Baffled and bewildered, the Egyptians drove their chariots into the sea, hoping to overtake the Jews.

In a normal world, horses pull the chariots. But at the splitting of the sea, the chariots turned, dragging horses and riders into the raging waters. Their orderly world collapsed into total chaos. "Let's flee from Israel. G-d is fighting for them against Egypt!" (Shemos 14:25) cried the Egyptians.

The Jews had plunged in until the water reached their necks, whereupon the waters from that point forward split. But when the Egyptians splashed in, even the shallow waters split. "Our guardian angel split the water on our behalf. This is not happening in the merit of those worthless Jews," they thought smugly. But events did not continue in their favor, for "Deep waters covered them; they descended in the depths like a stone" (Shemos 15:5).

The same pillar of cloud that had dried the seabed for the Jews turned the ground into a soggy swamp for the Egyptians. The chariots were stuck in the mud, unable to move. Then G-d sent the pillar of

fire. The mud bubbled and boiled, burning the legs of the Egyptians horses with painful blisters.

A single wheel broke off each chariot, setting the chariots into a violent side-to-side rock. Riders were tossed back and forth with their golden chariots, bones aching and breaking. Others were thrown overboard, tumbling into the slimy swamp, unable to extricate themselves.

The Waters Return

Hashem said to Moshe, "Extend your hand over the sea and the water will go back upon Egypt, upon its chariots and upon its horsemen" (Shemos 14:26). The Jews and the Egyptians were in the sea at the same time, the water surrounding them from all sides. Moshe asked G-d: "What are the Jews to do?" G-d then stretched out His hand and lifted His nation out of the sea, as it says, "He sent from on high and He took me, He drew me out of deep waters" (Tehillim 18:17).

> *A gang of bandits were threatening a father and his son. What did the father do? He held on to his son with one hand and fought off the evil bandits with the other. The son blessed his father, "May you have enough strength in both your hands-the hand that holds me and the hand you battle with."*

The Jews praised Hashem, "Blessed be both Your hands-the hand with which You led us through the sea, and the hand with which You thrust the Egyptians into the sea." As it says, "Your right hand, O Hashem, is awesome in power; Your right hand, O Hashem, crushes the foe" (Shemos 15:6).

(Shemos Rabbah 22b)

"Just before morning, Moshe raised his hand over the sea, and the sea returned to its normal condition. The Egyptians were fleeing the water, but G-d swamped the Egyptians in the middle of the water.

The waters came back and covered the cavalry and chariots. Of all Pharaoh's army that had followed the Jews into the sea, not a single one survived" (Shemos 14:27-29).

When the angel of the sea received permission to let the sea return to normal, he wanted to drown the Jews too. But the angel Gavriel, marching behind them, turned to the sea. "Look at the Jews. On their backs you can see two tzitzis and the knot of the tefillin." To the water in front of them he declared, "Look at the Jews. They have two tzitzis and the mitzvah of milah on their front." From the left, the Jews had the merit of tefillin placed on the left arm. And on the right stood the merit of the Torah they were to receive from G-d's right hand.

The water, standing like walls on either side, collapsed onto the Egyptians, an appropriate punishment for drowning Jewish infants in the Nile. The Egyptians, well aware that G-d punishes measure for measure, never dreamed of such retribution. The Egyptians specifically chose to drown Jewish babies, reasoning that Hashem would never drown them because of His pledge from the days of Noach. G-d had promised not to flood the entire earth-but He could flood a single nation, or draw them into the sea.

The waters of the Nile came to the Red Sea to pay the Egyptians for their heinous crimes. The four mighty rivers of Gan Eden-Pishon, Gichon, Chidekel, and Peras-came to the Red Sea to punish the Egyptians. One chilled them with icy water, another boiled them with seething water, the third tormented them with salty water, and the fourth drowned them in foul-smelling muck. All the waters of the world came to the Red Sea to take part in punishing the evil Egyptians.

While the Jews were still safely ensconced in their roomy tunnels, the towering walls of ice began to crumble. Egyptian chariot drivers and soldiers tried to escape, their eyes fearfully glued to the teetering towers. But alas, their feet were glued to the mucky seabed; they

could not move. Chunks of ice poured down, piercing painful holes in the bodies of the Egyptians.

The cold eastern wind that froze the waters of the sea for the Jewish people suddenly turned hot, melting the ice at an unnaturally rapid rate. With the water level rising so quickly, not a single Egyptian escaped.

The east wind also brought an epidemic. Egyptians came down with fever so high that it made their bodies shiver and their bones rattle. They vomited from nausea. Itchy sores covered their bodies head to toe, but they couldn't even scratch because their hands were holding tightly to their wildly swaying chariots. To make matters worse, worms came creeping out of their bodies.

The wildly swirling waves tore off their clothing, made their skin peel, and caused their bodies to break out in boils. Their agonizing cries could be heard for miles. The bodies of many Egyptians dissolved in the water, but they were restored to feel the full brunt of the pain. Then their bodies dissolved again.

Gleeful soldiers watched their Egyptians comrades tossed about by the waters. How happy they were not to be inside that mess! But G-d sent a strong wind that blew every single Egyptian into the raging waters to perish along with their friends. Even as they were tossed in the air, G-d tied the riders to their flailing horses, making them unable to escape.

Some Egyptians tried to use witchcraft or black magic to evade the raging sea. But the sea cried out, "G-d delivered them into my hands; I am not going to let them get away!" The water spouted upward, bringing down every single Egyptian escapee.

Other sorcerers grew magic wings, soaring above the tumultuous mess. But G-d commanded the angel Michoel, "Bring them down!" Instantly, Michoel grabbed them by their heads and flung them down into the sea.

The image of a large hand inscribed with various Egyptian magic formulas was suspended over the sea. Whichever form of witchcraft the Egyptian sorcerers tried to use, the hand quickly nullified.

Like Straw, Like Stone, Like Lead

Every Egyptian was punished in measure for his degree of cruelty. The best of the bunch sank straight to the bottom like lead, without much suffering. The in-between Egyptians sank like stones. And the truly evil Egyptians were thrown back and forth in the raging waters like weightless straw. The sea fought the Egyptians with great skill, as if it knew exactly what the Egyptians were up to.

There were three levels of the sea-the Yam Suf, Red Sea; tehomos, depths; and metzolos, bottom (Shemos 15:4,5). G-d churned the Egyptians in the sea as a ladle stirs a pot of soup. The ladle brings the thick ingredients from the bottom of the pot to the top and the top to the bottom.

Heavy chariots, loaded with riders and weapons, were lifted all the way to the clouds, then plunged from the heights to the bottom of the sea, falling upside down, horse on top of its rider, sometimes directly onto hard rocks. Unfortunate Egyptians cracked their heads and broke their bones, but still they hovered between life and death, feeling the full sting of torment.

Wellsprings deep inside the earth emitted their own waters to blend with the waters of the sea. The resulting churning whirlpool ripped apart the bodies and clothing of the Egyptians. Large fish swallowed Egyptians. Then came even larger fishes that devoured the ones that had swallowed the Egyptians. The mouths of the empty wellsprings opened to swallow a vast numbers of Egyptians, too.

During all this, all the inhabitants of Egypt watched. The land was raised higher than the sea so everyone could see the miracles taking place and fear the Jewish nation and their G-d. The Egyptians who remained behind, the spectators, understood that the parting of the sea was Divine retribution, not a quirk of nature. Once they recognized the hand of G-d, the waters of the sea flooded the land of Egypt, drowning all the Egyptians living there.

Washed Up

Semi-conscious Egyptians were washed up onto the shore of the Red Sea, along with their horses and chariots. But their souls did not leave their bodies right away. From their vulnerable position they saw the Jews, dry and safe at the water's edge. And the Jews saw them, too. The Jews witnessed the demise of Egypt's guardian angel along with its people.

The earth did not want to accept the Egyptian corpses. So the earth threw them back into the sea. But the sea did not want the corpses either. So the sea tossed them back out to the dry land. Back and forth, back and forth, from sea to shore they went, until G-d intervened. "If you will accept the Egyptians," G-d promised the earth, "you will not be punished for harboring the evildoers." Thereupon the earth accepted the corpses of the Egyptians.

Why did the Egyptians merit burial? When Yaakov died the entire Egyptian nation escorted his casket, paying their respects at the imposing funeral. In addition, the burial was G-d's reward to Pharaoh for saying, "G-d is just! It is I and my people who are in the wrong!" (Shemos 9:27). G-d never withholds reward from anyone. Also, Egypt was the instrument that brought about a tremendous sanctification of Hashem's name. Simply for this they deserved to be buried.

Soldiers from other nations who had joined the pursuit of the Jews marched into the sea alongside their Egyptian comrades. But while the Egyptians drowned, the foreign troops survived, witnesses to the downfall of Egypt and the mighty power of G-d.

Only one Egyptian survived this ordeal-haroah. He was swept away together with his military force, but G-d kept him alive. The mighty ruler of Egypt was sustained so he could tell the world about the great wonders and miracles G-d performed for His nation.

Countless treasures and vast wealth lay on the sand together with the dead Egyptians. Where did these valuable items come from? Didn't the Jews "drain Egypt of its wealth" (Shemos 12:35)? The Jews

had collected only the personal belongings of the Egyptians. Now Pharaoh's priceless royal treasury washed up on shore.

Pharaoh had induced his cavalry to join his pursuit of the Jews with gold and silver. Aside from these monies, beautiful golden ornaments decorated the horses and chariots that G-d had bound to their riders. All this washed ashore, loot for G-d's victorious nation.

The sight of every last Egyptian body was a comfort to the Jews. Even those that had sunk to the depths were tossed out on the shore. The Jews saw and they were not afraid anymore. "And Israel saw the Egyptians dead on the seashore. Israel saw the great power Hashem had unleashed against Egypt, and the people were in awe of Hashem. They believed in Hashem and in His servant Moshe" (Shemos 14:30,31).

Singing Hashem's Praises

Moved by the awesome moment, all the Jews were granted great prophetic inspiration. They sang Shirah in unison. The prophetic vision the Jews had at the parting of the sea was greater than the visions the great prophets had in the days when the Beis Hamikdash was standing.

Even the small children sang Shirah together with the mighty choir of all the sons of Israel. Everyone saw the holy Shechinah. Recognizing G-d's Omnipotence, children pointed their innocent fingers toward the Shechinah and proclaimed, "This is my G-d, and I will glorify Him" (Shemos 15:2)

Chapter 6

Korban Pesach

The Offering of the Korban Pesach

A Roman nobleman who lived during the era of the *Beis Hamikdash* once wrote a detailed account of the *Korban Pesach*, the preparations and bringing of the annual sacrifice that culminated on Pesach night. He was awed by the detail and diligence that every participant devoted to this holy practice. The text is quoted by the renowned Rabbi Yaakov Emden, in his *Siddur Bais Yaakov* from *Shevet Yehuda*.

The details in the Roman's letter, together with parallel descriptions the Sages give, provide a special glimpse into the glory of the Jewish nation during the time of the *Beis Hamikdash*. We pray for Hashem to have mercy on us and take us out of our long, dark exile, to participate very soon in the holy service of Hashem in the *Beis Hamikdash*, where we will witness its glory with our own eyes.

The Roman Noble's Letter

When the month they call Nissan begins, the king and the judges of the high court send forth messengers to all livestock owners in the entire region surrounding Jerusalem. Owners of sheep and cattle are summoned to bring their flocks to the Holy City. The vast multitude of pilgrims require many offerings for the holiday, as well as animals for food. Dealers are warned that whoever does not come with his flocks by the appointed time may have all his possessions confiscated on behalf of the Temple.

Five Types of Offerings

1. Before Pesach, Jews had to buy five different types of offerings:
2. *Olas R'eiah*- burnt offering to commemorate the occasion of appearing before G-d. Three times a year on the *shalosh regalim* (three pilgrimage holidays)-esach, Shavuos and Sukkos-ll Jewish men were commanded to appear before Hashem at the *Beis Hamikdash*. Each person was required to bring a *korban olah*, an offering that is entirely consumed by the fire on the altar, in accordance with the Torah command, "And they shall not appear before me empty-handed."

   (Shemos 23:15)

3. *Shalmei Chagigah*-eace offerings for the celebration of the holiday. For each of the three pilgrimage festivals, every man also had to bring a peace offering to Hashem. "Three pilgrimage festivals you shall celebrate for me during the year." *(Shemos 23:14)* The verse implies that celebration must be in a tangible manner, by offering an animal to Hashem and feasting on it. This offering was a *korban shlamim*, the majority of which was eaten by those who offered it.

4. *Shalmei Simchah*-eace offerings for rejoicing. Part of the holiday celebration was to eat meat every day. "Rabbi Yehuda ben B'seira says: In the time of the *Beis Hamikdash*, rejoicing was primarily through eating meat, as the verse says, 'You shall slaughter peace-offerings and eat there, and you shall rejoice before G-d, your Master.' *(Devarim 27:7)*" *(Pesachim 109a)* This, too, was a *korban shlamim*.
5. *Chagigas Arbaah Asar*-elebration offering of 14 Nissan. This was a voluntary *korban shlamim* that many opted to bring on the day before Pesach. Its meat was served to the family and other guests before partaking of the *Korban Pesach*, to fulfill the requirement of eating the *Korban Pesach* only when satisfied.
6. *Korban Pesach*-assover offering. Every Jew had to eat a *k'zayis* (olive-sized amount) of the lamb or goat. Any leftover meat became *nosar*, which had to be burnt the following morning. Before setting out to buy the *Korban Pesach* a buyer had to know how many people would be attending his meal, so he could find an animal of the proper size.

Avoiding Price Gouging

The *Sanhedrin* fixed an annual price for each category of animal, for fear that the high demand for animals would drive up the price-eaving G-d-fearing Jews with no choice but to pay astronomical prices. Since so many animals were needed, the messengers stipulated in their warning that anyone who dared charge higher than the fixed price could be punished. All his possessions could be confiscated by the court.

Inspecting the Animals

At that signal, flocks of sheep and cattle make their way up to Jerusalem. At Nachal Kidron, a stream east of the Temple Mount, the livestock pass through the rushing water to cleanse them of all dirt. This

is what King Solomon meant when he referred to the whiteness of flocks that "have come up from the washing." (Shir HaShirim 4:2) As they cross the hills to Jerusalem, the cloud of white wool blocks the view of any green vegetation. On the tenth day of the month everyone goes out to buy an animal, either a lamb or kid goat, since on the fourteenth day they will offer it as the Passover sacrifice.

While crowds of people are eager to make this precious purchase, the Jews have a rule that no one says, "Move out of the way" or "Let me go ahead" to anyone in line, even if it is their King Solomon or David. I asked the priests about this, for surely it is not polite etiquette to make an honored personage wait in line? They answered that there is no class ranking before G-d at a time when everyone is preparing for His service; how much more so during the actual Divine sacrificial service. During these times, everyone is equally important before G-d.

From the tenth until the fourteenth of Nissan, the animals were carefully inspected each day for any of seventy-three defects that could disqualify them from being offered as sacrifices. Trained experts posted in various locations across Jerusalem performed the inspections at no cost to the animal's new owner. The inspectors were paid by the official fund of the *Beis Hamikdash*, the treasury that accumulated each year from the annual half-Shekel contribution. Inspections took place daily, for four or five consecutive days. There are differing opinions whether inspections were conducted on the tenth of Nissan itself, the day the animal was purchased.

(Rashi, Arachin 12a)

Four days of observation and inspection correspond to the four letters of Hashem's holy Name, *yud-hey-vav-hey*. As an animal dedicated for the sake of Hashem, each successive day imbued a higher holiness, so a defect not apparent on one day was apt to be noticed the next.

(Chasam Sofer, Drashos, Parshas HaChodesh, 213)

Preparations for the Korban Pesach

On 13 Nissan, all Jews who had come to Jerusalem on pilgrimage immersed in a *mikvah* to purify themselves from all ritual impurities. Their new ritually purified status took effect that evening, enabling them to slaughter the *Korban Pesach* the next day, on 14 Nissan.

(Mizbach Avanim 18)

Utensils were also immersed on the thirteenth. Utensils used to prepare and eat the *Korban Pesach* required immersion only if they had become ritually impure according to Biblical law. Those that were *tamei* as a result of a stringency enacted by the Sages did not require immersion. For example, if a knife had come in contact with the carcass of a *sheretz* (small animal, see *Vayikra* 11:29-30), it had to be immersed before it could be used to prepare the *Korban Pesach*.

Any *korban* that a Jew became obligated to bring over the course of the year had to be offered before the next pilgrimage holiday, according to the commandment of "You shall bring it there." Any Jew who was obligated to offer a *korban todah*, a token of gratitude for surviving dangerous circumstances, had to fulfill his obligation by 13 Nissan, allowing one day and one night to eat the loaves of bread included in the *korban*. Since eating *chametz* is prohibited from midday on the fourteenth of Nissan until after Pesach, sufficient time had to be allowed to consume the meal offering. Though technically the *korban todah* could be offered on the morning of 14 Nissan itself, there would not be enough time to finish the *chametz* loaves before midday. Loaves would be left uneaten, transgressing the prohibition of *nosar*.

The Order of the Day

> *When the fourteenth day of the month arrives, heralds ascend a high tower in the Temple, which the Hebrews call the lul. It has a spiral staircase similar to our conferio. Blowing on the three silver trumpets they hold in their hands, they proclaim: "People of G-d,*

listen! The time has arrived to slaughter the Passover offering to G-d, Who has caused His Name to rest upon this great and holy House." When the people hear this proclamation they dress in festive clothing, because after midday it becomes a holiday for all the Jews, as it is the time of offering the sacrifice.

The task of awaking the *kohanim* in the *Beis Hamikdash* fell to a *kohen* named Gvini. When he called the *kohanim* in the *Beis Hamikdash* at dawn to the sacrificial service, his voice was so loud that it could be heard as far away as Jericho, a distance of ten parsangs (about 25 kilometers). The daily twenty-one blasts of the *shofar* sounded in the *Beis Hamikdash* were so loud that they, too, could be heard all the way to Jericho. As sacrifices were offered on the altar, the melodious voices of the *levi'im* singing their daily songs floated the long distance to Jericho.

(Tamid 3:8)

Two loaves left over from the previous day's numerous *korban todos* were set upon the roof of the *itztaba* (colonnade). Everyone gathered on benches atop the *Har HaBayis* to watch the two disqualified loaves. At the fifth hour of the day, a *Sanhedrin* representative climbed onto the roof and removed one loaf, signifying that it was time for the people to stop eating *chametz*. One additional hour remained until all *chametz* had to be removed from their ownership. At the end of the hour, the representative once again went onto the colonnade roof and removed the second loaf. That was the sign for everyone in Jerusalem to burn their *chametz*, which no Jew could have in his possession when he brought the *Korban Pesach*.

Abba Shaul, one of the Sages of the *Mishnah*, cites a different sign used by the people of Jerusalem. Two cows would be set to plow on *Har HaZeisim* (Mount of Olives) in full view of the whole of Jerusalem, as a sign that everyone could still eat *chametz*. When one of the cows was led away, it was time to stop eating *chametz*. When the second cow was led away, the hour had come for the *chametz* to be burned.

(Pesachim 14a)

After burning the *chametz*, everyone immersed in a *mikvah* to purify themselves before entering the holy *Beis Hamikdash*. Although anyone who had been *tamei* had already immersed the previous day, everyone did so again in preparation for the holy event.

The sacrifices of *Chagigas Arbaah Asar* and *Shalmei Simchah* were slaughtered in the few hours between the burning of the *chametz* and the *Korban Tamid*. At approximately 2:30 PM, the *Korban Tamid*, the second daily sacrifice, was offered on the altar of the *Beis Hamikdash*. The seven lamps of the golden *menorah* were lit, and all was in order for the *Korban Pesach*, the only sacrifice ever offered after the afternoon *Korban Tamid*.

According to the *Talmud Yerushalmi*, as the *Korban Pesach* was being slaughtered, the *matzos mitzvah*, *matzos* to be eaten together with the *Korban Pesach* that evening, were baked. Some still have the custom to bake *matzos* on the afternoon before Pesach. The *Mishnah* states that the men prepared the fire of the ovens while the women rolled and baked. The *matzos* of the time were not thin and crispy, as they are today. They were as thick as a *tefach,* the size of a fist-ver three inches thick! These *matzos* were only edible fresh out of the oven. When they cooled they hardened, making them impossible to chew. Fresh *matzos* were baked every day of Pesach except on Shabbos.

(Aruch HaShulchan, Chapter 459)

The Multitudes Present

Twelve Levites holding impressive silver staffs stand at the entrance of the great courtyard of the Sanctuary. Another twelve stand inside, holding golden staffs. The outside guards maintain order, ensuring that everyone enters calmly, without any arguments. They admonish the attendees not to hurt their neighbors in their hurry and haste. One Pesach, an elderly man and his sacrifice were crushed under the great pressure of the crowd. The Levites inside the entrance maintain order

among those leaving, ensuring that no one is jostled. They are also responsible for closing the gates when the Sanctuary reaches its full capacity.

The *Talmud* tells how one year King Agrippas wanted to know how many Jews offered the *Korban Pesach*. The *kohen gadol* ordered the *kohanim* to set aside one kidney from each sacrifice. *(Pesachim 64b)* They amounted to double the number of people who went out of Egypt-600,000 men, 600,000 women, 600,000 children and 600,000 elderly-,800,000 sacrifices!

(Maharam Schiff)

A minimum of ten adults participated in each *Korban Pesach*, so the number of participants totaled at least forty eight million. And this excludes Jews who were *tamei* on the day before Pesach or were distant from Jerusalem, unable to partake of the *Korban Pesach*.

The *Midrash* quotes the opinion of Rabbi Chiya that as many as forty or fifty Jews used to participate in every *Korban Pesach*. Bar Kapara felt that a hundred people could gather for a single *Korban Pesach*. So as many as four hundred and eighty million Jews came to Jerusalem to offer up the *Korban Pesach* every year!

(Eicha 1:2)

Rabbi Chanina once told a disbeliever that the land of Israel is called "*Eretz ... tzvi*- the land [like] a deer." *(Yirmiyahu 3:19)* Just as a deer's hide shrinks after it is skinned and can no longer stretch to cover the deer's original carcass-when the land of Israel is inhabited, there is ample space, but when it is sparsely populated, the land shrinks. The Divine Presence rested on the multitude of Jews who convened for the sole purpose of offering sacrifices to G-d. Hashem expanded the small confines of the land of Israel, Jerusalem and the *Beis Hamikdash* to accommodate the great numbers.

(Gittin 57a)

During the *shalosh regalim*, every courtyard had twice as many residents as the number of Jews who left Egypt. Each Jerusalem

resident had thousands of guests, including many children. Yet everyone still had ample living space, so Torah study, prayer and normal life could proceed undisturbed.

(Avos D'Rabi Nosson, chapter 35, Binyan Yehoshua)

There were ten miracles that occurred in Jerusalem at the time of the *Beis Hamikdash*:

1. Although many sacrifices were slaughtered as *Shalmei Chagigah*, none of them ever decayed. Nor did the smoke of roasting all the *Korban Pesach* sacrifices ever harm anyone's health.
2. Despite the vast crowds, no one was ever hurt or injured or broke any bones. No one was ever bitten by a snake; on the rare occasion that it did happen, that person suffered no harm.
3. No one was ever harmed by evil spirits.
4. Everyone's mind remained clear and composed despite the great tumult of vast numbers of people and the awesome revelation of Hashem's presence.
5. No one ever committed any sin even unwittingly while in Jerusalem, and no one transgressed the rules of eating the meat of *kodoshim kalim* (offerings of lesser holiness).
6. No fire ever broke out in the whole city of Jerusalem, guarded as they were by the fire burning on the altar.
7. The wall surrounding Jerusalem never collapsed.
8. On the day before Pesach, anyone ready to roast his *Korban Pesach* found a fire without delay. Although no large fires were permitted to curb smoke damage, the small fires quickly roasted everyone's *korban*, and all the meat was ready in time for *Yom Tov*.
9. When all the Jews assembled in the *Beis Hamikdash*, it was so crowded that their feet weren't standing on the ground—they were suspended in midair. But when they bowed to the ground, everyone had more than enough room-a full four cubits between each of them!

10. No had to go searching for a place to sleep overnight, nor did anyone ever say he was uncomfortable.

(Avos D'Rabi Nosson, chapter 39)

Entering the Courtyard of the Temple

Everyone entered the Sanctuary courtyard through the main entrance, which was ten cubits (approximately fifteen feet) wide and twenty cubits high-as high as a four-story building. The *levi'im* who stood guard, six on each side, asked various questions to those wishing to enter. When had they last immersed? Who checked their animal for defects? Did any of their invited participants for the *Korban Pesach* still possess any *chametz* or own an uncircumcised slave? Is the slaughtering blade ritually pure and was it checked for defects? All of these details affected whether they were permitted to offer a *Korban Pesach*. The *levi'im* randomly asked questions about ritual slaughtering to ascertain that they were qualified to perform it.

As more and more Jews arrived, the area became more and more crowded. The main courtyard of the *Beis Hamikdash*, the front area known as the *Ezras Yisrael* (the courtyard of Israelites), became full. The crowd overflowed into the *Ezras Kohanim* (courtyard of the priests) north of the area where the sacrifices were slaughtered. During the year, Israelites were not allowed in the *Ezras Kohanim* unless they had to do *semichah* (place their hands on the head of their sacrifice) or *tenufah* (waving parts of their sacrifice). For the purpose of slaughtering the *Korban Pesach*, which falls into the category of *kodashim kalim* (offerings of lesser holiness) which can be slaughtered anywhere in the courtyard of the *Beis Hamikdash*, Israelites were allowed to stand there.

Additional offerers filled the area south of the ramp leading up to the main altar, and even the area inside the northern, southern and western walls of the courtyard surrounding the *Beis Hamikdash*. But between the *mizbeiach* and *Beis Hamikdash*, the Torah allowed no one but the *kohanim* to enter.

The *Korban Pesach* could be slaughtered anywhere that was considered *Machaneh Shechinah*, including the entire courtyard. The *Ezras Nashim* was located fifteen steps down, east of the *azarah*, and was part of the *Machaneh Leviya* (abode of the Levites). That area was not designated for slaughtering the sacrifices.

Everyone stood in silence with deep awe and reverence. Other than the bleating of the lambs and goats, barely a sound could be heard. The entire procedure was completed wordlessly, for everyone understood what to do. They were guests in the *Machaneh Shechinah*, the abode of Hashem's Presence, the Royal Palace of the Supreme King of the universe, where every movement had to be measured and an improper stray thought could disqualify a sacrifice.

Daily miracles apparent to the physical eye made this holy place unique. "They stood crowded together, yet had ample space to prostrate themselves." *(Avos 5:7)* At every turn, the *mitzvah* of *Morah Hamikdash,* reverence for the Holy Temple, applied. No one who had even the slightest level of ritual impurity could enter the entire area, nor anyone who had just drunk a *reviyis* (about 4 ounces) of wine or whose hair had not been trimmed during the past thirty days. Shoes and torn clothing were banned; other than kings descending from King David, no one was allowed to sit down anywhere. Even someone who was ritually pure would not enter the *Beis Hamikdash* without first immersing himself again.

Closing the Doors

The Jews were divided arbitrarily into three different shifts for the offering of the *Korban Pesach*. *(Rashi, Shemos 12:6)* Abaye believed that when the shift was full, the courtyard doors closed miraculously on their own. Anyone was allowed to enter until they closed, without concern that there would be no participants left for the remaining shifts. Rava was of the opinion that the *levi'im* closed the courtyard as soon as it was full, without relying on miracles.

(Pesachim 64b)

The *Tiferes Yisrael*, a commentary on the *Mishnah*, writes that the doors closed to differentiate between groups: those admitted until then belonged to the first group, and those admitted later belonged to the next group. One group was admitted, the doors were closed, and then immediately reopened while the animals were slaughtered. The *Rambam* differs, claiming that the doors did not reopen until after each group finished offering its sacrifices.

When the doors to the Sanctuary closed on the day before Pesach, no Jew in the packed courtyard could be compared to the great *Tanna* Akavya ben Mahallel, who in humility and fear of sin sacrificed his *Korban Pesach*.

(Eiduyos 5:6)

The Process of the Sacrificial Service

A battalion of priests stand holding silver or gold vessels in their hands in front of the place where the animals are slaughtered. If a gold vessel rests in the hands of the priest at the head of the row, the entire row of priests has gold vessels; if it is a silver one, the entire row holds silver vessels. The orderliness adds to the beauty and splendor.

The priest at the head of the row receives one vessel of blood that flows from the throat of a lamb or goat, and he hands it to the priest next to him, and the next to the next, until the full vessel reaches the altar. The priest next the altar, in the very back of the row, returns the empty vessel to the front of the row, where another Jew waits to fill it with the blood of his sacrifice. This exercise is performed with such perfection that every priest receives one full vessel with one hand and returns another empty vessel with the other hand simultaneously, without delaying either vessel. The vessels appear to be flying back and forth like arrows from the bow of a mighty archer. The priests practice for this task thirty days before, vigilant for any possible error or problem they might encounter.

Any Jew was allowed to slaughter the *Korban Pesach*, but a *kohen* had to receive the blood into his holy vessel as it poured from the animal's throat. The animal was held tightly so its throat was directly over the vessel, allowing all the blood to flow straight in. The knife was removed immediately so any blood that remained on it would not drip into the vessel; this blood was not valid for sprinkling on the *mizbeiach*.

(Avodas HaKorbanos, chapter 48)

The slaughter of the animals proceeded with amazing speed:

In an average year there were about 4,800,000 *Korban Pesach* sacrifices. These were divided into three groups that entered and slaughtered their sacrifices consecutively. The *Talmud* says that most people tried to be in the first or at least the second group, and the final group consisted of the Jews who did not hurry to participate earlier. Accordingly, the first two shifts numbered at least 1,600,000 Jews and possibly many more, every man with his animal crowding the courtyard of the *Beis Hamikdash*.

This was aside from the *kohanim* in Jerusalem, all of whom were allowed to participate in this holy Divine service, regardless of whether their rotation was in service. Twenty-four family groups of *kohanim* each served at the *Beis Hamikdash* for one week at a time, but during special services, all groups were permitted to participate. On top of that, many *levi'im* were also present in the courtyard.

Slaughter of the *Korban Pesach* sacrifices began in the last third of the day and continued until *plag haminchah*, one and a quarter hours before nightfall. *(Shaagas Aryeh)* Almost five million Jews all had to slaughter their lambs in just over two hours-135 minutes. According to the math, over 35,000 animals were slaughtered every minute!

The base of the *mizbeiach* extended across the north and east sides for a total distance of 64 cubits (over 100 feet). No more than one hundred *kohanim* could possibly stand around this area, where the blood from the slaughter of each *Korban Pesach* was sprinkled. Since they needed space to maneuver vessels in both hands, less than one hundred *kohanim* stood around it, each at the back of a long row.

Estimating one hundred rows of *kohanim* and 1,600,000 animals to be slaughtered in each shift, each row passed over 16,000 vessels of blood back and forth in each of three shifts. And this was accomplished during the time it took to sing the *Hallel* twice! The *Mishnah* notes that the process never took so long that *Hallel* was sung a third time.

Each slaughterer had intent and pronounced that he was slaughtering his animal for "the purpose of the *Korban Pesach*, in the name of [its owners], for the sake of G-d, blessed be He, for the sake of [being consumed by] the fires [of the *mizbeiach*], for the sake of a pleasant fragrance before G-d, for the sake of pleasing [G-d]."

The first *kohen* in each row received the blood in the vessel he held in his right hand, without any assistance from his left hand. He recited the blessing, "Blessed are You, G-d, our Master, King of the universe, Who has made us holy with the holiness of Aharon, and commanded us the commandment of receiving the blood." He said he was receiving the blood for the purpose of the *Korban Pesach*, and in the name of its owners.

The filled vessel was passed immediately to the next *kohen* in the row. While handing it to him, the first *kohen* was required to walk forward rapidly. Simply handing it over disqualified the entire sacrifice. According to the *Mirkeves HaMishnah*, only the first *kohen* had to take steps, while the subsequent *kohanim* stayed in place as they passed the vessels.

The second *kohen* in each row received the vessel of blood from the first, and also had to recite his own *brachah* of "*holacha* (conveying) of the blood." He announced that he was performing this action for the purpose of the *Korban Pesach*, in the name of its owners. *(Rambam, Mishneh Torah, Hilchos P'sulei Hamkudashim, 1:22-24)* The vessel was handed rapidly down the line until it reached the *mizbeiach*.

The *kohen* at the foot of the line, standing next to the *mizbeiach*, also announced that he was sprinkling the blood for the purpose of the *Korban Pesach*, in the name of its owners and for the sake of Hashem. He recited the blessing of "...Who has made us holy with

the holiness of Aharon, and commanded us about the commandment of sprinkling." He sprinkled the blood on the *mizbeiach* and the empty vessel was returned to the next *kohen* in line, who quickly passed it back down to be filled once more. Each *kohen* received a vessel full of blood in his right hand, and in his left hand an empty vessel. Placing the vessel on the floor was impossible, for the blood could congeal and become unfit for sprinkling on the *mizbeiach*. Thus, the cone-shaped vessels, some full and some empty, flew continuously from hand to hand in opposite directions.

Practicing for the Great Day

For thirty days prior to *Erev* Pesach, the *kohanim* learned to deal with errors that might be encountered-what to do when a vessel of blood spills, how to correct mistakes. If anything out of the ordinary happened on *Erev* Pesach, the *kohanim* were able to calmly and quickly correct the mistake and move on with their job.

The Sounding of the Trumpets

> *Two priests bearing silver trumpets stand high on two columns. They blow the trumpets as each of the three successive groups begins to slaughter their sacrifices. This signals the priests [Levites] standing on their platform to start saying the psalms of praise in a voice of song and thanksgiving, accompanied by all their musical instruments which they bring out for this special occasion. Everyone offering a sacrifice also recites the psalms of praise. If the slaughter of the animals is not yet finished, they repeat their song.*

Musical sounds played a large part during the slaughtering of the *Korban Pesach*. When the trumpets sounded a *tekiyah*, everyone in the courtyard of the *Beis Hamikdash* bowed down to Hashem. *(Mizbach Avanim, chapter 26)* In place of the usual bronze flute, the song of

Hallel was accompanied by a wooden cane flute because its musical notes are especially beautiful.

(Arachin 2:3)

The powerful trumpet blasts were instrumental in driving out all foreign thoughts from the participants' minds. While offering the sacrifice, the owner needed perfect devotion to Hashem, Who has commanded to offer the sacrifice; even a slightly wrong intention could disqualify his sacrifice. But physical beings become inattentive to such exalted thoughts, so the loud sounds of trumpets served to awaken minds and rid one's head of all worldly thoughts.

(Sefer HaChinuch, Mitzvah 382)

The *Talmud* says that on *Erev* Pesach, the trumpets were sounded twenty-seven times. *Rashi* enumerates them: The *Korban Pesach* was slaughtered in three groups, and each group said *Hallel* up to three times. Once the courtyard doors were closed, but before *Hallel* began, two *kohanim* sounded three blasts-*tekiyah*, *teruah*, *tekiyah*. Prior to the two subsequent recitations of *Hallel*, the blasts were sounded again, totaling nine blasts per group for a grand total of twenty-seven blasts.

(Sukkah 54a)

Tosafos disagrees, pointing out that *Hallel* was not always said three times for each group, depending on how long the slaughtering lasted. Three blasts-*tekiyah*, *teruah*, *tekiyah*-were sounded before starting *Hallel*, and then during *Hallel*; before the Psalm 116, *Ahavti*; and before Psalm 119, *Hodu*, for a total of nine blasts per shift. Adding all three shifts together, there were twenty-seven blasts.

Skinning the Sacrifice

After slaughtering the sacrifice, all the participants exit, gathering in the courtyards. The walls of the courtyard are lined with iron hooks and spikes, where sacrifices are hung so they can be easily skinned.

There are many piles of staves lying there. In case no spikes are available, they support the stave on someone else's shoulder while skinning the carcass.

If someone could not find a spike that was not being used, he and the man in front of him would rest a stave over their left shoulders, both holding it with their left hands, while the sacrifice owner skinned the carcass with his right hand.

If the fourteenth of Nissan fell out on Shabbos, staves were not used. Instead, one would rest his left arm on the left shoulder of the man in front of him, hang the carcass over his arm, and skin it with his right hand.

Burning Portions of Each Korban Pesach

The owner of the sacrifice removes and hands over those portions designated for offering on the altar, and exits the Temple, happy and cheerful-like one who had gone to battle and emerged victorious. It has always been considered a disgrace among Jews not to offer the Passover sacrifice at its right time.

Designated portions of each animal were burned on the ten-cubit tall *mizbeiach*. The fat covering the innards, the fat covering the kidneys, the diaphragm, and a piece of the liver had to be thrown simultaneously into the fire. For a lamb, the fat of its tail was also included. These portions also had to be salted first. The ramp that led up to the *mizbeiach* was sixteen cubits wide (about twenty-five feet). In the center of the ramp lay a huge pile of salt. Several *kohanim* had the task of salting the fatty portions. Each sacrifice had to be salted and burned as a single unit, not to be mixed with portions of another sacrifice.

Several rows of *kohanim* extended from the courtyards, where the crowds busily skinned and separated their sacrifices, to the salting area on the ramp. Each *kohen* held a silver tray, one of the holy vessels of the *Beis Hamikdash (Rashi)* that was designed to hold the fatty portions designated for burning on the *mizbeiach*. The line moved forward until each *kohen* reached the foot of the *mizbeiach*, ascended the ramp, handed the tray to one of the salters, and immediately descended to bring another.

The *kohen* who was salting saturated the fatty portions with a handful of salt from the pile. He passed the tray to the closest *kohen* above him, who ran the tray to the ramp's top edge where it almost touched the *mizbeiach*. The portions from each sacrifice had to burn all at once—not one piece after another. So with his right hand, he threw all the fatty portions together into the blazing fire.

(Mizbach Avanim 46:7)

In honor of the *Korban Pesach*, the large woodpile on the *mizbeiach* was heaped with an extraordinary amount of wood, extending to the largest area possible. The fire was extra hot, consuming the fatty portions much faster than usual. The thick smoke from the well-fed fire rose straight up, a column rising toward the heavens. *(Avos 5:7)* Everything had to be burned before nightfall, since offerings from before *Yom Tov* could not be burned on *Yom Tov*, unless *Erev* Pesach was on Shabbos.

The Garb of the Kohanim

While doing their work, the priests wear red clothing, so if blood splashes onto their garment it is not noticeable. The garment reaches their knees; their legs and feet are bare. The sleeves are only elbow-length, so they do not hinder them during their work. On their heads they wear a small hat, tied around with a turban of cloth three cubits long. The high priest wears a white turban forty cubits long, according to what I was told.

The Roman could not have personally observed this scene, since non-Jews were not admitted into the *Beis Hamikdash*. In reality, the *kohanim* wore their usual white linen clothes, a hat, tunic, breeches, and girdle, which they were required to keep perfectly clean. They were not allowed to step on the ground where it was bloody from the slaughter of the sacrifices. While performing their holy tasks, such as passing vessels of blood to the base of the *mizbeiach* or transferring fatty portions from courtyard to ramp, their clothes had to stay at full length and could not be rolled up to avoid dirtying them.

(Mizbach Avanim 46:5)

Taking Home the Korban Pesach

After the portions were taken to the *mizbeiach* to be burned, each Jew spread out the skin of his *Korban Pesach* and placed the carcass inside. The skin of an animal can never become *tamei*, so the *korban*, wrapped tightly inside, was protected in case his attention was diverted as he carried it home. *(Ohr Sameiach)* He hoisted the animal onto his back, as Arabs do when they carry. *(Pesachim 65b)* The *mitzvah* was so precious that each man bore his heavy load like a porter.

(Yaavetz)

The skin of the *Korban Pesach* was given as a gift to the owner's Jerusalem host, a token of appreciation for opening his home for guests while the host himself stayed out in the yard to sleep. The skins of their other sacrifices were sold to their hosts for a low price, and the hosts in turn profited when they resold them at market value.

(Avos D'Rabbi Nosson, chapter 35)

Once everyone had gone home with their precious sacrifices in tow, only *kohanim* and *levi'im* remained. The almost empty courtyard was cleared in preparation for the next group, and the *kohen* gave the signal to start admitting a second, then a third, wave of slaughterers.

Roasting the Korban Pesach

> *The ovens where they roast their sacrifices are next to the doorways of their homes. I was told that this was in order to publicize their faith and because of the holiday festivity. After roasting it, they dine to the sound of psalms of praise and song, and their voices are heard from afar. No door in all of Jerusalem is locked on Passover night, in honor of the many passersby.*

In Jerusalem, thousands of special ovens were built in advance of the holiday, available for the millions of pilgrims to rent; they did not have sufficient time to build their own ovens when they arrived for Pesach. Wood was also for sale, although the price was very expensive—three *ma'ah* for a pile of wood, compared to a single *ma'ah* for a *Korban R'eiah*.

(Bava Metzia 30b)

The legs and intestines were cut off and rinsed before the roasting. The owner salted the carcass as is customary if he so wished. *(Rashi, Pesachim 74a)* The rest of the *Korban Pesach* was roasted whole, before cutting it into pieces.

The *Mishnah* says that the *Korban Pesach* was roasted on a long spit, not of metal but of pomegranate, a particularly firm wood. The *Korban Pesach* had to be roasted by fire, without any added water, which would disqualify the sacrifice. The wood for the spit had to be at least one year old, without any knots, so no moisture would issue from it. For the same reason, the length of the spit had to exceed the carcass so the cut ends would not emit any moisture into the meat. The spit pierced the animal at its mouth and extended to the tail end. The legs and intestines were hung on the spit next to the animal's mouth.

(Pesachim 74a)

The fire in the oven had to have high flames so the carcass was roasted by the actual flames, not from the oven's heat, as the Torah insists, "only roasted by fire." *(Shemos 12:9)* An animal lying on the hot coals would extinguish the fire and cook from the coal's heat. Instead, the spit was suspended in the air of the oven so the *korban* was roasted by the leaping flames.

(Tosafos, quoting Talmud Yerushalmi)

The verse in *Hoshea* says, "For the ways of G-d are straight; the righteous walk in them, while sinners stumble over them." *(Hoshea 14:10)* How can the same ways that enable some to walk straight cause others to stumble? Two individuals roast their *Korban Pesach*: one for the sake of the *mitzvah*, the other just to satisfy his hunger by eating a great feast. Although both roast it over the same fire, the one doing it for the sake of the *mitzvah* is "righteous," while the other "stumbles" over the identical action. *(Nazir 23a)* The Sages instructed that the *Korban Pesach* be eaten only once hunger has been satisfied, ensuring that feasting on the tasty meat was solely for the sake of obeying Hashem's command.

(Toras Elokim I, letter 22)

The Seder

In the time of the *Beis Hamikdash*, the Pesach *Seder* began with a full *Yom Tov* meal. A festive feast followed *Kiddush* and *lechem mishneh*, breaking of the bread using two *matzos*. Then the *Seder* was conducted over a single *matzah*. This *matzah* served as the *lechem oni* (the bread of affliction), interpreted by the Sages as the bread over which many answers are given-answers to the questions that constitute the *Seder*.

(Mordechai, Pesachim)

Once all the participants' hunger had been satisfied, the *Korban Pesach* was served. The Sages introduced this precaution so no one would try to hungrily chew the meat that adhered to the bone and

accidentally break it, transgressing the Torah prohibition, "And a bone in it you shall not break." *(Shemos 12:46)*

(Tosafos, Pesachim 70a, quoting Talmud Yerushalmi)

Opinions differ among Torah authorities about the procedure of the *Seder* meal.

- The *Rashbam* said that the *Seder* began with the blessing of "*al achilas matzah*-Blessed is G-d Who has commanded us to eat *matzah*." Then the participants would consume a *k'zayis* of *matzah* and recite "*al achilas marror*-Blessed is G-d Who has commanded us to eat *marror*" before eating the bitter herbs. Third, they said the blessing "*al achilas hazevach*-Blessed is G-d Who has commanded us to eat the sacrifice," and enjoyed the *Chagigas Arbaah Asar* offering until their hunger was satisfied. Finally, before partaking of the *Korban Pesach*, the *brachah* "*al achilas Pesach*-Blessed is G-d Who has commanded us to eat the Passover sacrifice" was recited. Then they ate the *Korban Pesach*. The *afikoman* was served in accordance with Hillel's opinion-a *k'zayis* of *matzah* and a *k'zayis* of *marror*, together with a *k'zayis* of meat from the *Korban Pesach*. The participants thus indulged twice in the meat of the *Korban Pesach*.

  (Rashbam, Pesachim 115)

- *Tosafos* believes that they did not eat *matzah* or *marror* separately before they ate *Korban Pesach*; all three delicacies were enjoyed simultaneously, according to Hillel's opinion. They ate the meat of the *Korban Pesach* only once.

  (Tosafos, Pesachim 115)

- According to the *Rambam*, each person took a *k'zayis* of *matzah* with a *k'zayis* of *marror* and dipped the two into the *charoses*. They recited "*al achilas matzos um'rorim*-Blessed is G-d Who has commanded us to eat *matzos* and bitter herbs" before eating the concoction. The *Rambam* permitted making separate blessings and eating the *matzah* and *marror* separately as well.

Second, they made the blessing on the *Chagigas Arbaah Asar*, and ate until their hunger was satisfied. Finally, they recited the *brachah* for the *Korban Pesach* and ate it. At the end of the meal, they ate the *afikoman* with a second piece of the *Korban Pesach*.

(Rambam, Hilchos Chametz U'matzah, chapter 8)

Eating the Korban Pesach

"[The *Korban Pesach*] shall be eaten in one house; you shall not take any of the meat out of the house to the outside." *(Shemos 12:46)* According to the Sages, a "house" refers to a prearranged *chaburah* (group) who planned to congregate and eat the *Korban Pesach* together. One was not permitted to start eating the *Korban Pesach* with one group and then change to a different group, even if both groups were assembled in the same building.

In Egypt on the night of the *Korban Pesach*, while Egyptian firstborns all over the land died, the Jews were commanded to remain safely inside their homes. At that time the Jews became free men, nobility. A king's feast is fully prepared in advance to be eaten in his palace dining hall in the company of a number of members of the royal retinue. Poorer people are not normally treated to a grand feast for large numbers of people; they send out portions to friends to be eaten in their own homes. The Torah instructs that the *Korban Pesach* be considered a royal feast, with the guests and delicacies fully prepared in advance and enjoyed together in the comfort of a single home.

(Sefer HaChinuch, Mitzvah 19)

The *Korban Pesach* could only be eaten on the ground level of a Jerusalem home. The roofs or upper stories of the tall buildings did not have the same exalted holiness found on the ground floor. *(Pesachim 86a)* How the Jerusalem hosts managed to make room on the ground floor for the multitude of Jewish neighbors who streamed to the holy city for Pesach was a wonder.

To maintain peaceful communal relations, a *chaburah* consisted of neighbors who lived in close proximity. No one should feel deserted by local acquaintances and friends, forced to participate in a *Korban Pesach* with strangers. Teachers of *mussar* (ethics) say that this shows how a Jewish *simchah* should be conducted, together with family and friends-unlike non-Jewish celebrations, which are often full of wild self-indulgence in the company of strangers they may never set eyes on again.

No partition or separation was permitted within a group. If something intervened, everyone ceased eating until it was removed. Every participant had to sit facing the *korban*. Once the procedure began no one was allowed to turn his face away, because he might appear to be partaking of a different *Korban Pesach*. A new bride, who might have been embarrassed to eat when everyone was watching, was allowed to turn aside while eating.

(Mizbach Avanim 59:1)

Two groups were permitted to conduct their *Seder* in the same home, but a partition was required between them to make it clear that they were separate groups. A small partition, even transparent, was sufficient, but each group had to face away from the other so they did not appear to be a single unit.

(Kesef Mishneh, Hilchos Korban Pesach 9:3)

The *k'zayis* of meat from the *Korban Pesach* had to be consumed within a designated time span of *k'dei achilas pras* (standard time required to consume a portion) in order to fulfill the obligation. *Halachic* authorities disagree on how long the time span was; opinions vary from two to eleven minutes. And the *Korban Pesach* had to be finished before midnight.

Immediately after eating the *Korban Pesach*, the used metal utensils had to be washed. The earthenware utensils were broken because they had absorbed the flavor of the *korban*. The *Korban Pesach* was so holy that anything that absorbed its taste was not allowed to be used for any other purpose.

(Tosafos Yom Tov, Zevachim 11:7)

Earthenware utensils used for any *korban* had to be broken before the following day. Since every *Yom Tov* meal included sacrificial meat, earthenware utensils were required in plenty. The Sages permitted buying utensils before *Yom Tov* even from those who were not as careful about the rules of ritual purity, so there would be sufficient utensils for everyone at every meal.

(Meiri, Chagigah 25a)

After the *Seder*, millions of Jews left their groups. Quarters on the ground floor where everybody partook of the *Korban Pesach* were crowded. Some walked out into the streets, while others escaped to the rooftops to sing *Hallel*, praising Hashem as loudly and with as much joyous song as possible. The sound from high rooftops carried over great distances; it was so loud that pedestrians below thought the roofs were collapsing.

(Mizbach Avanim, 59:17, Baal HaMaor)

The verse in *Shir HaShirim* says, "Let me hear your voice, for your voice is pleasant." *(Shir HaShirim 2:14)* Hashem tells His beloved people, "'Let me hear your voice' as you sing *Hallel* three times a year in Jerusalem." When the Jews sang *Hallel* after the Pesach *Seder*, their voices rose to the heavens, as the Aramaic saying goes, "The *Korban Pesach* was eaten in the house, and the *Hallel* breaks the roof."

Growing Closer to Hashem

The *Korban Pesach* commemorated the Exodus from Egypt, the night the Jewish nation became a "kingdom of nobility and a holy nation." *(Shemos 19:6)* Every year on that night the Jewish people act as princes, reclining as they dine and avoiding the bones of the *Korban Pesach.* Acting in a royal manner helps inculcate the high standards expected of an elevated people.

Why did Hashem command so many reminders of the miracles of the Exodus? A person's behavior is the primary influence on his

mind and soul. Even a wicked man can be aroused to reform his life by fulfilling the deeds required by the Torah. While initially he may not be fully sincere about Torah and *mitzvos*, the positive performance of good deeds will eventually bring about the sincerity. On the other hand, if someone of high standards stoops to lowly pursuits, he will likely fall from his previous level. Hashem gave the Jewish nation the Torah, with so many *mitzvos*, to occupy a person's mind and actions. Good deeds instill virtue, and earn the great reward Hashem has in store.

(Sefer HaChinuch, Mitzvah 20)

The lengthy preparation that culminated with the lofty meal of Pesach night left lasting impressions. Every Jew who witnessed the great purity of the *kohanim* as they performed the sacrificial service in the *Beis Hamikdash* was aroused to attain higher levels of closeness to Hashem and diligence in studying His Torah. "And you shall eat before G-d, your Master, in the place that He will choose to rest His Name ... so that you will learn to fear G-d, Your Master, all the days." *(Devarim 14:23)* The simple act of eating the *Korban Pesach*, as the verse says, in great holiness and purity, stirred a deep spiritual arousal in every participant.

(Tosafos, Bava Basra 21a)

"*Chasal sidur Pesach k'hilchaso, k'chol mishpato v'chukaso. Ka'asher zachinu l'sadeir oso kein nizkeh la'asoso*-the order of Pesach is concluded according to its laws, every precept and statute fulfilled. Just as we have been privileged to conduct it, so may we merit to perform it."

"*V'nochal sham min hazevachim u'min haPesachim*-and may we eat there from the sacrifices and the Pesach offerings."

Kashrus supervisors inspecting a wheatfield, making sure that no garlic plants are present, since garlic causes the wheat to become *chametz*. Preferably, the wheat is harvested in the afternoon when the sun has dried the stalks.

Garlic flower stalk bearing tiny bulbs and blossoms without seeds.

Garlic bulb; garlic bulbs grow underground.

Garlic flower with its bulb with which it grow underground

Tiny garlic bulbs falling from the garlic flower.

Kashrus supervisor cleaning the combine before the operator begins reaping and threshing the wheat

Kashrus supervisor riding on a combine, saying: *leshem matzos mitzvah*, "[this wheat is] designated for the mitzvah of matzah."

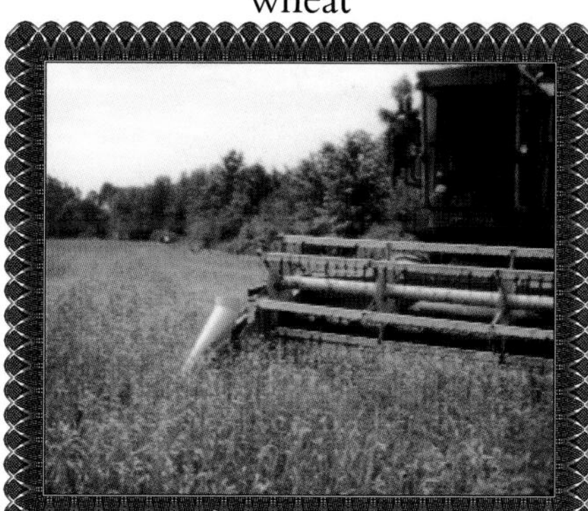

Combine harvesting and threshing wheat.

Cleaning truck container to hold the wheat.

Combines transferring wheat into grain truck.

Combine dumping wheat into grain container

Storage bin for wheat.

Machine transferring wheat into storage bin through the roof.

Kashrus supervisor sealing the roof of the storage bin.

Blower separating husks from wheat kernels.

Vacuum machine removing dirt from wheat kernels.

Sacks of wheat kernels stored in cool loft.

Wheat stalks.

Wheat kernels guarded from the time of harvesting.

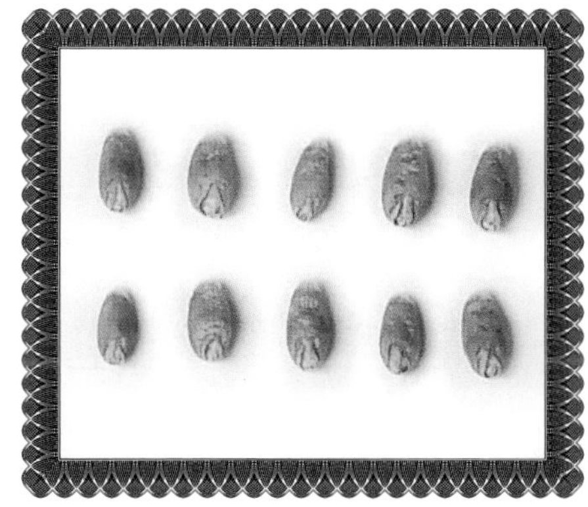

Wheat kernels with small cracks in the seed coat, beginning to germinate. Such kernels are *chametz.*

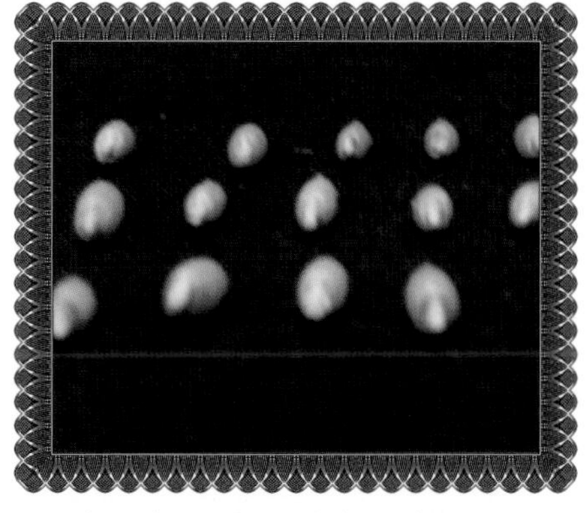

Wheat kernels with have begun to sprout and, therefore, are *Chametz.*

Hand-operated grinder.

Grinding kernels manually *leshem mitzvas matzah*.

Milling machine grinding wheat kernels into flour.

Wheat flour.

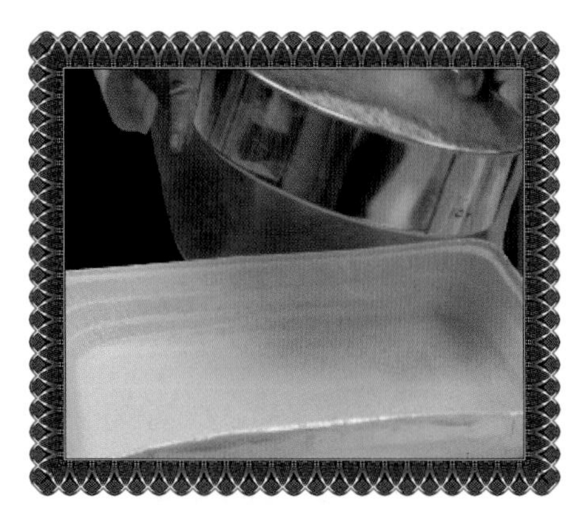

Manually sifting flour with hand operated sieve.

Sifting machine.

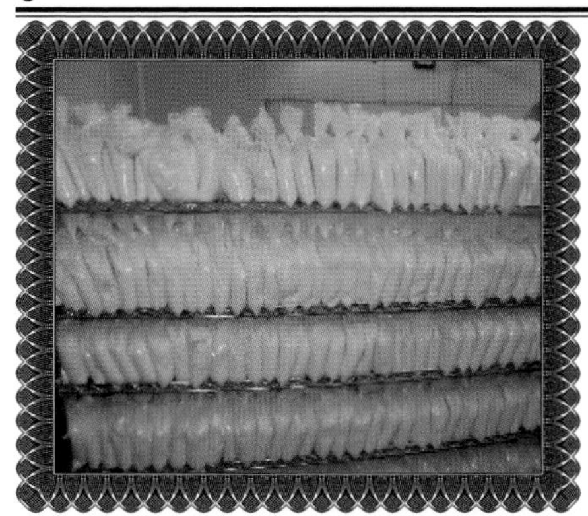

Three-pound bags of flour standing upright - not stacked - to keep the flour cool, preventing it from becoming *chametz*.

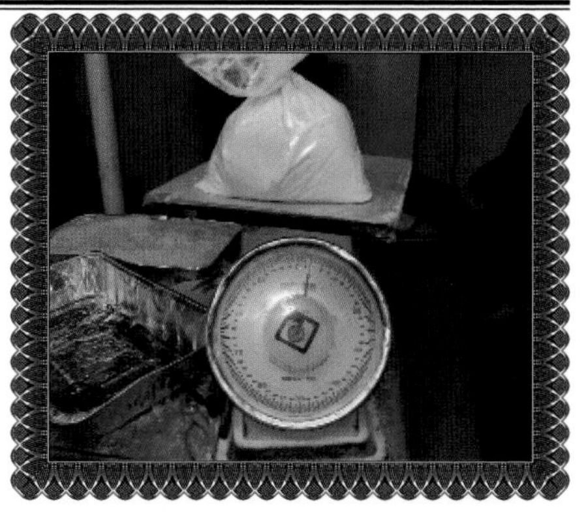

Scale set to weigh three pounds of flour, the amount used for baking one batch of matzos.

Electronic scale weighing three pounds of flour.

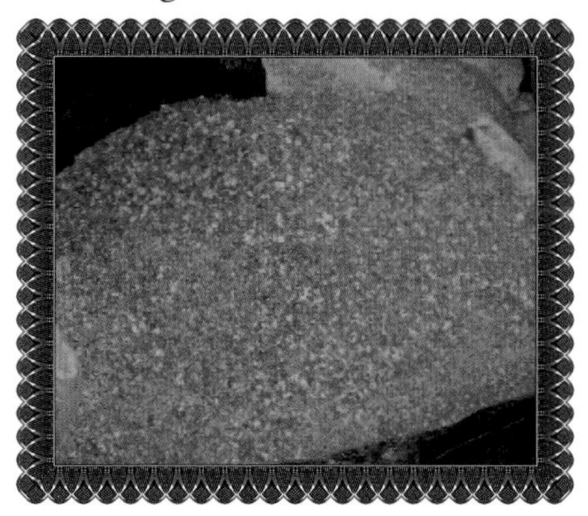

Bran, the broken husks of the grain which remain after sifting the flour.

Well from which the water for matzos is drawn.

Mayim shelanu - water which was kept overnight to cool off, because at night the water in the well becomes warm which hastens fermentation.

Pouring *mayim shelanu* into a strainer to remove any particles of *chametz*.

Electronic scale for weighing the amount of *mayim shelanu* needed for one batch of matzos

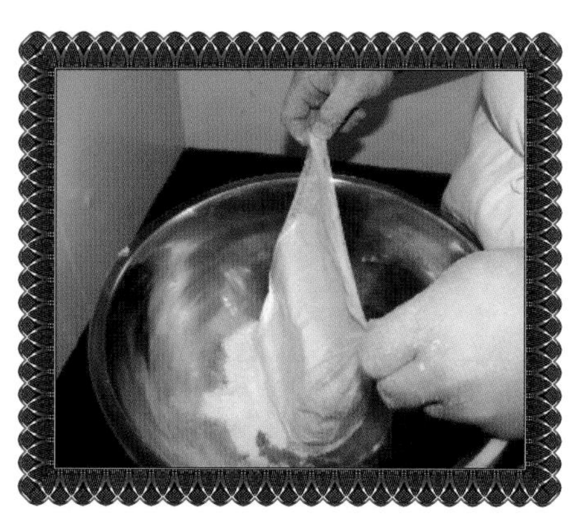

Pouring flour into mixing bowl.

Flour in mixing bowl.

Pouring *mayim shalanu* into mixing bowl.

Kneading the dough.

The kneading is completed.

The dough is ready.

The dough on the table, ready for processing. Note: The dough must be in constant motion, lest it become *chametz*.

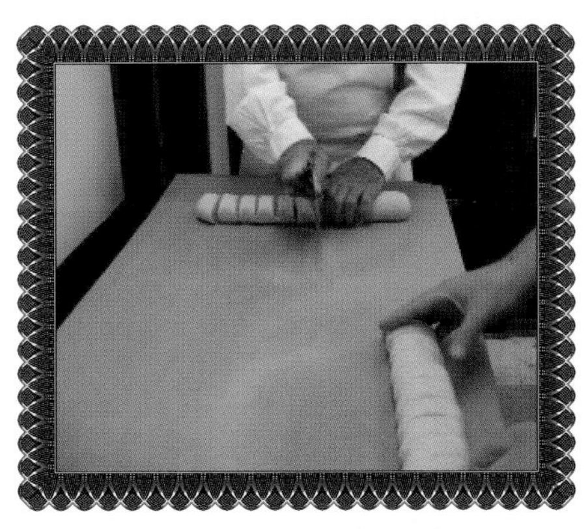

Cutting the dough. Each piece will become one matzah.

Giving the dough a round shape.

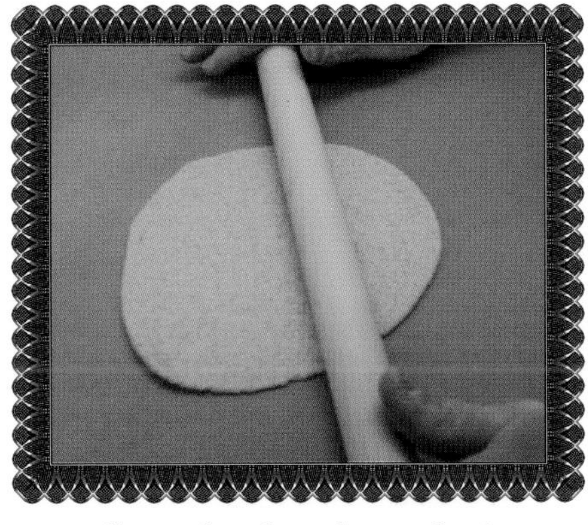

Rolling the dough to obtain a wafer-thin matzah.

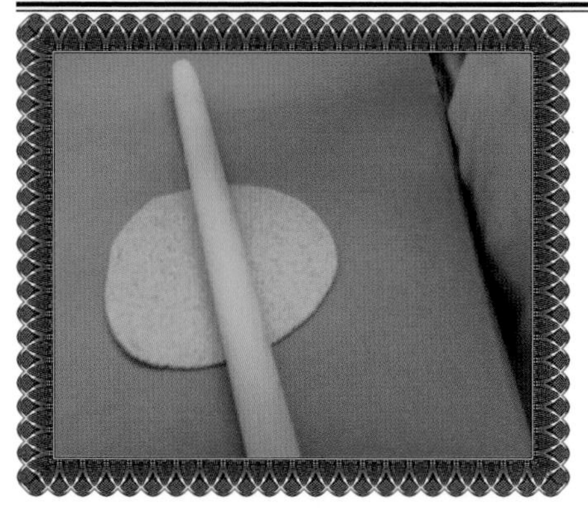

Turning the dough to obtain a round shape.

Punching tiny holes into the dough to prevent bubbles from forming during baking.

Punching tiny holes into the dough to prevent bubbles from forming during baking.

Placing the matzah dough on a long wooden pole.

Keeping the matzah pole away from the hot oven.

The oven is heated with wooden logs on one side.

Coal is used to heat the other side.

Wood burning on the right side of the oven.

Coal burning on the left side.

Placing matzos into the oven.

Placing two matzos into oven.

Watchful that no part of the dough folds back, as this would disqualify the matzah.

Shovel ready to remove the matzos from the oven.

A second shovel is needed in case a matzah became *chametz* in the oven, in which case the shovel is discarded.

Matzos baking in the oven.

Matzos arranged in two rows.

The matzos are ready.

Removing the matzos from the oven.

Leaving matzos at the oven door to dry out.

Placing the matzos in a basket.

Separating *challah* before packaging the matzos.

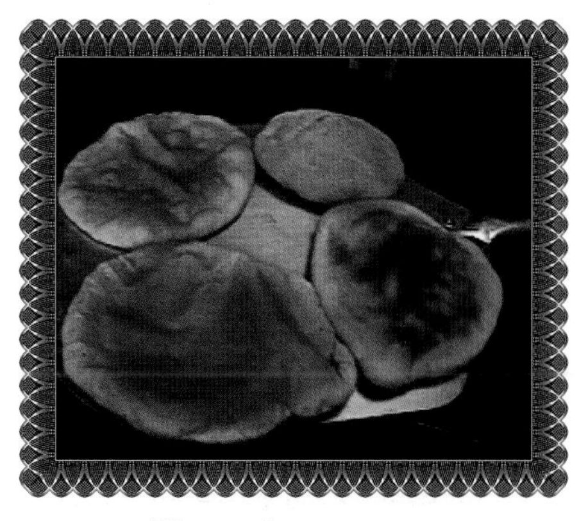

Yemenite matzos.

Partially doubled matzah, the doubled portion is *chametz* and must be discarded; the remainder is kosher.

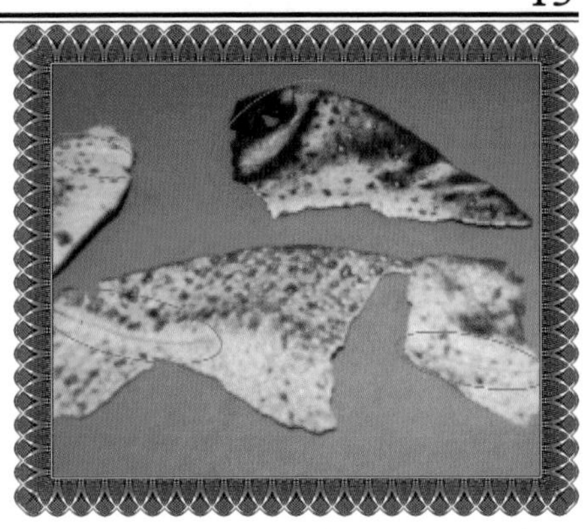

Pieces of doubled matzah.

A doubled piece inside a matzah.

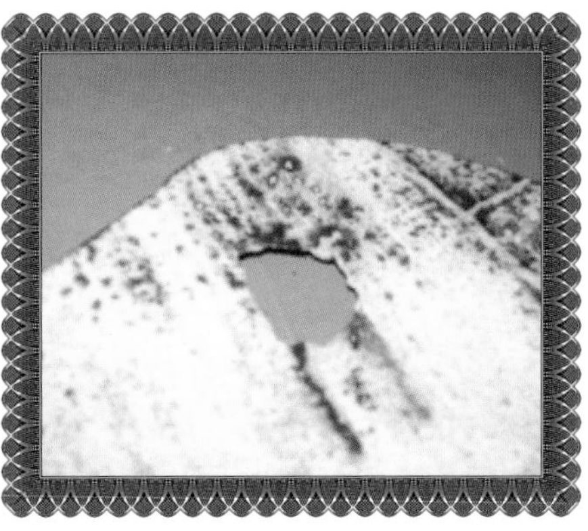

Doubled piece is removed along with an inch surrounding it; the remaining matzah is kosher.

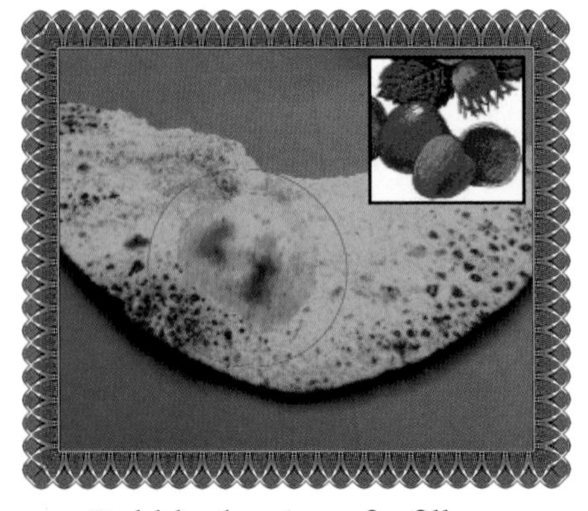

Bubble the size of a filbert (hazelnut) this part of the matzah is *chametz*.

Subtracting the weight of the box.

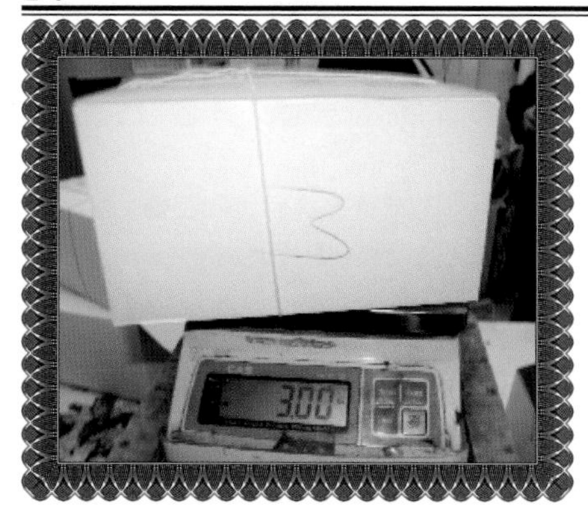

Three-pound box of matzos.

Box tied with loop, to allow opening on Shabbos and Yom Tov.

Mill for grinding matzah for matzah meal.

Grinding matzah.

Bags of matzah meal.

Cleaning utensils with mechanical brush.

Kashering the perforating tool with a blowtorch.

Smudged rolling pins after use.

Machine for cleaning rolling pins.

Poles for inserting matzos into oven.

Order of Kashering

Heating a brick.

Pouring hot water on the red-hot brick.

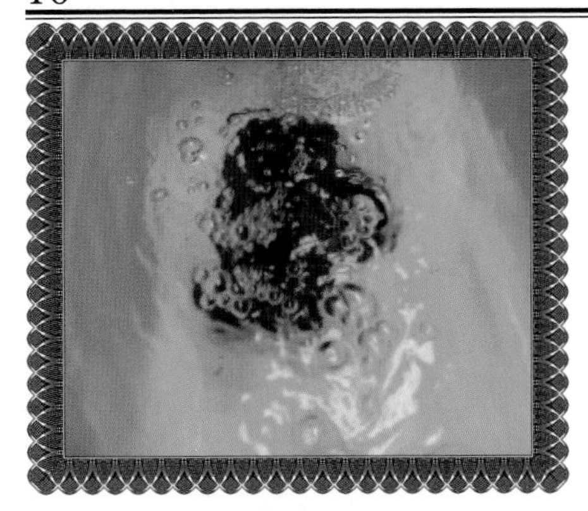

(Alternate method:) Filling the sink with hot water from faucet, then sliding the red-hot brick along the surface of the sink.

Bedikas Chametz, the Search for Chametz.

After reciting the *berachah*, ten small pieces of bread are placed together.

Others hide ten well-wrapped pieces of bread to be found during the search.

Burning the *Chametz*.

The Glorious Seder Table

The *Sefer Tiferes Shloma*, quoting the *Zohar*, says that both the Shabbos table and the Seder table are reflected in the heavenly realm, but the Seder table ranks higher in holiness than the Shabbos table. On Shabbos only a spiritual replica of the intentions of the Shabbos table appears in Heaven, but on the night of Pesach, not only the intentions of the Seder table are mirrored Above, but a virtual counterpart of the Seder table is present in Heaven. The essence of the Seder table - the matzos, the *maror*, and the four cups of wine are maniifest in Heaven and are presented to *Hakadosh Baruch Hu*, in fulfillment of the verse, This is the Table that is before Hashem (*Yechezkel* 41:22). And when the Mishnah (*Pesachim* 10:2) says: "They pour the first cup of wine for him" and "They then bring vegetables before him," it alludes to *Hakadosh Baruch Hu* conducting the Heavenly *Seder* along with us. At the heavenly *Seder Hashem* bestows on us His blessings for health, bounty, success, and for the redempton that is symbolized by the Four Cups.

Arrangement of the Matzos and the Seder Plate

The first matzah for Hamotzi (Kohen)

The second matzah for *Al achilas matzah* (Levi)

The third matzah for *Korech* (*Yisrael*)

Some use twelve matzos.

The *zero'ah* (shankbone) is placed on the right (to commemorate the *korban Pesach*).

The *beitzah* (roasted egg) is placed on the left (to commemorate the *korban Chagigah*)

The *maror* is placed below these items (it was eaten together with the *korban Pesach*).

The *charoses* is placed below the *maror* to the right (it is eaten with the *maror*).

The *karpas* is placed below the maror to the left.

The *chazeres* is placed below the *maror* and *karpas*.

Ke'arah with doors.

Romaine lettuce or endives for the *berachah* and for *koreich*.

Seder plate standing on legs to prevent it from crushing the matzos. Ground horseradish for *maror*.

Ground horseradish for *maror*, endives for *korech*.

Matzos in separate compartments.

Ground horseradish for *maror*.

Ke'arah below the matzos; matzos in separate compartments, the various symbolic mitzvah items on top of the matzos.

Large amounts of *maror*, *karpas*, celery, enough to give a *kazayis* to everyone sitting at the table.

Large measures for *maror* and *karpas*.

Large measures; boiled celery for *karpas*.

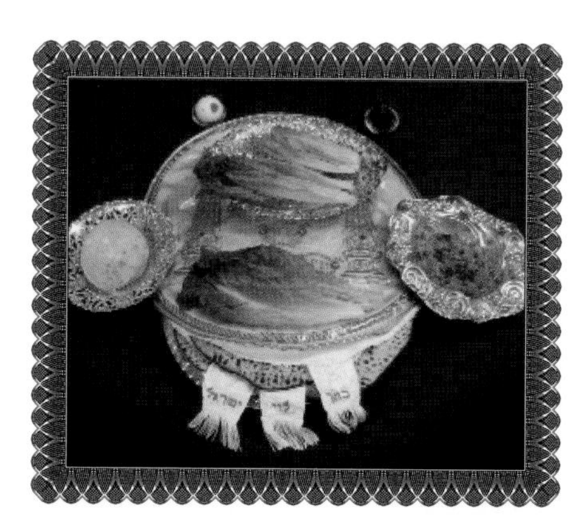

Large measures for all mitzvah items.

The matzos over the mitzvah items (*minhag belz*).

The mitzvah items arranged around the matzos (*Rema, Yaavetz*).

Some of the mitzvah items on top of the matzos, others alongside the matzos (*Arizal*).

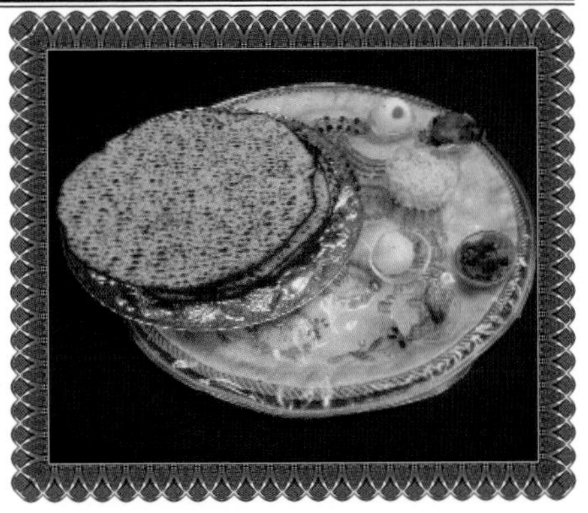

The mitzvah items on one side of the plate, the matzos on the other side *(Rabbi Shalom Sharabi)*.

The matzos on top of the Romaine lettuce, the *zero'ah* and the egg on top of the matzos, the other mitzvah items on the lettuce.

Using onions for *karpas* when celery was not available (*Chabad*).

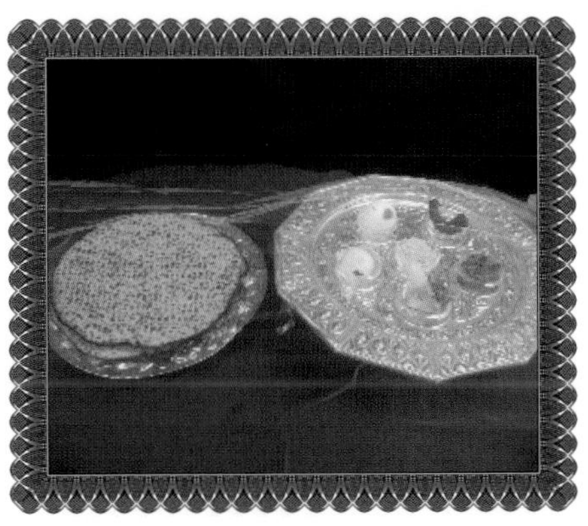

Covering the matzos and the mitzvah items (*Nesivos Olam*).

Covering the entire table with *maror*, "This night only *maror*!" (*Minhag Teiman*).

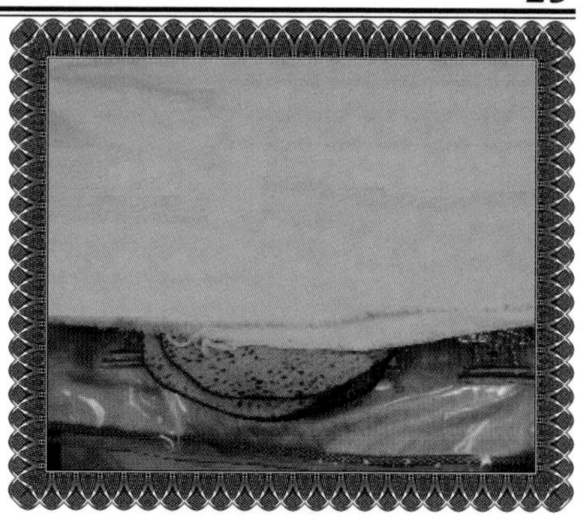

Covering the matzos and the mitzvah items.

Matzos separated and wrapped in long tablecloth, the mitzvah items on top, *charoses* in a spoon (*Minhag Chernobyl*).

Mitzvah items on top.

All mitzvah items placed on the matzos.

All mitzvah items on the matzos; during the recitation of the Haggadah the entire *ke'arah* is covered.

Ke'arah will all mitzvah items on the right side; on the left large quantities of the mitzvah items to be given to everyone at the table.

Two whole matzah, *lechem mishne* (*lechem oni*, bread of affliction).

Charoses made of apples, pears, pomegrantes, figs, nuts, almonds, cinnamon, and ginger.

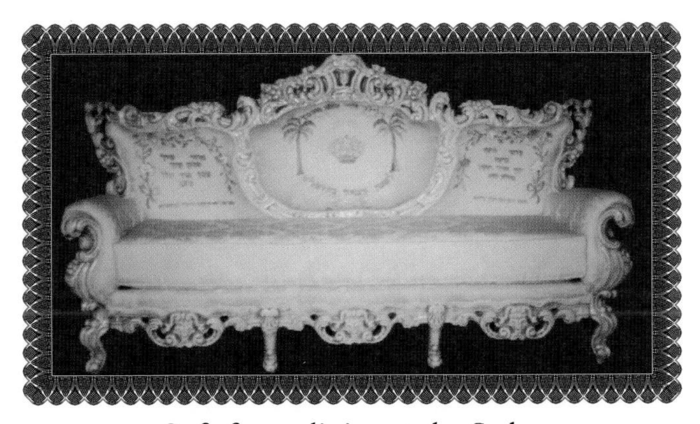

Sofa for reclining at the Seder ("tonight we must all recline").

The Seder

Kadesh: Kiddush is recited on the first cup.

Leaning on the left side we drink the first cup of wine.

Urchatz: Washing the hands in preparation for *karpas*. We do not say *Al netilas yadayim.*

Karpas; a bit of green vegetable, parsley, radish or potato.

We dip the *karpas* in salt water, say: *Borei p'ri ha'adamah*, and eat the *karpas*.

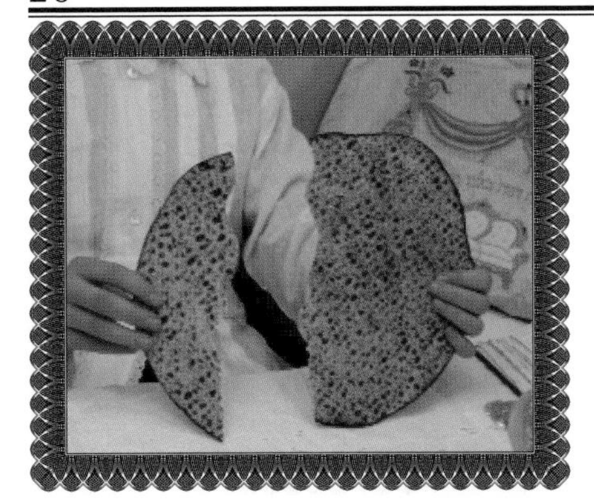

Yachatz: breaking the middle matzah into two pieces, hiding the larger part for *afikoman*, putting the smaller back on the *ke'arah*.

Some place the *afikoman* on the shoulder

Hiding the *afikoman* between two pillows.

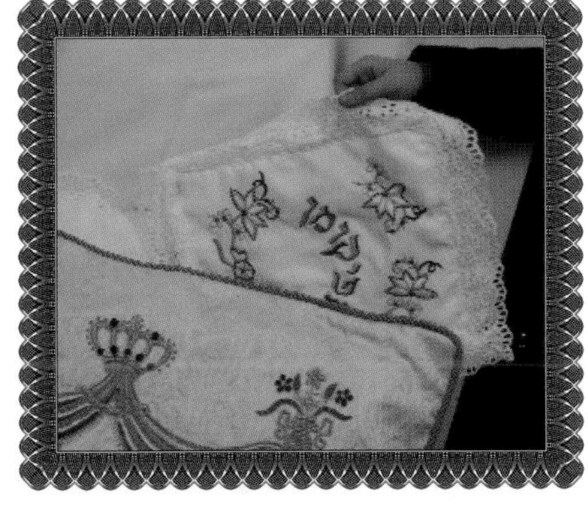

Child "stealing" the *afikoman*

Maggid; reciting the Haggadah.

Pouring the second cup.

The child gestures with his thumb while reciting the *Mah Nishtannah*.

In some circles the child claps his hands while saying the *Mah Nishtannah*. (*Belz*)

We cover the matzos and raise the cup when reciting *Vehi she'amedah*.

After *Vehi she'amedah* we uncover the matzos.

Spilling a drop of wine for each of the ten plagues.

Others dip a finger in the cup and dab a bit of wine onto the plate.

Pointing at the matzah when saying: "*Matzah zo*, This matzah which we eat..."

Pointing at the *maror* when saying: "*Maror zeh*."

Lifting the cup when saying the *berachah* of *Ga'al Yisrael*.

Drinking the second cup while leaning to the left.

Rachtzah; Washing the hands before the meal.

After washing one lifts his hands and says, *Se'u yedeichem kodesh*, Lift your hands in holiness."

Motzi. Saying *Hamotzi* while holding all three matzos.

Matzah. Holding only the top matzah and the broken matzah, we say the berachah of *Al achilas matzah*.

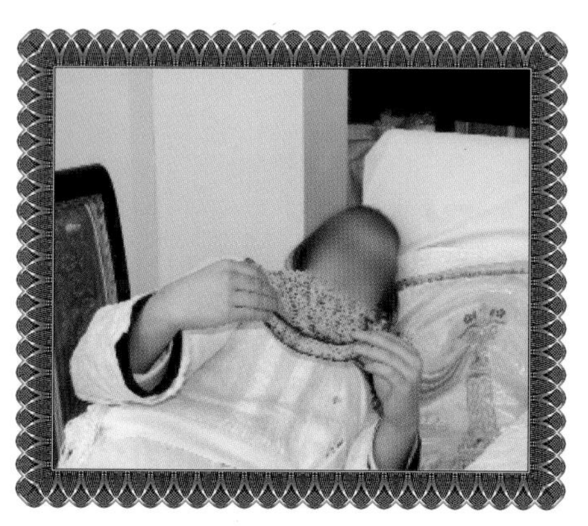

We eat of the top and broken middle matzah while reclining, holding the matzos with all ten fingers.

Maror. We take a *kazayis maror* (horseradish) dip it in *charoses*, and say the *berachah al achilas maror*.

Others eat endives or Romaine lettuce for *maror*.

Korech. Combining the matzah with *maror* (horseradish) and eating hem together.

Some combine the matzah with endives or Romaine lettuce for *Korech*.

Shulchan Orech. Eating the Yom Tov meal which includes eating eggs dipped in salt water as a reminder of *korban Chagigah.*

Tzafun. Retrieving the hidden *afikoman* to be distributed to everyone at the table.

Eating the *afikoman*.

Barech. Pouring the third cup and reciting *Birkas hamazon*.

Drinking the third cup while reclining.

Pouring the cup for Eiyahu.

A child opening the door for Eliyahu Hanavi.

Hallel. Pouring the fourth cup and reciting Hallel.

Drinking the fourth cup while reclining.

Nirtzah. Concluding the *Seder* with the hope that it was acceptable to Hashem.

Pesach Kugels

Maror kugel
(Bobov, Shabbos Pesach)

Charoses kugel
(Bobov, Shabbos Pesach)

Beet kugel
(Belz, Shabbos Pesach)

Esther kugel
second day of Yom Tov

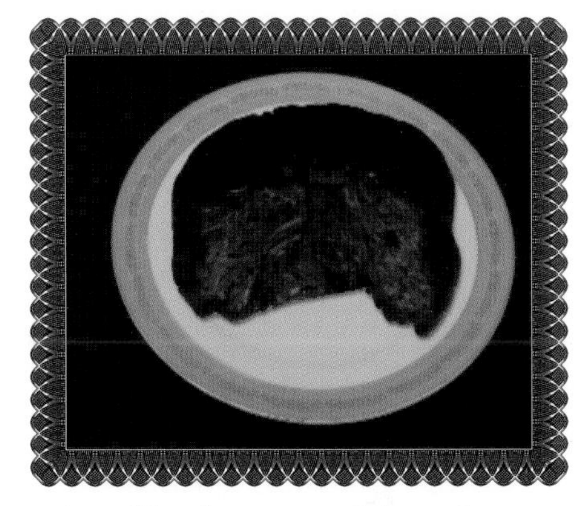

Kotzker matzah kugel
(for the last day of Pesach)

Ziben him'ln (seven heavens)
kugel (for the last day of Pesach).